Complete Guide
to Tested Telephone
Collection Techniques

ARTHUR WINSTON

PRENTICE HALL
Englewood Cliffs, New Jersey 07632

Library of Congress Cataloging-in-Publication Data

Winston, Arthur.
  Complete guide to tested telephone collection techniques / Arthur
Winston.
    p. cm.
  Includes index.
  ISBN 0-13-160185-7
  1. Collecting of accounts—United States. 2. Telephone in
business. 3. Telephone etiquette. I. Title.
HG3752.7.U6W56 1988
658.8'8—dc19

82-22321
CIP

© 1988 by

Arthur Winston

Printed in the United States of America

10   9   8   7   6   5   4   3   2

Prentice-Hall International (UK) Limited, *London*
Prentice-Hall of Australia Pty. Limited, *Sydney*
Prentice-Hall Canada Inc., *Toronto*
Prentice-Hall Hispanoamericana, S.A., *Mexico*
Prentice-Hall of India Private Limited, *New Delhi*
Prentice-Hall of Japan, Inc., *Tokyo*
Simon & Schuster Asia Pte. Ltd., *Singapore*
Editora Prentice-Hall do Brasil, Ltda., *Rio de Janeiro*

ISBN 0-13-160185-7

PRENTICE HALL
BUSINESS & PROFESSIONAL DIVISION
A division of Simon & Schuster
Englewood Cliffs, New Jersey 07632

To Audrey

About the Author

Arthur Winston is the founding partner of Winston & Morrone, P.C. His law firm is primarily engaged in the collection of delinquent accounts and commercial litigation. Mr. Winston has 35 years of experience in collection. His firm represents a wide cross-section of clients in the collection area ranging from several money center commercial banks, financial institutions, large wholesalers and manufacturers, to some of the major direct marketing firms in the country. Winston & Morrone also represents landlords, finance companies, distributors, franchisers, collection agencies, and a wide variety of other businesses.

Mr. Winston has written extensively for trade magazines on the subject of collection, and currently conducts a successful seminar for the Direct Marketing Association entitled "Law and Direct Marketing." He has also conducted many seminars on the subject of credit and collection before both national and regional associations.

Mr. Winston attended New York University before serving in the U.S. Army. Upon returning to civilian life, he attended New York University Law School and received a degree in law from New York University Law School.

Preface

This book was conceived more in the sense of a need than in the sense of an idea. The book represents a living diary of my personal and firm's experience in the collection field for a period of twenty years. Twenty years ago the practice of my firm turned from corporate and securities law to commercial law, contract law and litigation as well as emphasizing the collection of delinquent accounts. Needless to say, most clients wish to collect their debts without instituting suit. The ultimate device to achieve this purpose is the telephone call. In the early years it became very evident that a poor telephone call collected nothing but dust. On the other hand, a well-trained telephone worker could be almost as effective as an attorney attempting to collect *after suit*.

Many different approaches were tested in attempting to train telephone workers. The method most commonly used was for an experienced employee to hold the hand of the new telephone worker during the first thirty minutes to an hour of telephoning. This was inadequate because the teacher often forgot many of the basic rules, and discovery did not occur until the telephone worker made an error. Books on collection usually devoted only one or two chapters to the subject, and barely touched the surface of the problem.

Accordingly, a telephone script was born. It started with just one page, and grew to nine pages within a year. Thereafter, rap sessions between the telephone workers produced more problems and reasoned solutions. Slowly, the telephone script expanded into a text, which grew as my firm expanded, to over one hundred and fifty pages. This book is a rewriting of that text tailored to the needs of the creditor as opposed to the needs of the collection attorney.

The Debt Collection Practices Act reflected the views of government and the industry as to what should be allowed in the collection of a debt. In 1977 only collection agencies were subject to the Act. In 1986 attorneys became subject to the Act. Nevertheless, the Act has effectively set a standard for the use of collection efforts, and in the opinion of the author a creditor should comply with the Act (see analysis in Chapter 9) in the same manner as a collection agency or an attorney. An abusive or deceptive tactic is just that, whether performed by a collection agency, attorney, or creditor. There are references to the Act throughout the entire book, and the book is designed for compliance with the Debt Collection Practices Act. Before reading the first chapter, a review of the Act and the commentary by the Federal Trade Commission (see Appendix A) may be helpful in understanding the reasoning in the book.

There is a difference in the collection effort used with a consumer debtor and with a business debtor. The first eight chapters deal in general with the telephone effort, and in certain instances distinguish between the consumer debtor and business debtor. Chapter 9 discusses in depth the application of the Debt Collection Practices Act to the collection effort. The last six chapters separate the consumer debtor from the business debtor, and present the distinct problems that are encountered with each type of debtor.

Dialogues are heavily employed throughout the book since our telephone workers over the years made extensive records of their telephone conversations. We utilize, in addition to the telephone text, cassette tapes to illustrate a proper and effective telephone collection call.

I have also provided sample letters to support a telephone call, but I urge the reader not to use my vocabulary or sentence structure. The best letter is one written by the creditor to reflect his own personality and business philosophy.

Arthur Winston

A Note About This Book

Today, the collection of delinquent accounts is heavily regulated at both the federal and state level, and in many instances even at the county and city level. No attempt has been made to review, include, or comment upon all the laws and statutes which are in existence that affect the collection effort. Although a state may not have enacted a law similar to the Debt Collection Practices Act, the principal federal law affecting collection, each state probably has passed laws dealing with deception, misrepresentation and fraud, unfair business and unfair practices, and similar types of laws which may affect the collection effort.

In addition, exceptions exist to every general statement of the law; and each general statement cannot be used to fit a particular set of circumstances until a thorough examination of all the facts is made in conjunction with an examination of all the laws and the decisions of the courts which interpret the laws.

Laws and statutes are continually amended, revised, and repealed, and court decisions may be reversed or rendered obsolete by more recent decisions or decisions of a higher court. The references to the laws are designed to provide an overview that may influence telephone collection, and the limited materials presented merely reflect what generally exists at the time the book was written.

In view of the above, and the fact that only a very small sampling of state laws have been considered, a review of the federal and state laws and court decisions which affect the collection effort of each creditor should be made and should be monitored continually.

The book is not intended to be a substitution for consultation with an attorney. Consultation is not only recommended but encouraged.

All names and addresses used in the illustrative dialogues are fictitious, and bear no resemblance to and are not intended to be actual persons, firms, or businesses. Any similarity is purely coincidental.

How This Book Will Help You Dramatically Improve Your Telephone Collection Techniques

The goal of this book is simple: to help you improve your collection efforts by persuading the debtor to pay. The thrust of this book is directed at the telephone collection effort. While the telephone is just one of the tools that can be used in an overall collection procedure, it is unquestionably the most productive tool—if you know how to utilize it properly.

Each chapter offers sample telephone dialogues between collector and debtor, with follow-up commentary on how effective the dialogue was. In addition, collection tips, checklists, and sample forms are provided to help you streamline your telephone collection process.

Here are just some of the many features each chapter offers.

CHAPTER 1 shows why combining telephone calls and follow-up letters effectively helps you convince more debtors to pay. Some of the topics include

- credit checking
- how to produce the impact of two calls for the price of one
- tips on selecting a collection agency
- how to comply with the Debt Collection Practices Act

CHAPTER 2 analyzes the basic ingredients of a collection telephone call, separating it into four main components called the "golden keys" to a successful effort: (1) a positive identification, (2) the foundation for a demand of payment, (3) stating your bottom line—that payment is due—and (4) a closing statement.

CHAPTER 3 offers you the eight most-often-heard excuses on why the debt cannot be paid—and guidelines for responding to these excuses.

CHAPTER 4 tells how to leave a message that will reach the debtor, including

- special situations and how to handle them
- leaving messages with a business debtor
- what your message should contain to be sure it reaches the debtor
- tips on leaving messages with recording devices and answering services

CHAPTER 5 will help you negotiate a successful settlement by showing

- how to motivate the debtor to offer a settlement
- the art of timing
- the dangers of "bidding" against yourself
- five rules of installment indebtedness that you can break—and one that you cannot

CHAPTER 6 covers the basic ingredients necessary for training your department

- costs involved in training telephone callers
- the telephone script—why it is essential for your training program
- training procedures, such as group training, one-on-one, taping calls, and record keeping
- monitoring telephone calls
- cost factors in making long-distance calls

CHAPTER 7 explores the different types of techniques available for obtaining payment, such as

- how to use the "pause" to encourage cooperation
- dealing with a "yes...but" response
- tips on offering the debtor ideas for sources of funds
- how to handle uninterested or argumentative debtors
- what to do when a debtor uses abusive language

CHAPTER 8 discusses the impact of stalling techniques and offers guidelines for dealing with them, including

- how to respond to seven of the most often-used clichés
- popular stalling techniques—and how to offset them
- how to avoid miscellaneous telephone delays

CHAPTER 9 gives an overview of the Debt Collection Practices Act, with special emphasis on legal boundaries and limitations, including

- why a creditor should comply with the Act
- limitations on threatening suit
- definition of covered parties and type of debt
- problems with consumer and third parties
- harassment and abuse
- misleading representation

CHAPTER 10 discusses the art of obtaining an accurate telephone number. Some of the subjects discussed include

- credit applications and order forms
- guidelines for obtaining home telephone numbers
- unpublished numbers
- making the most of telephone directories and telephone information
- wrong numbers

CHAPTER 11 deals with the procedures of a "business-to-business" approach for dealing with debtors, and how it differs from a consumer debtor. Some of the topics included are

- different business debtors require different treatment
- types of indebtedness (including installment debt, time and demand loans, and secured loans)
- size of business debtor and indebtedness

CHAPTER 12 details the most frequently heard business excuses and advises how to respond to them. Everything from the well-known "the check is in the mail" to "trouble with the computer" is covered—and clear, decisive answers for each are offered.

CHAPTER 13 covers special legal problems encountered with businesses, including

- bankruptcy
- assignment for the benefit of creditors
- when debtor goes out of business
- why you should use skip tracing

CHAPTER 14 offers an in-depth look at consumer excuses, with emphasis on how to tell if they are sincere or merely a ploy to stall payment. Included are claims of

- medical troubles
- financial troubles
- domestic or family troubles
- debtors on limited incomes
- divorce

CHAPTER 15 covers the distinctions found among various consumer debtors and how they can affect the collection process over the telephone, including

- size of debt
- homeowner versus apartment dweller
- children as debtors
- what to do when debtor is deceased

In addition, a detailed five-part appendix offers federal and state laws affecting collection, the monitoring and taping of telephone calls, and dishonored checks, and general information that can help you save time and money.

In all, you'll find this a useful and informative resource tool for improving your telephone collection effort and securing the money owed from the debtor.

Contents

A Winning Combination: Letters and Telephone Calls

WHY THE INTERPLAY BETWEEN LETTER AND TELEPHONE IS CRITICAL TO YOUR COLLECTION EFFORT STRATEGY

Any general will tell you that the key to a successful military operation consists of the foot troops and the artillery. For a collection manager the principle is the same: send forth a series of letters (the foot troops), and follow up with the telephone call (the heavy artillery). Although this book concentrates on the "artillery" of a telephone collection effort, it's critical that you first understand the importance of the interplay between letter and telephone. In effect, this chapter will show how a telephone call without a letter is very much like using the heavy artillery without the foot troops.

This chapter discusses other procedures which affect the collection effort and the cost comparisons between the various collection devices such as credit checking, registered and certified mail, invoices and statements, Mailgrams, and third-party letter-writing agencies.

The successful merchant, wholesaler, or manufacturer incorporates the losses incurred by bad debts into the price of the product or service. Average bad-debt write-offs can range from less than 1

1

percent to 2 percent to as high as 15 percent to 20 percent depending upon the industry, the service, the size of the firm, the average size of the debt, and a multitude of other factors, one of which is the strength of the internal collection effort.

Most businesses, large or small, new or old, consider marketing to be their most important priority, followed by production, finances, personnel, and so forth. Perhaps this is as it should be; for if the product or service cannot be sold, there is no justification for being. But the disturbing fact is that the collection of delinquent accounts, on a scale of 1 to 10, is somewhere down at minus 1 or minus 2 on the list. The only time the collection effort reaches the top ten priorities is when the cash flow slows down to a trickle. At this point the collection manager receives a telephone call, or even a personal visit, from the chief operating executive. In smaller enterprises the chief operating officer, described more commonly as the owner, may even make a few collection calls on the largest open accounts. Contact is then made with the attorney or the collection agency, and the account is referred to them. Later a status report is sought, and an estimated time of arrival of the remittance is requested. But by this time, such action is probably too late and totally inadequate

COST COMPARISONS TO OTHER COLLECTION DEVICES

The thrust of this book is directed at the telephone collection effort. While this is just one tool to be used in an overall plan and procedure, it is unquestionably the most productive tool if properly utilized. The use of the telephone should be placed in perspective when considering the cost of all the devices available for the collection effort. The telephone is more expensive than the use of invoices, statements, dunning letters or Mailgrams, but less costly than registered and certified letters. The use of a third-party letter-writing agency may be comparable to a telephone call, but the letters are usually not as effective as the telephone call. If the account must be sent to a collection agency/attorney, the cost of the outside agency/attorney is enormous compared to the cost of collecting by using a telephone call.

The cost of mailing one invoice ranges from $.35 to $.42 to cover postage of $.22, about $.02 or $.03 for the cost of the invoice and the envelope, about $.04 for stuffing and mailing, and a few pennies for computer time and labor, and about $.10 for typing the invoice and the name and address, depending upon how complicated the invoiced item is. Sending several invoices or several statements may run this cost over $1.00. Mailgrams also cost less than $1.00, but registered or certified mail requesting a return receipt will run over $1.50. A set of four third-party letters may run from $1.60 to $6.00 depending upon the agency that is used. A collection agency or attorney usually charges a contingency fee extending from 15 percent to 50 percent of the amount collected. A telephone call should cost an average of around $1.50 to $1.75.

PROPER CREDIT CHECKING: THE FIRST LINE OF DEFENSE IN THE CAMPAIGN TO CONTROL LOSSES

Proper credit checking will prevent a bad debt. Such a simplistic statement begs the question. While the first mercantile credit agency was organized in the middle of the 1800s, and Dun and Bradstreet is over 100 years old, the credit society in which we live did not really come into being until after World War II. Prior to that time, the principal extension of credit to the consumer was the mortgage on his home and a local charge account at the general store until next payday. Lending for business purposes was common much earlier. The extension of credit was both secured and unsecured, and perhaps the best example of secured lending was the 90 percent margin accounts which prevailed on Wall Street prior to the crash of 1929. Each margin account was secured by securities which were systematically sold as the prices declined, eventually triggering the worst depression our nation has ever known.

In today's society the extension of credit is an art. The laws controlling interest, credit advertising, and preventing discrimination are numerous and complicated. Each organization has its own forms for obtaining financial information concerning the prospective borrower. Credit procedures vary from firm to firm. Articles and books appear each year to guide the American businessman. Seminars flourish at luxury hotels. Credit reporting agencies, such as TRW and Hooper Holmes, have created huge data bases on consumers. Financial information and payment experience are provided by local business and trade associations. Dun and Bradstreet is still with us.

The growth of the credit industry has turned the granting of credit into an art form. Credit losses are a way of life. If the losses are too high, credit becomes more restrictive. If the losses are small, credit becomes more lenient. Somewhere in between, there is an acceptable level of losses that the average business is willing to endure. Every means should be used to train and educate credit personnel to reach this ideal plateau.

USE AND FREQUENCY OF INVOICES AND STATEMENTS

Repeated invoices and statements to a delinquent debtor is probably the device used by most businesses to respond to a delinquent debt. The temptation to use statements is sweetened by the apparent attractiveness of the tiny labels that are easily affixed to the statement. The gentle words "reminder of a past due debt" which grace these labels seem to persuade the businessman that something is being done to collect the debt. In fact, the probability is that the gummed label merely serves to dress up the drab statement before it is discarded. While invoices and statements should be used, their repeated use beyond a 60-day period after the debt is due is certainly not warranted and adds nothing to the collection effort. Actually, the invoice is the mildest form of dunning, and a statement, with or without a rubber stamp or attachment, is really no improvement. By the time the debtor receives the third invoice or statement, he or she is making payment in response to the dunning letter or telephone call of another creditor.

HOW THE INTERPLAY BETWEEN
COLLECTION LETTERS AND TELEPHONE CALLS WORKS

Collection letters, or dunning letters, are a subject unto themselves. The collection letter has a very definite purpose and place in the collection effort. To be most effective, it must be used in conjunction with the telephone call, for it complements and, in fact, increases the effectiveness of the telephone call.

How to Get the Impact of Two Calls for the Price of One

When a debtor receives a letter after the telephone call, his first memory is of the prior telephone call. Accordingly, the net result is a free second telephone call. For this reason, a follow-up letter should always be mailed after a telephone call. While telephone calls may be made without the use of letters, their efficiency may be reduced by as much as 20 percent to 30 percent. The cost of the letter is minor compared to the cost of the telephone call. *Again, be certain to mail a letter after each telephone call.*

The Ingredients of an Effective Letter

The contents of the letters, the type of stationery, the format of the letter and envelope, how often the letters should be mailed, how many letters should be mailed, and who is to sign the letters could fill hundreds of pages. Nevertheless, some basic concepts are presented as an introduction to the telephone collection call.

Basically, there are four types of collection letters.

1. *Notice:* The first is the notice or reminder letter, stating that the account is past due, or a simple reminder that the customer has ignored the statement and the creditor is now requesting payment. There are no consequences for nonpayment set forth in this letter.

2. *Customer Relations:* The second letter is a customer relations letter. The creditor inquires whether there is any reason why the debt has not been paid. The letter seeks information as to defective merchandise, late delivery, inadequate services, shortages, or any other reason that might justify nonpayment. *This is never used as a first letter unless it is combined with a first letter.*

3. *Collection letter:* The third letter is the true collection letter. The creditor insists that the debtor pay the debt. The letter is direct and to the point.

4. *Consequence letter:* This is the final written notice. The creditor states that some further consequence will take place if payment is not made within a prescribed period of time. The promised action usually takes the form of referral to a third-party letter-writing agency, a collection agency, or a referral to an attorney.

The initial communication to a consumer requires certain information under Section 809 of the Debt Collection Practices Act if the collector is subject to the act, i.e., collection agency or attorney. A creditor is usually not covered by the act.

Three Special Keys to a Series of Letters

1. *Series of Letters:* While there are basically only four types of collection letters, it is quite possible to mail a series of eight letters consisting of two notice letters, two customer relation letters, two collection letters, and two consequence letters, or any combination thereof. At the same time, a series of only two letters may be mailed by combining the notice and customer relation letter into one letter and then combining the collection and consequence letter into another letter.

2. *Special Types of Letters:* Other types of letters are appropriate to specific situations. After a message is left on the telephone, a special letter should be prepared and mailed a day or so later advising the debtor that a telephone call was made and of the fact that a debt is due, etc. Special letters should be prepared for situations where the debtor promises payment, pays on account, wants to return merchandise, or whatever other situation indicates a follow-up letter.

3. *Trick to Writing the Letter:* I know of instances where consultants are paid hundreds and thousands of dollars to write a series of collection letters. In my experience the best collection letter is the one written by the owner or the collection manager, for this truly reflects the policy and attitude of the business and its owners. Letters should be integrated with telephone calls and each letter should convey the appropriate message. While many books are available with hundreds of examples of letters, here are several suggested formats for letters to be mailed after the telephone calls.

FORMS FOR LETTERS TO USE WITH TELEPHONE CALLS

CUSTOMER PROMISED PAYMENT

Re:
Refer to:
Amount:

Dear   :

You promised to make payment of the above amount, but as yet, we have not received payment.

If we do not receive payment by Monday, May 7, 198X, this claim will immediately become subject to referral to a collection agency/attorney for further action.

Very truly yours,

CUSTOMER PROMISES INSTALLMENT PAYMENTS

Re:
Refer to:

Dear   :

This is to acknowledge that you have agreed to make _____ payments of $_____ until the full balance above is paid.

We shall expect your payments promptly each _____ and we have marked our records accordingly.

If you fail to make these payments, we will be forced to refer this claim to a collection agency/attorney for further action.

Very truly yours,

PARTIAL PAYMENT BY CUSTOMER

Re:
Refer to:
Amount:

Dear   :

This is to acknowledge receipt of your part payment in the sum of $_____ leaving a balance of $_____ due to us.

If we do not receive said balance within the next ten days, this claim will immediately become subject to referral to a collection agency/attorney for further action.

Very truly yours,

REQUEST FOR INVOICE

Re:
Refer to:
Amount:

Dear   :

With regard to your request for an invoice, please find same enclosed.

In the event we do not receive your check by Monday, May 7, 198X, we will have no other alternative than to refer this matter to a collection agency/attorney for further action.

Very truly yours,

CUSTOMER WANTS TO RETURN MERCHANDISE

Re:
Refer to:
Amount:

Dear   :

We agree to allow you to return the merchandise and full credit will be given for same. Please ship the merchandise prepaid to the address set forth below.

Please insert the account number on the label on the outside of the package in the left-hand corner of the address. Also, at the same time you mail the merchandise, please send copies of shipping receipt or evidence of shipment to us making sure to include the account number with your address.

Of course, if we do not receive the merchandise by Monday, May 7, 198X, we will have no alternative but to treat this account as open. In such event the account will then become immediately subject to referral to a collection agency/attorney for further action.

Very truly yours,

CUSTOMER CLAIMS MERCHANDISE RETURNED

Re:
Refer to:
Amount:

Dear   :

We find no record of your merchandise being returned.

I would appreciate you forwarding to me some type of receipt from the Post Office or shipping carrier indicating that you did ship the merchandise.

If you will forward to me a copy of such evidence, we shall make another effort to check that the merchandise was returned, and the credit will be issued to your account.

If we do not receive such evidence by Monday, May 7, 198X, we will have no alternative but to treat this account as unpaid. In such event, the account will then become immediately subject to referral to a collection agency/attorney for further action.

Very truly yours,

CUSTOMER CLAIMS PAYMENT

Re:
Refer to:
Amount:

Dear   :

With regard to your claim of payment, we have checked this against our records and we have no record of your payment.

We would appreciate you forwarding to us a copy of the front and back of the check in order that we may trace down exactly what happened to your payment.

If we do not receive the copy of your check by Monday, May 7, 198X, we will have no other alternative but to treat this account as unpaid. In such event the account will then become immediately subject to referral to a collection agency/attorney for further action.

Very truly yours,

CREDITOR CANNOT LOCATE PAYMENT

Re:
Refer to:
Amount:

Dear   :

This is to acknowledge your recent check.

Unfortunately, we are unable to make the appropriate entry on your account since we do not have sufficient information to locate your account.

Accordingly, we would appreciate you submitting the following:

1. Please advise us of the account number and the proper address and ZIP code.

2. If you do not have the account number, please give us the date when you ordered the merchandise, and type of merchandise you ordered.

3. Please forward to us all documentation and correspondence you received from us.

We thank you for your cooperation in this matter, and please be certain to return this letter with the above information.

Very truly yours,

FOLLOW-UP LETTER

Telephone workers should have the authority to require a follow-up letter after the telephone call. The following is a suggested form:

REPORT BY TELEPHONE WORKER
FOR MAIL FOLLOW-UP LETTER

Invoice #	Name and Address	ZIP Code	Amount
_____	_____	_____	_____
	_____	BL _____	RP _____
		CC _____	RM _____
	_____	ES _____	POD _____
		INV _____	PO _____
			OTHER _____

	_____	BL _____	RP _____
		CC _____	RM _____
	_____	ES _____	POD _____
		INV _____	PO _____
			OTHER _____
	_____	BL _____	RP _____
		CC _____	RM _____
	_____	ES _____	POD _____
		INV _____	PO _____
			OTHER _____

CODE: BL—Balance Letter   RP—Promised payment

CC—Copy of check letter   RM—Return merchandise

ES—Evidence of Shipment   POD—Proof of Delivery

INV—Invoice   PO—Purchase order

OTHER—

TIPS ON SELECTING A COLLECTION AGENCY OR ATTORNEY

In each of the previous letters a choice is afforded to the creditor to either use a collection agency or an attorney. If such a statement is employed in a telephone call, a choice also must be made as to whether to use a collection agency or attorney. Both serve separate and distinct purposes in most instances, but in many areas they overlap and either will achieve the desired purpose.

Collection Agencies

Procedures: Collection agencies are organizations designed for the sole purpose of collecting debts. The procedures they use consist mostly of letters and telephone calls. In some instances representatives of the agency may visit the debtor, but this is becoming quite rare in today's environment. Agencies do settle and resolve disputes between the debtor and creditor, and do negotiate modifications and extensions of loans, but leave to the attorneys the preparation of the legal documents where same are required.

Association and Licensing: The American Collectors Association, a national association of collection agencies, has in operation a code of ethics for its members. Operating a collection agency for one year or more in those states not requiring licensing, being bonded by state law or by the association are some of the requisites for membership. Some states have enacted licensing statutes which require the agency to register in the state in order to collect a debt in that state. Usually, a registration fee is required for licensing and bonding in those states that require it. Most states have statutes which contain the normal prohibitions against deceptive and abusive collection, but at the same time the laws vary from state to state. The Debt Collection Practices Act was originally designed to cover only collection agencies, but now has been expanded to cover attorneys who engage in the collection of debts.

Fee Structure: Most agencies handle claims on a contingency fee basis. The third-party letter-writing agencies charge a flat fee for writing a collection letter. Few collection agencies charge a fixed amount or an hourly charge for services rendered in the collection of a debt whether or not the debt is paid.

Liability: The agency is liable for its negligence, errors, and omissions, and liability insurance is available to cover errors and omissions.

Institution of Suit: A collection agency cannot institute suit without engaging the services of an attorney. This is probably the basic distinction between a collection agency and attorney. If a collection agency cannot collect the debt by letters or telephone calls, the creditor has the option to retain his own attorney to commence suit or utilize an attorney engaged by the collection agency. Most collection agencies recommend that the creditor use the agency's attorney.

Attorneys

Lawyers and law firms in this country engage in the practice of law in wide and diversified fields. Many of them will undertake the collection of debts, and some of them engage primarily in the collection of debts. I am considering here only those firms which are primarily engaged in the collection of debts.

Procedures: An attorney overlaps the collection agency to the extent that the attorney may also use letters and telephone calls to collect the debt. Naturally, the attorney will settle or compromise the claim, and is able to prepare the necessary legal documentation for any modification or extension. The licensing statutes that apply to collection agencies do not apply to attorneys, and attorneys may collect a debt by letter or telephone call in a state where the attorney is not admitted to practice law. But if the attorney wishes to institute suit in the state of a debtor where the attorney is not admitted to practice, the attorney must retain an attorney who is admitted in that state. The attorney may institute suit against the debtor in a state where he is admitted to practice law.

Law Lists: Several firms have compiled lists of attorneys by state and city who engage primarily in the collection of debts, and seek referrals of collection cases from collection agencies and other attorneys. These attorneys are usually bonded by the firms publishing the list to protect the creditor from an attorney collecting money but failing to remit the money to the creditor. If the debtor resides outside the state, both the collection agency and the attorney must retain an attorney admitted to practice law in the debtor's state in order to institute suit, and both the collection agency and attorney utilize the published lists to retain attorneys in other states.

Admission to the Bar: In every state a lawyer must pass an examination and appear before an admission committee composed of attorneys before he or she is admitted to practice. The lawyers of every state have organized a state bar association which monitors, regulates, and disciplines each attorney licensed to practice in the state. Each bar association has promulgated canons of ethics which control the practice of law by the attorneys licensed to practice in the state. In 1986,

Congress amended the Debt Collection Practices Law to require attorneys who engage in this type of practice to comply with the provisions of the act. The Federal Trade Commission will probably issue commentary sometime in 1988 as to the application of the law to attorneys.

Fee: An attorney may handle the collection of a debt either on a contingency basis or on an hourly basis. In the case of an hourly basis, the attorney charges for the time spent in the collection effort.

Liability: Attorneys are personally liable for negligence, errors, and omissions; and malpractice insurance is available to protect the client.

Making the Choice

The selection of a collection agency or attorney will depend upon many factors as described above. The continual use of the collection agency or attorney should depend upon performance. For this reason, whenever a creditor must determine whether to refer the claim to a collection agency or attorney, we use the phrase "collection agency/ attorney." The creditor may then make his own selection and eliminate the words "collection agency" or "attorney" from the letter or telephone call.

Whether to Use Registered and Certified Mail: The use of registered or certified mail is not recommended principally because the cost is almost comparable to a telephone call. If the debt is large enough to warrant a registered or certified letter, then it is important enough to employ the telephone. Perhaps the only exception is when the debtor does not answer the telephone or the creditor is wary of leaving messages. Whether the debtor will pay more attention to a registered letter as opposed to responding to a telephone call is very questionable. If the number is unlisted, perhaps this method might be used.

Mailgrams—Are They Worth the Cost? Mailgrams are a relatively new ingredient in the arsenal of collection devices, born during the 1970s. Prior to that time, the telegram was always available, but certainly cost equivalent to the telephone call. Furthermore, the freedom of creative composition was limited by the increase in cost for every word recited. Western Union recognized a potential market for transmitting a large volume of the same message to different recipients. The economy of the same message produced a substantial reduction in price per unit message. Since time was not a factor, the Postal Service was used for delivery. Because of the use of the Postal Service for delivery as compared to the all-American youth who delivered the telegram on a bicycle, a Mailgram became more economical than a telephone call and a telegram. Mailgram costs could be as low as $.30 to $.50 per Mailgram, depending upon volume. In its infancy, many firms utilized the Mailgram with great success as a collection tool. The Mailgram was unique. The debtor had never encountered a document of this nature. His association with telegrams was of illness, disaster, and death. The Mailgram was undoubtedly read, and its similarity to the telegram was obvious. The net effect on the debtor was most impressive. The results were exceptional.

Unfortunately, the very effectiveness of the Mailgram was the cause of its downfall as a collection tool. Its popularity among collection managers spread quickly. Its use became quite common as imitators sprouted everywhere. "Speedgrams," "Quickgrams," "Rapidgrams," and all sorts of "grams" could be purchased at a fraction of the cost of a Mailgram, inserted in an official-looking envelope, and mailed to the naive debtor. As the businessman and consumer became accustomed to the use of the Mailgram, the sight of one in the morning mail no longer frightened the recalcitrant debtor. When the substitutes began to usurp the original, its usefulness as a collection stratagem came to pass. Although the Mailgram on a volume basis may be cheaper than a telephone call, its perception by the recipient is that of "just another letter."

A sidelight to the above story is that Western Union was fully aware of this frustrating development. Success breeds imitation, and in this instance, imitation ruined the original. Western Union tried to persuade the Federal Trade Commission that the use of collection device imitators was misleading since each one was trading on the vast telegraph system of Western Union and the impact, urgency, and importance of the telegram and Mailgram. Of course, only Western Union had such a system in place. The Federal Trade Commission agreed, and stated that imitators of the Mailgram may be engaging in misleading advertising of the product. Unfortunately, the horses had already left the barn.

Impact of Third-Party Letter-Writing Agencies: This concept was born when a collection manager realized that collections improved if a different organization attempted the collection effort. The debtor seemed to recognize that the creditor was now spending money to collect and thus was serious. Third-party collection agencies filled the need. Their name and address, bearing the "collection agency" logo, was marketed and their form letters sold for a price per letter, somewhere between $.35 and $1.00 per letter. The agency would mail the letters and collect the checks and deliver them to the creditor. Responses to the incoming mail were either undertaken by the agency or the creditor depending upon the financial arrangement. Whether third-party letter-writing agencies are a substitute for telephone calls is certainly a question to consider.

The cost of the third-party collection agency letters is a very important factor in the decision. Some agencies agree to mail a set of four letters for a price as high as $6.00. Other agencies might do the same for the sum of $.35 to $.60 for each letter, so that a set of four letters would cost $1.40 to $2.40. A telephone collection call costs between $.30 to $1.50 per telephone call plus approximately $.50 to $.75 for wages and another $.10 for preparation of the account, making a total of about $.90 and $2.25 or more as a maximum. Another $.60 must be added to the cost if the telephone number must be obtained by use of AT&T information.

If each series of third-party letters costs between $1.40 and $6.00, certainly an evaluation should be made as to where to best spend the collection dollar. Using only third-party letters after a series of letters mailed by the creditor is, admittedly, relying too heavily upon letters, only one of many collection devices. A debtor will be ready to ignore a third-party collection letter as well as a letter mailed directly by the creditor. The final analysis must be whether more is collected by the third-party letter-writing agency or by a telephone call, assuming the cost of both are the same. Of course, the lower the price, the more attractive the device, providing the net collections are equal.

Advantages of Contingency Fees: A comparison of the fixed fees for a set of letters compared to the contingency fees charged by collection agencies also may provide startling results. The more sophisticated creditor overwhelmingly appears to favor the contingency relationship with a collection agency rather than paying the established charge for a certain number of letters. The exception to this policy arises in those situations where the average balance due is so small that the agency will only accept it on this basis.

DEALING WITH THE DEBT COLLECTION PRACTICES ACT

Section 812 of the Debt Collection Practices Act provides the following concerning the furnishing of certain deceptive forms:

(a) It is unlawful to design, compile, and furnish any form knowing that such form would be used to create the false belief in a consumer that a person other than the creditor of such consumer is participating in the collection of or an attempt to collect a debt such consumer allegedly owes such creditor, when in fact such person is not so participating.

(b) Any person who violates this section shall be liable to the same extent and in the same manner as a debt collector is liable under Section 813 for failure to comply with a provision of this title.

Section 813 deals with the civil liability of a party who does not comply with the Act. See Appendix A for the Debt Collection Practices Act.

1. *Condition Under Which Creditor Becomes Subject to Act:* Under this section a creditor may become subject to the Debt Collection Practices Act. Furthermore, three things happen. First, the creditor becomes subject to the Act; second, the creditor is automatically in violation of the provisions of the Act; and third, the creditor becomes subject to the civil liabilities set forth in Section 813.

2. *Violating the Act by Using In-House Collection Agency:* The section was designed to prohibit a creditor from organizing a pseudo in-house collection agency. The creditor created the ABC Collection Agency to write letters to its debtors. The collection agency existed in name only. It operated from the same office but used a different address from the creditor. The collection agency employed no one, for the employees of the creditor were used to prepare and mail the letters. In all respects a hollow shell resulted. The purpose was to influence the debtor to believe that a third-party agency was being paid to collect the debt. These facts present a clear case of a creditor designing a letter to create a false belief in a consumer that a person other than the creditor is participating in the collection of a debt when in fact the creditor is the one performing all the acts.

3. *Purchasing Form Letters Prohibited:* The section was also targeted at the phenomenon of debt collection forms. Creditors have always realized that debtors are more likely to pay a debt if the debtor believes that the creditor has turned the debt over to a third-party collection agency. Nevertheless, creditors are sometimes unwilling either to pay the contingency fees charged by agencies or the fixed rate charged by collection agencies to mail a third-party letter, commonly called "flat rating." The practice then developed of the sale by a collection agency of one or more letters on the letterhead of the agency requesting that the debtor make payment directly to the creditor. The creditor prepared and mailed the letters and arranged to have the responses delivered to a post office box or different address. These letters create the false impression that the collection agency is involved in the collection of the debt, when in fact there is no participation by the collection agency except for the sale of the letters. This would probably be a violation of Section 812 of the Debt Collection Practices Act.

BEFORE YOU MAKE THE TELEPHONE CALL: A CHECKLIST

☐ Train and educate the credit personnel.

☐ Do not use invoices or statements after 60-day period.

☐ Collection letters fall under these categories:

—notice letter

—customer relation letter

—collection letter

—consequence letter

☐ Collection letters are to be integrated with telephone calls.

☐ Special letters for special situations are needed.

☐ Registered and certified mail are not effective.

☐ Mailgrams have lost their effectiveness.

☐ Third-party letter-writing agencies are reviewed.

☐ Section 812 of the Debt Collection Practices Act is considered.

—Condition under which creditors become subject to Debt Collection Practices Act.

—In-house collection agencies prohibited.

—Purchasing form letters prohibited.

CHAPTER 2

Four Golden Keys to an Effective Telephone Collection

The most important thing to remember is that the object of the telephone call is to collect money, not to make telephone calls. Anyone can make telephone calls, but only the successful caller collects money.

This chapter analyzes the basic telephone call and separates it into its elementary components. Understanding the components will enable telephone workers to utilize the basics to their fullest extent to persuade the debtor to pay, which is the ultimate purpose of this book.

I have separated the telephone collection call into its four most basic ingredients. The collection telephone call must contain these four golden keys to successful collection:

1. Identification
2. Foundation
3. Demand for payment
4. A closing statement

Without these four ingredients, a telephone call may be totally ineffective for the following reasons:

1. If the debtor does not recognize the creditor, the debtor will not know to whom to send the check.
2. If no foundation is laid, the lead-in is inadequate to support the demand for payment.
3. If a demand for payment is lacking, then the telephone call has no purpose.
4. If the closing statement is omitted, the debtor will not be motivated to mail the check.

GOLDEN KEY 1: POSITIVE IDENTIFICATION

Always confirm that you are speaking to the correct person. For example:

1. Is this James Jones at 235 Main Street?
2. Is this the Speedy Cleaning Company on Route 66?

After you are certain you are speaking to the correct person or firm, the next step is to identify yourself.

Suggested Methods of Identifying Yourself

1. "I am calling from the offices of XYZ Hotel Corporation."
2. "This is the office of XYZ Commuter Line."
3. "This is the accounts receivable department of the XYZ Construction Corporation."
4. "This is the collection department of the XYZ Mortgage Corporation."
5. "This is the loan workout department of XYZ Bank."
6. "This is the revolving credit department of XYZ Department Store."
7. "This is the patient account department of XYZ Hospital."

Business-to-Business Collection Calls

When calling a business, ask to speak to the owner first. If the owner is not available, ask to speak to the bookkeeper. If the debtor is a large business, ask first to speak to the accounts payable department and then the bookkeeping department. If all of the above are not available, speak to anyone who is in charge or who is authorized to accept a message.

If the debtor is a corporation, speak to any of the corporate officers: comptroller, financial manager, treasurer, credit manager, bookkeeper, vice-president or the president.

Business-to-Consumer Collection Calls

When calling a consumer, ask to speak to the individual debtor. If the spouse of the party answers the phone and the debtor is not available, communicate as if the spouse was the debtor.

COLLECTION TIP: When Debtor Will Not Come to the Telephone. There are times when the collector suspects that the debtor will not come to the telephone in response to a telephone call from the XYZ Corporation. The use of the name of the telephone worker could be used in place of the XYZ Corporation until the debtor is actually on the phone. You should identify the XYZ Corporation as the caller at that time.

GOLDEN KEY 2: FOUNDATION FOR DEMAND FOR PAYMENT

A telephone call is weak and ineffective without a proper foundation. A foundation consists of advising the customer of the length of the delinquency, the number of bills or invoices that were sent and ignored, the number of collection letters mailed and ignored, and any prior telephone calls made and ignored. The purpose of the foundation is to strip the customer of any defensive argument. The moment the customer realizes a creditor is dunning him, the first thought is to obtain some form of extension of time and avoid an immediate payment. The purpose of the foundation is to surround the customer and allow no opening for the customer to claim ignorance of the debt or the fact that the debt was delinquent. The foundation might take the following form.

Six Typical Phrases to Use as a Foundation

1. "XYZ Corporation has sent several statements, and your bill is past due over 60 days."

2. "Your invoice is 60 days old and we have sent you several statements, all of which have been ignored."

3. "We have written you several letters and called you once."

4. "Your charge account is 60 days in arrears and you have ignored three letters and one telephone call."

5. "Your mortgage payment is two months in arrears, and we have sent you two delinquency notices. You are already incurring substantial late charges."

6. "Your rent is due on the first of the month, and now you are two months in arrears. You have ignored two 30-day notices."

The foundation should be presented immediately after the identification, but it may come either before or immediately after the demand for payment.

Prior Promise to Pay

The very best foundation is to cite a prior written or oral promise by the customer to pay. Ninety-five percent of the population attempt to keep their promises, and a broken promise should be utilized to its fullest extent. Imposing a feeling of guilt on a customer is the surest road to obtaining payment. Therefore, use a prior broken promise at the beginning, in the middle, and at the end of the telephone conversation, when possible. When the debtor previously promised any specific action, reference should be made to that action:

1. You promised payment.

2. You promised to return the merchandise or equipment.

3. You said you would check your records.

4. You said you would speak to your husband.

5. You said you would check with your bookkeeper.

6. You said you would send in two payments and we did not receive them.

7. You said you would send the form to Blue Cross, but we have not received their check.

Perils of a Personal Relationship

If the debt is a large business-to-business debt, the foundation is even more important, especially if there is a personal relationship between the parties. Prior promises should open the conversation immediately after the identification. Do not allow the conversation to drift from its main purpose. Remind the debtor about his promise. Try to develop a guilt complex on the part of the debtor. Nevertheless, in all cases you should use the demand for payment and the closing statement.

COLLECTION TIP: *How to Handle Nasty Responses.* Do not become too friendly or too nasty. The debtor may still do business with you after the debt is paid. If the debtor does business or resides in the community, becoming nasty will achieve nothing. The closing statement should be of the negative type (see page 29 at the end of this chapter) wherein the creditor promises not to take further action if the payment is received within the prescribed time

---

GOLDEN KEY 3: BOTTOM LINE—DEMANDING A PAYMENT

When you demand payment, you should do exactly that. Do not use "please," and do not "ask" for money. Certainly, do not plead or beg for money. Even if the debtor is a person with whom a personal relationship exists, a firm demand should be made.

Seven Suggested Methods to Demand Payment

1. We must have full payment by Monday, May 7.
2. We insist on full payment by Monday, May 7.
3. Full payment must be made by Monday, May 7.
4. Your check must reach our office by Monday, May 7.
5. The last day for the March installment is Monday, May 7.
6. The revolving charge account must be brought up-to-date by Monday, May 7.
7. We must have the mortgage payment by Monday, May 7.

COLLECTION TIP: *Use a Specific Date.* Always use a day of the week and a date, such as Monday, May 7. Do not use "within a week," "by next week," "within seven days," "within ten days," or "by next Monday." The debtor may perceive the other phrases differently than the creditor, and the debtor may not accurately remember when the telephone call was received. Two weeks may have passed and the debtor may believe the call took place a few days ago. The use of a day and a date is much more effective.

Eight Ways to Emphasize Payment

Of course, an effort should be made to emphasize the demand for payment. The tone of voice, the deliberate slowing of delivery, the sincerity, and the clarity of the words all contribute to the positive impression on the debtor. In addition, the use of other phrases as lead-ins to the demand can be used, depending upon the circumstances:

1. The party is over, and we must have payment by Monday, May 7.
2. If you intend to make payment, now is the time to pay, and payment must be received by Monday, May 7.
3. The moment of truth has arrived, and we must insist upon the charge account being brought up to date by Monday, May 7.
4. This is the last telephone call you will receive from the loan department, and payment must be here by Monday, May 7.
5. This is the end of the road, and the rent must be paid by Monday, May 7.
6. So that we can clear this up and give you proper credit, your check must reach our office by Monday, May 7.
7. We are coming full circle, and we must have payment by Monday, May 7.
8. We have given all the extensions we are going to give, and we must have the mortgage payment by Monday, May 7.

The examples are endless, and dictated solely by the relationship that has been established with the customer.

The Danger in Asking Questions Concerning Payment

A well-established rule is never to ask a question unless you know what the answer will be. The lawyer that does not adhere to this rule will encounter many surprises at a trial. Similarly, the telephone worker should never ask "when payment will be made." This is one of the major mistakes in telephone collection calls. Imagine being asked, "When can you make payment?" The obvious answer is, "When I have money in the bank." The same answer can be used for, "When will the check go out?" Another common question is, "Will we have your check by Monday, May 7?" The answer is, "No, not for two or three weeks." Do not open the door for such answers. This type of reply will occur often enough without an invitation. Of course, the rule does not apply to the situation where you are seeking financial and personal information concerning the debtor or trying to locate the debtor. In these instances asking questions is an art. (See Chapter 14, "Consumer Excuses: How to Tell If They Are Sincere.")

TESTED TIP: Timing of Demand for Payment. The best of both worlds suggests a demand for payment immediately after the foundation and again just before the closing statement.

COLLECTION TIP: Name, Rank, and Serial Number. You should always advise the debtor of the name, address, and ZIP code of the creditor, including to which department or person the letter and/or payment should be addressed. The debtor should be told to write this information on a piece of paper. This rule has no exceptions and applies even when the debtor states that he knows the address, or that he has a letter from the creditor, or that he has mailed all his prior payments to the same address, or that he claims he just visited the creditor two days ago. Although the debtor should have this information, the prime reason to give it again is for emphasis—to impress on the debtor how urgent it is that he pay.

GOLDEN KEY 4: CLOSING STATEMENT MUST END TELEPHONE CALL

The general rule is that a closing statement must be made at the end of every telephone call. *A closing statement is a concise statement of the consequences which will take place if the debtor does not pay.* Normally, this means that the creditor will refer the claim to a collection agency for letters and telephone calls, or to an attorney for collection and institution of suit. This closing statement will be used in 90 percent of the telephone collection calls.

Some Warnings About Making Threats

Threat to Refer Claim to Collection Agency or Attorney: Section 807, subdivision 5, of the Debt Collection Practices Act provides that a violation of the act takes place where the creditor threatens to take any action which cannot be taken legally or that is not intended to be taken. Therefore, it is imperative that action threatened be taken. If referral to a collection agency or attorney is the essential ingredient of the closing statement, then the creditor must refer the claim to a collection agency or attorney. Implications that action is intended although never taken can also violate this section. An in-depth discussion of this section appears in Chapter 9, "Legal Boundaries and Limitations: The Debt Collection Practices Act."

Warning—Time Within Which an Intended Threat Will Take Place: If your letter or telephone call states, "We insist on payment by Monday May 7, or else we must immediately forward the action to an attorney," or if you imply that the matter will be referred immediately to the collection agency/attorney and then wait for three or four months before referral, this may constitute a misrepresentation under the Act. A simple statement that the matter will be forwarded to an attorney probably allows for more time to start the procedure of referral than using the word "immediately" or "within a week."

Strict Application of Closing Statement: The closing statement should be used in the following instances:

1. When the debtor has promised payment.
2. When the debtor has claimed payment.
3. When a message is left (in some cases). (See Chapter 4.)
4. When the debtor has promised to return goods.
5. When the debtor wishes to return merchandise.
6. When the debtor claims merchandise was returned.
7. When the debtor states he is unable to pay.

In brief, a closing statement should be used at the end of the telephone call.

There are three exceptions to this rule:

1. Where the intent is to utilize two or more calls, the closing statement should be used only when making the last call.
2. When leaving a message with a child, employee or third party who apparently is not involved with the collection process, a

closing statement should never be used. The same rule applies to anyone who takes a message, but apparently has no interest in the collection process or no relationship with the debtor. (See Chapter 4.) In general, closing statements on consumer debts should be left only with the individual consumer or spouse.

3. A closing statement should not be used in leaving a message on a recording device. (See Chapter 4.)

Seven Effective Closing Statements

1. If the rent is not received by Monday, May 7, this matter will be referred to our attorney for further action.

2. We must have the February and March payments by Monday, May 7, or else the matter will be forwarded to our collection agency/attorney to take whatever action is necessary to collect this debt.

3. We must insist on payment by Monday, May 7, or we will send this to our collection agency/attorney to enforce payment of this debt.

4. If two installment payments are not received by Monday, May 7, this matter will be referred to our attorney, who may institute suit by service of a summons and complaint.

5. If we do not receive your check by Monday, May 7, this claim will be delivered to our attorney to take the necessary action to collect this debt.

6. If the computer printer is not returned so that we receive it by Monday, May 7, this claim will be referred to a collection agency/attorney.

7. If you do make payment to the outpatient customer account department by Monday, May 7, you can avoid this matter being referred to our collection agency/attorney.

Three Special Alternative Closing Statements

Just as there are ways to emphasize a demand for payment, there are three different approaches to the closing statement.

a. I will put the file on the manager's desk, and if a check is not received by Monday, May 7, the matter will be referred to a collection agency/attorney.

b. If you intend to pay, now is the time to pay. Next week will be too late. By then this matter will have been referred to a collection agency/attorney.

c. If the matter is referred to an attorney, and suit is started, it may cost you additional court costs and expenses.

d. If payment is not received by Monday, May 7, then the debt will be referred to a collection agency/attorney.

Warning—Threat to Report to Credit Agency. The threat of reporting the delinquent credit of a consumer or business to a credit reporting agency is intentionally omitted here. To utilize this type of a statement, either the creditor, the collection agency, or the attorney *must* report the matter to a credit reporting agency. *The action promised or threatened must be done.* Usually, the burden of reporting falls on the creditor. If the creditor is reporting to the major reporting agencies, then the creditor may utilize this additional weapon. If the collection agency is reporting, then the statement should be confined to them. A copy of the Fair Credit Reporting Act appears in the appendix.

COLLECTION TIP: Identifying Geographic Location of Attorney or Collection Agency. If, for example, you mention a "Chicago" attorney or "Chicago" collection agency in your closing statement, the geographic area should be where the debtor resides or does business. If the creditor is located in Boston, and the debtor is located in Chicago, the debtor would be more concerned about a referral to a Chicago attorney. The collection agency/attorney will have the means to forward this matter to the Chicago attorney. Of course, a closing statement does not have to include a geographic area but may be limited to a referral to a collection agency or attorney, depending upon whose services will be used.

Negative Closing Statements

The basic closing statement may not be suitable for all situations, and in order to react to the different circumstances, alternative responses are available and illustrated here.

1. *Negative Closing Statement:* This is a weaker closing statement properly used in response to a promise of immediate payment or return of the goods. "Be certain that you mail your check by Monday,

May 7, so that it will not be necessary for this matter to be referred to a collection agency/attorney for further action or institution of suit."

2. *No Alternative Closing Statement:* The debtor has claimed payment, and the creditor feels that there is a possibility the debtor is correct. "You must forward a copy of the front and back of the cancelled check so that it can be credited to your account, since the money must have been incorrectly credited. If we do not receive the copy of the check by Monday, May 7, then we will have no alternative but to assume you did not pay and will refer this matter to a collection agency/attorney." You may also use this approach if the telephone worker wishes to blame the company policy for the hard line, such as, "Our policy is that we cannot carry a delinquency in house longer than 30 days. I have no alternative but to insist on payment by Monday, May 7, and if payment is not received by Monday, May 7, I will have no alternative but to refer this matter to a collection agency/attorney."

A negative closing statement is less effective, but should be used where the debtor is expressing good faith in an effort to pay and has made a promise of some form of payment.

The closing statement is omitted in most examples of dialogue provided in the book due to expediency. Actually, where appropriate, the closing statement should be used at the end of each dialogue.

Warning—Fulfillment of Threat or Promise: Always remember that the creditor must take the action promised or threatened. If the claims are not referred to a collection agency or attorney, then a statement to that effect must not be made. The same applies to any other action. What is promised or threatened must be fulfilled. If it is not, then the creditor may be exposing himself to liability for deceptive and misleading collection practices either under the Debt Collection Practices Act or under federal or state law.

EXAMPLE ILLUSTRATING ALL FOUR KEY INGREDIENTS

When it is our intention to make only one telephone call, the one telephone call should include all of the four golden keys: identification, foundation, demand for payment, and closing statement. If a series of two calls are being used, then the first call should include the first three components and the closing statement should be omitted since it is your intention to make another call before taking any further action. Furthermore, the customer may be retained if payment is received and no closing statement is made.

If the second call is made, all four ingredients: identification, foundation, demand for payment, and a closing statement should be repeated. The telephone caller should remember to use as part of the foundation a reminder about the first call and any promises made by the debtor.

Here is an example of a typical collection call. "Dr." stands for "Debtor" and "Cr." stands for "Creditor."

Identification:

Dr: Hello.

Cr: This is the XYZ Bank. Is Mr. Kelly there?

Dr: I'm Mr. Kelly.

Cr: Mr. Kelly, I am calling about your auto loan which is presently two months in arrears.

Dr: Who is this?

Cr: Mr. Clark.

Dr: I paid that two weeks ago.

Cr: My records show no payment. Perhaps you addressed the mail incorrectly. How much did you send?

Dr: I sent $450 for one month, so I am only one month in arrears.

Cr: The monthly payment on this loan is only $189.

Dr: Oh!

Foundation

Cr: We sent you several notices in the mail about this payment, and we have received no reply. Also, your payment book should still show open payments for these two months.

Dr: Oh! I sent money on my other loan.

Demand for Payment

Cr: Well, we must have the payment immediately.

Dr: OK. I will try to get it to you in a few weeks.

Cr: That will not be good enough. We must have it this week.

Dr: Well, I guess I could make it from the next paycheck.

Closing Statement

Cr: Fine. Then, it will be unnecessary for me to put this loan on the referral list to an outside attorney for institution of suit. I will look for the payment next week by Monday, May 7.

Dr: OK, by Monday, May 7.

Cr: Fine, thank you.

Checklist
1. Identification
2. Foundation
3. Demand for payment
4. Closing statement
    a. negative closing statement
    b. no alternative closing statement

CHAPTER 3

Seven Frequently Used Excuses and How to Respond to Them

This chapter deals with the proper approach to the most frequently used excuses to delay or avoid payment. A well-trained and well-educated telephone worker should be able to respond to the excuse offered and then still proceed with the problem of convincing the debtor to arrange payment of the debt. The excuses most often used are:

1. Promises of future payment
2. Debtor claims payment
3. Claims merchandise was returned—or needs to be
4. Claims he never ordered or received merchandise
5. Wants an invoice or statement
6. Medical troubles
7. Financial troubles

The telephone caller's response must be a reaction to the excuse for nonpayment. This requires a case-by-case approach in each telephone call. If the debtor is receptive and promises payment, an effort should be made to retain the debtor as a customer. The debtor's refusal to pay any money or refusal to return the merchandise warrants further action. The situations that fall between the two ends of the spectrum dictate an attitude on the part of the caller that falls somewhere between the extremes.

EXCUSE 1: PROMISE OF FUTURE PAYMENT

The most powerful excuse for a debtor to use is a promise of future payment. A promise to pay may not be defined technically as an excuse, but in reality, this promise buys more time and is a very persuasive device to forestall any action by the creditor. How the telephone worker reacts to this offer of good faith will often determine whether payment is actually made as promised, or as more frequently happens, another telephone call becomes a necessity. Sometimes promises of payment delay further action for weeks, months, and even longer.

Always Demand Payment in Full

Always request and expect payment in full whenever the debtor promises payment. Often, the telephone worker will respond to a promise of payment by inquiring as to "how much do you intend to pay." This response should never be a question. A request for the full amount should always be made.

Example:

Dr: I don't have the money right now.
Cr: But we must have payment by Monday, May 7.
Dr: Well, maybe I can send a little.
Cr: You don't understand. We must have payment in full by Monday, May 7.
Dr: But I can't pay the full amount.
Cr: This bill is over three months past due.
Dr: Suppose I pay half of it now and the balance....

Example:

Dr: I think I can pay next week.
Cr: We shall expect $500 (or whatever the full amount of debt) by Monday, May 7th.

The Right Response to Partial Payment

When the debtor responds that only a partial payment can be made, a serious attempt to obtain a commitment for the balance must be made at that time. Acceptance of the offer of a partial payment is only half the battle. You should insist that the debtor obligate himself to a *specific date* within which the balance will be paid. Offers of payment by "next month," or "in two weeks," should be translated immediately into a day and a month. Next month should become "by May 1st" and two weeks should become "by Wednesday, May 21st." The first day of the month is the best day to select since the debtor will be more likely to remember this day as a payment day. While payment may not be received or mailed on that day, the debtor will remind himself of the day, and will send the payment a few days later. If the day is the 10th day of the month, a greater chance exists to forget the day.

Example:

Cr: This is Mrs. Clark concerning the balance due to Dr. Jones

Dr: Yes, I know about this, but I can't possibly pay that money now I just do not have it.

Cr: The balance is only $80 and this debt is almost four months past due, and you have made absolutely no payment on the account.

Dr: Well, maybe I can send you a little and the balance in a month or so.

Cr: A little is not enough.

Dr: I just don't have the money right now.

Cr: We must have at least half immediately.

Dr: I can't send that much.

Cr: Well, exactly how much will you be able to send now?

Dr: How about $20 now?

Cr: So we will receive $20 by next Monday, May 21st.

Dr: Yes, by next Monday.

Cr: That leaves the balance of $60 and we will expect this on July 1st.

Dr: Well, I hope I'll be able to send it by then.

Cr: Mr. Reagan, we must have a specified time in order to permit you to pay this amount out.

Dr: OK, in about two months.

Cr: That is too long. July 1st is a month and a half. Surely, you can do it by then.

Dr: OK.

Cr: Then we will receive $20 by May 21st and $60 by July 1st.

Dr: Yeah, I can meet those payments.

How to Use the Installment Payment Plan to Collect the Debt in Full

Some debtors will only be able to pay the balance they owe in installment payments. Other debtors only think of repayment in terms of installments since originally the loan or extension of credit was cast in installments.

Explaining the Installment Schedule: For the debtor who is only able to pay in installments, a weekly or monthly schedule should be worked out explaining the due dates and the amounts of each future payment. The best approach is to choose a day of each week or a date of each month, preferably the first day of each month.

Example.

Cr: All right, you owe $5,000 and we will accept $500 per month until the full balance is paid and you can pay the interest after the last payment of principal.

Dr: I'll send the $500 in a few weeks

Cr: Make the payment on the first of May and on the first of each following month. That way you will know a payment is due the first of every month.

Dr: But I pay my rent on the first of the month. I need another week.

Cr: We will allow a grace period of one week, but the records will show that your payment is due on the first.

Dr: OK.

Demand for a Lump Sum: When regular payments are promised in writing and the debtor has fallen behind in these obligations, the aim is to bring the loan up to date. Collection of the past due payments in one lump sum is the main objective, and then the debtor may be permitted to continue making the regular payments. If this is not possible, you should attempt to obtain at least some of the past due payments. Of course, failing to accomplish this, the resumption of payments is the primary concern.

Example:

Cr:　You are three months in arrears in your monthly payment of $300 per month. We will need $900 within the week, or we will have to refer this to our attorney.

Dr:　I can't pay that amount. I just finished paying my auto insurance and $1,000 in repairs on my car. I can pay a couple of hundred.

Cr:　Well, pay $600 within the week and on the next installment payment due the first of next month, add another $300.

Dr:　Suppose I pay $300 next week, and $300 every two weeks until I am caught up. How does that sound?

Cr:　That sounds OK. So we will have $300 by May 21st, and $300 on June 3rd, and $300 on June 17th, and every two weeks until July 10th.

Will the Debtor Deliver on His Promise? Evaluating the credibility of the debtor's promise is very significant. A promise to resume payments when the promise obviously will not be kept is certainly not the ideal situation. Intimidation may produce this promise, but the creditor must be realistic. Sometimes, a smaller payment should be considered if the amount and schedule can be maintained.

Smaller payments are better than none at all. Some creditors take the position that the monthly payment should never be reduced. This position is basically shortsighted, since the essence of every installment payout is to receive a payment every month or every week, regardless of the amount. At least, a chance exists that the payments will continue and the loan will be paid. If the monthly payment cannot be made by the debtor, the debtor will be more likely not to send any payment rather than sending a smaller payment. Thus, strong reasons exist for considering reduced monthly payments. The schedule can always be reviewed every three months, and at that time further efforts may be made to increase the monthly payment.

COLLECTION TIP: Always Note the Date and Day. Whenever the debtor promises a payment of any type, remind the debtor exactly when the payment is due. Use specifics, such as "Monday, May 7," or "next Monday, May 7." Do not invite misunderstandings by utilizing such phrases as: "next week," "a week from Monday," "ten days from today," "two weeks from today," etc. The exact point of beginning (i.e., when you called) is often not recalled by the debtor. After two weeks pass, the debtor may believe the telephone call was made only a few days ago and two weeks still remain for payment. A specific date and a specific day are essential to an effective telephone call.

Example:

    Cr: We must have payment by Monday, May 7.

or

    Cr: We must receive payment no later than Monday, May 7.

COLLECTION TIP: *Get It in Writing*. When agreeing upon a payment schedule, advise the debtor to send a letter with the first payment, setting forth the payment schedule. This commitment provides the creditor with something in writing, and the debtor has reaffirmed the indebtedness as well as emphasized in his own memory the payment schedule.

COLLECTION TIP: *Cutting the String*. The creditor must establish a firm policy of when the string must be cut and when further action must be taken. But the collector must respond properly so that the "cutting the string" is supported by the foundation previously laid by the collector. One broken promise may or may not be enough to "cut the string." Certainly, two or three broken promises should be sufficient to cause referral to a collection agency/attorney. The reasons for the broken promises and whether any partial payments have been made are important considerations which may defer referral to a collection agency/attorney.

THE DOOMSDAY WEAPONS—FORECLOSURE AND EVICTION

When a creditor has security for a loan, a different situation exists between the creditor and the debtor. Although most promissory notes to banks, lending institutions, mortgage lenders, and finance companies enable the lender to accelerate payment of the balance due, and resort to the security, employing this threat to compel a promise to pay sometimes only creates more problems for the lender. Most borrowers are aware that their loan can be accelerated and that their machinery and equipment, their automobile or their real estate, can be foreclosed and sold to satisfy the loan. A premature threat often ruins the relationship between the borrower and the lender. The frightened borrower crawls into a shell and makes promises that will never be kept. The debtor slowly and surely retreats into a corner from which there is no escape other than the inevitable foreclosure. Use this threat sparingly, and only when absolutely necessary. Exploiting this vulnerability will not lead to an orderly resumption of payments, which happens to be the singular aim of all lenders.

The same rule holds true for the landlord. The tenant knows that eviction is the ultimate leverage that rests in the hands of the owner of the property. The consumer realizes that the telephone company may disconnect his telephone and the furniture store may repossess the furniture. The threat of such action is a powerful weapon, and should not be used indiscriminately. Many telephone workers representing these types of creditors immediately employ this weapon to drive home a hard-core collection effort. Some use the threat before any effort is made to find out why the debtor has not made the regular payment. The argument is made that this is the only thing the debtor understands. But this threat should only be used after all other efforts have failed, and certainly the threat should never be used on the very first telephone call, no matter how unsuccessful it may appear to be. The borrower or tenant should have an opportunity to consider the situation. The debtor will certainly consider the strong possibility that the creditor will exercise the options available and this will certainly be a factor in his decision to pay.

Why a Closing Statement Is Effective Even When a Debtor Has Promised to Pay

It is a common error to forget to use the closing statement when a debtor promises that a check will be mailed at once. "The check is in the mail" is the oldest joke in the collection industry. A high percentage of those promises are not kept. Many sophisticated debtors use the promise of payment as a device to stall and obtain an extension of time. The debtor waits for another telephone call and then repeats the same routine. A promise of immediate payment does not necessarily mean payment. A promise of immediate payment without a closing statement is equivalent to an invitation to the debtor not to pay.

It can be argued that it is unfair to threaten to refer an account to a collection agency/attorney if the debtor has just promised payment in full. Nevertheless, there are variations of the closing statement which would be appropriate. An example of a negative closing statement would be as follows:

- We will hold up reviewing the account for referral to our collection agency/attorney until Monday, May 7, but no later.
- If we receive your check by Monday, May 7, it will not be necessary for us to forward this account to our collection agency/attorney.
- If we do not receive your check by Monday, May 7, then we will have no alternative but to refer this matter to our collection agency/attorney, so please be sure it is mailed in time.

EXCUSE 2: THE DEBTOR CLAIMS PAYMENT

Whenever the debtor claims that payment was already made, the immediate response must be that "the creditor has no record of receiving payment." The reason for the careful wording of the response is to protect the creditor in the event the debtor is correct. If the office is uncertain, the follow-up response is to ask the debtor for a copy of the front and back of the check. With this information the creditor should be able to determine if the check has been credited to another account by misposting, has been deposited in the wrong checking account, or has been incorrectly credited for some other reason.

Of course, if the office records are up-to-date and accurate, and the telephone worker is certain that this excuse is a stalling device, the approach of the creditor should be stronger. A clear and concise statement should be made that the payment has not been received and a new check should be mailed at once. An offer should be made to accept the excuse that the postal service lost the letter, but at the same time extra emphasis should be placed on the sending of a new check.

Never Ask for a Check Number

Never ask when the check was sent! The debtor will leave the telephone to pull out his checkbook and ruffle through the pages. After an extended period of time, the check number and date will be furnished to the creditor. Both bits of information are useless except as an indication of the debtor's sincerity. The check number contributes nothing of value. If it were several months ago, the debtor would have already made a statement to this effect. If the check was recent, the same would be true.

Of course, for every rule there are exceptions. The name of the bank would be useful after a judgment is obtained, for this information would enable the creditor to attach the bank account to satisfy the judgment. So therefore, if it is a claim which you believe will be ultimately referred to an attorney for suit, obtaining the name of the bank may be helpful at a later date.

Very often the debtor will state that he either "made payment or will make a payment." More than likely the debtor has not made payment, and it is his intention to immediately send the payment. In this instance, treat the response as a promise of payment.

Often when the debtor claims payment within the last few days, the debtor is trying to terminate the telephone call and in fact has not mailed the check. The following replies might be used:

1. We must have the check by Monday, May 7th. If we do not receive it by Monday, May 7, we will be forced to refer the loan to our collection agency/attorney.

2. As long as we receive a copy of the front and back of the cancelled check or a new check by Monday, May 7, we will not have to refer this matter to our collection agency/attorney.

Refusal to Furnish Copy of Check: Considerable resistance may be encountered to a request for the debtor to send a copy of the front and back of a check. The debtor does not wish to spend the time and effort necessary reviewing his bank statement and stubs to locate the particular cancelled check. If the debtor is reluctant to supply a copy of the front and back of the check and asks for reimbursement for the cost of the copy (and the request appears to be sincere), the recommendation is to mail a check for $.50. Experience indicates that in most instances the debtor will send the copy of the check and sending the $.50 is worthwhile. Usually, the check has been misposted in some manner and the opportunity to remove the debtor from the delinquent account or delinquent loan list and retain him as a customer is worth the effort.

Response to Refusal to Send Copy of Check: If the debtor still refuses to send a copy of the check, the following approach might be tried:

"Sir, if someone claimed they made payment to you and you had no record of receiving the check, you certainly would want to see the check and the endorsement to find out how that check was diverted from the proper account. You certainly would appreciate the cooperation of the party who sent the check. This is what we are asking. We want to know what happened to the check. We want to know who received credit, who received the money."

If that approach fails, try the following:

"You realize that the account is still open and if we do not receive your check or a copy of the check, we will refer this claim to our attorney, and it is possible that both of us may have to appear in court. You will show the check in court and we will then find out to whom it was credited. Certainly this would be a waste of time and money. It would be a lot easier if you just sent us a copy of the check now, and save both of us all this trouble."

COLLECTION TIP: Closing Statement. Whenever a debtor claims payment, always use the closing statement and use a specific day and date. Depending upon the attitude of the debtor, a strong closing statement, a weak closing statement, or a negative closing statement should be used. But always use a closing statement.

Example:

Cr: This is Frank at Wally's Service Station. We still have not received your check for $450 for that transmission job.

Dr: Frank, I sent that check in over three months ago.

Cr: Well, we never received it.

Dr: Well, I did send it.

Cr: Could you send me a copy of the front and back of the check?

Dr: Frank, that means hours looking through my checkbook. Why don't you look through your records. I am sure it is easier for you.

Cr: Well, we have carefully examined our records and we know that we have not credited the check to your account. If we did receive it, then someone else received credit. We certainly would like to straighten this out, and the only way we can do it is with a copy of the front and back of the check.

Dr: Well, that's your problem.

Cr: It is really *our* problem. We must straighten this out since your account shows an open balance, and, Wally, we will refer this to our attorney if we can't resolve this problem.

Dr: Well, OK, I will take a look at my checkbook.

Cr: We must resolve this before the first of next month in order to close our books at the end of the month, so please be certain we receive your check before the first of next month so it will not be necessary to refer this to our attorney.

Dr: OK!!OK!! I will send it to you.

Cr: Thank you very much, and believe me, this is certainly the best way.

The closing statement was not utilized until the debtor exhibited substantial objections to the request for a copy of the front and back of the check. Most debtors, when confronted with this explanation, will cooperate quite readily.

EXCUSE 3: THE MERCHANDISE WAS RETURNED—OR NEEDS TO BE

What to Do When the Debtor Claims the Merchandise Was Returned

When a debtor claims that the merchandise was returned, the obvious response is to ask the customer to send the postal receipt, public carrier delivery receipt, United Parcel receipt, or any other appropriate receipt. The customer should be advised that the creditor has no record of receiving the merchandise and that the account is still open and marked unpaid. Determine the manner in which the merchandise was returned, when it was returned, how it was packed, and the address where it was mailed or shipped.

One key question to ask is the condition of the merchandise when it was shipped.

Example:

Dr: Green and Son Painting Co., Mr. Green speaking.

Cr: This is the Sturdy Office Furniture Company and we are calling concerning the bookshelf that we shipped last month.

Dr: Who is this?

Cr: This is Mr. Clark.

Dr: Well, Mr. Clark, the bookcases were not wood like you said, but more like cardboard; and as soon as I put some heavy books on the shelves, the shelves sort of caved in.

Cr: Well, we didn't say they were....

Dr: Anyhow, we shipped them back to you in the same crates as we got them.

Cr: When were they shipped?

Dr: A week ago.

Cr: How did you address them?

Dr: I put labels on with your address and paid for the shipping charges.

Cr: What condition were the shelves in? Were all the shelves caved in or just one shelf? Did you test just one bookshelf or all four?

Dr: I only tested one, and just one shelf caved in. You could probably repair it.

Cr: Mr. Green, if you would have examined the bookshelves, and the labels on the bookshelves, you would have seen that there was no representation that they were made of wood. It clearly said....

Dr: I don't care what it said, I know what the salesman said.

Cr: Well, when we receive it, we will inspect the condition and will make a decision then as to what we should do. If the shelves are damaged, you will be responsible. If the shelves are in good condition, I will recommend to accept them, since our policy is to give a full refund if there is no damage to the merchandise.

Dr: OK, you do what you want.

Debtors frequently return merchandise to avoid payment. The philosophy is the same whether it is a consumer or a business. The merchandise is either not needed anymore or is broken; or, as in most instances, the debtor just does not have the money and has chosen to live without the merchandise.

The problem arises when the creditor has not received the merchandise, and the debtor does not have the receipt or does not wish to find the receipt and send it to the creditor. The following are examples of the approach to use to persuade the debtor to send you the receipt.

1. "Until such time as we receive evidence of shipment to us, we must treat this account as open and unpaid and we will have no alternative but to refer this claim to a collection agency/attorney."

2. "It will be necessary for you to furnish us with evidence of shipment since our records do not indicate receipt of the merchandise. If we do not receive evidence of shipment by

Monday, May 7, we will be forced to refer this claim to a collection agency/attorney."

HELPFUL HINT: *Inspect Before Accepting*. When the customer has said that the merchandise was returned, always advise the customer that an inspection must be made before the return will be accepted. Until the merchandise is received, no inspection can be made.

Dealing with a Debtor Who Wants to Return the Merchandise

Frequently, the debtor will offer to return the merchandise for a variety of reasons which may range from damaged goods, a shortage, the wrong model number, the wrong color or material, or a wide assortment of reasons. A settlement may be in order, and a whole chapter in this book (Chapter 5, "How to Negotiate a Successful Settlement") has been devoted to the negotiation of a settlement. If the creditor has decided to accept a return of the merchandise, there are certain procedures which should be followed.

First, determine what is the condition of the item. If it is totally damaged and worthless to the creditor, neither the expense, time or effort should be expended in arranging for this valueless item to be returned to the possession of the creditor. Once this hurdle is overcome, the next item to be considered is whether the debtor will package the merchandise so that it will arrive in reasonably saleable condition. If the original packaging is available, the battle should be won. If not, then it is up to the telephone worker to evaluate whether the debtor is able to and will properly package the merchandise. Questions should be asked depending upon the type of debtor and the type of merchandise. Where a consumer is involved, careful attention should be given if the merchandise is fragile and the original packaging is no longer available. In any event, the problem must be addressed.

Dr: I am going to send back the clock radio.
Cr: Does the clock work?
Dr: The radio has static, and the clock works...I think.
Cr: What do you mean, "you think"?
Dr: Well, I never used the clock. It works, but not correctly.

Cr: How will you pack it?

Dr: I have some packing left over from a TV I bought, and I have a box from a pair of shoes. Don't worry, it will be packaged properly.

A closing statement is still recommended in all cases where the debtor promises to return the merchandise. A weak or negative closing statement should be used.

1. Please return the computer to _____. Be certain that it is shipped by Monday, April 30, so that we will receive it by May 7. If we do not receive it by May 7, we will have no other alternative but to refer this matter to a collection agency/attorney.

2. Please do not make us refer this matter to a collection agency/attorney so be certain that you ship the merchandise by Monday, April 30.

COLLECTION TIP: Separate Letter. The debtor should be advised to write a separate letter to the credit or collection manager on the day the merchandise is shipped. This will achieve two purposes: First, the creditor will know the day the merchandise was shipped and can alert the shipping department to expect the shipment and also to notify the credit or collection department when the merchandise arrives. Second, if the letter is not received, the creditor will know that the goods have not been shipped. Thus, a second telephone call can be made immediately without waiting the additional time necessary for the shipping department to search and confirm that the goods were not received.

Accepting the Offer of Return: The wisest course is to accept a return of the merchandise in all of the above instances since economically it will benefit both parties. The exception of course is merchandise that is broken or seriously damaged. Soft goods require inspection upon receipt. Items that are expensive and fragile, such as television sets and electronic equipment, definitely require inspection. The type of item is the key factor in deciding whether or not to accept a return.

Example:

Cr: This is Mr. Clark from the Star Wars Computer Center. We received a notification that you refused to accept the credit card charge for your personal computer.

Dr: That is right. It doesn't work. You know that. I have spoken to Charlie six times.

Cr: We were under the impression that the problem had been taken care of.

Dr: Well, it worked for a while, but even after I brought it in for the second time, it still did not work properly. I want to return it.

Cr: But Charlie said it was working perfectly when it left our store the last time.

Dr: Well, maybe, but it went on the blink the next day.

Cr: Did you drop it off the table?

Dr: No. I didn't touch it. It never accepted the first diskette.

Cr: Well, we can't make a decision until we receive the computer and inspect it.

Dr: Well, how do I ship it?

Cr: I think it would be best if you brought it in and let the owner look at it.

Dr: OK. I will call you to tell you when I am coming in.

Cr: Can you bring it in this week?

Dr: I don't know.

Cr: Well, can we make an appointment?

Dr: OK. Next Tuesday at 3:00 P.M.

Cr: We will see you then.

In this instance a closing statement was not used since it wasn't indicated, but a negative closing statement could have been used. If a second call was made, a closing statement should be used.

EXCUSE 4: MERCHANDISE WAS NEVER ORDERED OR RECEIVED

Debtor Maintains He Never Ordered Merchandise

When the debtor claims he never ordered the merchandise and never heard of the creditor, the following steps are in order:

1. Verify the name and address.

2. Verify to whom the order was shipped.

3. Verify whether a purchase order is on file.

Of course, if there was a mistake in the record keeping or shipping instructions and no purchase order exists, the only alternative is to apologize to the party on the telephone for the inconvenience. The creditor should be aware of the law on unsolicited merchandise. The debtor has a right to retain the unsolicited merchandise. (See Chapter 9, "Legal Boundaries and Limitations.") The creditor may request the return of the goods, but cannot insist on the return. Whether the creditor must advise the debtor of the law is a delicate question. As far as the author knows, there is no reported decision in the Courts on this issue.

Valid Order: On the other hand, if it appears that the creditor has a valid order and the shipping instructions were carried out properly, the following responses might be used:

1. "We do not ship unsolicited merchandise. You ordered the merchandise and we shipped it to your address" (and where appropriate, say "We have a shipping receipt"), "and therefore we must insist on immediate payment. If we do not receive payment by Monday, May 7, we will have no alternative but to refer this matter to a collection agency/attorney."

2. "Our records show that you ordered the merchandise and we shipped the merchandise to your address. If we do not receive payment by Monday, May 7, we will have no alternative but to refer this matter to a collection agency/attorney."

Signed Order: If the creditor has a signed purchase order, and the shipping instructions were properly executed, the creditor should present a stronger position:

"We have a signed purchase order and a delivery receipt. You ordered and received the merchandise. If we do not receive payment by Monday, May 7, we will be forced to refer this matter to a collection agency/attorney for further proceedings."

Current Records Should Be Available: In any of the above situations, current records should be available to the telephone worker. If the telephone worker is uncertain, the debtor will have to be advised that the records will be checked. The telephone call is totally wasted, for the debtor will do absolutely nothing until another call is made. This applies whether the debtor is truthful or is merely stalling.

> **COLLECTION TIP: Business Debtor.** With regard to a sale to a business, often an employee orders and the owner is not aware of this. If a name appears on the purchase order, advise the owner of the name. Also, ask the owner to inquire among his employees to determine if the employees know the whereabouts of the merchandise.

Debtor Says He Never Received the Merchandise

A debtor frequently admits that he ordered the merchandise, but claims he never received it. The shipping receipt is the paper that the debtor signs upon receipt of the goods. The receipt is issued by United Parcel Service, the Postal Service, a public carrier such as a railroad, a trucking concern, a shipping line, an airline, a private carrier such as Federal Express or Emery Air Freight, or any other private firm which engages in the delivery of goods and merchandise. If a receipt is available, and the records of the creditor clearly disclose shipment and receipt by the debtor, the following dialogue should be used:

Cr: This is Mr. Clark of the Downtown Department Store. We shipped a high-density reading lamp three months ago, and we have sent you two statements, but we still have not received payment.

Dr: I never received the lamp, and I usually do not pay for what I do not receive.

Cr: We have a receipt showing you received the lamp.

Dr: Who signed it?

Cr: It appears that Mary Thompson signed it. Is that your wife's name?

Dr: Yes, but she says she never got it.

Cr: Well, we will be glad to send you a copy of the receipt, but we still must have payment by May 7. I will mail the receipt today so you will have it by May 2.

Dr: Well, we still did not receive the lamp.

Cr: Sir, we delivered the merchandise and have proof of delivery. If we do not receive payment by Monday, May 7, we will be forced to refer this matter to a collection agency/attorney.

Dr: I will speak to my wife.

Cr: Please do, and we will expect payment by May 7.

Dr: OK.

Cr: Thank you and goodbye.

Dr: Goodbye.

Requesting Written Statement of Nonreceipt: If the telephone worker's documentation clearly shows shipment and receipt, but the debtor is adamant that the merchandise was not received, the creditor might request that the debtor set forth in writing a letter stating that the merchandise was not received. The reason for requesting the letter is that the creditor may furnish it to the firm that shipped the goods (United Parcel, Postal Service, Public Carrier, etc.) so an investigation can proceed. The creditor may carry insurance coverage on valuable effects, and in this instance, a letter of nonreceipt is very important. Very often such a request will prompt the debtor to discover the goods and payment will be received.

The appropriate response in this instance would be:

"We would appreciate it if you would write us a letter stating that you never received the merchandise and we will forward it to our carrier who will investigate this matter. Of course, if we do not receive a letter by Monday, May 7, we will be forced to refer this matter to a collection agency/attorney."

Shipping by Post Office: Some merchandise is shipped by mail, such as books, magazines, etc. and the creditor has no receipt showing delivery. It is a difficult situation if the debtor is claiming he never received the book. While you may prove your case in court, the amount involved usually does not warrant such action. The best approach might be as follows:

Cr: This is Mr. Clark from the Business Publishing Company. We shipped our best-selling book, *Office Administration*, three months ago, but we have not received your payment of $49.95 despite two statements and two letters.

Dr: What book?

Cr: The name of the book is *Office Administration*. We have a purchase order from you.

Dr: Yes, I remember ordering it, but I don't remember receiving it.

Cr: Well, it was shipped on February 20.

Dr: That's fine, but we never got it.

Cr: Mr. Thompson, we sent you two statements in March, but you never responded to them.

Dr: Probably never got them, or didn't know what they were about.

Cr: But you do remember ordering the book.

Dr: Yes, I ordered it, but those statements came in when I was very busy.

Cr: Then, you do remember the statements?

Dr: Yes. I guess so.

Cr: Well, why didn't you contact us then?

Dr: I don't know. I told you, I was busy.

Cr: Do you remember receiving the collection letters?

Dr: Look, I didn't receive the book.

Cr: Perhaps one of your employees took the book when it came in, and is either reading it or took it home.

Dr: I don't know.

Cr: Well, Mr. Thompson, our firm shipped the book, and we expect payment. If we don't receive payment by Monday, May 7, we will refer this to a collection agency/attorney. Perhaps we can avoid this if you will check with your other employees to see if you can locate the book.

Dr: OK, I will look around.

Cr: I am sure you will find it.

Dr: I hope so.

Cr: Thank you and goodbye.

Dr: Goodbye.

Comment on Dialogue: Perhaps the debtor will not pay, but at least the telephone worker has delivered an excellent effort.

COLLECTION TIP: Correct Name and Address. Be certain that you have the correct name and address. Many of these problems are the fault of the creditor since the merchandise is shipped to a party with the same name but different address or to the correct party at a wrong address. Be sure you check your records.

EXCUSE 5: DEBTOR WANTS PROOF OF OBLIGATION

Debtor Wants Invoice

Invoice: When a debtor requests an invoice for the first time, agree to mail it to the debtor, but always use a closing statement. The closing statement can be a weak closing statement or a negative closing statement, but always use a closing statement.

1. "We will send the invoice to you by Friday, so you will receive it by Monday. We shall expect payment by return mail. If we do not receive payment by Monday, May 7, we will be forced to refer this matter to a collection agency/attorney."

2. "The invoice will be in the mail today. We shall expect payment by Monday, May 7. If we do not receive payment by Monday, May 7, we will be forced to refer this matter to a collection agency/attorney."

Second Request for Invoice: If a second request is made for an invoice, the debtor should be reminded that an invoice was already sent. This is obviously a stall, and a second invoice should not be sent. At this point, you have been forewarned that the debtor is merely stalling. The sooner action is commenced, the sooner payment will be received.

Give Debtor the Benefit of Your Doubt

However, situations occur where an invoice should be furnished to the debtor. In some instances, an invoice is lost and the debtor is quite sincere in his embarrassment in not paying. The telephone worker must use judgment in evaluating the credibility of the debtor. Perhaps 80 percent of the requests for invoices are an effort to postpone action by the creditor, but 20 percent may be legitimate. The line of distinction is difficult. Therefore, when in doubt, afford the debtor the benefit of that doubt and send the invoice. Failure to do so will produce a debtor who has no record of the indebtedness, and these circumstances will never result in payment. A debtor who has no bill or invoice will not pay!

On the other hand, the large class of debtors who use this method of deferring payment are not worthy of considerate treatment. The creditor should not send an invoice, should advise the debtor that an invoice is not being sent, and should use the strongest closing statement.

Example:

Dr: Frank's Diner.
Cr: Is Frank there?
Dr: Frank who?
Cr: The owner, Frank McDougal.
Dr: OK, I'll get him.
Dr: Frank speaking. Who is this?

Cr: This is Mr. Young of the General Paper Company. We shipped you an order of paper products three months ago; we have not received payment.

Dr: I have no record of receiving the order. Why don't you send me an invoice? I will need an invoice to check it out.

Cr: Mr. McDougal, we shipped the order three months ago and have sent three invoices and two statements. We also sent you two letters. We are not going to send another invoice. This bill is long past due and will be sent to a collection agency if payment is not received by Monday, May 7.

Dr: Don't get upset. All I'm asking for is an invoice. After I get it, I'll send you a check.

Cr: Mr. McDougal, I am not sending an invoice because two were already sent to you. I must have payment by Monday, May 7.

Dr: How do I know how much to pay without an invoice?

Cr: The amount is $980, and mail the check to General Produce at 100 Main Street, Center City, 12345. Do you want me to repeat it?

Dr: No, I know your address. You say $980.

Cr: Yes.

Dr: OK. I'll check this out.

Cr: Please do, so it will not be necessary to send this to a collection agency.

Dr: You won't have to do that.

Cr: I'm sure it will not be required. I will look for your check on Monday, May 7.

Dr: OK.

Cr: Goodbye.

Comment on Dialogue: The creditor came on very strong, and tried to soften the effect towards the end of the telephone call. But, the creditor's effort to soften was somewhat incomplete, and the net effect was a very firm collection call. Obviously, the creditor felt that the request was merely an effort to delay payment.

The same rules apply to requests for statements. The first one should be sent, but a second request usually should be denied.

EXCUSE 6: DEBTOR HAS MEDICAL PROBLEMS

Determine Duration of Illness

The first step is to determine whether the debtor is suffering from a brief or a serious illness.

Brief Illness or Minor Injury: If it is a brief illness or minor injury, where the recovery will take place within a few weeks, and the debtor will be returning to work, express concern and wish the debtor a speedy recovery. If the debtor seems sincere, a short extension may be in order. Nevertheless, the thrust of the telephone call should target the benefits of making payments even when a minor problem is encountered. Suggest that the debtor use funds in his bank accounts, or borrow or utilize other reserves to pay the bill to bring the account up-to-date.

Serious Illness or Injury: If it is a serious injury or illness which will incapacitate the debtor for a prolonged period of time, a somewhat different method must be used. Determine the extent of health insurance coverage the debtor has to evaluate the impact on the debtor's resources. A thorough discussion of the debtor's financial resources should be made, including the ability to borrow by conventional means, as well as through relatives and friends. Perhaps in these circumstances a recasting or refinancing of the obligation is in order.

Example:

Cr: I am sorry to learn of your injury, and I want to wish you a speedy recovery.

Dr: Thank you.

Cr: This loan must be brought up-to-date for it is over three months in arrears.

Dr: But I am not working, and I have to feed the family and pay the rent and electric company.

Cr: Well, I'm sure you have some savings. Perhaps you can withdraw enough money to make two payments.

Dr: Savings are for emergencies. If I didn't have that money when I was injured, the family couldn't survive. Anyhow, there isn't much left.

Cr: How about borrowing the money? We do need at least two payments to prevent this matter from being sent to an attorney.

Dr: I doubt if my father would lend me any more money, since he covered some of the doctor bills, but I might ask him.

Cr: You realize how important it is to maintain a good credit standing?

Dr: Yes, I know that.

Cr: So please don't make it necessary for us to refer this matter to a collection agency/attorney.

Dr: No, I will speak to my father, and maybe if he says no, I may be able to get the money somewhere else. I'll call you next week.

When Debtor Is Confined to Bed

If the debtor claims confinement to bed and inability to converse over the telephone because of an injury or illness, compliance with the request is necessary. An effort should be made to talk to the wife or husband or other close family member. A telephone call should never be made to a hospital. The course of action to take if the illness is serious is to return to using letters.

Cr: Is Mr. Thompson home?

Dr: Yes, but he is in bed.

Cr: To whom am I speaking?

Dr: This is his wife.

Cr: This is the Orange National Bank.

Dr: Is this about the loan my husband has?

Cr: Well,...

The Debt Collection Practices Act restricts contact with third parties except spouses. This problem is discussed more thoroughly in Chapter 4, "How to Leave a Message That Gets Through to the Debtor."

COLLECTION TIP: The Unwritten Clause. A cavalier attitude will produce a debtor who may very well hang up the telephone. The psychology of the debtor is that the illness or injury is an act of God. As such, the debtor believes an unwritten clause has been included in the loan agreement or contract entitling the debtor to an automatic extension of the debt until such time as the debtor recovers. The job of the telephone worker is to persuade the debtor that his personal misfortune does not create this unwritten clause.

EXCUSE 7: DEBTOR HAS FINANCIAL PROBLEMS

Business

Coping with the business debtor that encounters financial problems requires the patience of a saint and the diplomacy of a peacemaker. Basically, the business debtor is not your adversary; your adversaries are the other creditors with whom you are competing. The business debtor with financial problems has baked a pie with six pieces. Unfortunately, eight creditors have been invited for dinner. Some of the creditors will go hungry.

Repayment—A Game of Chance: The story goes that a very aggressive creditor kept calling this businessman at least once a week for several weeks about a debt for several thousand dollars. Finally, in the last two weeks the creditor called twice. Each time, a message was left, since it seemed the businessman was always out, in conference, or on the telephone. On the last call, the debtor picked up the telephone call, and the conversation continued like this·

> "You know, you have been calling for the last month and giving me a pain in the neck· We know we owe you the money We owe lots of people money. We have lots of problems, but we are trying. Each week we put the names of all of our creditors in a hat, and we pick out about four or five creditors. On Monday, we send them checks. Now, if you keep on calling and being rude to our receptionist, I am going to instruct our bookkeeper to not even put your name in the hat."

The moral of the story is that if the debtor is still in business and operating, he is trying to pay his debts. Whether he will be successful or not is another question. In any event, the operation of his business indicates that money is coming in, since payroll and rent are being met. Normally, some money should be left over to pay old debts. The problem is to convince the debtor to choose you as the lucky creditor.

Therefore, if the business fails to pay after a reasonable number of telephone calls, do not continually use more telephone calls. At least two calls should be made, but not more than three or four calls. Stronger action is warranted since other creditors are receiving the money. At this point referral to a collection agency/attorney is recommended.

Obtaining Easy Payments: Most businesses are attuned to making installment payments, and this may be the answer in dealing with businesses. Of course, if it is a small amount, the entire balance must be demanded. However, a larger amount is suitable for a payout plan and the entire telephone call should be targeted at making an agreeable arrangement with the debtor to reduce the debt to "easy" installments. The offer of a payout plan should include a larger lump sum down payment, but this should not be a stumbling block if the debtor refuses.

Never ask the debtor when he thinks he will be able to pay. Always make a reasonable suggestion first. Then, permit the debtor to suggest an amount. This prevents a ridiculous offer of $10 per month as a starting figure. Once a figure has been presented by the creditor, the responsive offer will at least be in the same neighborhood, or else no responsive offer will be made. The conversation might sound like this:

Cr: It has been three months since we installed the partitions in your office and there is still a balance due of $5,000.

Dr: I know, but business has been very bad and I have been barely able to meet payroll.

Cr: We also have to meet payroll, and we do not want to have to refer this to our attorney. Can we work out a payout plan?

Dr: I don't know. I owe some back real estate taxes and…

Cr: How about $1,500 down and $1,000 per month?

Dr: Are you kidding? I couldn't even pay $500.

Cr: Well, how much can you pay?

Dr: The very best I could do is $200 per month starting in 60 days.

Cr: That is no good. I must have some money now. Can you pay me $500 in a week?

Dr: Next week is the first of the month. I have rent to pay.

Cr: What about on the tenth of the month?

Dr: Possibly.

Cr: And $500 a month after that?

Dr: I can't meet that. I'll only default.

Cr: How about $400?

Dr: $300 is the best I can do.

Cr: $350 for three months and then we'll talk again.

Dr: OK, that sounds good.

Cr: Then, $500 by the tenth of next month, and $350 a month after that, beginning on the first of the next month.

Dr: OK.

While it is not an ideal telephone collection call, the first hurdle has been passed. It is important to follow up a few days before the tenth to be certain the debtor sets aside the $500 to meet this obligation. Of course, if no offer is received, the next step is further action with a collection agency/attorney. See Chapter 5 on "How to Negotiate a Successful Settlement," p. 86, "Bidding Against Yourself."

Warning—Communication: Repeated telephone calls amounting to harassment will not achieve the purpose of obtaining payment. After the first call, you should be able to evaluate whether this debtor will make installment payments. If the reaction is negative, other action must be considered. Be certain to explore all the alternatives, and don't put yourself in a corner with strong language. The idea is to further communication, not to cut off communication.

Consumer

Ask Questions About the Debtor's Financial Situation: The same rules apply to financial problems of the consumer as apply to medical problems. Constant inquiry must be made to enable the telephone worker to reach a decision as to the proper course of action. While the financial excuse may be a facade to enable the debtor to delay payment, asking the routine questions will smoke out whether the debtor is sincere or just masquerading. The following should be asked:

"How much do you earn?"

"How much is your rent?"

"Are your rent payments current?"

"How much do you pay each month on your mortgage payment?"

"Are your mortgage payments current?"

"Do you have an IRA?"

"Do both you and your spouse work?"

"What kind of automobile do you own?"

"Do you have any loans?"

"Are the payments on the loans current?"

"Are you living in a condominium or cooperative?"

"Do you expect a tax refund?"

"Are your credit card payments in arrears or current?"

"Do you have a bank account?"

"Do you own any stocks?"

If all of the above questions were answered by the debtor, this would paint a fairly accurate picture of the debtor's financial condition. The purpose of the questions are to determine whether the debtor really has a severe financial problem, and whether his resources can be marshalled to pay the debt. Each question should be pursued to obtain additional information until the telephone worker becomes confident that the entire story has been told.

Example:

Dr: I know my loan is four months in arrears, but I just don't have the money. You really don't want to repossess a four-year-old Volkswagon that is all beat up.

Cr: No, I guess not; but how do you pay the insurance on the car in New York? That is probably over $1,000.

Dr: I borrowed that from my mother-in-law. I told her that if she didn't lend me the money, I would not have a car to visit her.

Cr: Sometimes mothers-in-law come in handy. Does your wife work?

Dr: Yes, she works part time at a lawyer's office. She doesn't get paid much.

Cr: Can you tell me the name of the lawyer?

Dr: No, I don't want you to bother her; she doesn't even know the loan is behind four months. Maybe I can pay $10 a month. Is that OK?

Cr: Well, I don't know. Is your mortgage four months in arrears also?

Dr: No, I have to pay the mortgage. I don't want my house taken away.

Cr: How much do you pay a month?

Dr: About $700.

Cr: Does this include taxes?

Dr: No, I pay that separately.

The conversation continues as long as information is being gained. If the debtor becomes evasive and refuses to answer, the conclusion is obvious that he has the money but it is being diverted somewhere else. At this point, other action is warranted.

Outrageous Excuses for Nonpayment: The excuse of financial trouble can produce some of the most bizarre and outlandish reasons for not paying, as the following statements illustrate:

"My dog needed a cataract operation and it cost over $500."

"Roto-Rooter cost over $300."

"I invested in a floating gambling casino that was docked outside the three-mile limit, and the ship sunk."

"My boyfriend left and took all my money."

"I was mugged and all my bankbooks were stolen. It will take me six weeks before I can finish the paperwork to withdraw my money."

"The seven-year locusts came and wiped me out."

"The van just disappeared.... I didn't report it to the police because my wife also disappeared with the van."

Most blatant excuses attempt to use the unusual as evidence of credibility. The more bizarre, the better it sounds. The best response is careful and persistent questioning.

RETURNED CHECKS: ANOTHER EXCUSE FOR DELAYING PAYMENT

When clients refer returned checks to our office for collection, they are treated separately and distinctly from any other type of indebtedness such as unpaid loan payments or open accounts. Creditors must also consider a returned check as a different type of indebtedness and one that requires special handling. Of 44 billion checks processed in 1986, after redeposit of one percent, about 3/10 of one percent remain unpaid, that is, a total of about 132 million checks.

Determine Why Check Was Returned

A returned check is a check which has been mailed or delivered to the creditor in payment for some service or merchandise. The creditor has deposited the check in its bank account, and the check was transmitted through the federal clearance system, and presented for payment at the debtor's (issuer's/maker's) bank. Normally, the debtor's account would be debited and the monies transferred to the creditor's bank and then deposited (credited) to the account of the creditor.

Under certain circumstances the debtor's bank will not debit the debtor's account, but will return the check to the creditor's bank marked "Unpaid." The reason why the check is returned is significant and does have an impact on the type of telephone call to be made.

Relationship Between Bank and Creditor: The relationship between a bank and its depositor is that of a lender and borrower. The depositor is lending his money to the bank to be paid out pursuant to the depositor's written instructions (the written check signed by the depositor). Of course, the lender has agreed to borrow the money only on certain terms and conditions, including charges for certain actions, and according to rules and regulations as to certain procedures. The banking departments, both federally and in each state, also exercise control over the depositor and the bank in accordance with the laws passed by Congress and the respective states.

The check may be returned for a variety of reasons, the most frequent ones being:

1. *Uncollected Funds:* The debtor has deposited sufficient funds to cover the amount of the check, but the funds are traveling through the federal clearance system and have not as yet been credited to the debtor's account.

When a check is deposited in a bank account, three to ten days were usually required for the check to clear (going through the federal clearance system), depending upon whether the check was drawn upon a local bank, a bank outside the immediate locality, or in a nearby or distant state. In some instances two and three weeks were needed to clear the check. Recently, a law was passed to require the banks to substantially reduce the time within which a depositor's account must be credited.

2. *Insufficient funds:* The debtor has not sufficient funds on deposit to cover the amount. In short, the check will not be paid unless the debtor makes another deposit.

3. *Account Closed:* This terminology is self-evident. However, the creditor should realize that both the bank and the depositor make mistakes, and sometimes accounts that are closed may be reopened.

4. *Stale Date:* This designation indicates that the date of the check is "unreasonably" old (stale) in relation to the date of deposit by the creditor. This decision by the bank is usually "bank policy" for the purpose of protecting their depositors. The reasoning is that a check dated three or four months ago may have fallen into the wrong hands,

for normally, creditors deposit checks immediately. The proper course would be for the creditor to require the debtor to replace the check with a check dated currently. Failing that, an attorney should be consulted, so that the check may be properly presented for payment to the bank.

5. *Payment Stopped:* The debtor has instructed the bank to refuse payment. The debtor may have delivered this instruction to the bank for a variety of reasons, including defective merchandise, nondelivery, shortages, or any other breach of contract.

With regard to checks issued for services or merchandise where the check is not exceptionally large, the check may be redeposited in situation 1, 2, and 3, whether a business or consumer debtor. With regard to situation 4, perhaps a telephone call or letter to the debtor would be appropriate. As to situation 5, inquiry should immediately be made as to the reason for the stop payment. In other situations such as installment loans or large checks, in situations 1, 2, or 3 the creditor must realize that a serious financial problem exists, and redepositing the check may be granting the debtor an extension of time.

Do Not Threaten Criminal Prosecution

In the 1930s the confidence man would suddenly appear in a small western town and issue several dozen checks to unsuspecting merchants for both cash and merchandise. Before the checks were returned by the bank upon which they were drawn (usually marked "Account Closed," since the name on the check was either fictitious or deceased), the confidence man had driven across the state line and was planning to execute the same scam in another town. Finally, laws were passed and this type of scam became a criminal offense punishable by a fine and imprisonment.

The Essential Ingredient: In order to criminally prosecute a party for bouncing a check, an essential ingredient to be proved at the trial is the *intent* of the party *not to pay* the check and to *defraud* the party to whom the check was delivered. In cases where the confidence man issued 10 or 20 checks to merchants on a nonexistent checking account, the proof was relatively easy.

The Most Frequent Excuses: Proving a case against the businessman or the consumer is totally different. The debtor has usually issued just one check to a creditor, and this one check has been returned by the bank. The excuses for nonpayment of the check could be any of the following:

1. I did not know it would take so long for the checks I deposited to clear and be credited to my account.

2. I just hired a new bookkeeper who I thought was more experienced than to issue a check against uncollected funds.

3. My bookkeeper's clerk added incorrectly, and we thought we had the money in the account.

4. A check bounced which we deposited, and this caused the insufficient funds.

5. The bank closed the account and we did not get notification. We thought the account was open, and we would have instructed the bank to pay the check and debit a different account at the bank.

6. We just moved and my wife forgot about notifying you, for she notified the other creditors by sending them a different check.

The excuses are endless because in most cases the debtor does not intend to defraud the creditor, but is truly trying to pay the bill. For these reasons it is obvious that the debtor has not committed a crime under the statute, for the requisite intent is missing. For most felonies and misdemeanors, "intent" is usually a necessary ingredient of the proof to obtain a conviction.

Warning—Threatening Criminal Prosecution: Clearly, a threat that nonpayment of any debt will result in arrest or imprisonment is a violation of the Debt Collection Practices Act (Section 814 subd. 4). The creditor is not subject to the Act, but should certainly abide by these sections (see Chapter 9, "Legal Boundaries and Limitations.") To intend to take some action, there must be substantial reason to believe that the debtor did intend to defraud the creditor. The Debt Collection Practices Act also prohibits taking any action that cannot be legally taken or that is not intended to be taken (Section 814 subd. 5). Where one check has been returned for insufficient or uncollected funds, intent to defraud would be difficult to prove. Therefore, a creditor who knew, or should have known that the debtor did not intend to defraud, and who still threatens criminal action may very well expose himself to violations of the Debt Collection Practices Act or some other similar statute which may apply to creditors. Thus, no threat of criminal prosecution should be made, mentioned, or *even inferred.*

Emphasis is deliberately placed on the word "inferred," for inferring criminal prosecution could be just as bad as threatening criminal prosecution. The following are some examples of "inferring" a threat of criminal action:

1. "You know you can get into a lot of trouble by giving me a bounced check."
2. "You know if I decided to prosecute, you might go to jail."
3. "A bum check could be a ticket to real serious problems with the authorities."
4. "You don't want to spend any time in jail for issuing a bum check."

When to Consider Prosecution: Nevertheless, in those instances where there are many checks from the same debtor issued to the same creditor under suspicious circumstances, an intent to defraud may exist. Of course, if the amount is large or the debtor has issued checks to other creditors, circumstantial evidence might be strong enough to support "intent." Where the intent to defraud becomes obvious, the creditor should consider reporting the matter to the appropriate authorities for criminal prosecution. In some instances where a conviction is obtained, the Court will direct the defendant to make whole or partial restitution.

A copy of the New York Penal Law dealing with this will be found in Appendix C: Dishonored Checks.

Double Recovery Laws on Returned Checks

Many states, including New York and California, have passed laws which provide for double and triple recovery of the amount of the check in those instances where the debtor has issued a check which has been returned unpaid by the bank (these states are Arizona, California, Colorado, Idaho, Indiana, New York). Other states provide for recovery of the amount due plus the costs of suit and protest fees (Connecticut, Delaware, Florida, Hawaii, Illinois, Maine, Maryland, Massachusetts). Some states, in addition, allow for reasonable attorneys fees (Florida, Illinois). A few state laws are more complicated (Colorado, Minnesota).

Most of these laws provide very detailed procedures that the creditor must undertake before the creditor will be able to utilize the law to enforce its provisions. Most of the laws require strict disclosure and notice provisions which take the form of conspicuous posters at the counter where the check is delivered, disclosing clearly the contents of the statute, or a written notice, sometimes by registered or certified mail, clearly appraising the debtor of the rights of the creditor. The New York law actually provides an example of the form for the notice letter to the party who issued the dishonored check.

The creditor should examine the law in its own state and make the decision whether or not to use the provisions of the law in a telephone communication to the debtor. Advising the debtor of the existence of the law may require the creditor to proceed under the law unless the creditor expressly states that no proceedings will be taken. While this may appear to be an anomaly, the explanation is that referring to the law implies the creditor will use the law. Therefore, unless the creditor intends to use the law, it should not be referred to in the collection telephone call.

A copy of the New York and North Carolina laws will be found in Appendix C.

Additional Ammunition

There is no question that the creditor should utilize the existence of a returned check to assist the creditor in the collection of a debt. If the check has been issued after the service was rendered or the merchandise has been shipped, the debtor has acknowledged that the creditor properly performed the service or the creditor has delivered what was ordered to the satisfaction of the debtor.

In those circumstances where the check has been delivered prior to delivery of the merchandise, such as in the direct mail industry where the debtor is ordering from a catalog, the creditor cannot make these assumptions even when the check is returned for insufficient or uncollected funds. The debtor might have deliberately withdrawn money from the bank because the merchandise was defective so that sufficient funds would not be available to pay the check.

But in most cases this is not the situation, and the creditor should use the returned check as an additional foundation to strip the debtor of any defenses to payment. The normal case presents the situation that the debtor does not have funds to pay, and is certainly unable to meet his debts as they are coming due. In telephone contact with the debtor concerning a bad check, two important points are self-evident:

1. The check should be used as additional foundation.
2. The debtor has a serious financial problem.

COLLECTION TIP: Redepositing a Check. Should a creditor redeposit a check, request a new check or insist upon cash, a money order, or a certified check. This decision depends upon a variety of circumstances. If the debtor is a business, inquire if the business is operating and what the financial condition is. If the business is sound, perhaps the creditor should redeposit the check. Other things to consider are: Is it worthwhile to insist on cash or a money order when the amount is very small? Is the debt substantially in arrears? Does the debtor have a good record up to now of making payments? Obviously, the creditor must use his best judgment and make his decision accordingly. The creditor should insist on a money order or certified check if the debt is large, substantially in arrears, or if the debtor has a serious financial problem. Of course, the chances of receiving this may be small, but the creditor must realize that redepositing a check or accepting a new check is merely granting the debtor an extension of time.

Example:

Cr: Is Mr. Taylor there?

Dr: This is Mr. Taylor.

Cr: This is the Western Finance Company. Your check for the last two payments was returned for insufficient funds.

Dr: I know, the bank told me. Redeposit the check. It will clear this time.

Cr: I am sorry, we cannot do that.

Dr: OK, then I will send you another check.

Cr: That is not what I mean. By the time we get another check, or redeposit your old check, another payment will be due; and you know when this happens, I have to prepare the papers to re-possess your car. We must have the entire amount due in cash or by money order at our office by Monday, May 7.

Dr: I told you it was a mistake. Just redeposit the check and everything will be OK.

Cr: Mr. Taylor, we cannot extend you further time. We must have the cash payment by Monday, May 7.

Dr: Well, maybe I can have one payment to you by then.

Comment on Dialogue: Some finance companies do not believe in advising the debtor in advance when his car will be repossessed.

The philosophy is that the debtor either will continue in arrears, or will hide the car in anticipation of further action.

Example:

Cr: Is Mr. Morris there?

Dr: Mr. Morris here, who is this?

Cr: This is Phil from Arctic Air Conditioning. Your check for $850 bounced higher than a kite.

Dr: I had to meet payroll last week.

Cr: I have payroll to meet also. I gave you an extra 90 days, and now you give me a bum check.

Dr: Just redeposit the check and I will see to it that it clears.

Cr: Look, I did the work. The air conditioning is working fine, isn't it? I sent you bills, and you didn't pay. You send me a check that bounces. If I do not get paid within the next three days, I am going to refer this matter to my attorney and let him sue you. I am not going to wait, and I am not going to redeposit the check. And don't bring me another check, I want cash, a money order, or a certified check.

Comment on Dialogue: The last comments by the creditor were an excellent foundation. The problem is that the creditor has backed the debtor into a corner. Even if the debtor could pay half in three days, he probably would not make the offer. Be careful of this trap.

Warning—Request by Debtor to Return Bounced Check: Some sophisticated debtors will request that you return the bounced check before they will issue you a new check. If suit should be required, a dishonored check is solid evidence that the debtor was satisfied with the service or merchandise and that the debtor intended to pay. Do not return the check until you receive the new check, and then return the old check.

Example:

Dr: My wife made a mistake. The account was closed by mistake. I will send you a new check for $19 as soon as you return the old check to me.

Cr: I will return this check to you as soon as I receive the new check and the new check is paid.

Dr: Yeah, but how do I know that you will not deposit both checks?

Cr: Well, first, you could put a stop payment on this check. Second, we do not charge our customers twice. Third, if we do not receive a new check within three days drawn on a different account, we will be forced to forward this to a collection agency for further action.

Comment on Dialogue: Although the creditor could deposit both checks, the creditor should impress upon the debtor his integrity and honesty by virtue of the fact that the service or merchandise was delivered to the debtor based upon the fact that the creditor trusted the debtor.

CHAPTER 4

How to Leave a Message That Gets Through to the Debtor

A large number of telephone contacts will be with someone other than the debtor. Whether to leave a message, what kind of message to leave, and the manner and method of leaving a message will be covered in this chapter.

GUIDELINES TO FOLLOW WHEN LEAVING CONSUMER MESSAGES

Debt Collection Practices Act

Even though creditors are not subject to the Debt Collection Practices Act, the position of a creditor should be that the Act has become a standard in industry and creditors should comply with the Act. (This premise is more fully discussed in Chapter 9.)

Communication with Third Parties: The Act contains several sections dealing with communications with third parties. Section 805 (b) should be read carefully for it contains a provision prohibiting contact with third parties except:

1. To acquire location information.
2. With the prior consent of the consumer given directly to the debt collector.
3. With the express permission of the Court.
4. As reasonably necessary to effect a post-judgment judicial remedy.

Unless suit has been started, or the debtor has granted permission, the best policy is *not to leave a message with any third person* concerning the debt of a consumer. (See Chapter 9, "Legal Boundaries and Limitations.")

Special Situations and How to Handle Them

Leaving Message with Spouse: Section 805(b) of the Debt Collection Practices Act provides that no communication may be had with any other person other than the consumer except as provided in Section 801. Section 801 deals with acquiring location information, so it appears that you may communicate with the spouse for the purpose of acquiring location information. This would appear to limit the conversation with a spouse, for such an inquiry would probably surprise and at the same time insult the spouse. Nevertheless, under Section 805(d) the Act expressly states that the term "consumer" includes the consumer's spouse for purposes of Section 805 only. Therefore, the law allows a full communication with the spouse in the same manner as the consumer would be treated, and of course this would include any rights under Section 801 that deal with location information.

The Federal Trade Commission acknowledges that no advisory opinion has been issued on the point nor is there any mention of this in the commentary. The posture is that despite the confusion, this is the logical result of Section 805(d).

Accordingly, communication with the spouse may proceed in the same manner as you would talk to the consumer.

Dr: Hello.
Cr: This is the National Bank, Mr. Clark speaking. Is Mr. Graham home?
Dr: No, this is Mrs. Graham.
Cr: Well, Mrs. Graham, we have written your husband several letters and made two telephone calls concerning this past due loan....

This exception does not apply to brothers, sisters, parents, children or relatives of the consumer. These relatives are considered third parties, and contact with them should be limited in accordance with Section 801 which sets forth the ground rules for purpose of acquiring location information about the consumer.

Section 805(d) does include an exception for parents of a minor, providing the consumer is a minor. If the consumer is under eighteen years, you may talk to the parents in the same manner as you would speak to a consumer. Remember that you will be unable to threaten suit since a minor in most states can disaffirm a contract. Yet, under some states a parent is responsible for the necessities of a minor.

Section 805(d) also allows you to speak to a guardian of a minor in the same manner as you would speak to a minor, and also speak to the executor or administrator of an estate of the consumer in the same manner as you would speak to the consumer.

In summary, you may speak to the spouse in the same manner as you would speak to the consumer. You may also speak to an executor or administrator of an estate in the same manner as you would speak to the consumer who is now deceased. You may also speak to the parent or guardian of a child in the same manner as you would speak to the child, except you may not threaten suit against the parent or guardian for you cannot sue a child, since a child under eighteen can disaffirm a contract in most states. The exception to the last rule concerning minors is that parents and guardian in most states may be sued for those items sold to a minor which are necessities.

How to Handle Messages to Children: Obviously, messages should not be left with children:

1. The chances of the message being transmitted properly are very slim, and as a matter of fact, there's a good chance that the message will never be transmitted.

2. The parents will probably be very distraught that their child knows that the parent is unable to pay his bills.

3. This annoyance may not only result in antagonism to the creditor, but the parent may even consult an attorney to ascertain if suit may be brought against the creditor.

HELPFUL HINT: Determine Age of Child. The simple way to discover the age of a person is to ask. In almost all instances, all children under the age of 18 will respond accurately.

This rule about children also applies to children visiting the household such as friends, babysitters, or neighbor's children performing chores in the house. In short, messages should not be left with children.

Dealing with Friends: The same rule generally applies to relatives who are visiting the debtors. A friend is a third party, and contact should be limited to acquiring location information. Leaving a message with friends who happen to pick up the telephone is extremely dangerous and should be avoided, as is illustrated in the following dialogue:

Dr: Hello.

Cr: May I speak to Mr. Stevenson?

Dr: He's not here; he just went out to the store to get some paint. He will be back in a few minutes.

Cr: Who is this, please?

Dr: This is his neighbor. We are working on a picket fence between our properties. Can I help you?

Cr: Well, I don't know.

Dr: Well, give me the message; he will be right back.

Cr: This is Mr. Edwards from the Friendly Finance Company.

Dr: The what?

Cr: The Friendly Finance Company.

Dr: Does he have a loan with you?

Cr: I'm sorry, but I cannot discuss that with you.

Dr: He must be in arrears.

Cr: Sir, could you just tell him we called?

Dr: Oh, I will tell him, and I will also tell him that I am not going to lend him the $5,000 for his business. He didn't tell me he wasn't meeting payments on his personal loan. Am I glad I picked up this phone!

Third Parties Passing Through: Identifying the caller as a "bank" might produce the same undesirable results as the previous dialogue shows. Third-party contacts require great care and insight. Therefore, do not leave messages or identify yourself to plumbers, exterminators, gardeners, washer and dryer service men, electricians, TV repairmen, painters, carpet installers, piano tuners, tutors, decorators, baby sitters, nurses, housesitters, dog sitters, domestics, maids, butlers, or any other persons who just happen to be in the house of a consumer.

Nonresidents: Leaving messages at telephones of third parties should not be done. Leave only the name of the person, the name of the creditor, and the telephone number. Do not leave the name of the creditor if it is indicative of a "lending" or "delinquent" situation.

Warning: Leave Name, Rank and Serial Number Only, When Dealing with Employers: Leaving a message with an employer is a very dangerous action and may lead to serious legal consequences. If the debtor's standing as an employee is affected by the employer's knowledge of his indebtedness, the creditor may expose himself to liability. Losing a promotion because the employer discovers the employee is in debt (and the employer may be justified in this action to reject the promotion to protect itself in the case of a sensitive position, such as a bookkeeper) may be the catalyst for the institution of suit by the employee against the creditor. If the employee-debtor is fired as a consequence of the message, the damages may be substantial. *Talking with employers about the debts of employees is dangerous* and should be avoided at all costs. No message of any kind should be left, and the entire conversation should be limited to name, rank, and serial number, i.e., the name of the company, the name of the person, and telephone number. In addition, leaving such a message is a violation of Section 805(b) of the Act.

Warning: Name of Company: If the name of the company indicates a lending institution, you should use only the collector's name when leaving a message in any sensitive or dangerous situation. (See Debt Collection Practices Act, Section 804.)

Example:

Cr: May I please speak to Mr. Charles?
Dr: He is at a meeting now.
Cr: Well, may I leave a message?
Dr: Yes.
Cr: Tell him Mr. Lawrence called. My number is 555-1234.
Dr: Anything else?
Cr: No, just ask him to return my call, please.
Dr: OK.
Cr: Thank you.

Identify the Employer: Section 804 (1) of the Debt Collection Practices Act states that when communicating with any person other than the consumer, the telephone worker shall only identify himself, state that he is confirming or correcting location information, and only, if expressly requested, identify his employer. Analyzing this sentence, one must consider the other side of the warning. The telephone worker must identify himself, but must not identify his employer unless specifically requested. If the third party specifically asks the telephone worker for the name of his employer, the telephone worker may properly respond, even if the name indicates a lending position or a delinquent account.

Do Not Tell Third Party That Debt Is Owed: Section 803 (2) of the Debt Collection Practices Act states that the telephone worker cannot tell any third party that the consumer owes a debt. The telephone worker may say that "it is personal" or "I prefer to talk to him about it" or words of similar meaning.

HOW TO LEAVE MESSAGES INVOLVING A BUSINESS DEBTOR

Four Tests for Leaving a Message at a Business

The simple way to inquire whether the person answering the telephone will take a message is to ask. The question should be phrased to include the following:

1. Whether the person talking on the telephone agrees to take a message.
2. Will the person talking on the telephone convey the message to the debtor?
3. Is the person talking on the telephone authorized by the debtor to take the message?
4. Does the person talking on the telephone identify what his or her relationship to the debtor is, and does this relationship cloak the person with apparent authority to take a message?

You must ascertain if the employee has been directed by the debtor to take messages, and if he is answering the telephone in response to said directions. The degree to which this is pursued depends upon the circumstances of each situation. In many cases it is obvious to all that the employee has apparent authority by virtue of his or her position, such as a secretary or office manager. In other instances, the line of demarcation is not as clear, and further efforts to clarify the authority must be made. Other times it is quite evident that the employee may have authority to answer the telephone, but has no authority to take a message. Here is an example of two types of questions that should be asked:

1. Q: Do you have authority to take the message?
   A: Yes.
   Q: Will you please be certain the owner gets the message?
   A: Yes.
2. Q: Can you take a message for the boss and be sure he receives it?
   A: OK, what is it?

Specific Situations Involving Business Debtors

Specific situations will now be discussed and examples of dialogues will be reviewed.

Leaving Messages with a Partner–Officer: Messages usually may be left with partners or officers of a corporation. Take care to inquire first. If dealing with a very large corporation and a very low-level officer, perhaps questions as to his or her authority should be made:

Dr: Black and Christopher. May I help you?
Cr: This is the ABC Computer Company, Steve Kent talking. May I talk to the owner?
Dr: The owner is away for two weeks. I'll give you Mr. Williams.
Dr: This is Mr. Williams.
Cr: This is Mr. Kent from ABC Computer.
Dr: What's the problem?
Cr: With whom am I talking?
Dr: I am a partner in the accounting firm.
Cr: How large is your firm?
Dr: We have 37 accountants, and I just became the thirty-seventh.
Cr: I think you had better switch me back to your receptionist.

The problem here is threefold. The junior partner probably has no authority to take a message for a delinquent bill of $10,000; second, he probably knows nothing about it; and finally, little attention will be paid when it is transmitted.

Leaving Messages with Financial Personnel: Controller, Financial Manager, Treasurer, secretary, and bookkeepers or assistants to any of these titles are all appropriate persons with whom messages can be left.

When to Leave Messages with Employees: Messages may be left with employees provided that the employee has apparent authority to accept the message. In some cases, the employee is hired specifically to take messages, such as secretaries, nurses in doctor's offices, and other employees whose jobs consist of answering the telephone for someone else. The question of authority becomes blurred somewhat when dealing with mechanics in a gas station, barbers in a barber shop, a foreman in a factory, a programmer in a computer service bureau. The answer is to make diligent inquiry as to the person's authority and right to take a message.

Example:

Dr: Julia Williams Real Estate, may I be of service to you?
Cr: This is the Clark Printing Company. May I speak to Mrs. Williams?
Dr: She is out showing a house. Are you interested in purchasing or renting?
Cr: No. When do you expect Mrs. Williams?
Dr: Not for at least an hour. Maybe I can help you?
Cr: What do you do there?
Dr: I am a sales agent. I have several excellent commercial spaces for rent.
Cr: I am not interested in renting space.
Dr: Well, what is this about?
Cr: I think I should speak to Mrs. Williams.
Dr: Well, I run the office when she is out. You might say I am her office manager.
Cr: Are you familiar with our company?
Dr: Yes, you printed the brochures that came out fuzzy, and we haven't paid you yet.
Cr: What do you mean?
Dr: Well, if you wait a minute, I will get the brochures...

Leaving Messages with Sales Employees: Very often the person answering the telephone will be a salesperson such as a sales clerk in a retail store, a marketing salesman in a regional office, an insurance salesman in a regional office, etc. Messages may be left with this type of employee, but only after judging exactly what the party's position is within the organization. The danger is that the person answering the telephone may be the person running the office, may be an entry-level employee, or somewhere in between.

Dr: ABC Ribbon Company, Miss Green speaking.

Cr: This is Mr. Carey from Southern Mills. Is Frank there?

Dr: No sir. Mr. Jordan is away. May I help you?

Cr: Are you the bookkeeper?

Dr: No sir. I am a sales representative. All our bookkeeping is done from a central accounting office. Would you like the telephone number and address?

Cr: No, but when will Mr. Jordan return?

Dr: On Monday.

Cr: Please have him call me.

Independent Contractor: Sometimes an independent contractor such as an electrician, copy machine repairman, typewriter repairman, or air conditioning service man may pick up the telephone. As with the consumer, do not leave a message with "third parties passing through." The name of the firm, person, and telephone number is appropriate.

---

*COLLECTION TIP: **When in Doubt.*** The above rules are but guidelines for the telephone worker, but the ultimate decision to leave a message with a third party depends on careful inquiry, general rules, and common sense. One rule supersedes all others, "When in doubt, do not leave a message."

COLLECTION TIP: Refusal to Take Message. If a party, whether a proper or improper party, refuses to take a message, do not attempt to leave a message. Using persuasion or forceful tactics will not help, for the message will probably never be transmitted; and if it is transmitted, the message will probably be transmitted incompletely or inaccurately.

> **COLLECTION TIP: Find Out Who Is the Debtor.** When the secretary, teacher, or doctor ordered for his own account instead of the business, school, or hospital, be very careful of the extent of the message that is left. If the order indicates any doubt as to who made the order, a very limited message should be left until a determination is made as to the liability of the business.

WHAT YOUR MESSAGE SHOULD CONTAIN TO MAKE SURE IT REACHES THE DEBTOR

The contents of the message depend upon with whom you are communicating. If the person answering the telephone falls into the classification of one who has obvious authority to accept a full message, then a full message should be left including:

1. Identification
2. Foundation
3. Demand for payment
4. The closing statement

See Chapter 2 ("Four Golden Keys to an Effective Telephone Collection") for a detailed discussion of these key elements of a collection call.

> **COLLECTION TIP: Pens and Pencils.** When leaving a message, start with, "Can you write this down for him?" or "Do you have a pencil and paper to write this down for the owner?" Hopefully, these preliminary statements will eliminate the situation where after a message is left, the person says "Wait a minute, I will get a pencil."

How You Say It Is as Important as What You Say

The most important ingredient of leaving a message is the tone and attitude of the telephone worker. A message that is left in a monotone with little emphasis will be transmitted to the debtor in the same way. A message that is left with concern and interest will be communicated in the same way. For example:

1. "Please tell the owner that XYZ Company called, and he owes $1,500 for software that was delivered six months ago. If we don't receive the check by Monday, May 7,...(give closing statement)."

    Transmission: "Someone called about some software you bought and you owe them money."

2. "Please tell the owner that he owes $1,500 to the XYZ Company for software and this bill has been past due for the past six months, and that this will be the last call before we refer this to our attorney for collection. Be very certain that the owner receives this message, because if we do not receive his check by Monday, May 7,...(give closing statement)."

    Transmission: "The XYZ is going to send this to their attorney unless you pay the $1,500 by Monday, May 7."

Examples of poor messages could cover many pages. The main thrust is to leave a good message with all the interest, forcefulness, and concern that a telephone worker would express if the money owed was owed to the telephone worker himself. In short, how would the telephone worker talk to a friend who owed money to him for three months? The approach would certainly not be matter-of-fact. The voice would rise and fall depending upon the emphasis on certain phrases, for example:

1. "I *must* have the money by Monday, May 7."

2. "This is the *second time* you have promised."

3. "I am *not* going to call again. I *insist* on payment by Monday, May 7."

4. "If you intend to pay, *now* is the time; next week may be *too late.*"

5. "This is the *final* call before...."

The telephone worker must leave the message with the third party in much the same way as if the debtor himself was on the receiving end of the telephone call. A message is transmitted with the same emphasis as it is received, and usually with somewhat less emphasis. Therefore, a message should even be more aggressive and forceful than when speaking to the debtor.

LEAVING MESSAGES WITH RECORDING DEVICES AND ANSWERING SERVICES

Tips for Leaving Messages with Answering Services

The rules that apply to leaving a message with a third party, such as a secretary, are also applicable to answering services. The party answering is a live person who has been engaged to accept messages. Therefore, a full message can be left and should be left with a high degree of intensity. Most answering services record the messages and then read them back over the telephone to the client. The message taker will add something to the message when conveying it to the client. The major problem with answering services is that they refuse to accept a lengthy message and only want the name and address. The only solution is to be persistent.

Example:

Dr: Dr. Jones' Office. Do you wish to make an appointment?

Cr: No. This is the ABC Medical Supply Company

Dr: Give me your name and number, please

Cr: First, please tell him that his bill for $550 has not been paid for .. "

Dr: I'm sorry, but I can only take the name and number.

Cr: I think you should take the whole message, since we are referring this to our attorney for suit and I am certain the doctor would like to know about this.

Dr: OK, but....

How to Leave Messages with Recording Devices

Recording devices present the problems of limited time and communicating within a vacuum. The difficulty in talking to nothing is evident when one spends time playing back the messages. The recommendation is to prepare a script for the telephone worker to read so that it will be a purely ministerial act. This will not produce the best results, but it will achieve the desired purpose. The best results come from a concerned and forceful message delivered in the same manner as if one were leaving a message with a secretary.

Remember that when the debtor listens to the tape, the creditor has a captive audience, for the debtor will listen to each word with no interruptions. He will not turn off the machine since there is probably another message following the collection telephone call.

Dr: You have one minute to talk. Please start after the tone.

Cr: This is the 14th Street Realty Company. You have not paid your rent of $550 for the month of May. We must have it by May 23. Be sure you take care of this matter immediately, or...(closing statement).

Warning: Beware of What You Say: Remember that everything that is said over a recording device is written in stone. Be sure no profane or obscene language is used, and be certain that the information left is accurate and that *the party is the correct debtor.*

Obtain Name of Other Person: When leaving a message, an effort should always be made to obtain the name of the person answering the telephone. Nevertheless, the effort expended to obtain the correct name should be limited. The correct spelling is not as important as having the semblance of a name. If it is a complicated name, do not waste the time obtaining the correct spelling, provided that the name is clear enough for identification. If the party answering the telephone refuses to furnish his name, do not insist upon it, since really nothing can be done to force the party to furnish his name. Identify the party as a "female employee," "male worker," "secretary, female, young," or "male waiter."

CHAPTER 5

How to Negotiate a Successful Settlement

The subject of settlements is so broad that entire books have been written about negotiating a settlement. The art of persuasion, the technique of influencing people, and the use of intimidation and psychology all contribute to the proficiency needed to effect a reasonable settlement. Actually, the list of skills necessary to negotiate are endless, and no attempt is being made to cover the huge area of how to deal with people and bend them to your way of thinking.

This chapter covers some very basic concepts of settlement including the timing of the settlement, the invitation to settle, bidding against yourself during a settlement, arrangements for resuming installment payments, and the circumstances under which the creditor does make the first offer.

THE ART OF TIMING IN A SETTLEMENT

Whenever a debtor offers to return merchandise, alleges defective merchandise, alleges a shortage of merchandise shipped, alleges damaged merchandise, or other circumstances of a similar nature, an effort to settle is the recommended procedure. Whenever the debtor lodges any complaint coupled with the possibility of a return of the goods together with a refusal to pay, an attempt to settle is the proper course. The cost and expense of accepting a return of the goods is substantial. If the settlement amount is greater than the cost and expense of accepting a return of the goods, restoring the goods to a saleable condition and reselling the goods, then a settlement makes good sense and should be explored.

"Adjust" Rather Than "Settle": The better word to use is "adjust" rather than "settle." An offer to settle sometimes carries the implication that the party offering to settle is in the wrong. Actually, an offer of settlement is being made to expedite the matter and provide the best of both worlds to both parties. The question of who is wrong does not come into play. The word "adjust" also implies some incident of guilt but in my judgment to a lesser degree. My preference is "adjust" rather than "settle."

Let the Debtor Make the First Offer: The purpose is to start the negotiation process without admitting any weakness. The problem is that weakness is directly associated with the party who initiates the process. Therefore, if you make the first offer of settlement, you are already at a disadvantage. The only question remaining is the extent of the disadvantage.

How does one commence settlement negotiation without making the first offer? The question begs the answer. Have the debtor make the first offer. The art of persuading or manipulating the debtor to open the settlement negotiations, however, requires some thought and anticipation.

AN INVITATION TO DINNER: HOW TO MOTIVATE THE DEBTOR TO OFFER A SETTLEMENT

The psychology of the debtor is to offer nothing since the debtor prefers not to pay. The job of the telephone worker is to send out carefully engraved invitations to the debtor to make an offer of settlement. These invitations can take many forms, such as the following.

Ten Lead-In Statements

1. "What do you think we ought to do about this problem?"

2. "We are two intelligent people. We ought to be able to solve this disagreement."

3. "I wish I knew how to help you."

4. "I guess the only alternative is a lawsuit, but neither of us want that."

5. "Well, you can't return it and I can't fix it. What do we do now?"

6. "If you will not give in, I certainly will not. Stalemates do not help either party."

7. "I really don't know what to do about this."

8. "Should we fight or compromise?"

9. "Should we be stubborn or intelligent?"

10. "Let's resolve the problem."

After the debtor has been invited to dinner, the appetizer should be served to whet his curiosity as to what the future holds. The following are some examples of how to entice the debtor further into the arena of settlement negotiations, and encourage him to order the main course, i.e., the settlement.

Eleven "Appetizers" That Encourage a Debtor to Settle

1. "Let's work this out."

2. "Let's compromise."

3. "Let's reconcile our differences."

4. "Let's make an arrangement."

5. "Let's talk—I will concede...if you will concede."

6. "Let's meet halfway."

7. "Let's straighten this out."

8. "Let's give and take a little."

9. "Let's negotiate a little."

10. "Let's each of us give a little."

11. "Let's each of us bend a little."

Examples of how these phrases might be used:

Cr: We shipped the shirts on March 1, just as you asked.

Dr: But they didn't get here until March 25.

Cr: That doesn't seem possible. We sent it United Parcel. How could it have taken that long?

Dr: Well, it came two weeks after the sale, and we couldn't fill many of the orders. Now it will not move until Christmas.

Cr: Well, let me check with United Parcel.

Dr: What good will that do? Whatever the reason, it did not get here on time. We called you a week before and every day for a week during the sale. Charlie kept telling us it would arrive the next day.

Cr: Well, I don't know what to say.

Dr: There's nothing to say. We are going to return the entire order. There is nothing else we can do.

Cr: Well, we are not going to accept the return. Even if it did come late, you did not tell us it was for a special sale. Charlie only found out about the sale a few days before the sale.

Dr: We're still shipping it back.

Cr: We will not accept the return. Shall we fight this in court, or are we going to try to straighten out our problem?

Dr: It's up to you.

Cr: Do you think you could sell them at Christmas?

Dr: I don't know.

Cr: Look, let's try to solve the problem.

Dr: What do you mean?

Cr: I don't know, but we ought to be able to work this out.

Dr: How about a discount?

Cr: That depends upon how much.

Dr: Well, I have to carry these shirts for three more months.

Cr: OK, I can understand that.

Dr: How about 30 percent?

Cr: Are you kidding?

Comment on Dialogue: Notice the first step was an invitation followed by suggesting an alternative way to sell the merchandise. Even if the creditor knows this suggestion will not be accepted, the alternative should be employed before the key phrase, "Let's try to solve the problem."

Another example:

Dr: The desk came with a huge scratch right down the middle of the top.

Cr: You should make a claim against the carrier.

Dr: That's your problem, not mine. I'm just not going to pay for it. You better pick it up within the week.

Cr: The cost of picking it up is prohibitive.

Dr: I guess I'll have to throw it out and let the garbage men pick it up.

Cr: I guess the only alternative is a lawsuit, although I'm sure both of us really don't want that.

Dr: You can sue me. There is no law that says I have to accept a desk with a long huge scratch down the middle.

Cr: No, but you will have to retain an attorney to defend the suit. The end result may be that you will pay a few dollars less, but make no mistake, you are not going to keep the desk and not pay for it. Perhaps we should make an effort to resolve our differences.

Dr: That may be a good idea. What do you suggest?

Cr: Can you get someone to repair the scratch?

Dr: I don't know, but if I do, will you pay the bill?

Comment on Dialogue: This invitation to a settlement was disguised by a threat of a lawsuit. The technique is to soften the threat before the debtor is frightened. Still, the debtor must be led down the garden path, because the debtor may not recognize the opportunity until it is presented several times.

BIDDING AGAINST YOURSELF

"Bidding against yourself" means that you do not make the first offer of settlement. Basically, your offer is a demand for the full amount of the debt. Since the debtor has made no offer, an offer of less than the full amount competes with the only offer on the table, i.e., your demand for the full amount. Carried forward, if the debtor rejects the reduced amount, a lower offer is now competing with the reduced offer. Playing a game by oneself produces a loser.

Example:

Dr: The computer paper is all but useless. Your delivery truck left it outside the door, and in that downpour, the water leaked right through the cartons. Ninety percent of the paper is no good. You can have it back.

Cr: The carton should protect the paper from the water. This is the first time we ever heard of water seeping through. Have you checked the paper?

Dr: Yes, we checked it. About 10 percent is good.

Cr: Well, that seems illogical since even if water did go through, the paper in the middle should be dry as toast.

Dr: Well, it isn't.

Cr: OK, I'll take 25 percent off the bill, so send us a check for $900.

Dr: That's ridiculous when over 80 percent of the paper is soaked through. You'll have to do better.

Cr: OK, I'll take off a third. Send $800.

Dr: If you saw the thunderstorm, you would understand. I told you almost 80 percent of the paper is spoiled and cannot be used. I'll be glad to ship it back.

Cr: Well, my last offer is 50 percent, and I'll take a check for $600.

Dr: No way. That's out of line.

Cr: I am not making any more offers. That's it. Take it or leave it.

Dr: I'll tell you what. I think maybe 25 percent of the paper was good, and just to be fair, I'll send a check for $300.

Cr: Look, my bottom figure is $500.

Dr: How about $400?

Cr: No way.

Dr: OK, $425.

Cr: Make it $475.

Dr: $450.

Cr: $450. We have a deal.

Comment on Dialogue: The debtor was in control during most of the negotiation. The creditor started at $1,200, reduced the offer to $900, then $800, and finally $500. During this time the debtor did not even enter the bidding. The only one attending the auction was the creditor. The creditor's statement that this was his last offer was about three offers too late. By the time the debtor began to counter-offer, the creditor was down to $600 from $1,200. While the debtor only improved on this figure by $150, the battle had already been won and the victor was only picking up the pieces. On the other hand, the debtor bid against himself at the end of the conversation when he increased his bid from $400 to $425.

When the Bank or Financial Institution Retains a Lien on Collateral

Where the bank or financial institution does retain a lien on collateral, the extent of the pressure is whether the lender really wants to recapture the collateral. If the security is a seven-year-old car, two-year-old furniture, or a five-year-old motorcycle, the lender's philosophy is that of an unsecured lender who does not place much value on the security and is ready to extend the payment plan in the same manner as an unsecured lender.

Cr: Your auto payment is now three months in arrears.

Dr: I know. I used the money to repair the car. The third time the transmission broke down, I almost pushed it into the river.

Cr: We loaned you the money to buy the car. We did not guarantee how it would operate. Now, what about your monthly payments?

Dr: What about them? You'll find all three mixed-up somewhere in the transmission. The best I can do is start paying again next month, unless the transmission goes again. Then I'll mail you the name of the car dealer who has your payment.

Cr: Starting to pay next month is not enough.

Dr: It's the best I can do.

Cr: You must pay at least one of your past payments. Suppose you send me two payments for the next three months?

Dr: Buddy, are you kidding? I can barely meet the one payment with all the money this car is costing.

Cr: Well, you must make some dent in your back payments.

Dr: I can't pay anything.

Cr: How about $100 per month plus your regular payment?

Dr: Maybe I can pay $25 per month

Cr: That is a very small amount.

Dr: Well, maybe $50, but that's all.

Cr: OK, we'll try that for three months.

Comment on Dialogue: The creditor recognized that the car was of little value, but tried to bargain from strength. Probably, the additional payment will not be made, but a likelihood exists that the monthly payments will be made.

Threat of Eviction or Foreclosure

The threats of eviction or foreclosure are powerful weapons. But by their very nature, mention of them is inadvisable unless their use is intended imminently. By threatening eviction, and not evicting, the strength of the threat is almost destroyed. Accordingly, work out the problem and do not mention eviction or foreclosure. By your tone and attitude the mortgagor will fully understand his predicament.

Cr: This is the third time that I have called about your arrearages. Your payments on your mortgage must be brought up-to-date.

Dr: I know, but the thunderstorm washed away the north 60 acres, and I lost all the seed and fertilizer.

Cr: I understand, but you know that your mortgage is guaranteed by the FHA, and they set the guidelines. I am only doing my job. I understand your problems.

Dr: Well, maybe I can start picking up the missing payments in about 60 days, for then the soybeans will be in and the prices should be up.

Cr: You realize that this condition cannot go on indefinitely. I strongly suggest that next month you make a partial payment on your arrearages. This is very important.

Dr: OK. I understand.

INSTALLMENT INDEBTEDNESS: FIVE RULES WHICH MAY BE BROKEN AND ONE RULE TO KEEP

The goal of the creditor is to resume the monthly installments as well as collect the arrearages. The telephone worker will have to face many decisions in the quest to accomplish this purpose.

Rule One: The difficulty is that once a reduction in payments is granted, the debtor will **never** resume paying the original amount. "Never" is a harsh word but in this instance the prediction lies close to the truth. Therefore, *the first rule is to avoid reducing the monthly payment.*

Rule Two: If the debtor agrees to resume the monthly payments, any additional amount in excess of the monthly payment to be paid with the monthly payment is acceptable, even if this amount is as little as $5. This result produces a resumption of the monthly payments plus a reduction of the arrearages. *The second rule is to arrange some commitment to reduce the arrearages, no matter how small.*

Rule Three: Never extend the period of time between the payments more than the original period of time between the payments. This means that if the loan provides for monthly payments, the loan should remain a loan with monthly payments. Do not accept the debtor's offer to resume payments in 60 days, at which time the debtor will make three payments. A payment must be made at least each month, no matter how small. Allowing a longer period of time between payments causes the monitoring procedure to deteriorate. The reason that weekly is better than biweekly, biweekly is better than monthly, and monthly is better than quarterly is that the creditor will recognize a problem earlier when the debtor misses a payment. *The third rule is to refuse to extend the period of time between payments longer than the original period of time between payments.*

Rule Four: The next ideal result is to compress the period of time between payments. Thus, if the original period of time was 30 days, the new period of time between payments should be weekly or biweekly. *The fourth rule is to compress the period of time between payments whenever possible.*

Rule Five: Whatever arrangement is made, the settlement should be short term. The longest arrangement should be no more than a period of six months, and the shortest could be for 30 days. The idea is to contact the debtor again and try to increase the payments. The shorter the period of time between the contact, the more opportunity exists for increasing the payments. *The fifth rule is that settlements reducing the amount of the monthly payment should be short term.*

The One Rule Not to Be Broken: Unfortunately, rules are made to be broken; more often than not the above rules will be broken when attempting to settle with a debtor. Circumstances do arise where the rules cannot be applied, and in the great majority of the situations, all of the rules do not work all of the time. Accordingly, there is one last rule to apply where the other rules do not work.

Whatever the excuse for failure to send the monthly payment and whatever the circumstances of the debtor, never leave the telephone without a determined effort to obtain some payment in some amount at least each month. This applies if the amount of the outstanding balance is $5,000 and the monthly payment is only $5.

This rule has actually been applied. Although many may disagree, and state that such a settlement is ridiculous and not worth the time and effort, the results produce cash to the lender. The circumstances, of course, must warrant such action, and such circumstances do not happen very frequently. If the debtor at one time originally warranted a $5,000 loan, the debtor must be the type of borrower who may once again enter business or the job market and warrant a loan of this size.

We represented a bank, and a teller siphoned off over $15,000 in cash from depositors over a period of four years. The teller did this by shortchanging the depositors and occasionally dipping into the unattended cash boxes of his fellow tellers. At any rate, he was finally caught and he confessed. The money was used for doctor bills for his terminally ill wife. These bills far exceeded his medical coverage, and in addition, he sought unapproved medical help which was not covered by medical insurance. He signed a confession of judgment, and was sentenced to three years in prison. He was paroled in 14 months and freelanced as a landscape engineer. His wife had died. He lived in a small apartment, and had undertaken to raise his two small girls who were cared for by his sister during his incarceration. His salary was $400 per week. He offered to pay the bank $35 per month. We accepted the offer, and he paid that $35 for almost three years. He then raised the payments to $50 a month. Now the debtor has been making payments for over five years, and may very well continue for another five or ten years. The important element is that the bank is receiving payments on a continuous basis.

The point is that each case is different. If the situation supports $5 a month, then $5 a month is what should be collected. Naturally, the telephone worker must inquire as to the circumstances and history of the default. The extent of verification of the financial condition of the debtor depends upon the balance due, but the telephone calls to the employer, to the debtor's bank, and to the landlord can assist in confirming the debtor's financial position. If the debtor is a business, the rule is the same. Confirmation of the financial condition of the business can be supported by financial statements; or if outside confirmation is in order, a physical and personal inspection can be made and inquiry to banks, suppliers, vendors, credit bureaus, etc., can be made.

Of course, if the circumstances and the amount of the debt allow, arrange for the consumer or business debtor to appear personally at the creditor's place of business. Personal contact is far superior to the telephone, and will normally achieve much better results.

Summary of Five Rules:

1. Avoid reducing the monthly payment.
2. Reduce the arrearages, no matter how small the monthly reduction.
3. Refuse to extend the period of time between payments.
4. Compress the period of time between payments.
5. Any arrangement must be short term.

First Offer of Settlement: The rules of the first offer of a settlement are the same in dealing with an installment indebtedness as with any other indebtedness. The creditor should try to persuade the debtor to make the first offer of an arrangement. The telephone worker directs and guides the debtor into the type of reconciliation that is being sought. Let us examine how this might develop.

Cr: Your business time loan is three months in arrears.

Dr: I know, but business has been awful. It seems no one is buying file cabinets anymore. Maybe everything is going onto computer discs and we are fast becoming a world without paper. I wonder if the paper mills are faced with this problem of discs replacing paper. Do you think the evening newspaper will eventually be put on a disc and then we will go home at night and see the daily news on the screen of our computer?

Cr: Mr. Victor, I do not predict the future. I only know that your loan is three payments back, which translates into $4,500 in arrears.

Dr: I know, I know. I think things will pick up in October and November, and I will be able to resume payments by December 1.

Cr: That is too long a time.

Dr: Well, it is impossible to make any payments sooner. I have payroll and my quarterly taxes to make I just hired a credit and collection manager to work on my outstanding receivables, and I hope he will begin to collect some money. He will cost me a weekly salary also, but I think I need someone like him.

Cr: That is a step in the right direction. But I need a payment now, and some arrangement with regard to the arrearages.

Dr: I cannot turn garbage into gold. I just don't have the money.

Cr: Well, you know I would prefer to give you the extension, but I don't set the policies of the bank.

Dr: Look, I know you have a lien on my inventory. Can you use about 50 file cabinets? I also have about 25 desks.

Cr: We don't want to hurt you, but we must do something.

Dr: What do you suggest?

Cr: I don't know, but I'm sure both of us can work something out.

Dr: I'll pay $1,500 on December 1; and I'll pay an additional $500 towards the open three payments; and I'll continue the $500 until the arrearages of $4,500 is paid. How does that sound?

Cr: Well, not bad, but I cannot wait until December 1. That's more than two months away. I must have a payment now and another one on November 1.

Dr: Impossible.

Cr: How about $1,000 now and $1,000 on November 1. Don't forget that if you wait until December 1, you will then be behind almost $7,000 and not $4,500.

Dr: How about $500 now and $500 on November 1.

Cr: No, give me $500 now and $1,000 on November 1.

Dr: OK.

Comment on Dialogue: The telephone worker was able to persuade the debtor to make the first offer. But the telephone worker was adamant on extending the period of time between payments. At least the creditor will know whether the debtor is making any progress in his business.

Another example:

Cr: Your balance on your VISA card is close to the $2,500 limit, and we have not received a payment for two months.

Dr: I was fired.

Cr: I am sorry to hear that. Are you looking for a new job?

Dr: Of course, but so far I've found nothing.

Cr: Well, the bill must be paid.

Dr: I have to use my money for my family until I get another job.

Cr: I understand that, but you must get started on paying this.

Dr: Well, I guess you can sue me; because I can't pay now.

Cr: Both of us don't want to do that. I'm sure we can work this out.

Dr: Not until I get a job.

Cr: When do you expect that?

Dr: Who knows?

Cr: Let's be realistic. You should get a job within a month.

Dr: I hope so.

Cr: Well, we must have a payment this month. Otherwise, the account will be taken away from me and the next step will be taken.

Dr: What is that?

Cr: Look, are we going to try to resolve this problem? We are both reasonable persons. We have a problem. Let's be positive and see what we can do.

Dr: I really have no money.

Cr: Can you make a small payment now?

Dr: How much is small?

Cr: How much can you pay?

Dr: How about $10?
Cr: That will take 10 years.
Dr: I know that, but for just a few months.
Cr: How about $100?
Dr: That is too much. I don't have $100.
Cr: How about $50?
Dr: I can't get up $50, either.
Cr: Well, that is the bare minimum we will accept.
Dr: What about $25?
Cr: Well, could you make that $35?
Dr: OK, $35 per month.
Cr: But in three months we'll take another look at this.
Dr: OK.

Comment on Dialogue: The telephone worker made one mistake of bidding against himself: when the debtor rejected $100, instead of offering $50, the telephone worker should have said that $100 is just too little and then waited for another offer from the debtor.

WHEN FIRST OFFER IS MADE: EXCEPTION TO THE RULE

The cliché states that "rules are made to be broken." Nevertheless, there are instances where the only alternative is to make an offer of settlement before the debtor makes the offer. If all efforts to persuade the debtor fail, then the telephone worker senses that a settlement or arrangement is the desired course of action. If the information obtained presents an opening for an offer, the creditor should surely use the opportunity. Certainly, where the adjustment bears some relationship to the problem in terms of money, an effort should be made to adjust the bill. Examples are as follows:

Example 1:

Cr: How much merchandise did you receive?
Dr: I only received four hard discs instead of six.
Cr: Well, maybe you can send me two-thirds of the bill now and let me investigate what happened to the other two discs.

Example 2:

Cr: What was wrong with the chair?
Dr: There was no way to adjust the height.
Cr: Can you fix it?

Dr: Well, I will have my maintenance man look at it. I suppose he can fix it.

Cr: Suppose we adjust the bill for $35?

Example 3:

Dr: I missed the last payment because the state tax audit assessed me $9,000 and I paid only the most necessary bills last month, and probably will not be able to resume payments on the copy machine for another three months.

Cr: Well, if no payment is made, the claim must go to an attorney for suit and that will only cost both of us additional money. Maybe you can make a small payment for the next three months so we will not have to take any action.

Example 4:

Dr: I lost my job and I must feed my family.

Cr: We know you will find a new job, and we certainly do not want to add to your burden. But we must receive monthly payment of some kind. How about a very nominal payment for the next three months until you get a job and are back on your feet?

Example 5:

Cr: We must have a small payment on your loan.

Dr: I have no money and I just can't pay anything.

Cr: Well, how about a small payment of $50 per month?

Comment on Dialogue: Obviously, in each instance the telephone worker is bidding against himself. Of course, a strong endeavor should be made to persuade the debtor to make the first offer of a settlement, but if nothing else works, some attempt should be made to settle.

HELPFUL HINT: Immediate Payment. When a settlement is finally resolved, a basic approach to consummate the settlement is to impress upon the debtor the urgency of immediate payment. Impress the debtor with the importance of the final settlement by forcefully conditioning the settlement upon the fact that "payment must be received within one week or the settlement offer will be withdrawn." The debtor perceives that a good bargain was made, and the debtor will probably make the payment.

Cr: OK, we will settle for $550.

Dr: Fine, I'll send you a check.

Cr: Well, this settlement is conditional upon receiving your check by Monday, May 7. If we do not receive it by then, consider the offer withdrawn for all purposes.

Dr: What does that mean?

Cr: That means if we do not receive the check by Monday, May 7, we will refer this to our attorney to sue for the full amount of $750. In short, you are getting a good deal and we want our money within the week. Otherwise, the deal is off.

Dr: OK.

COLLECTION TIP: Refuse Written Confirmation of Settlement. If the debtor requests written confirmation of the settlement, the answer should be in the negative. The letter will take several days to be prepared and several more days to be sent. In the interim many things could happen which might change the mind of the debtor, including a summons being served by another debtor, a medical problem, a fire, a flood, etc. Advise the debtor to write "paid in full" on the reverse side of the check or on the front of the check (see below "PAID IN FULL CHECKS"). *In most jurisdictions* (see Chapter 9) this will protect the debtor, for when the creditor deposits the check, the creditor is consummating the settlement. Of course, if the settlement involves a large sum or other terms and conditions, insist that the debtor write a letter to accompany the payment.

PAID IN FULL CHECKS

A discussion of settlement procedures would not be complete without considering the impact of the Uniform Commercial Code Section 1-207 on the established concept of accord and satisfaction. Generally, the law was well settled that if a purchase and sale or an item of indebtedness was disputed, and one party offered a check in a lesser amount, endorsed said check with the notation "paid in full" (or words of similar import), and the recipient deposited said check, the matter was effectively settled since an accord and satisfaction had taken place.

For example, a businessman buys a printer for $1,000. The seller makes certain representations as to the performance and capabilities of the printer. The businessman interconnects the printer to the computer and finds that the printer is unable to perform certain functions. The businessman complains, and the seller states that the only representations made were those contained in the manufacturer's brochure. In any event, a dispute arises over what was and was not said. The buyer states he still can use the machine and sends a check for $700 in full payment to the seller. The buyer recites on the reverse side of the check that "this check is in full payment of the printer" and accompanies the check with a letter basically saying the same thing. The seller deposits the check. The matter is now settled, and the seller would be unsuccessful if he sued for the balance of $300. An accord and satisfaction has taken place.

The above result was the law as it always existed. Section 1-207 of the New York Uniform Commercial Code states:

> Performance or Acceptance Under Reservation of Rights:
>
> A party who with explicit reservation of rights performs or promises performance or assents to performance in a manner demanded or offered by the other party does not thereby prejudice the rights reserved. Such words as "without prejudice," "under protest," or the like are sufficient.

The above section appears to state that if the seller wrote on the check the magic words "without prejudice," the check could be deposited and the seller could sue the buyer for the balance of $300 and an accord and satisfaction would not be available for a defense.

At the time of writing this book, the above interpretation has been generally adopted over the last ten years by more than a half dozen states, including New York. This interpretation has been rejected by more states than have accepted it. Nevertheless, there are over thirty states that have not considered the question. In some of these states lower court cases have been working their way toward the appellate courts for a decision as to whether the particular state will adopt the interpretation that Section 1-207 changes some of the basic tenets of accord and satisfaction.

Therefore, it is incumbent for every creditor to realize that the law in this area is still unsettled. Although the vast majority of states still do not follow this recent change, creditors should consult with their counsel to be certain of the status of the law in their state.

CHAPTER 6

Cost Guidelines for Hiring, Training, and Evaluating Telephone Workers

An untrained soldier is just as much a liability as an untrained telephone worker. We have tested newly hired telephone workers against experienced telephone workers. We provided the newly hired with the training manual, but with no other form of training. The results can only be described as total disaster. When I use the word "total," I do not use it generically, but literally. One of the newly hired telephone workers made as many as 50 telephone calls without producing one collection. A test for a particular client in the direct-mail industry provided for 50 telephone calls, and the average success rate was 6 out of 50 accounts. Compare these figures with an average of 16 out of 50 accounts collected for experienced, well-trained telephone workers. The message is very clear. Training is not only strongly recommended, it is essential to any efficient telephone collection program.

This chapter will cover the basic ingredients in training your department including hiring telephone workers and training them, as well as monitoring telephone calls by taping, verification, and use of dummy calls. In addition, we'll also take a look at the cost factors involved in doing business by telephone, such as long distance calls and interstate directory assistance

GUIDELINES FOR HIRING

Whether résumés are sought or a telephone number is used in the newspaper advertisement, the key to the selection of a telephone worker is to hear the voice over the telephone. The supervisor is seeking a clear, crisp voice with a normal tone. The applicant should also speak in proper English, not slang or street talk. A foreign accent should not disqualify the applicant as long as the applicant is speaking the English language clearly.

Questions to Ask Prospective Employees

Of course, the normal procedures should be used in hiring a telephone worker as with any other future employee of the business Nevertheless, a few additional questions might be added:

1. Do you have any problem with making collection calls to consumers or businesses?
2. Have you ever received any collection calls yourself?
3. Do you like to spend time on the telephone?
4. Would you work part time or full time?
5. How many hours would you like to spend on the telephone?
6. Have you ever been a telephone receptionist?
7. Have you ever done other telephone work, such as fund raising or volunteer work?

An example of such an interview over the telephone follows. The assumption is that the interviewer is satisfied with the voice, the clarity, and the grammar. "Int." stands for Interviewer and "App." stands for Applicant in the following dialogue.

Int: Hello.

App: I am calling in response to your advertisement for a telephone collection worker.

Int: Do you have any experience?

App: What company is this?

Int: This is the Space Tool Company

App: I've never done collection work, but I have used the telephone a lot.

Int: What have you done?

App: I made sales calls for my last employer, and once I called for the local library to collect past due books.

Int: How did you like doing that?

App: It was OK, no problem.

Int: How do you feel about collecting debts from your fellow consumers?

App: Well, I pay my bills. They should pay theirs.

Int: Well, this job requires you to be on the telephone six hours a day, three hours in the morning and three hours in the afternoon. Do you think that is too much?

App: I don't know. I've never spent that amount of time on the telephone What is the rate of pay?

Int: The salary is very good. The time you are not on the telephone will be devoted to clerical duties.

App: That seems like a lot of time on the telephone. Maybe four or five hours would be enough

Int: Well, maybe you should come in and we will talk some more

THE COST OF TRAINING

The cost of training is the one expense factor which is worth spending, since the return will be astronomical. One well-trained telephone worker is worth five untrained telephone workers. Testing at our own offices have shown that a thoroughly trained worker will recover more money in one week than an untrained worker will recover in five weeks. The chasm between them in terms of profitability for the employer is so great that it makes the Grand Canyon look like just another ravine.

A telephone worker is a representative of the firm, and in many instances, should be able to collect the money due to the firm as well as retain the customer for future business. The disposition of the telephone worker and his or her perception by the customer are just as important as any good will ambassador. Therefore, the general demeanor of the telephone worker should be positive, and the firm should expend time and effort to project the philosophy of the creditor before any time is devoted to the basics of collection.

Learn by Doing—The "Easy" Way to Train

The normal approach to training is to hire a new telephone worker and have a supervisor or another telephone worker spend an hour or two with the new employee, stay with the telephone worker during one or two telephone collection calls, and thereafter answer whatever questions are asked. The immediate urgency is to put the person on the telephone to collect money. Needless to say, this is probably the very worst scenario under which to train a telephone worker.

Of course, before the first telephone call is made, the telephone worker must be fully prepared with the records of the debtor. Whether these records are on accounts receivable ledgers, in credit files, on three-by-five cards, or on a computer screen, the records and all the information concerning the debtor must be readily available.

THE TELEPHONE SCRIPT:
KEY TOOL FOR ANY TRAINING PROCESS

The most important tool for training is the preparation of a telephone script. A script may be simple, or it may list a multitude of situations that will face the telephone caller. It may merely cover the circumstances of how to lay a foundation, the customer relations approach, and the demand for payment.

Suggested Details to Include in Your Telephone Script

- Leaving a message.
- Response when customer claims payment or promises payment.
- Response when customer claims he never received the merchandise or wishes to return the merchandise.
- Response when borrower or tenant claims not enough money is available for the monthly payment.
- How to handle the customer who wants an invoice after several invoices have been sent.
- The parameters for making a settlement, including the extent of the discretion of the telephone worker.
- The borrower or customer who states he will complain to a governmental authority, such as the office of the attorney

general, office of district attorney, newspaper, and radio-TV consumer action groups, the Better Business Bureau, or the Federal Trade Commission.

- The response to the business who refers you to the central office.
- To what extent should the telephone worker absorb profane or abusive language.
- The response when the business claims the employee personally ordered the merchandise.
- The customer pleads he is on social security.
- To what extent you wish to investigate the demise of a customer.
- The debtor has filed bankruptcy.
- The leverage of security for the loan, and how to use it.
- The approach to use with attorney, doctors, churches, and governmental agencies who are customers.
- The message to leave for the businessman who is never in.
- The borrower who is falling farther and farther behind.
- The installment payer who only pays after three letters and two telephone calls.
- The child who answers the telephone.

The following situations can also be included:

- The owner says "go ahead and sue me."
- The customer who says "you are not going to bother me for such a small amount."
- The installment borrower who wants a moratorium for three months.
- The debtor who states "you can't get blood out of a stone."
- The debtor who says he never heard of the creditor.

Some of these situations have already been covered in this book, and those which have not been covered will be covered in later chapters. While this book is a rather complete telephone script in itself, it is directed at a wide variety of creditors and businesses. Both consumer and business debtors are considered, and both sellers, lenders, renters, and lessors are treated. The creditor preparing a telephone script should confine the manual to his own product, whether it be goods or money, and also confine the script to either a consumer or a business, depending upon which debtor is being sold.

The above examples are limited only by the number of situations that your employees may face. As the telephone calls are made and the telephone workers present their problems to the supervisor, the supervisor should record the solutions to each problem. Thus, the script is born. A four-page script could be better than a twenty-page script if it is clear, concise, and to the point. An outline type of narrative is suggested, so that the telephone worker may memorize the basic ingredients. See Figure 6.1 (pages 104-105) for the basic outline of a telephone script.

Background Information

This information should be delivered to each new telephone worker. It should furnish background of the company, the corporate philosophy of collection, an introduction as to how the debts arose, and what efforts have been used prior to the telephone call.

A brief example is as follows:

The Display Counter Inc. has been in business for over 40 years. The company sells a wide variety of display counters to department and retail stores. These counters are either wooden, metal, or glass, and are suitable for a wide variety of products to be displayed. The counters cost between several hundred dollars and a thousand dollars. They are sold all over the country, and are delivered from three different factories located in the far west, the south, and the northeast. The sales are made by salesman, most of whom have been with the company for many years.

We stand behind our products, and we will accept a return of the product if it is justified. Before the telephone worker receives the account, the debtor has received a telephone call from the salesman to determine what the problem is. If there is a dispute, the salesman makes every effort to resolve the problem. After the salesman and sales manager determine that the debtor should pay the amount due, it is referred to the collection department. At that point, the collection department sends three letters demanding payment. When the letters are unanswered, or the excuse for nonpayment is unacceptable, the matter is placed with the telephone worker.

Figure 6.1: Outline of Basic Telephone Script

1. Basics of a telephone call
   a. Identification—"This is the XYZ Corp."
   b. Foundation—"We have sent two invoices and one letter."
   c. Demand for payment
   d. A closing statement—"If the matter is not paid, we will refer this to our attorney for suit."
   e. Use of negative closing statements
2. Responses to the following situations:
   a. Promise of payment—demanding full payment
   b. Partial payment—terms available
   c. Installment payments—minimum amount
                            maximum time
   d. Claim payment—procedure to request copy of front and back of check
   e. Claims merchandise returned—procedure for obtaining evidence of shipment
   f. Wants to return merchandise—procedure and address where to ship, separate letter and inspection before acceptance
   g. Wants invoice or statement—first and second request
   h. Medical troubles—business or consumer
   i. Financial troubles—business or consumer
3. Leaving messages
   a. Consider Debt Collection Practices Act
   b. Consumer
      (1) spouse
      (2) child

(3) relatives
(4) friends
(5) employers
c. Business
(1) Employee
(2) Bookkeeper
(3) Apparent Authority
d. Recording devices and answering services—contents of message
4. Settlements
a. Bidding against yourself
b. Installment payments
5. Technique
a. Pause
b. Arguments
c. Monotony
d. Yes—but...
6. Responses to clichés
a. "Go ahead and sue me."
b. "Don't threaten me."
c. "The check is in the mail."
d. "I'll check my records."
7. Legal considerations
a. Debt Collection Practices Act
b. Fair Credit Billing Act
c. Fair Credit Reporting Act
d. Other applicable federal laws
e. All applicable state laws which apply to the creditor

Testing

The applicant should have ample time to read and digest the script. Permitting the applicant to have the opportunity to review the script at home might be advisable. Many employees merely scan the script and hope to rely on the verbal training. In order to deter this type of approach, a statement should be made to the applicant that a test will be taken by the applicant, prior to making any telephone calls, to determine whether the telephone worker is prepared. This promised test sometimes is enough to cause a more careful and considered reading of the script. A printed test should be submitted to the telephone worker to evaluate the extent to which the script was absorbed. True–false questions probably are sufficient. The test will enable the employer to distinguish between the interested and uninterested employee.

Here is an example of some typical test questions which require true–false answers and the appropriate answers.

- You can settle any dispute involving $500 or less for any amount. (May be true or false.)
- Ask a child his/her age to find out whether the child is under 18 years old. (True.)
- Do not accept a return of merchandise where the customer's name has been imprinted. (May be true or false.)
- Always send an invoice when the debtor requests an invoice. (False.)
- If the bookkeeper is sick, ask to speak to the owner. (True.)

TRAINING PROCEDURES

Group Training

Whether to use group training or one-on-one training is somewhat academic. If several new telephone workers are employed at once, group training is the most economical method, although perhaps not the best method. If group training is selected, the supervisor should always provide adequate time for one-on-one training also. We found that telephone workers are uncomfortable and do not learn as much in group training. The workers are uncomfortable because they believe that their fellow worker is learning quicker and progressing faster. As a result, the worker usually crawls into a shell, asks no questions, and finally either quits or asks to be transferred. Use the group session as a lecture, and answer all questions. Do not use it as a testing arena to see which workers are best prepared. Use the tests and the one-on-one sessions to determine whether your telephone worker is properly prepared.

The group sessions should be elementary and instill in each person the essentials of the basic telephone call. The elements of the call, the most frequently faced situations, and the types of messages to leave should be more than sufficient for the first session. In fact, the elements of the call may even be enough depending upon the audience. The next sessions may deal with other topics. The table of contents of this book may be helpful in planning your sessions.

Copies of the Debt Collection Practices Act may be distributed, or at least excerpts from the act. Prohibited practices under the Act should be emphasized.

One-on-One Training

One-on-one training is the most effective and durable type of training. This training involves the supervisor spending one to two hours with the telephone worker. This format should cover the following schedule:

1. Answering questions concerning the manual or other topics.
2. Reviewing incorrect answers on the test.
3. Listening to a training tape of telephone collection calls between the supervisor and a debtor.
4. Listening to the telephone worker's first telephone call.
5. Critiquing the first call and listening to several other calls.
6. Monitoring at least one call by listening on the extension telephone.
7. Reviewing the records and paper work that must be posted.

This type of training is most appreciated by the prospective telephone worker, and the results will justify the time and effort contributed by the supervisor.

Taping Calls

Title 18 of the USCA Sections 2510 and 2511, subdivision (a)(c)(d) (see Appendix A) allows the taping of a telephone conversation with the consent of either party. This is the federal law, and is also the law in most states, but not all states. (See Chapter 9, "Legal Boundaries and Limitations," Taping and Monitoring.) Since the telephone worker consents to the taping, the consent of the debtor is not required, and the telephone call may be taped and reused for training purposes. Some states, such as California, require the consent of both parties to the taping. This area of the law is changing radically due to the increase in telemarketing. Since the taping of telephone calls is an essential ingredient of training, it is strongly recommended that this aspect of the law be fully monitored, not only federally but also in the respective states, to become cognizant of any changes in the state law, which may affect your procedures.

Tapes as a Training Tool: The use of audio-cassettes of telephone conversations of other telephone worker's conversations with debtors is a very powerful training tool. These cassettes are made in the regular course of business, and thus may be made without the consent of the debtor (except in some states, as mentioned above), providing, of course, the consent of the telephone worker is obtained. The telephone taping of the supervisor's calls should be played back to each new telephone worker both at group sessions and at one-on-one sessions. During the taping, the supervisor should point out the good and bad points of each telephone call. Sometimes a tape of some poor and ineffective calls should be used to illustrate what should not be said on the telephone. The supervisor's tapes should be permitted to be played at home many times so that the feeling and thrust of the telephone call can be absorbed by the telephone worker.

HELPFUL HINT: Training Tapes. Rather than use actual telephone calls to live debtors as training tapes, the supervisor should arrange a telephone call to one of the better telephone workers and use a prepared script where the telephone worker is playing the part of the debtor. This script might teach more in a shorter time to a new telephone worker than using actual live telephone calls.

Record Keeping

Usually very little time is devoted to teaching record keeping. Yet poorly kept records will cost the creditor dearly. A follow-up system on telephone calls is absolutely essential. Either index cards postdated to a monthly index of days or using a daily diary to post date telephone calls are adequate. Computer docketing systems may be used, where the computer will give a daily printout of the collection calls to be made when payments are not received. Any system is sufficient providing it does the job.

Utilizing short-hand abbreviations to reflect the "collection activity" is necessary so that less time is used to record what took place. A list of abbreviations that our office uses is set forth in Figure 6.2 (page 111). Every call should be recorded with the date and time and the person who made the call, as well as the collection activity that took place. An abbreviated entry and its proper translation is set forth below:

Abbreviation	*Translation*
4/5—3 P—AR—LM w/sp.	April 5, 3 P.M., Arlene, left message with spouse.
4/9—7 P—AR—Dr. pp 4/20 $1,000.	April 9, 7 P.M., Arlene, debtor promised payment of $1,000 by April 20.
5/1—9 A—BR—LM bkpr/ck rcd/wcb 2 dy.	May 1, 9 A.M., Bruce, left message with the bookkeeper who said she would check her records and call back within two days.
5/4—9 A—BR—Bkpr vct/LM own.	May 4, Bruce, bookkeeper on vacation. Left message with owner.
5/11—2 P—AR—NA.	May 11, 2 P.M., Arlene, no answer.
5/12—9 A—AR—BS/NA/LM/ To C/A wk.	May 12, 9 A.M., Arlene, busy signal, no answer, left message, send to collection agency in a week.

HELPFUL HINT: Time to Call. Breakfast, lunch, and dinner times are not the ideal times to call a consumer debtor. On the second and fourth Friday of the month is probably not the best time to call a business debtor since payroll is probably being distributed and everyone is preparing for the weekend. Monday morning may also not be the best time to reach the owner of a small business.

The Debt Collection Practices Act prohibits calling the consumer debtor except between 8:00 A.M. and 9:00 P.M., but a careful reading of the section does allow calling at other times if more convenient for the debtor (not the creditor). Nevertheless, in either case, the telephone worker should record the time of day that contact was made so that there is a better chance of reaching the debtor at the same time on the next telephone call.

HELPFUL HINT: Time Changes. The Debt Collection Practices Act prohibits the calling of the debtor before 8:00 A.M. and after 9:00 P.M. with certain exceptions (see Chapter 9). This time period applies to the time when the debtor receives the telephone call at his location and not the time when the creditor makes the telephone call. Each telephone worker should have a time zone map so that no mistakes are made. Usually, the local telephone book contains a map which indicates the change in the time zones.

The length of the script is a function of the experience of the supervisor and the nature of the creditor. For example, a bank would not need the sections that deal with the return of merchandise. A landlord could omit settlement negotiations. On the other hand, the script could be expanded in those sections which most often confront the creditor.

TRAINING: A CONTINUOUS PROCESS

Training is not indigenous to hiring. Many creditors decide that once a telephone worker is trained, the telephone worker is trained forever. The well-trained telephone worker does not review the telephone script, and the memory of the training declines as a direct function of how long ago the training was completed. If the creditor doubts the veracity of these conclusions, ask for a training tape five months after the telephone worker was trained and compare it with a

Figure 6.2: List of Suggested Abbreviations

The following list of abbreviations is used by our telephone workers on their reports. Variations are suggested according to the needs of each particular industry.

AMT	amount
AGMT	agreement
ASST	assistant
ATT	attention
ATTY	attorney
BAL	balance
BC	bad check
BEG	beginning
BIZ	business
BKPR	bookkeeper
BKRPT	bankrupt
BRO	brother
BS	busy
CB	call back
CC	copy of check
CIR	circuits as in "circuits" busy
CNL	cannot locate
CNOM	claims never ordered merchandise
C/N	correct name
COMPT	comptroller
CP	claims payment
CTO	come to office
CUST	customer
CR	credit card account
CRM	claims returned merchandise
CNRM	claims never received merchandise
DCB	don't call back
DECD	deceased
DEF	defective
DIFF	different
DIS	disconnected
DV	divorced
DTR	daughter

Figure 6.2 (continued)

△	debtor
△/C	debtor called
EMPL	employee
ES	evidence of shipment, shipping receipt, UPS receipt, post office receipt
EM	each month
EW	each week
EMP	employed
EOM	end of month
EOW	end of week
EVE	evening debtor's time
FTHR	father
F/D	final demand
F/N	final notice
FAD	forwarding address
FT	family trouble
GTOR	guarantor
HA	home address
H/P#	home telephone number
HB	husband
HT	health trouble
HU	hung up
INFO	information
INT	interest
JB	job
JDGMT	judgment
KM	moved
KU	unknown
LANG	language problem
LL	landlord/landlady
L/D	long distance
LM	left message
LMAS	left message answering service
LMTR	left message tape recorder
M/R	mail return
MDSE	merchandise
MTG	mortgage
MTHR	mother
MGR	manager

Figure 6.2 (continued)

MO	money order
MT	money trouble
N/FA	no forwarding address
NA	no answer
NG	no good
NIS	not in service
NL	no listing
NLE	no longer employed
#	number
OFC	office
OOB	out of business
OOO	out of order
OOW	out of work
OOH	owns own home
OPER	operator
ORIG	original
PY	payment(s)
PRP	partial payment
PT	patient
PC	private corporation
PD	paid
PDP	promise direct payment
PIF	paid in full
PL	personal letter
PM	afternoon debtor's time
POB	place of business/employment
PO	purchase order
POD	proof of delivery
PP	promises payment
PREV	previous
RCP	receptionist
RF	refused
RCPT	receipt
REFD	referred
RP	refused payment
REL	relative
REPO	repossess or repossessed
RES	residence
RESP	responsible

Figure 6.2 (continued)

RET	returned
SAT	Saturday
SECY	secretary
SIS	sister
SAL	salary
SE	self-employed
SVC	service
SWCHBD	switchboard
SGL	single
TB	telephone book
TMR	tomorrow
TEMP	temporary
T/R	tape recorder
UNP	unpublished
UPS	United Postal Service
VCT	on vacation
W/	with
WF	wife
WM	will mail
WI	wants invoice
WKG	working
W/O	without
WP	wrong person
WRG	wrong
WRM	will return merchandise
WTRM	wants to return merchandise

tape one month after the worker was trained. The difference will be startling.

The message is obvious. Training is a continuous and never-ending process. A well-organized department will do the following for the newly hired collection worker:

1. Allow sufficient time to read and digest the manual.

2. Hold a group training session.

3. Hold a one-on-one training session for at least one to two hours.

4. Allow a new hire to call on the telephone for three hours, with one hour being taped.

5. Have a one-on-one session for critiquing tape and listening to one or two telephone calls.

6. Allow a new hire to call on the telephone for four to six hours, with one hour being taped.

7. Hold a one-on-one session to critique tape.

8. Verify several telephone calls.

9. Continue procedure until satisfied with performance.

For experienced telephone workers, do the following:

1. Have each telephone worker submit a one-hour tape each month.

2. The supervisor will verify at least six calls each month for each telephone worker.

3. At least once a month, or more often, a group meeting should be held to exchange ideas and discuss problems and unusual situations.

4. One-on-one training by a supervisor should take place at least every 90 days.

These standards are suggested where the telephone collection staff ranges from five to twenty or more persons. As with all other standards or rules, exceptions depend upon circumstances. Of course, where the staff is only one or two persons, adjustments must be made. But the general principles still remain, and tapes should still be submitted, verification should still take place, and it is essential that one-on-one training take place at least twice a year.

The telephone script should be constantly revised and updated. The group sessions should provide substantial material for the script. Legal counsel should be required to advise your department concerning any changes in the law which could affect the collection effort.

Training is the foundation of any successful collection department. No substitute exists.

HELPFUL HINT: Vacation Layoffs. We have found that telephone workers who are absent for two or three weeks due to a vacation or illness are not very efficient when they return to work.

> Their interest and memories seem to slow down. We always
> schedule the telephone worker for a short one-on-one training
> session before the worker is permitted to resume making tele-
> phone calls.

Warning—The Litigious Society: Good training will produce
many side benefits, the principal one being that the telephone worker
will not expose the creditor to suits by the debtor or to violations of the
law. A well-informed telephone worker will not get carried away by his/
her own emotions or by a sophisticated debtor to commit an act which
would give rise to a law suit or a violation of the law. Twenty years ago,
there were few laws on the books dealing with collection of debts.
Today, many exist both nationally and within each state. Training is
not only advisable in order to produce the best results, but absolutely
essential to protect the creditor from litigation or violation of the law.

MONITORING THE TELEPHONE CALL

Section 18 USCA 2510 subdivision (5)(a) allows employers to
monitor its employees' calls by means of a monitoring device installed
by the local utility company. Nevertheless, monitoring programs must
be conducted in the ordinary course of business, must be limited in
time and scope, and must not be used to spy on employees. The
federal laws permit the states to pass more restrictive legislation, and
many states have taken advantage of this by requiring informed
consent of the party to be monitored, beep tones, and disclosures to
the recipient that the call is being monitored. Therefore, it is absolutely necessary that the law of the respective state be known (see
Chapter 9, "Legal Boundaries and Limitations").

Using Extension Phone to Monitor

The federal law is clear that an employer may monitor a telephone worker by listening to the telephone conversation on an
extension telephone. The employer must conform to the standards of
the federal law (see Chapter 9, "Legal Boundaries and Limitations").

The employer must still be certain that there are no more restrictive state laws before utilizing this procedure.

Recording the Collection Call

In this procedure the telephone worker records his or her own telephone calls on cassette tapes, and submits the tape to the supervisor for review. Normally, an hour of telephone calls is taped, which is about 5 to 17 completed calls. The assumption is that the telephone worker will erase a particularly poor call, and replace it with a better call. Permit this procedure, for the telephone worker has recognized the mistake and will correct it in future calls. The mistakes the supervisor discovers are usually mistakes that the telephone worker does not realize are being committed. These mistakes will be repeated continually unless the supervisor recognizes and corrects them.

We recommend that the telephone worker submit a one-hour tape at least every month. The training that is forgotten increases with time, and if the telephone worker is not continually monitored, the presentation by the telephone worker will become weaker as time goes on.

Dummy Calls

Another device to monitor the telephone worker is the use of dummy debtors spread over the geographic area where the telephone calls are being made. The usual procedure is to substitute a dummy telephone number in place of a number of a debtor who has no telephone listing. The dummy may be any one of a number of persons, including members of the family, other supervisory personnel, friends and relatives, or even business acquaintances who understand the problem. Of course, the dummy must be prepared to receive the call and must be instructed on how to respond to the telephone worker.

A short memorandum should be furnished to the dummy debtor explaining the reasons for the telephone call, the response to the collection call, and an explanation of the report that grades the performance of the telephone worker.

The report might use the following format shown in Figure 6.3.

Figure 6.3: Telephone Worker Performance Sheet

Name_____

Address _____

Name of Debtor _____
    (Stage Name)

Date Call Received _____

Time of Call _____

Amount of Debt _____

Name of Telephone Worker Calling _____

Use the Reply Checked

_____ Promises payment in a few weeks

_____ Claims never ordered the merchandise

_____ Claims that you have no money to pay

_____ Claims that you lost your job

_____ Claims that your bookkeeper is on vacation for one month and
    she or he is the only one who can help you

_____ States that your receivables are very slow and you can't start
    paying for three months

Was the Following Information Left?

_____ Account number or invoice number

_____ Name and address of employer

Figure 6.3 (continued)

General Evaluation

_____ Effective

_____ Passive

_____ Uncertain

_____ Informed

_____ Weak

_____ Other _____

Respond Yes, No, or Maybe

_____ Have an interest in the call.

_____ Sound monotonous.

_____ Was call rushed?

_____ Was delivery organized?

_____ Did caller have accurate information?

_____ Was a date given when payment had to be made?

_____ Did the caller speak clearly?

Other Remarks: _____

_____

Signature_____ Date_____

The letter to the perspective dummy debtor might read as follows:

Dear _____ :

Our firm employs telephone workers to make telephone calls to consumers and businesses for the purpose of collecting past due debts for our firm for merchandise shipped to these customers. It is with respect to this effort that we are seeking your help. Our telephone workers are thoroughly trained. However, we must be certain that they are performing their duties efficiently and that they are complying with all the rules and procedures that we prescribe as well as the federal and state laws which govern debt collection.

We are asking you to assume the role of a debtor who allegedly owes our firm money. When you receive the telephone call, the telephone worker will identify himself as employed by our firm and will ask to speak to the fictitious debtor. You are then to respond in accordance with the instructions on the attached form, and use your discretion and imagination in order to carry on a conversation with the telephone worker. Do not be unusually difficult or unusually cooperative. Vary your approach with each call. You are to complete the form after each telephone call.

It is imperative that other family members know about this letter and form so that they will not say it is a wrong number when the telephone worker asks for the assumed name.

If you have any questions, please call _____.

Thank you.

The amount of payment for services in preparing this type of form depends to a large extent upon the type of person who is the dummy. Relatives and friends may be insulted, but acquaintances may be delighted with a payment. How many calls will be received by one person is also a factor. We pay our dummy debtors for each report they submit to us so that we receive a carefully considered review of the telephone call. If the same report is being received on all calls, the dummy is showing no interest and the only alternative is to replace the dummy with someone who has an interest.

HELPFUL HINT: Dummy Debtors. Do not conceal the fact that you may use dummy debtors. It is important to disclose the existence of the dummy debtors as soon as the new telephone worker is hired.

Verification That Call Was Made

Another device to monitor telephone workers is personal verification. The supervisor calls the same debtor sometime later. (See Debt Collection Practices Act as to restrictions on frequency of calling.) The supervisor then asks a set of questions designed to determine the performance of the telephone worker. The call might sound like this:

Dr: Hello.

Cr: This is Mr. Grant from the Space Tool Company. May I speak with Mr. Boxer?

Dr: This is Mr. Boxer.

Cr: Did you receive a call from Mr. Noble about your debt to the Space Tool Company?

Dr: Yes, he called me. I said I would pay the bill in two weeks.

Cr: Well, we are just verifying his performance. Was he courteous?

Dr: I guess so.

Cr: Did he give you all the information you wanted?

Dr: Yeah, I guess so.

Cr: Did he answer your questions?

Dr: Yeah.

Cr: Did he speak in a business-like manner?

Dr: Look, he did his job and he was nice and all that. If you want me to grade him, I charge extra.

Cr: Well, I am sure you understand this is our procedure for monitoring collectors.

Dr: Yeah, I wish some of my other creditors would monitor their collectors.

Cr: Well, thank you very much.

Comment on Dialogue: Normally, debtors will not furnish too much information, but it usually is enough to make an evaluation.

Evaluating the Telephone Worker

The supervisor may wish to evaluate each telephone worker to determine the most competent ones. The most competent should receive the most pay, and at the same time, the most responsibility. The following review may assist in making said evaluation:

1. The extent of preparation
2. Clarity in speaking
3. Using the Four Golden Keys
4. Delivery of closing statement
5. Interest in the call and its result
6. Motivation, including voice projection
7. Elimination of arguments
8. Use of transferring calls
9. Complaints from debtors
10. Compliance with Debt Collection Practices Act
11. Consistency of performance
12. Attendance record

HOW MANY CALLS TO MAKE:
THE IDEAL SCENARIO

A competent and experienced telephone worker engaged in simple, undisputed telephone calls with small balances should complete between 10 and 20 telephone calls in an hour. The wide difference between the number of calls that could possibly be made in an hour is a function of how many no answers, busy signals, wrong numbers, or operator-assisted calls are made and, of course, the duration of each telephone call. In addition, the telephone worker must keep records and make entries to record what transpired with each call, and the extent of this record keeping also affects production. The ideal situation is to allow no more than 3 minutes for each telephone call multiplied by 10 telephone calls to equal 30 minutes of actual speaking time on the telephone in each hour. Busy signals, no answers, wrong numbers, operator-assisted calls, and normal dialing should account for another 15 minutes. This leaves 15 minutes for record keeping. Of course, if the record keeping is kept to a minimum, the number of calls should be increased. This should be the scenario where the account is a small amount and relatively simple.

Complicated accounts, disputed accounts, revolving credit accounts, or delinquent loans certainly require more time, and in some situations, completing three telephone calls an hour is excellent, depending upon the problems with each account. The length of each call could vary between 5 minutes and 20 minutes, depending on a wide variety of factors, the most important one being the amount of the balance.

Needless to say, this ideal scenario is difficult to achieve. But at least there is now a clearer picture of what your goal should be. The purpose of this book and this chapter is to clearly delineate the steps to achieve this goal.

LONG DISTANCE CALLS: COST FACTORS

AT&T Versus Private Companies

The cost of long distance telephone calls varies somewhat between AT&T and the private companies such as MCI and SPRINT. The rates of each company are changing on a daily basis, and companies have been formed to evaluate telephone bills by measuring the destinations of the telephone calls, the times they are placed, and the average lengths of the calls. After this information is placed in their computers, a decision is made by the computer as to which utility is the most economical.

WATS Lines

WATS lines certainly are an alternative, but their costs are changing as the telephone companies compete. AT&T reduced the WATS charges in New York by almost 25 percent. There is a substantial installation charge; and, of course, in New York, there is a monthly charge whether or not the line is being used. The billing is usually based on a fixed hourly charge for the first ten hours of talking, and then a reduced hourly charge for any additional hours. Of course, other types of lines can be rented. The subscriber is charged for the time the telephone line makes a complete connection.

> *COLLECTION TIP: Penny Wise, Pound Foolish.* As was previously stated, the WATS line carries a monthly charge whether or not the line is used. This pressure to use the line sometimes is the main reason that untrained telephone workers are allowed to make telephone calls. This should not happen. Failure to correctly train the telephone worker will be more costly than the money wasted in not using the WATS line. In short, train the telephone worker properly before allowing use of the telephone.

What It Costs for Interstate Directory Assistance

The cost of looking up telephone numbers across state lines (interstate directory assistance—IDA) as of the writing of this book is $.60 for each information call and $.30 for each number if one operator furnishes two numbers on one call to information. Under the new system, the operator must be informed at the beginning of the call that there is to be a request for two telephone numbers. Most of the regional companies are now on computer, and if a number is requested, the response is by a computer which disconnects after furnishing the number. A few regional telephone companies and some AT&T area codes are still manual, but this relic is slowly and inexorably disappearing. Presently, the Direct Marketing Association and other large users are lobbying in Washington to reduce this charge for information calls. Their argument is that AT&T could not justify this charge, and the charge discriminates against the heavier users of this service. The Direct Marketing Association, at this writing, is presently awaiting a decision from the U.S. Court of Appeals for the District of Columbia. The chances of success for a reduction appear to be very slim.

EXPENSES OF TELEPHONE COLLECTION

The expense of preparing the work for the telephone worker may cost as much as $10 to $15 per hour. The cost of a dictated letter is almost $4, while a form letter may be only $.40. The accounts must be selected, must be aged, must be pulled and must be arranged and sorted. Whether the company is on computer or doing it manually, a certain amount of time must be devoted to these procedures. If a telephone caller works 30 accounts an hour with 15 completed calls, the 30 accounts must be properly prepared with current information to enable the telephone worker to communicate with the debtor.

A summary of these expenses indicates the following:

	Low	Med	High
Wages of telephone worker	3.35	6.00	15.00
Looking up numbers—30 numbers	4.50	7.50	15.00
Cost of telephone—1 hr	5.00 (local)	25.00	45.00
Preparation of 30 calls	10.00	12.50	15.00
	22.85	51.00	90.00
Indirect expenses	——	——	——
Management, training	——	——	——

The cost of placing a telephone worker on the telephone can vary from \$22.50 per hour (of local calling) to \$90 per hour...a very significant expense. In addition, indirect expenses such as rent, electricity, taxes, fringe benefits, vacations, etc., which are allocable to the specific department have not been mentioned. Therefore, if the telephone worker does not collect money, or collects very little money, the expense of seven hours on the telephone will vary between \$210 to \$630 per day. This also excludes all the other miscellaneous expenses of management: supervisors, coffee breaks, and one other very important item—*training*.

Cost Justifications

A collection letter could cost \$4 if the letter is dictated to a secretary. Most firms use form letters and simply complete the name and address; and in this instance, the cost could be as low as \$.40 per letter. Thus a telephone call is more economical than a dictated letter, but less economical than a form letter.

Another formula for using a telephone call is the concept of accelerating payment for a given number of days. For example, say the average outstanding balance of the customer is \$10,000. A telephone call produces a \$1,000 payment in 10 days, rather than a letter which produces payment in 30 days. The accelerated payment produces \$1,000 cash to the creditor 20 days earlier. If the creditor borrows money at 12 percent per annum, the creditor would save \$10 per month on \$1,000 or \$6.66 for 20 days. The \$6.66 would certainly pay for the expense of the telephone call.

CHAPTER 7

Techniques to Obtain Payment

A technique is defined as, "knowledge applied to accomplish a desired aim." A technique is *not* a response to the position adopted by the debtor. A technique should be the instruments used and not the ingredients which are instrumental in obtaining payment of the debt from the debtor. Good techniques convince the debtor that payment should be made, and poor techniques create more difficult situations.

The following discussion outlines a few avenues to pursue while discussing the payment of the debt. The good technique is the "bridge over the water." The poor technique is "the boat that is slowly sinking."

USING THE "PAUSE" TO INDUCE COOPERATION

This technique consists of making a statement...then waiting and pausing. The natural reaction of the debtor is to "fill the void" or "fill the silence." Accordingly, the debtor responds. The debtor who makes no response of any nature is indeed very difficult to handle. A telephone collection call involves two people, and involving the debtor is most important. Many telephone workers do not allow the debtor an opportunity to talk. Using this technique at the beginning of the call should involve the debtor and induce a response. Whether the response is positive or negative, at least the dialogue has commenced. For example, use a strong foundation and then a pause:

Dr: Hello.

Cr: Is Mr. Diamond there?

Dr: Yes.

Cr: This is the Friendly Finance Company. We are calling with regard to your installment loan which is presently past due three months.

Dr: Yes.

Cr: We have sent you two invoices, written two letters, and tried to reach you by telephone last week, and your account is now 90 days past due...*pause.*

Dr: Well,...We have problems....We didn't get the letters....Last week I was out of town, etc.

Comment on Dialogue: At least, the call is started and now the telephone worker can begin to do the job of collecting money.

Dr: Hello.

Cr: Is Mr. Stuart there?

Dr: Just a minute, I'll get him.

Cr: All right, I'll wait.

Dr: Hello, who is this?

Cr: Is this Mr. Stuart?

Dr: Yes.

Cr: This is the Interstate Bank; your auto loan is now two months in arrears.

Dr: Yeah, Yeah.

Cr: Well, Mr. Stuart, this is serious. We must have a payment on this account...*pause.*

Dr: I don't have any money to pay.

Cr: Well, you do know that a payment *must* be made...*pause.*

Dr: You wouldn't really take the car back after I have paid over $3,000 on it.

Cr: Mr. Stuart, we wish to bring your loan up-to-date.

Dr: But I can't make a payment of $700 to cover the two payments in arrears.

Cr: But I must have some payment immediately...*pause.*

Comment on Dialogue: The pause is used throughout the dialogue to invite a response. Waiting for the debtor to answer is very important, even if the pause lasts for a few seconds or as much as five seconds. At that point the debtor might ask, "Are you still there?" The response should be, "Yes, I am here and still waiting for an answer." The creditor should never ask the debtor whether the debtor is still there. If the debtor refuses to answer the question, and the silence lasts over 10 seconds (or what seems like a long time), the creditor should continue with a negative closing statement in one last attempt to persuade the debtor to answer.

COLLECTION TIP. To Pause or not to Pause. The pause is normally used after a statement of fact and not after a question. If a question is used, a pause does not come into play since a question begs an answer. When a statement of fact is presented, the pause is used to invite an answer even though no question has been asked.

Cr: Your loan is three months in arrears and has been in arrears almost from the very beginning.

Dr: But I have been paying regularly each month. I've never fallen behind more than three months. That's a plus.

Cr: Your pattern of paying 30 days late is unacceptable to the bank. Payments on a revolving credit loan must be current and be made each month in the required amount...*pause.*

Dr: What do you mean current?

Cr: I mean you must bring your loan up-to-date and then continue to make payments on a current basis.

Another example:

Cr: We must insist upon payment.

Dr: But I shipped the stuff back weeks ago. I'm not going to pay for something I don't have. You have it. You are not going to have the stuff and get payment also.

Cr: Our policy is to accept a return of merchandise only within 30 days of the sale...*pause.*

Dr: So I didn't ship it back within the 30 days. So what?

Cr: We provide for a return in 30 days so we will be able to dispose of the merchandise for a reasonable loss. We do this to stand behind our goods. But when you ship it back three months later, we have no use for it. We cannot dispose of it for any price, and we have no alternative but to throw it out. Since our loss is due to the fact that you had the use of it for three months, and then decided to return it, we are insisting on payment... *pause.*

FIVE WAYS TO MOTIVATE DEBTORS TO PAY

Debtors, as well as everyone, are susceptible to human greed. If the debtor feels that something else may be gained, or that a benefit will be derived from doing something, a new motivation may exist to pay the indebtedness. The telephone worker's goal is to integrate these enticements into the presentation to induce the debtor to recognize the advantages of paying. Some examples follow:

1. *Remind Customer About His Credit Record:* A reminder to the debtor that future credit might be affected by his continual delinquency may help to persuade the debtor to pay. *You should not threaten to report the debtor to a credit reporting agency unless this procedure is actually being used.* Be careful not *to imply* that the debtor's failure to pay will affect his future credit unless the creditor does report to a credit reporting agency. (See Appendix A for Fair Credit Reporting Act.) This area is very delicate, and implications concerning being denied future credit are possible violations of the Debt Collection Practices Act. Section 814 of the Debt Collection Practices Act prohibits the use of a false representation to collect a debt. Advising the debtor that his credit would be impaired would appear to be a false representation unless some action was taken to try to impair that credit reputation. (See Chapter 9, "Legal Boundaries and Limitations.") If you do report to a credit reporting agency, you might use the following statements:

   a. "If you fail to bring your account up-to-date, we will be forced to report the account to a credit reporting agency."
   b. "If you expect to buy on credit again, it would be wise to bring your account up-to-date; if not, we will be forced to report you to a credit reporting agency; and this will affect your future credit if an inquiry is made to the credit reporting agency."
   c. "I am sure you do not want this delinquency to affect your future credit."

2. *Appealing to Customer's Integrity:* Every person respects an honest person, and addressing the debtor as an honest person appeals

to the debtor's reputation among his friends and in his community
The thrust should be that honest persons pay their debts, and that this
is the proper and right thing to do. Some examples are:

   a. "As an honest and respected person, I know you recognize your
      duty to pay this debt."
   b. "The right thing to do is to pay, and I know you feel this way."

A dialogue might develop as follows:

Cr: The bill is over four months old.
Dr: I know, but I can't make any payment. I don't have the money. You
         will just have to wait.
Cr: I need a payment this month.
Dr: I want to pay, but I can't do the impossible.
Cr: I know you want to do the right thing, and I know basically that
         you are an honest person, and I do believe you, but I must have a
         payment this month. How do we solve this problem?

3. *Appeal to Credit Standing:* Every person has a responsibility to
his family. Emphasizing this responsibility in terms of obtaining credit
may be used, but remember to consider the problem when the creditor
is not using a credit reporting agency. *If you are not reporting to a credit
reporting agency, do not use this technique.*

Try to create a guilty feeling in the debtor that he is disappoint-
ing his family. While this technique may seem very negative, in the
hands of an experienced telephone worker, using it at an opportune
time may be very successful. An example:

   "You owe it to your family to maintain a good credit profile.
Please do not injure it by continuing this delinquency." (If reporting
to a credit reporting agency, see Appendix A.)

4. *The Friendly Creditor:* Many creditors use the ploy that "credit
was extended when you needed it" and we were your friend in need.
This may not work, since there are too many sarcastic responses that
could be made by the debtor. A sarcastic response only tilts the
telephone call off-center, and sometimes provokes an unneeded retort
by the telephone worker. When this happens, the telephone call will
never accomplish the desired results.

5. *Time, Effort, and Money:* Saving the debtor time, effort, and
money certainly is attractive. The time and effort are somewhat
elusive, but the money becomes more seductive. If the loan carries
interest charges, late charges, or other penalties, these possibilities

should be brought to the attention of the debtor. Every debtor finds late charges and additional interest or penalties totally repugnant; and if said charges may be avoided, the debtor may make a more determined effort to pay. Examples follow:

    a. "If payment is not received by the end of the month, there is an additional late charge of 1 percent. Certainly, you don't want any additional expenses."

    b. "Interest is not charged if the payment is received within 30 days after the charge is made; but after that 30-day period, interest accumulates at the rate of 12 percent a year."

    c. "There are substantial charges if the loan is not paid when due "

    6. *Peace and Security:* An appeal may also be made to the social needs of the debtor, such as:

    1. "You may be faced with a medical emergency and really need credit, and because of this situation on your record, you may be denied credit." (Say this only if reporting to credit reporting agency.)

    2. "When you pay this bill, you will have no more worries and will be free to enjoy life."

    3. "Having all your bills paid will enable you to have the security to face and enjoy life."

Of course, the last three statements leave the telephone worker very vulnerable to a quick retort or a put-down. The effectiveness of these statements is dependent entirely upon the right place, the right time, and the right debtor.

THE "YES...BUT" RESPONSE

"Yes...but," implies agreement with the debtor. Both parties are on the same road towards discharge of the indebtedness, but what is being proposed may need further clarification. This approach builds a bridge to the debtor in that the creditor is at least partially agreeing with the debtor. This partial agreement is interpreted by the debtor as sympathy. If the debtor reaches for this sympathy, an arrangement will become easier to accomplish.

Example:

Dr: Hello.

Cr: This is Mr. Murphy from the Technical Laboratory Supply Company. Who is this?

Dr: Dr. Clark. What company is this?

Cr: The Technical Laboratory Supply Company, and this deals with the outstanding bill for a sterilizer upon which there is a balance due of $1,200.

Dr: Yes, I know, but I am having a difficult time starting a practice, and I can't quite make enough to pay all the bills for all of the necessary equipment to practice as a dentist. You have to give me some more time. I am trying to meet almost $2,000 in payments a month. I've been just about making it, but last month I had a virus and was in bed for almost three weeks and I couldn't do anything for almost the whole month. I only worked four days the entire month.

Cr: *Yes,* we understand the problems in starting a practice. We have helped many young dentists. *But,* bills still have to be paid, and you are over four months in arrears We must have a payment

Dr: Just where am I going to get the money?

Cr: Your account has not received a payment since April

Dr: I didn't know it was that far behind

Cr: Well, it is, and you have been running in arrears for the past six months.

Dr: All right. I will try to make a couple of double payments to catch up.

Cr: Then we will receive $260 for the next two months instead of $130.

Dr: Yes, I think I can handle that.

Cr: And what about after that, can you increase the monthly payment 50 percent, to $195 until you are caught up?

Dr: I will do my best.

Cr: OK. I will write this arrangement down. Please be certain that you keep it, so that it will be unnecessary to forward this to an attorney for legal action. This will be referred to an attorney if the payments are not continued, for your account has been running in arrears too long. We must bring it up-to-date.

Dr: I understand. That's $260 for the next two months and $195 a month until I'm caught up.

Cr: That's right. And I'm sure you will be able to meet these payments. Young practices have a way of building. You are not the first dentist we have helped launch.

Dr: I hope so, but there are so many bills and the patients do not pay right away, at least not my patients.

Cr: Why don't you see if the bank might help you with your receivables, or possibly refer you to someone who might help you collect the receivables?

Dr: Maybe that's an idea.

Cr: Don't worry. All of a sudden it will all come together.

Dr: I hope so.

Cr: It will. Don't worry.

Dr: Thanks. Goodbye.

Cr: Goodbye.

Comment on Dialogue: The problems of a new practice are self-evident. The creditor acknowledged them, and even repeated his understanding of them at the end of the telephone call. This type of debtor may be an excellent customer in the future. The creditor does not want to sue, but will usually extend the payments as long as some payment is received. The idea is to develop an empathy with the debtor so that the debtor recognizes that you understand his problem.

Another dialogue:

Cr: We sold these fork lifts to you over five months ago, and there is still a balance due.

Dr: Well, business is very slow and I can't pay all my bills. I am doing the best I can.

Cr: *Yes,* we know that the economy is very weak, *but* bills still have to be paid and your bill is very old...*pause.*

Dr: Well, I can't pay you with money I don't have. I don't have to tell you what happened to the lumber market. Prices fell out of bed. I think that I lose money on every sale I make. All you have to do is read the papers.

Cr: *Yes,* I know how tough the lumber business is. We've sold machinery to other firms like yours, *but* they are managing to pay their bills.

Dr: You said managing to pay their bills. Then they are having trouble, too.

Cr: Yes, we know things are difficult and we will try to help you work this out.

Dr: Well, what are you suggesting?

Cr: The balance due is $3,700, and it was due three months ago.

Dr: I know the details.

Cr: We will need payment of the whole amount by the end of the month.

Dr: Are you kidding? The most I could pay is about $500 at the end of the month.

Comment on Dialogue: The creditor acknowledged the problems in the industry and this produced the first interest by the debtor to make payment. Notice that the debtor asked the creditor to bid against himself ("What are you suggesting?") and that the creditor adroitly avoided this trap.

COLLECTION TIP: Repeat and Summarize. An important point to remember is not to start the response with *"Yes, but* bills still have to be paid." Always, summarize and repeat what the debtor has alleged, "Yes, we know the economy is weak...." This establishes a rapport with the debtor, and the debtor now feels that the creditor has some understanding of his problem. This enables the debtor to talk more freely.

TIPS ON OFFERING THE DEBTOR
SUGGESTIONS ON SOURCES OF FUNDS

The telephone worker must be aware of the many sources of money available to the debtor. A suggestion to the debtor as to possible methods of raising monies sometimes produces a favorable response. To utilize this device, the telephone worker must be alert to the most common origin of monies. Consider the following sources of money available to a consumer:

1. The most obvious source is checking and savings accounts.

2. A not-so-obvious place where funds can be found is a safe deposit box. Many people leave cash, jewelry, gold, silver, and other valuables, all of which may readily be converted to cash.

3. In the past few years the stock market has produced substantial profits, and many consumers are now in the market both with stocks and bonds.

4. Mutual funds, money market funds, Keogh plans, IRAs (individual retirement account), and a wide assortment of other types of funds are now available to consumers.

5. Pension plans, 401 fund plans, and profit-sharing plans are all created by employers, but the employee has access to the monies in these funds under certain terms and conditions. In addition, some of these types of plans are empowered to lend to an employee.

6. Loans from banks, loan companies, and credit unions. Credit unions are particularly oriented to lending monies to their members who have financial problems, and sometimes at interest rates below the rates charged by other lending institutions.

7. Many consumers are not aware of the fact that the cash value of insurance policies may be borrowed—and usually at very favorable rates of interest—below the current rates charged by banks and loan companies.

8. Employers often have in place procedures to lend their employees monies, especially those who have many years of service. Even small businessmen will lend an employee some money to help him or her out of a financial problem.

9. Under the new Tax Reform Act, equity loans (formerly called second mortgages) are the rage since interest is still deductible for these loans, whereas interest on automobile loans is not deductible starting in 1987.

10. Many consumers receive tax refunds, and this should not be overlooked if the consumer is being dunned during the early part of the year.

11. Consumers with credit cards or debit cards can usually obtain a small amount of cash to meet a monthly payment.

12. Occasionally the debtor has loaned money to someone else, and may have neglected to seek repayment.

13. Loans from friends and relatives may be suggested, but such an inquiry may alienate the debtor. Use this inquiry carefully.

An example of how to use this device is as follows:

Cr: This is the National Bank, and we are calling about your installment loan which is over three months in arrears.

Dr: Who is this?

Cr: Mr. Clark from the loan workout department.

Dr: I am only two months behind, not three. The next payment is not due until next Thursday.

Cr: The payment is due this Monday. Next Thursday is the last day of the 10-day grace period.

Dr: Oh! Well, I will try to make a payment next week, or probably the week after, when I get paid.

Cr: Where are you working now?

Dr: Where I always worked.

Cr: Where is that?

Dr: I don't want you calling my employer.

Cr: Don't worry, I won't do that. How long have you been working there?

Dr: Almost nine years, and if you leave me alone, your loan will get paid, too.

Cr: I know that, but we do have a problem now. Perhaps you could speak to your boss, and he might lend you enough to pay off this loan, or at least the arrearages. You know, the interest rates he would charge would be a lot less than the bank is charging you, especially now that you are past due.

Dr: I doubt if he would give me a loan.

Cr: Has he ever given anybody else in your office a loan?

Dr: Well, only once I can remember when Harry's wife was in the hospital.

Cr: Well, he might help you. All he can say is "no"; and he might say "yes."

Dr: You know, what have I got to lose?

Another example:

Dr: I have no money to pay you. You might as well sue me, for then I will have three months to accumulate some money to pay you.

Cr: You really do not want us to sue you. I am sure if you gave this some thought, you will be able to make these two payments. I'm sure you can find some money somewhere.

Dr: Well, maybe you are a magician and can produce money out of thin air.

Cr: I am not a magician, but I could make some suggestions.

Dr: OK, then make some.

If the debtor is a business, the availability of money is greatly enlarged. Some examples:

1. Accounts receivable can be pledged to a bank or finance company, or assigned to the creditor as payment for the indebtedness.
2. Machinery and equipment may be mortgaged.
3. Loans from banks may be increased.
4. The principal owner can usually obtain additional monies if a personal guarantee is offered.

The list is endless and is only limited by the ingenuity of the creditor, based upon his knowledge of the business of the debtor. The important point to remember is to ask and suggest whenever the opportunity presents itself.

COOPERATIVE VERSUS UNCOOPERATIVE DEBTORS

There is a vast difference between affirmative communication and negative communication. The difference lies in whether the debtor is cooperative or uncooperative.

A cooperative debtor deserves a positive and optimistic dialogue. Whether the debtor will or will not ultimately pay is immaterial. Providing an opportunity for payment in a positive atmosphere is important. Thus, where the debtor promises to instruct his bookkeeper to mail the check the same day, the creditor should accept the offer at face value (at least the first time around) and make an appropriate closing statement, such as:

Dr: I will send a check out today.

Cr: Good. Then, we will have payment before the end of the week, and will not have to forward this to our collection agency/attorney.

—or—

Dr: I will have the bookkeeper send a check by the end of this week.

Cr: Then, your rent check will be in our office by May 15. Good, so I will not have to send you the 30 day [3 day] notice, and I am sure you will be more careful next time and pay your rent by the tenth of next month.

—or—

Dr: I'll send two payments by the end of the month.

Cr: If we receive them by the end of the month, it will not be necessary to send this to an attorney for institution of suit. I'm sure you don't want a suit, and neither do we, so please be certain you don't forget to send the payments.

Communicating with a Difficult Debtor: Of course, if the debtor is uncooperative, a strong and forceful technique is required. An attempt to accelerate referral to a third party, such as an attorney or collection agency, certainly will grasp the attention of the debtor. The debtor may realize that his recalcitrant attitude has caused him further harm, and that being rude and obnoxious will not achieve the goal of obtaining an extension. At this point, the debtor may become more reasonable, and the telephone worker will at least have an opportunity to communicate with him.

Cr: Twenty-four cartons of corrugated boxes were shipped to you over six weeks ago, and we have a shipping receipt.

Dr: I don't care what you have. We never got the boxes. Maybe you shipped them to Outer Mongolia, for they would have gotten there quicker.

Cr: Look, we shipped the boxes, we have a receipt for them, and you received them. Now, why don't you pay for them?

Dr: I didn't receive them, and I'm not paying for them.

Cr: Well, if we don't receive a check within two weeks, we are going to refer this claim to our attorney for immediate institution of suit.

Dr: Do whatever you please. I don't pay for things I don't receive, and don't try to intimidate me.

Cr: You know, I'm not waiting two weeks. I am going to speak to my attorney today, and you will get a summons and complaint served on you by tomorrow.

Dr: Look, I really did not get the cartons. I don't see how you can have a receipt.

Cr: I have a receipt from the carrier signed by your receiving department.

Dr: Look, get the receipt and read me the name of the person.

Cr: I don't have it here, but I will call you back in a few minutes.

Dr: Make it ten minutes, and let me double check with my receiving department.

Comment on Dialogue: The creditor must be prepared to act on the threat. If the debtor hangs up after the threat, speak to his attorney "today."

WHY PRECISENESS IS SO CRITICAL

Use specific words and specific dates and times for eliciting promises to pay. A promise to pay "within a week" is only significant if the debtor remembers the exact date on which the telephone call was received. A statement to the debtor that the account is delinquent is only significant if the debtor is told how many months delinquent. A statement to a borrower that the mortgage payments are behind is not significant unless the debtor is told how many payments are in arrears and the total amount of the arrearages. A statement to a debtor that the revolving credit balance has not been paid is not significant unless the debtor is told how many payments are in arrears and how much has to be paid until the debtor can utilize the account again.

Examples:

1. "We must have payment by Monday, May 7."
2. "Your payments are in arrears three months, and with a monthly payment of $130, that means a total of $390 is due."
3. "The invoice was for $850 and the merchandise was shipped on April 1, and the balance due is $850."

MOTIVATING THE TELEPHONE WORKER

The telephone worker who treats the debt as his own debt is the truly motivated telephone worker. Finding such employees is difficult. But using a telephone worker who is not motivated may very well be a waste of time and effort, for the results pale in comparison with the interested telephone worker. Rather than concentrate on the well-motivated telephone worker, the supervisor should concentrate on identifying the telephone worker who has no interest and is merely going through the motions, reciting words, or sounding as if a script is being read.

No dialogue on the printed page can illustrate a motivated telephone worker. The interest in the call is exhibited in the tone of voice, emphasis on certain phrases, attentiveness, and overall sincerity. A training tape (see Chapter 6, "Cost Guidelines for Hiring Callers) will reveal to the supervisor these elements which combine to create an efficient telephone worker. These qualities distinguish a telephone call that collects money from one that collects dust.

Helping Callers to Overcome Monotony

The worst pitfall for a telephone worker is "monotony." Unfortunately, by continuing to make the same telephone call over a period of months and perhaps years, the telephone worker reaches a point where the presentation sounds like a recording. The words selected are the same for each telephone call, and the order of the phrases, demands, questions, etc., also are similar. The emphasis is always placed in the same place, and the opening and closing sentences are the same. The end result is a telephone call that is the equivalent to an automatic dialing and recording device. In short, the telephone worker does not listen to the debtor, but only says what has been said a thousand times before.

Again, the best way to recognize this is to listen to the training tapes on a regular basis. The telephone worker does not realize his or her own fatigue. Monotony has overtaken the presentation. The telephone worker is astonished when their tape is played back for them.

Another effective control is to monitor the reports by the dummy debtors. Weak or passive attitudes are symptoms of monotony.

The best cure for this problem is a moratorium for a few days or a transfer to another department for a week. Then, a fresh start should be made with a training session. The supervisor should monitor the particular telephone worker for a period of several months to be certain that the condition does not reappear. Frequently, the telephone worker lapses back into the same bad habits. Continual monitoring and training is essential.

Somewhat similar to monotony is the "sing-song" style or rhythmic up-and-down elevation in the tone of the voice. Boredom or fatigue is usually the cause. While this condition is just as troublesome as the problem of monotony, the solution is for the supervisor and telephone worker to listen to the tape of the telephone worker. Continual monitoring and taping is beneficial in overcoming both these problems.

HOW TO REACT TO THE UNINTERESTED DEBTOR

The telephone worker should always react to the debtor. If the debtor is sincere and displays an interest in repaying the debt, then the telephone worker should display the same interest. If the debtor seems not interested, then the telephone worker must become forceful and aggressive in order to gain the attention of the debtor.

The owner, bookkeeper, or controller of a business is aware that to maintain a good credit reputation, bills must be paid. The consumer in recent years has also become more concerned about his credit profile. But some consumers have no intention of dealing with the creditor again and do not care whether the bill is paid. In fact, some businesses adopt the same attitude after a decision has been made not to deal with the creditor any longer. In both of these instances, a strong and forceful presentation must be made to persuade the debtor that the creditor means business and will continue to press for payment, even if this includes referral to an attorney and finally, suit. Consider the following:

Dr: Hello.

Cr: May I please speak to Mr. Rose?

Dr: This is Mr. Rose.

Cr: This is the Outdoor Flower Corporation. We sent you seeds three months ago, and despite several letters, you still have not paid your bill of $125.50.

Dr: Yeah.

Cr: We must have payment by Monday, May 7.

Dr: Yeah.

Cr: If we don't receive payment, then the matter will be referred to our attorney for further action.

Dr: Yeah.

Cr: I shall then expect your check...*(pause)*.

Dr: ...*(silence)*.

Cr: Well, I assume you are not paying, so I will not wait until Monday, May 7, but will refer this matter to our attorney today and let them take immediate action.

Dr: Wait a minute. I didn't say I wouldn't pay.

HOW TO HANDLE ARGUMENTATIVE DEBTORS

The telephone worker should never become personally or emotionally involved in the telephone call. Provocative statements made by the debtor should be ignored totally. Some statements by the debtor do not require a response, and any response by the caller would result in negative communication. In short, permit the debtor to score in this particular inning. The purpose is to win the ball game.

If the debtor transfers his complaints with the creditor to the telephone worker, this personal attack should be disregarded and the telephone worker should continue with the conversation as if the attack was not made. *Never apologize for the creditor.*

Violation of these precepts will only lead to an argument with the debtor. This is the very worst scenario and will only cause a difficult and recalcitrant debtor to become totally uncooperative.

Example:

Cr: The carpet was laid over three months ago and we still haven't received the balance due.

Dr: You did one lousy job. The carpet buckled already in a few places, and your installers did not connect the carpet, and it is turning up at the ends.

Cr: I was there, and I could see no buckling.

Dr: Well, you must either be blind or stupid.

Cr: Don't call me stupid. No one calls me stupid.

Dr: I called you stupid, and I'm someone.

Cr: Look, you owe the money; and if it's the last thing I do, I am going to make sure you pay for it.

Dr: Well, it may be the last thing you do, but I'm not paying for your lousy work.

Cr: We'll see.

Comment on Dialogue: This is probably the worst possible result for a telephone collection call.

Transfer the Call if You Have Trouble

Many sophisticated supervisors of collection departments employ this device as a basic procedure. In short, the telephone worker is encouraged to transfer the call to another telephone worker or supervisor any time control over the telephone call is being lost. This may happen in any of the following situations:

1. The debtor is screaming.
2. The debtor is using profane or abusive language.
3. The debtor is accusing the creditor of violating a law, and at the same time, the debtor may be threatening to sue the creditor.
4. The debtor is threatening to report the creditor to some governmental agency, such as the Federal Trade Commission, an office of the Attorney General, a consumer affairs office or a similar authority.
5. The debtor is threatening to report the creditor to some civil authority such as a newspaper action line or a radio or television action line, or some entity such as the Better Business Bureau.
6. The debtor is just being totally obnoxious.

The theory is that the "transfer" will enable the new telephone worker to begin from the beginning, and thus enable the debtor to start over since the new telephone worker has not heard the abuse and threats. This concept does work, and should be used when appropriate. The difficulty is convincing the original telephone worker to acknowledge that a new worker may do a better job. The telephone worker sometimes feels that such an abdication means that he is not peforming his job properly. Actually, transferring the call is an excellent procedure, and the telephone worker should be praised whenever he utilizes this device properly.

When the Debtor Threatens to Report the Creditor to a Governmental Authority

In a situation when a sophisticated debtor is threatening to report the creditor to the Attorney General's Office or some other governmental agency, the best approach is to assure the debtor that the matter will be looked into immediately, that contact will be made with the client, that this matter will be held in abeyance, and that the debtor will be recontacted. Do not try to dissuade the debtor from reporting to the governmental agency. Such an attempt will only encourage him. In most instances, this threat is merely a threat, and will not be carried out if the creditor displays an interest in solving the problem.

DEALING WITH ABUSIVE LANGUAGE

On those occasions when you are faced with a difficult debtor on the telephone, there are several things which must be kept in mind when dealing with this type of debtor.

A difficult debtor is the type of debtor who falls into one of the following categories:

1. *Screaming Debtor:* This is the debtor who is screaming over the telephone claiming he doesn't owe the money, or that he has already paid the money, or that the creditor has agreed not to take any further steps.

2. *Threatening Debtor:* This debtor threatens to report the creditor to the Federal Trade Commission, the Attorney General's Office, the Federal Reserve Board, the District Attorney's Office, the Better Business Bureau, the Consumer Fraud Division, a newspaper, radio, or television action line.

3. *Profane Language:* This debtor uses profane language over the telephone and his vocabulary consists of nothing better than four-letter words.

It is very difficult to speak to a debtor who is screaming or using profane language. If the problem cannot be identified or solved, the telephone call should be terminated just as quickly as possible in order to give the debtor time to calm down. In such an instance, one course of action would be to tell the debtor you will look into this further and the matter will be held in abeyance until you contact him. It is important to say proper good-byes so that the debtor does not feel that you are hanging up the telephone. Another alternative would be to transfer the call to a supervisor. The debtor may be satisfied that his screaming produced additional attention, and at this point the debtor may communicate the problem and seek a solution.

Sometimes, the debtor will be screaming in such a continuous way that it will be absolutely impossible to terminate the telephone call. In this instance, advising the debtor that you "have another telephone call coming in on the other line and you must say good-bye now," will probably be a more diplomatic way to terminate the telephone call. As an alternative, transferring the call might even be better.

The follow-up to this call should be a letter, rather than another telephone call, because a second telephone call may only produce a second encounter with a screaming debtor or more profane language. On the other hand, if you know what the problem is and you have resolved it, then a second telephone call would be in order.

How to Respond

Identify Problems: In all instances, the primary goal of the person on the telephone should be to try to determine exactly what is the problem or complaint of the debtor. Too often, between the screaming, threats, and profane language, it is impossible to find out what the complaint is. As soon as you are able to identify the problem, the major difficulty in dealing with the particular debtor will disappear. The most important thing to remember is to attempt to identify the problem.

Assurance to Debtor: Accordingly, after you are able to determine what the problem is, the immediate response to the debtor should be that you will investigate the problem. Before this series of thoughts are communicated to the debtor, the debtor should be assured that the matter is being held in abeyance until the problem is resolved.

Listen: Another thing to remember is that it pays to listen to the debtor on the telephone. If you allow the debtor sufficient time to talk, you will be able to recognize the problem, and perhaps even be able to solve it during the same telephone call. So, therefore, when the debtor wishes to talk and air his grievance, it's better to spend the additional time on the telephone and listen to the complaint.

SUMMARY CHECKLIST OF TECHNIQUES TO ENCOURAGE PAYMENTS

1. Using the "pause" to induce a response.
2. Reminding the debtor that his future credit might be affected by his continual delinquency.
3. Appealing to the debtor's honesty and integrity.

4. Appealing to the debtor's responsibility to his family and to keep his good credit standing.

5. Proposing that the creditor is the friend of the debtor.

6. Showing the debtor how to save money.

7. Agreeing with the debtor—the "yes—but" technique.

8. Using affirmative communication for a cooperative debtor.

9. Using specific dates, days, and time periods as well as amounts.

10. Never arguing with the debtor.

11. Responding forcefully to the uninterested debtor.

12. Monitoring training tapes and dummy debtors to recognize monotony.

13. Identifying the problem with a screaming debtor.

14. Transferring the call to someone else.

15. When a threat is made to report the matter to a governmental agency, assuring the debtor that the matter will be investigated, the debtor will be called back, and that the matter will be held in abeyance until the creditor calls the debtor.

16. Reviewing the sources of funds which may be available to the debtor.

CHAPTER 8

How to Deal with Stalling Techniques

During the course of a telephone conversation certain clichés and stalling techniques will be encountered repeatedly by the telephone worker. The proper response often will enable the creditor to convert the conversation to a promise of payment. Failure to deliver a proper reply usually will enable the debtor to obtain an extension of time, provide a "valid" excuse for nonpayment, or force the creditor to use the closing statement without any opportunity to negotiate a settlement or to question the debtor.

Another significant problem is the length of the telephone call. Long telephone calls cost money; short telephone calls save money. If the results will be the same regardless of the length of the conversation, the better choice is the short telephone call. After covering some of the most common clichés and stalling techniques, some skills for shortening a telephone call will be discussed.

HOW TO RESPOND TO SEVEN OF THE MOST OFTEN-USED CLICHÉS

"Cliché" in the *Webster's New Collegiate Dictionary* is defined as "a trite expression or phrase, or a hackneyed theme or situation." These phrases usually stem from a desire to express a lack of money in such a way that will produce sympathy from the creditor. A lack of preparation will leave the telephone worker speechless. The sophisticated debtor is relying on the fact that the telephone worker is a novice who will be frustrated in the search for a reply. Let us consider a few clichés.

1. "You Can't Get Blood from a Stone"

Of course, one can't get blood from a stone. The creditor, however, is not seeking blood from a stone. This type of cliché is also found in other similar type phrases (e.g., "pound of flesh"); it must be attacked on a frontal basis, and immediately set aside so that the conversation can proceed in a normal course.

Cr: This account is over five months past due.

Dr: I know, but I haven't worked for five months.

Cr: The account must still be paid.

Dr: You can't get blood out of a stone.

Cr: We do not want blood from a stone, we want payment of this debt.

Dr: But that's the same thing.

Cr: Sir, let us talk about this debt in which you are five months in arrears. We cannot continue these arrearages. Just how bad is your financial situation?

Dr: Very bad.

Cr: How much could you afford to pay?

Dr: Well, the most I could pay....

Cr: We must have payment by Monday, May 7.

Dr: No way; it just can't be done.

Cr: Well, it will have to be done because my supervisor has advised if it's not paid, the matter goes to our attorney.

Dr: Your boss wants his pound of flesh.

Cr: No, he doesn't; he just wants repayment of the loan. That's a reasonable request.

Dr: Reasonable!! I don't have the money now.

Cr: Well, when?

Dr: In about a month.

Cr: A month!! That's too long. We have payroll to meet also.

Dr: Well, maybe in two or three weeks.

> *COLLECTION TIP: "How Bad Is Your Financial Situation?"* The use of the question "how bad are your finances" often extracts from the debtor a favorable response. I don't know exactly why, but somehow the phrase conveys understanding and compassion; and the debtor seems to grasp at the opening. Try it yourself, and see if you elicit the same results.

2. "Go Ahead and Sue Me"

How many times a debtor has made this offer to the creditor! Such a statement is more in the nature of absolute frustration than an invitation to the creditor to proceed. The last thing the debtor really wants is to be sued. The response must be firm, but at the same time the door must be left open to permit the debtor to enter into the conversation positively. A few examples:

Dr: I don't pay for damaged goods that I can't use. I'm sending the whole thing back.

Cr: But you have kept the goods for six weeks.

Dr: So what?

Cr: You should have notified us.

Dr: I have more important things to do. I just got around to it now.

Cr: But because of your delay I can't dispose of the goods. The order gave you ten days to return. I'm not going to accept a return. I don't have to.

Dr: Well, go ahead and sue me, because I'm not paying.

Cr: Well, our attorney would love to have the business, if that is what you really want; but don't you think we can work this out?

Dr: Yeah, take back the merchandise.

Cr: Under the written order, I don't have to do that.

Dr: I don't care about the written order. If you want money, sue me.

Cr: As I said, if a suit is what you want, I will arrange to have my attorney serve you with a summons and complaint within the week; you'll have to pay an attorney to represent your side.

Dr: I'll represent myself.

Cr: Whether you use an attorney or represent yourself, a lot of time will be wasted. Let's look at this intelligently.

Dr: What do you mean by "intelligently"?

Cr: Well, I mean we should try to see each other's point of view and try to settle this so attorneys will not get most of the money.

Dr: Well, what do you have in mind?...

Comment on Dialogue: As long as the debtor keeps talking, there is a chance to negotiate a settlement. The effort by the debtor to close the conversation by inviting a suit was carefully handled by the creditor. The creditor created several openings, none of which the debtor walked through, except perhaps the last opening. Perhaps this will be an instance in which the matter must be referred to an attorney, but at least the creditor will have made a sincere effort to avoid this.

Dr: I have been out of work for the past three months.

Cr: Then, you should not have ordered a cashmere jacket from our catalog for $305.

Dr: I have no money. Go ahead and sue me.

Cr: Our job is to collect this debt, and if suit is what you want, we will be glad to arrange it unless you would rather arrange for payment of this debt.

Dr: Do you want to take the food out of my mouth?

Cr: We have to insist on the bill being paid. How it is paid is up to you.

Comment on Dialogue: A promise of payment may not be of much value in this type of situation. But an effort must be made, and in some instances this type of retort does produce results.

3. "No Authority to Order"

This ploy is often used by the employer to persuade a creditor that if a lawsuit was instituted against the debtor, the creditor would not be successful. Nevertheless, many circumstances enter into the question of liability.

If the employee had "apparent authority" to order, the employer is liable. If the employee is an officer of the corporation, such as a controller, vice-president, treasurer, or president, certainly this party has apparent authority to order. If the employee is in the purchasing department, is an office manager, or is an employee who ordered from the creditor in the past, a strong case could be presented to hold the employer liable. Even the secretary of an officer or a bookkeeper in a small firm might acquire this authority if they have dealt with the creditor in the past. Such employees as waitresses, mechanics, bartenders, sales clerks, file clerks, barbers, receptionists, construction workers, factory workers, foremen, policemen, and similar classes of employees would encounter serious difficulty in proving that they had authority to order for their employer. Whether or not an employee has apparent authority also depends upon the amount of the order, the conditions under which the order is placed, past dealings with the debtor, size of the firm, and many other circumstances. We recommend that an attorney be consulted before a decision is made.

Example:

Cr: The calculator was delivered by United Parcel Service, and we have a receipt for delivery from Janet Adams.

Dr: Mrs. Adams is no longer with us, and anyhow she had no authority to order calculators.

Cr: She signed as a bookkeeper. If she was employed by you at the time she ordered the merchandise, the firm is legally responsible for the debt.

Dr: Well, she may have said she was a bookkeeper, but she wasn't. She was just an order clerk, who accepted orders and put them through.

Cr: Well, perhaps someone told her to order the calculator.

Dr: No one told her, because we don't have it. She probably took it with her when she quit. I don't have it and I don't intend to pay.

Cr: How long was she with you?

Dr: I don't know, about two years.

Cr: Did she ever work in the bookkeeping department?

Dr: For a few months.

Cr: Did she ever do any ordering?

Dr: Stop cross-examining me.

Comment on Dialogue: The employer may be telling the truth, but the creditor started to ask questions to seek more information. The more information available the better chance the creditor has of making a judgment as to whether to proceed with suit.

4. "Don't Threaten Me"

This phrase is often used as a reply to a closing statement advising the debtor that the matter will be referred to a collection agency/attorney if payment is not made by a specific date. The response should be firm and uncompromising. The answer given by the telephone caller is often the prelude to an attempt by the debtor to make a settlement. Do not overlook this signal. Try immediately to develop a dialogue towards some type of settlement.

Cr: If we do not receive payment by Monday, May 7, we will be forced to refer this to our attorney for immediate institution of suit and service of a summons and complaint.

Dr: Don't threaten me.

Cr: Sir, we are not threatening you. We are merely stating what may happen in the event you do not make an arrangement to pay your debt. Now, can we talk about how you intend to pay this indebtedness?

5. "Why Bother Me for Such a Small Amount of Money?"

A sophisticated debtor is aware of the cost of instituting suit for a small balance of under $500. In New York, the cost of serving and filing a summons and complaint is about $30, plus the services of an attorney. Most attorneys across the country who are listed on national lists of commercial attorneys require a suit fee of between 5 percent and 10 percent of the outstanding balance. In addition, to cover the out-of-pocket expenses of filing suit in connection with a case, an advance to an attorney for costs between $50 and $75 is not unusual. Thus, for a balance due of $200 to $500, an attorney would request to commence suit the total sum of at least $100, which includes disbursements of $50 and a suit fee of $50. Obviously, in most instances a prudent business is not about to risk $100 on the probability of collecting $200. Thus, the sophisticated debtor has sound arguments for the prediction that the creditor will not start suit on a small balance.

Nevertheless, this tactic to frustrate a creditor must be addressed with a quick and solid answer. An example is as follows:

Cr: If you continue to be immovable, we will send this to our attorney and instruct him to commence a suit against you.

Dr: Stop the bull. For a few hundred dollars you are not going to sue me. The expense of suing is more than the bill.

Cr: We deal with large and small claims, and our attorney also deals with large and small claims. If you feel we will not forward this to our attorney for suit, there is but one way to find out.

Dr: Don't be cute. I know the dollars and cents of it.

Cr: Well, Mr. Dent, cute or not, it will be referred and suit will be started no matter what you think, unless of course, you want to make an arrangement.

Comment on Dialogue: The creditor should now refer this matter for suit even though the amount is very small. (See Chapter 9 on "Legal Boundaries and Limitations".)

6. "There Is a Law Against That"

The solution to this strategy is to know the law. Knowing the law in your own state is essential, but when you cross state lines, a different problem arises. The debtor from a remote state claims that a law exists prohibiting the creditor from saying something during the telephone call. A variety of reasons may be given:

1. telephone calls are only permitted between 9:00 A.M. and 6:00 P.M.
2. messages are not allowed to be left
3. you are not licensed in this state
4. the law prohibits you from threatening me
5. there is a law against harassment
6. the law says you can't speak to me, only to my attorney

Familiarity with the Debt Collection Practices Act will solve most of these allegations. Unfortunately, in a few states, laws do exist which may directly affect the telephone call and are more restrictive than the Debt Collection Practices Act. The American Collectors Association (ACA) publishes a magazine for the benefit of its members, which are principally collection agencies. This association does stay abreast of the change in the laws, but I know of no association for creditors which will keep you informed of every law in every state that affects collection. Consult with your attorney.

Another solution is similar to a drill sergeant's advice to new recruits: "When in doubt, salute." If in doubt as to whether the law mentioned by the debtor might exist, be courteous, hang up, and then consult with your attorney. In general, it is my opinion that you will discover that most laws upon which debtors rely do not exist and are figments of their imaginations.

7. "The Check Is in the Mail"

This infamous phrase has acquired the reputation of being the most-often-used sentence in the English language or the most-often-told lie. Yet, the phrase is still a very effective device to obstruct the creditor's effort to collect. If the creditor accepts this statement without qualification, the creditor is entering a silent agreement with the debtor to make another telephone call when the check is not received. Nevertheless, sometimes the statement is accurate and a check was mailed. Is there an easy way to distinguish the truth from the lie? One recommendation is to treat all such promises as exactly that—a promise to pay and nothing else. For every such promise, a closing statement should be used. The only difference is that what appears to be sincere may warrant a negative closing statement (see Chapter 2), and what appears to be an obvious ploy to delay will warrant a very strong positive closing statement. For example:

Dr: I mailed the check yesterday myself. It was for $250 and I am sure you will have it in your hands by Monday.

Cr: Fine, because this loan was scheduled to be referred to our attorney for suit. Of course, when we receive the payment by Friday, May 12, your loan will then be up-to-date and it will not be necessary to take this action.

Another example:

Dr: Hello.

Cr: Is Mr. Presley there?

Dr: Who is this?

Cr: This is the United Finance Company. Is this Mr. Presley?

Dr: Yes.

Cr: Your loan is two payments in arrears.

Dr: I sent in the check two days ago. You should be receiving it on Monday.

Cr: I'll look for your check on Monday. You understand that if we do not receive it, this matter has been scheduled for referral to a collection agency.

Dr: Don't worry, you'll get it.

Cr: I'm sure I will, but I just want you to know the status of your loan. It might be a good idea to call us on Monday, May 7 to be certain that we received your check.

STALLING TECHNIQUES AND HOW TO OFFSET THEM

Debtor Never Heard of the Company

This strategy is often used in direct mail sales where the creditor is located thousands of miles from the debtor. The proper approach is to be confident that the merchandise was shipped and received, and then question the officer or office manager to convince him to try to locate the merchandise.

Dr: Hello.

Cr: This is the Marvin Computer Supplies Company.

Dr: Who?

Cr: The Marvin Computer Supplies Company with regard to your bill for $305 which is past due for 60 days.

Dr: I never heard of you.

Cr: With whom am I speaking?

Dr: This is the owner.

Cr: Is this the Stevens Gift Boutique?

Dr: Yes, but I never heard of you.

Cr: We shipped a box of paper, some diskettes, plus one game program

Dr: I still never heard of you.

Cr: We only ship against an order and we have a receipt from United Parcel.

Dr: Who gave the order?

Cr: Ralph Kaplan, at least it looks like that.

Dr: No such person at our firm.

Cr: You do have a computer?

Dr: Yes, an Apple IIC.

Cr: Well, this program will operate on an Apple. Someone there must know about this order since you did receive it.

Dr: I never heard of Kaplan and I don't order game programs.

Cr: Did you recently receive a box of paper?

Dr: I think so, but I thought that came from the store where we bought the computer.

Cr: Did you receive statements and invoices from us?

Dr: Yeah, but I threw them away. I thought you made a mistake

Cr: Well, we made no mistake.

Dr: Could that name be Hogan?
Cr: It might be. Do you have a Ralph Hogan?
Dr: Yes, we do.

Request for a Breakdown of Payments

An installment borrower sometimes uses this tactic to delay sending in a payment. Combined with this contrivance is a protest that the creditor has not credited all the payments made by the debtor. A similar strategy is to advise the creditor to double-check the records, since the debtor is sure that a mistake has been made. The only answer is to have the records available, have confidence that the records are accurate, and express that confidence. A strong position should always be taken. Of course, offer to send the payment history or whatever other information is requested after the delinquent payments are received

Cr: Your loan is five months in arrears.
Dr: That can't be I'm only two months back Your records must be all mixed up.
Cr: Our records show your last payment on May 7, and you have made a total of only six payments and by now eleven payments should have been made.
Dr: Send me a breakdown showing the dates and amounts of each payment. I know I made at least nine payments.
Cr: We have only six payments, made in September, October, December, January, February, and March.
Dr: Send me a breakdown, then we'll talk.
Cr: Whether you made six or nine payments, you are still in arrears, and we must have a payment
Dr: Look, you are wrong. I'm not making a payment until I get a breakdown from you with all the information.
Cr: As soon as we receive a check for three payments, we will forward to you a detailed payment history showing the date and amount of each payment as well as the other information on your loan. But if we don't receive a payment by Monday, July 7, we will refer this loan for suit to our attorney. Please understand that our records are accurate. You must have forgotten or perhaps confused this loan with some other indebtedness upon which you are making payments.
Dr: Well,...

Comment on Dialogue: If the debtor fails to respond, then the only alternative is to refer the matter to a collection agency and/or attorney.

> **Dr:** I sent in a check three weeks ago.
>
> **Cr:** We have no record of your check.
>
> **Dr:** Your records must be all fouled up. I think you ought to double-check your records, since I know I sent in a check.
>
> **Cr:** As of this morning, our records show no payment and the account is still open for $870. Either send us a new check, or a copy of the front and back of this check that you say you sent three weeks ago. I will hold the account for ten days to receive a new check or a copy of the old check. If I receive neither, the matter will be referred to a collection agency and/or attorney.

Lost Address

The response to this is simple. Furnish the correct address and set a very short time limit for payment.

> **Dr:** We lost your address, and don't know where to send the check.
>
> **Cr:** Please get a pencil and paper.
>
> **Dr:** I have it.
>
> **Cr:** The name is the Johnson Envelope Company, 744 Main Street, Greenville, New York 99999. Have you got it?
>
> **Dr:** Yeah.
>
> **Cr:** We will expect your check within four days, by Monday, May 7. If we do not receive it by that date, this claim will be referred to our collection agency for further action. Do you understand that?
>
> **Dr:** Yes.

Lost Invoice

The response to this stalling technique is quite different from the situation where the debtor lost the address. The debtor is now requesting that a new invoice be sent by mail. This means the debtor is seeking an extension of two weeks, for a few days will pass before the invoice is sent, a few days to send the check, and a few more days in the mail. If the debtor already has received an invoice, or several invoices, a strong attitude should be presented. Some clients feel that the first request for an invoice should always be granted, despite the delay. This is not necessarily true. If the debtor already has possession of at least two invoices sent at different times by the creditor, sending a third is merely acquiescing to his attempt to delay payment. If only one invoice has been sent by the creditor, perhaps then the request for an invoice should be granted.

Dr: I need an invoice to pay the bill. We can't pay a bill without one.

Cr: We already have sent you two invoices.

Dr: We don't have either one. What do you want from me? Send me an invoice and I'll get your bill paid.

Cr: You did get the merchandise.

Dr: Nobody is arguing that. All I want is an invoice.

Cr: This bill is over 90 days past due. It is scheduled to be referred to our collection agency in five days for further action. I will give you information over the telephone and I will send an invoice when I receive payment. But I am not stopping the referral to the collection agency. It is up to you whether you want the account sent to them. We must have our check in five days, or make no mistake, the bill will be sent to the collection agency.

Dr: OK, give me the information.

—or—

Dr: I can't pay your bill because I lost your invoice.

Cr: OK. We will send you a copy today in the mail, and we will expect a payment by Monday, May 7. If we do not receive the payment by that date, we will be forced to refer this claim to our collection agency.

"I'll Check My Records"

This ploy also requires a strong rebuttal, with emphasis on a short extension and immediate referral. Most debtors are fully aware of their debts. No time is needed to check records. This applies to individuals, small firms, medium firms, and large firms. An argument might be made in favor of medium and large firms if the amount outstanding is small. Nevertheless, for medium or large firms, the time necessary to locate an account payable on the computer may only be a few seconds. Accordingly, a strong presentation is recommended.

Cr: This bill is pretty old.

Dr: I don't know anything about it. I'll have to check my records.

Cr: Well, we are going to refer this claim to our attorney if payment is not received by Monday, May 7.

Dr: Do what you want. I still have to check my records.

Cr: Unfortunately, I have no choice; our firm has a strict policy on open accounts. On Monday, May 7, it goes to our attorney. That's it.

Dr: I will check our records today.

Cr: You should have checked your records after each letter we sent you. If you don't know about it, someone in your firm does. In any event, unless we receive payment by Monday, May 7....

Vacations, Quitting, or Hospitalization Delays

When reaching the owner or a senior officer concerning a past due debt, the creditor is very apt to find that the bookkeeper, treasurer, and/or comptroller either quit, left for an extended vacation, or just entered the hospital for a serious operation. Naturally, the debtor needs time to sort out the records or await the return of the indispensable person who pays the bills. Sometimes, a lower-level employee is reached and the boss or the vice-president in charge of paying bills is away on an extended business trip, usually out of the country. Of course, the business does operate; employees are paid, rent is paid, telephone bills are paid. Quite frankly, these excuses should be recognized for what they are—simple and blatant strategies to extend the due date of the loan or the debt. Accordingly, the treatment should be the same as if no excuse was offered.

Dr: My bookkeeper just left and my books are in turmoil. We don't think she did anything for the past six months. Deposit slips are missing, check stubs haven't been completed, and the payable ledger is chaotic. We have an advertisement in the paper and it will take at least a month to sort this out.

Cr: We cannot wait a month. Please get a pencil and I will give you all the information you need to pay the bill. When I receive the check, I will be glad to send you a duplicate invoice. Nevertheless, if we do not receive payment by Monday, May 7, this matter will be referred to our attorney for immediate institution of suit. So please take this information down and send us a check.

Another example:

Dr: The accounts payable supervisor just left on a three-week vacation and she said all the bills were paid.

Cr: Well, our bill has not been paid and it is past due for three months.

Dr: I can't do anything until she returns. Company policy says she has to approve payment of bills, and no bills get paid while she is away.

Cr: We can't wait three weeks.

Dr: Unfortunately, you have no choice for no check will be issued while she is on vacation.

Cr: I will be glad to give you the information if you want it, but that is your policy; our policy is that bills must be paid on time. So today I will send the claim to our attorney for suit. You will probably receive a summons and complaint before she returns. It seems silly to pay the additional interest and costs of a suit, and to retain an attorney, just because your accounts payable supervisor is on vacation. But that's up to you. Our attorney will have the claim within a few days.

Comment on Dialogue: The purpose in each instance is to impress the recipient of the call, whether the owner, officer, or person replacing the bookkeeper or accounts payable supervisor, with the urgency of paying the bill. This may cause the recipient to take the necessary steps to arrange for the payment of the bill. Success will not occur all the time, but this approach is generally rewarding to the creditor.

Central Accounting Office Referral

With all the franchise operations that have blossomed in the past 30 years, referral to a central accounting office is not an uncommon request by the debtor. In many instances, the central accounting office arranges for the payment of the payables of the fast food outlet or the retail outlet. Furthermore, central accounting offices do have problems and often will just neglect or lose a bill for one of its franchises. The franchisee may have approved the bill and sincerely thought that it had been paid. The request for the creditor to contact the central accounting office also may be sincere with no effort being made to delay or avoid payment. The problem is that the creditor will be ignored at the central accounting office, whereas the franchisee, by comparison, has full recognition. Accordingly, the collection effort must be directed at the store, and normally a telephone call should not be made to the central accounting office.

Dr: All of my bills are paid by the central accounting office. Here is the phone number and you call them.

Cr: Charlie, you owe me the money, not the central accounting office. You call them up because they will listen to you, not me.

Dr: What makes you think they listen to me? If they listened to me, your bill would have been paid.

Cr: I will wait ten more days, and then...

Dr: Look, I can't do anything for you. I have approved the bill and sent it to central accounting. If you talk to them, maybe you can get something done. I sure can't.

Cr: Charlie, I know your problem, but it is your problem and not my problem. If I do not receive a check by Monday, May 7, this claim will be referred to an attorney for immediate institution of suit.

Dr: What good will that do? Central accounting will only pay when they receive an invoice.

Cr: Send the summons to the central accounting office and maybe they will pay then. It is too bad, for by that time, the credit agencies will pick up that you are being sued. Charlie, I'm sorry, but it is your problem to get them to pay our bill.

Dr: OK, I'll try one more time.

Comment on Dialogue: The net effect should prompt the manager to call the central accounting office himself, and results are usually positive. The appeal for help by the manager, expressing his utter frustration with the central accounting office is certainly reasonable and deserves understanding. Yet, succumbing to these entreaties will not solve the problem, but will only delay the payment of the debt. The manager is the one who must act.

"My Spouse Pays the Bills"

Using a third party as the one responsible for paying the debtor's bill is again an attempt to avoid accountability now.

Dr: I don't know whether the bill was paid or not, since I leave all of that to my wife.

Cr: May I speak to your wife?

Dr: Oh, she is not home now. She is visiting her sick mother for the next two or three weeks.

Cr: I certainly hope her mother recovers, but we cannot wait for that period of time for payment of this bill. We must have payment by Monday, May 7 or.

Delaying Tactics

1. *Another Telephone Number:* Occasionally, the recipient of the call will refer you to another telephone number to reach the debtor. At this point, a decision must be made as to whether to leave a message or to try and reach the debtor at the new number. We recommend to leave a message wherever possible. Calling the new number may result in a no answer, a busy signal, a wrong number, or a wrong person at the right number. In the first instance, a person has been reached who knows the debtor and is in a position to transmit a message. In the second instance, the likelihood of reaching the debtor is probably no better than a 50-50 chance.

2. *Handling Request to Hold the Line:* Some sophisticated debtors use the tactic of keeping the creditor waiting on the telephone. The collaborator is usually the receptionist, the wife, or the employer. In any event, the creditor is left waiting and the debtor has no intention of talking to the creditor. Finally, in frustration, the creditor hangs up. Some creditors will wait a few minutes, an hour, several hours, or even a few days and then attempt again to contact the debtor. Recognize that if the debtor is using this device, a second attempt will only produce another stalling technique. Refer the claim to a collection agency/attorney. Do not make another call.

3. *Responding to a Lack of Interest:* This basically is also a contrivance to delay payment, although the debtor who displays a lack of interest is not displaying a high level of intelligence. The response must be a forceful closing statement with great emphasis on immediate action. If this produces no interest in the debtor to communicate positively, the only alternative is to close the conversation.

Dr: Hello.
Cr: This is Mr. Jackson of the Green Department Store.
Dr: Yeah.
Cr: About your revolving credit account. You haven't made a payment in three months.
Dr: Yeah.
Cr: We must have a payment of at least $150 within the next week.

Dr: Yeah.

Cr: You are going to make a payment of $150?

Dr: I don't know.

Cr: You don't know what?

Dr: What?

Cr: If we don't receive a payment of $150 by Monday, May 7, this account will be referred to our collection agency. You know what that means.

Dr: Yeah.

Cr: Your credit may be affected since we do report to credit reporting agencies.

Dr: Yeah.

Cr: Then I will not wait. I will refer this to the collection agency today, with a notation to take immediate action.

Dr: OK, goodbye.

Warning—Checking Your Records: One of the cardinal rules of telephone collection is never to advise the debtor that you will check your records and call again. The debtor will do absolutely nothing until you call again, and be assured that at least three calls will have to be made before the debtor actually is reached again on the telephone. Sometimes personal contact will never be made until the claim is referred to a collection agency/attorney.

Profane Language

There is really no adequate response to the use of profane or abusive language by the debtor. The debtor employs this device as a substitute for an adequate response to a demand for payment. This debtor is not sophisticated enough to utilize a stalling device, and being caught by surprise, resorts to profane language to shock the creditor. The only response is to terminate the telephone call as quickly as possible, and take the next step in the collection procedure.

Evasive Answers

When the debtor is evasive, or wanders or rambles on, interrupt immediately and return the discussion to the purpose of the call.

Dr: I couldn't make the payment because my truck had an accident and I had to replace the tire, even though the tire was only bought a month ago....

Cr: I'm sorry to hear that, but we must arrange for payment of this loan.·

—or—

Dr: Well, you see, last month I had to lend some money to my brother, and he was supposed to repay it within a week; but you know how these things happen. My brother was in an accident and....

Cr: I am sorry to hear that, but let's return to why I made this telephone call to you....

—or—

Dr: I know I haven't paid, but I was operated on last month and they removed the largest stone you ever saw. I was on the operating table for over....

Cr: Well, I'm glad to see you have fully recovered. About the payment of this bill....

The Danger in Asking Questions: Certain questions should never be asked. Never ask where or when the check was mailed. In response to this question, the debtor will leave the telephone to examine the checkbook and attempt to locate the date of the check. This wastes time. The solution to the problem is never to ask questions unless you are seeking information concerning the debtor's financial background and the debtor's ability to pay. This rule applies even more so to asking the debtor, "When will you send the check?" or "When will we receive the check?" The debtor might answer with, "After I receive the invoice," or, "After I get my breakdown of payments," or, "In two months," or perhaps, "In one year." To return to a basic tenet, the creditor should set the time when payment is to be received, and always use a date and a day of the week.

Some bad examples:

Cr: When can we expect a payment?

Dr: I don't know exactly. Our computer writes the checks, and unfortunately it's been down for the past two weeks. We hope to get it going within a few days. So after the essentials, maybe in two or three weeks, we'll start issuing checks.

—or—

Cr: When will you return the merchandise?

> **Dr:** Well, right now it's under a pile of packages. I guess we'll get to it in about two weeks, and then we have to pack it and arrange for a carrier. I guess in about a month or so.

Coping with "Hold the Line"

If the party answering the telephone advises you to wait so that the debtor may be called, a long wait may ensue before the debtor comes to the telephone. If the call is being made long distance, communication of this to the original party answering the telephone may prompt him to move a little faster to bring the debtor to the telephone and thus save a few minutes of long distance charges.

> **Dr:** Hold on a minute, I'll get my husband.
> **Cr:** This is a long distance call, so I would appreciate you calling him to the telephone now.

Small Talk

A pleasant voice can lead the telephone worker into a discussion of weather or geography. For example, the debtor might want to discuss good old New York (if that is where the creditor is located). Speculation on the weather forecast is also pleasant conversation. But this conversation costs in time spent by the telephone worker (which is paid for by the creditor) and also increases the cost of the telephone call. Ignore these comments and go directly to the subject of delinquency and payment. Polite statements will channel the conversation back to the question of payment.

> **Dr:** Isn't it a beautiful day outside?
> **Cr:** The weather is fine, but the problem is your delinquency.

—or—

> **Dr:** I was in New York last summer, and it is really a great city for a tourist, especially Broadway and....
> **Cr:** Yes, New York is a fine city, but the matter that must be discussed is your loan.

Sophisticated Debtor: If the debtor appears to have no intention of promising payment and is merely going in circles to keep the conversation moving, and has all the characteristics of a knowledgeable and sophisticated debtor, the best advice is to demand payment, use the closing statement, and hang up. No effort should be made to answer questions, furnish history of the account, or explain why the creditor is insisting upon payment. The cost will be time and money, but the result will be the same.

OFFSETTING MISCELLANEOUS TELEPHONE DELAYS

Ask if Pen and Paper Are Available for Taking Your Message

When a message is being left, be certain that the debtor has a pencil and paper and is writing the information. Nothing is more frustrating than to be told after all the information has been communicated, "Wait a minute. I'll get a pencil." To avoid this, before the message is left, ask the debtor:

"Do you have a pencil and paper to write this down?"

"Would you please write this down on a piece of paper?"

Avoid Conversations with Children

Do not spend unnecessary time when a child answers the telephone. Immediately ask for an adult or a parent. If any difficulty is encountered with the child, advise the child that the telephone call is "important."

Cr: This is Mr. Peters from the High Tech Electrical Company.

Dr: Yes, who is speaking?

Cr: Mr. Peters. How old are you?

Dr: Six, but my birthday is next month and mommy is going to give me a party.

Cr: Is your mommy there?

Dr: She said I could invite all my friends from school and...

Cr: What is your name?

Dr: Melissa, and my middle name is...

Cr: Melissa, this is a very important call; please put your mommy on the telephone right now.

Dealing with Answering Services

Answering services which are manually staffed present problems in two areas. First, sometimes a lengthy amount of time is spent waiting for the operator to take a message. The caller is put on hold while the operator tends to other calls. When this difficulty occurs, hang up and call again, hopefully then the operator will not be so busy. On the second time around, a comment might be made that the first call was disconnected. Sometimes, the reaction will be that the operator will take the message immediately.

Second, operators in manually staffed answering services are often quite busy and do not want to take a message longer than a name and telephone number. Nevertheless, if more information must be furnished for the debtor, an effort must be made to impress upon the operator the importance of the message. This can be accomplished by the tone of voice, the use of words such as "important," "imperative," etc.

Dr: Please hold on a minute.

Cr: Please tell Mr. Emory that Mr. Adams called regarding his past due bill.

Dr: Just give me your telephone number.

Cr: This message is very important. I strongly suggest that you take everything down.

Chapter 9

Legal Boundaries and Limitations: The Debt Collection Practices Act

The art of collection of delinquent accounts was hardly regulated just a short 10 or 20 years ago. Nevertheless, in order to correct the abuses of many collection agencies, the federal government created the Debt Collection Practices Act. The states, and even some cities, also became active, and many passed a wide variety of laws controlling abusive collection practices. The consumer decade of the 1970s also produced many other laws to protect the unsuspecting consumer, including the Fair Credit Billing Act and Fair Credit Reporting Act. An informed creditor must be aware not only of the federal laws, but also of the state legislation that has been passed, and in some instances, even the county and city legislation. In Appendices A and D, I have set forth the three major federal laws and the laws passed by three states and one city to control and regulate debt collection, as well as other laws which may affect telephone collection.

The Debt Collection Practices Act was passed on September 20, 1977, and took effect six months later. The act was passed by an overwhelming majority of exactly one vote in the House of Represent- atives as an amendment to the Consumer Credit Protection Act (15

U.S.C. 1601 et. seq.), and its purpose was to prohibit abusive practices by debt collectors, i.e., collection agencies and attorneys. The act does not apply to creditors.

The Federal Trade Commission issued a Statement of General Policy and Interpretation on the Debt Collection Practices Act in 1987. While the commentary is not binding on the Federal Trade Commission and is not considered an advisory opinion or trade regulation, it does interpret the prior opinions of the commission and clarifies the interpretations of the statute. In short, it should be carefully reviewed in conjunction with the Act itself whenever reference to the Act is made to solve a particular problem.

This chapter considers both the Act and the commentary.

WHAT THE ACT COVERS—AN OVERVIEW

Collection Agencies and Attorneys—Not Creditors

The Act originally covered third-party debt collectors, known as collection agencies. The Act did not apply to the majority of *creditors or attorneys*. The reason for this distinction is that creditors were merchants and thus interested in maintaining their reputation in the marketplace and did not need regulation by the government. Furthermore, the creditors would not be as likely to engage in unfair practices as collection agencies whose prime purpose was to collect debts and present a strong reputation to the public. With regard to attorneys, the legislators acknowledged that lawyers were bound by the code of ethics promulgated by the respective bar associations of each state, and believed that covering attorneys would be overregulation of the profession. Nevertheless, in 1986 the exemption covering attorneys was eliminated, and attorneys are considered to be debt collectors if they engage in debt collection. The impact of eliminating this exemption has produced some confusion, and will probably produce some advisory opinions to explain the application of the Act to attorneys.

Whether creditors will ultimately be covered by the Act is not certain. Nevertheless, a Congressional committee is reviewing this question, and somewhere down the road the probability exists that creditors may be subject to all the terms and conditions of the Debt Collection Practices Act.

Consumer Debts Versus Business Debts

The Act was limited to the type of debts being collected, and defined "debt" as any obligation of a consumer to pay money arising out of a transaction in which money, property, insurance, or services which are the subject of the transaction are primarily for *personal, family, or household purposes.* Thus, the Act does not apply to *business debts*—only to consumer debts, and only consumer debts for personal, family, or household purposes.

Is the Creditor Subject to the Act? If the above statements are adopted at face value, *the creditor is not subject to the Act* because the law only applies to debt collectors and is even further limited to consumer debts. Accordingly, it appears that the creditor should feel no compulsion to comply with the terms of the Act or any of its implications. If the creditor accepts this position, walking on water should be as easy as jogging. Actually, every creditor who engages in collection activities should be fully aware of every section of the Debt Collection Practices Act and should comply not only with the terms of the act but also with the purpose, intent, and spirit of the Act.

An explanation of this unequivocal necessity begins with the telephone call to the debtor at three o'clock in the morning. The debtor awakens with a start and slowly lifts the telephone from the receiver. The first words are "This is the ABC Department Store and your account is six months in arrears." The last words could sound something like this, "and if we don't get payment by tomorrow, you will receive another call at about the same time tomorrow night, so I suggest you get plenty of sleep at your job tomorrow." Perhaps this is an extreme example, but the purpose is served to illustrate a clearly abusive collection tactic. Under the Debt Collection Practices Act this tactic, when used by a collection agency, would be prohibited. Can the creditor who is not subject to the Act use this despicable tactic without fear of violating the Act or any other law? The answer must be in the negative.

Customs and Standards Maintained in the Collection of Debts

The Debt Collection Practices Act does not apply to creditors, only to third-party collectors, such as collection agencies and to attorneys. Consider the problem if the above tactic was performed by a creditor and presented to the court in a lawsuit, and further consider the dilemma of the judge presiding at the trial. The Act has established standards for collection, and violation of these standards indicates that the particular practice should be prohibited. The judge clearly understands that the tactic is abusive and prohibited under the Debt Collection Practices Act, but he is powerless since the Act cannot be applied to a creditor. The judge is resourceful, and decides to research the state laws as opposed to the federal laws (the Consumer Credit Protection Act is a federal law that applies to all states). Most states have laws prohibiting deceptive advertising, deceptive pricing, deceptive procedures, or unfair and deceptive business practices. The precise wording varies from state to state, but the general principles remain the same.

The judge finds an appropriate statute to fit the offending act, and finds the defendant guilty under the state law. The judge has relied on the Act to determine if the practice violated the Act, and then the plaintiff's attorney provided the appropriate statute or the judge himself searched and found a violation of state law. While perhaps ideally the judge should not use this type of reasoning, in reality this is what may happen. The net effect on the creditor is the same.

What has happened is that the enactment of the law has created a set of customs and standards in the collection of a debt. If these standards are not maintained, the plaintiff, prosecutor, or judge will look elsewhere to compel the offending creditor to adhere to the guidelines set forth in the Act. Basically, the arbiter will not have to strain to find some law, regulation, or ethic to satisfy his needs. Many of the laws have been in place for years, and, in fact, the Debt Collection Practices Act is a reflection of all of these laws. Many states and other jurisdictions have adopted a "little" Debt Collection Practices Act with either very few deviations or no changes from the federal law. For example, New York City adopted the Act and required both creditors and attorneys to be subject to the Act. Massachusetts has a similar Act—the Mass. Gen. Laws. Ann. 93A & 2(b)(c) 1972, and New Hampshire has an "Unfair, Deceptive, and Unreasonable Collection Practices," N.H. Rev. Stat. Ann. & 358-C (2) 1975. (See Appendix D.)

Compliance by the Creditor Is Recommended: The creditor should comply in all respects with every section of the Act, and also should determine what other laws exist in its state that apply to collection procedures. A strong recommendation is made that creditors comply, regardless of whether a consumer or business obligation

exists, for the three o'clock telephone call is just as abusive if the debt
is a business obligation. Needless to say, compliance with state and
local laws is just as important as compliance with the federal law.

Complaints to Governmental Agencies

A difficult situation arises when the debtor asserts that a complaint will be filed with a governmental agency such as the office of
the District Attorney, the office of the Attorney General, the Federal
Trade Commission, the Banking Department of the respective state,
the Federal Communication Commission, the Insurance Department
of the respective state, the Consumer Fraud Commission, or any other
administrative agency, either federal, state, or local, which has jurisdiction over the business of the creditor. The same problem is
presented when the debtor alleges he will call the TV or radio action
line, the consumer advocate in the local newspaper, or the Better
Business Bureau.

Treat every threat of this nature as very real and imminent. Few
actually carry out their threats, but your concern is the person who is
sincere and aggrieved. Therefore, it is incumbent upon the creditor to
have a procedure in place to handle this type of telephone call.

Such a call should be immediately removed from the telephone
worker and referred to the supervisor, manager, or officer of the firm.
Principally, the caller wants attention and referring the call to
someone higher in the corporate or business structure will often
satisfy the disgruntled debtor. At that point, every effort should be
made to obtain as much information about the problem from the
perspective of the debtor. Needless to say, excessive effort should be
used to resolve the matter.

The creditor should not try to dissuade the debtor from carrying
out his threat since this will only encourage the debtor. The debtor
will perceive that the creditor is afraid of such action, and the debtor
will take an even stronger stand. Assure the debtor that he has every
right to report the creditor to whatever agency he wishes as long as the
facts are reported accurately. The important point is to return to the
problem and try to resolve it.

Frequent complaints from debtors with respect to business practices will cause governmental agencies to investigate the business. But
assuming the business is operating properly and complying with the
laws, the major problem is simply the time and effort spent in
responding to the inquiries from the administrative agencies. In

addition, such publicity from television, radio, newspapers, or other media is usually not helpful and rarely complimentary to the business.

Telephone Worker Call:

Dr: The salesman said I could return the merchandise.

Cr: Sir, that is correct providing it is returned within 30 days.

Dr: That is not what the salesman said.

Cr: Well, sir, we must insist on payment.

Dr: I left it at the store and I'm not paying for it.

Cr: Did the salesman accept it?

Dr: He had a memory failure. That's why I left it.

Cr: Sir, we must insist....

Dr: I'm going to call the District Attorney. This is fraud. First, you tell me I can return it and then after I return it, you ask for payment. We'll see what the D.A. says.

Cr: Sir, perhaps you should speak to my supervisor.

Dr: Good idea.

Telephone Worker Call:

Cr: We have no record of your payment.

Dr: Well, I have my canceled check and I'm not paying you twice.

Cr: We want our money once only, and so far you haven't paid it.

Dr: This must be a con job. I'm going to report this to the Attorney General's office and let them get after you. You are not going to intimidate me when I have a canceled check.

Cr: Can you get the check and read to me the date of deposit on the reverse side, and the endorsement on the check?

Dr: I'm not doing anything. I have my check and you can talk to the Attorney General.

Cr: Now, we need information to see...

Dr: Forget it, you are not going to con me. Goodbye!

Cr: I think you should speak to Mr. Douglas, the supervisor. Please hold on.

Supervisor Call:

Cr: This is Mr. Douglas, the supervisor of The Friendly Department Store. I understand you had a problem with Mr. Adams.

Dr: No problem. I'm going to write to the Attorney General.

Cr: That is your right, and I will not dissuade you. But in the meanwhile, can you help me to straighten this out? Do you have the check handy?

Dr: I have the check

Cr: Could you please get it for me and maybe we can resolve this now?

Dr: I'm still going to contact the Attorney General.

Cr: Fine, but if I can solve the problem now, it will be much easier for both of us.

Dr: OK, hold on for a minute...

Unordered Merchandise

The law is very clear that the mailing of unordered merchandise may be treated as a gift by the recipient who may retain, use, discard, or dispose of it in any manner without any obligation to the sender. There must be a clear and conspicuous statement attached to said merchandise informing the consumer of his rights and, of course, no bill may be mailed to the consumer. (See Appendix A.)

KEY SECTIONS OF THE ACT AND HOW THEY AFFECT COLLECTION EFFORTS BY TELEPHONE

The Debt Collection Practices Act is many pages long and divided into 18 sections. A copy of the Act appears in Appendix A. The sections which affect telephone calls will be discussed in depth, *but the other sections should also be carefully reviewed by the creditor.*

During the early part of 1986, the Federal Trade Commission issued a commentary on the Debt Collection Practices Act. The Commission stated that a significant part of their activity was the issuance of informal staff interpretations of the Act by the Division of Credit Practices. There were over 210 interpretations which were contained in three large volumes. The volumes were not cross-referenced and not indexed. Some interpretations were superceded or overruled by court opinions, by subsequent interpretations, or by consent judgments. Other interpretations were inconsistent with the Act or its purposes. After these startling but true admissions by the Commission, the Bureau of Consumer Protection staff chose to "streamline" the interpretations by issuing a section-by-section commentary on the Debt Collection Practices Act. The Commission requested public comment on the proposed staff commentary for 60 days after publication. It is assumed that after the commission reviews the comments of the public, the commentary may be revised or amended. In this book, we will review the commentary as *originally* issued by the Federal Trade Commission. *It is strongly suggested that the reader carefully review the commentary which appears in Appendix A and monitor any revisions or amendments issued by the Federal Trade Commission.*

Section 803—Definition of Covered Parties and Type of Debt

This section deals primarily with the definitions of the type of party covered, type of communication, and the type of debt covered.

The commentary states that the term "communication" does not include a request for the consumer to return the call if there is no reference made to a debt. With regard to the definition of "debt," an overdue medical bill or a dishonored check is included within the definition. Fines and taxes are not treated as debts.

A debt collector includes any person who uses any instrument of interstate commerce or the mails in any business, the principal purpose of which is the collection of any debts, or regularly collects or attempts to collect debts owed to another.

Third-Party Involvement: The Act also covers *creditors* who use names other than their own to attempt to indicate that a third party is collecting the debt. Thus, if the creditor uses a name other than his own in a telephone call, such as representing that a *nonexisting collection agency is calling, the creditor becomes subject to the Act.* Many creditors used a collection agency name in their collection efforts since they wished to avoid the collection agency's fee. The "collection agency" did not exist except on paper. The address was across the street and the mail drop collected the mail for the creditor to open. The "collection agency" had no employees, no office, and no other business. The result was an in-house collection agency, which the Act is designed to prevent from operating. If a creditor uses a false name, the creditor loses his exemption and also is in violation of the Act. The purchase and use of forms from collection agencies is more completely covered under Section 812, which is discussed below.

Exemption of Creditor: The law specifically excludes any officer or employee of a creditor who, in the name of the creditor, collects debts for the creditor. This is the principal section which excludes creditors from coverage of the Act. Actually, the only way a creditor presently may become subject to the Act is to violate Section 804 as described below or Section 812.

The commentary specifically prohibits the use of a salaried attorney as an employee who collects debts and uses stationery to indicate that the attorney is employed by someone else or is independent and separate from the creditor. This appears to be directed at the in-house counsel who writes collection letters or makes collection telephone calls and uses a different address or different telephone number from the creditor. It ties in with Section 807 (3) which prohibits the false representation that an attorney is collecting the debt in any manner other than is disclosed. The commentary also under Section 807 (3) refers to the situation where a creditor (not a debt collector) uses an attorney's name, rather than his own, in his collection communications. In this instance two things happen: the creditor loses his exemption and violates this provision. The commentary states that the creditor's collection division also must be clearly labeled as affiliated with the creditor.

There are several other exclusions:

1. An officer and employee of the United States.

2. Any nonprofit organization which performs bona fide consumer counseling.

3. Any attorney at law collecting a debt as an attorney on behalf of and in the name of a client, but the Act includes attorneys who are engaged primarily in the collection of debts. On July 9, 1986 the exemption for attorneys was eliminated entirely as to all attorneys who "regularly" collect or attempt to collect debts owed or due another.

4. Any person serving or attempting to serve legal process on any other person in connection with the judicial enforcement of a debt.

The Way Consumers Were Located: In bygone years, a collection agency or creditor would call a neighbor ("Nb.") with the following ruse:

Cr: This is Mary Smith, a nurse at the ABC Hospital. John Jones' wife was just brought in and we are trying to reach Mr. Jones. Can you tell me where he works?

Nb: Oh, is she hurt badly?

Cr: Well, the doctor is examining her now, but it is important that her husband get here to sign the necessary forms, and she's been asking for him. Can you help us reach him? Do you know where he is?

Nb: He works at the ABC Insurance Agency on 43rd Street and Main. I don't know the number.

Cr: That's OK, we can get it. Thanks very much.

The justification for this action was that the debtor was concealing where he worked, so therefore the creditor was entitled to use deception to find out where the debtor worked. The devices were innovative, mostly based on false injuries or appeals to greed. Common ones based on greed were

1. "Mr. Jones just won first prize in the DEF sweepstakes. Where can we reach him?"
2. "Mr. Jones' uncle just left him $500,000 in his will, and we have been retained to find him. Can you help us?"

Comment on Dialogue: Of course, the neighbor or friend should have asked many questions, including what hospital, how did you get my number, why didn't his wife tell you where he is, why wasn't his address on the entry form of the sweepstake, and the uncle should have known where he was if he was leaving him $500,000. By playing upon greed and eagerness to help, people do not ask questions and are quite ready to furnish what they perceive as harmless information.

Locating the Debtor—804: This section requires a debt collector communicating with any person *other than* the consumer to identify himself, state he is confirming or correcting location information concerning the consumer, and only if requested, identify his employer. The *other person* is any person other than the debtor, either a friend, neighbor, relative, employer, former employer, or any firm with which the debtor does business. The creditor must basically state that the creditor is trying to locate the consumer and no statement should be made that the consumer owes a debt. Of course, if the creditor's name would indicate a debt is owed, it should be revealed only if requested. Where a creditor is seeking location information, the telephone call might be similar to the following ("Tp" equals Third Party):

Cr: This is Mr. Waterson of Cotten Clothes, Inc. We are trying to locate John Winter. Can you help us?
Tp: He hasn't worked for us for the past three months.
Cr: Do you have an address for him?
Tp: I can't get it for you today. Call back in the morning.
Cr: Ok, thank you.

Communication should be only made *once* unless the earlier response is believed to be erroneous or incorrect and such person now has correct or complete location information or such person requests a call back to obtain the information. This was designed to preclude numerous telephone calls which are designed to exert pressure on friends, relatives, or neighbors.

The commentary specifically allows a debt collector to use an alias as long as the name and identity of the collector can always be determined. Accordingly, we do recommend the use of an alias for all telephone workers since telephone workers do not favor furnishing their correct name to debtors.

Section 805—Communication Problems with Consumer and Third Parties

This section deals directly with the problem of communicating with the consumer and third parties.

Communication with Consumer: Without the consent of the consumer or a court order, no communication with the consumer shall be made at any unusual time or place, or a time or place known or which should be known to be inconvenient. In the absence of knowledge of circumstances to the contrary, 8:00 A.M. until 9:00 P.M. is considered a convenient time at the consumer's location. The consumer's location seems to mean residence or job location, but contacting the consumer at his job location presents different problems which will be discussed later in this chapter. If no one answers the telephone between those times, and sufficient calls have been made, a telephone call at another time is more convenient to the debtor since the debtor is not available during the hours of 8:00 A.M. and 9:00 P.M. But abuse of this device probably would constitute harassment and be a violation of the Act.

The staff commentary used very careful language to limit and extend communication with the debtor. First, the consumer cannot be called at any time or any day that credible information exists to indicate it is inconvenient to the consumer. While this certainly is an extra burden, no attempt was made to define what credible information means except to say the source could be the consumer. Thus, if the consumer says, "Don't call me in the mornings or evenings" and during the day he works, it appears that the debt collector must decide whether this is "credible" information. Second, the commentary allows that a call on Sunday is not *per se illegal* if the debt collector does not have such information. Why the staff used this language "per se illegal" is difficult to comprehend, but, notwithstanding same, it appears that the commission is still not totally comfortable with collection calls on Sunday.

In this particular section the term consumer includes the spouse of the consumer or parent of a minor. Accordingly, it appears that messages may be left with spouses and parents of minors.

Referral to an Attorney §805(a)–2: The Act has several paragraphs, including one in this section, which compels contact with an attorney once an attorney has made an appearance in the matter and no further contact with the consumer is permitted. Of course, if the attorney fails to respond after a reasonable time, and reasonable efforts have been made to contact, recontact with the debtor is allowed.

Communication with Third Parties §805–(b): The second part of this section expressly prohibits communication with third parties except for location information, a court order, a judicial remedy after a judgment, or unless the third party is an attorney for the debtor. The target of this section is to control contact with the employer of the consumer where the consumer is most vulnerable. The provisions prohibit this type of contact except for location information, and, of course, no mention is to be made to the employer that a debt is owed.

Contact with Employer: The creditor should recognize that contact with an employer is fraught with dangers which far exceed the violation of the Debt Collection Practices Act. If the debtor suffers any damages due to this contact, you may be exposing yourself to liability. The debtor losing his job or failing to obtain the promotion as a result of contact with the employer is not beyond belief, especially with those employers who are sensitive to employees being in debt, such as banks, race tracks, or any business where the employee handles cash. A message left with a department head in a university may affect a promotion when it was discovered that the professor was heavily in debt. Do not leave any information with any fellow employee that the consumer owes a debt, and be careful that the consumer is not talking to you where he may be overheard. Ask the consumer if his surroundings furnish a degree of privacy. For these reasons, contact with a debtor at his place of employment should only be done by a thoroughly trained telephone worker, and diplomacy and tact must be the order of the day. Therefore, in view of the severe restrictions set forth in the Debt Collection Practices Act, contact with an employer always presents some danger.

The commentary expressly warns the debt collector not to call the consumer at work if there is reason to know that the employer forbids the communication.

Cr: May I please speak to Mr. Mahoney?
Tp: I'll get him.
Cr: Is this Mr. Mahoney?
Dr: Yes. Who is this?
Cr: This is Mr. Bradford of the XYZ Finance Company. Can you talk to me about your loan?
Dr: In the middle of this place? Are you kidding?
Cr: Can you go to another phone in another room?
Dr: Yes, wait a minute.

Warning—State Laws Prohibiting Contact with Employer: A number of states do prohibit employer contact, such as New York under the New York General Business Law, Section 601.

Right to Require Ending of Communication

While the Act does not require that the debtor be advised of his rights, the section also enables a consumer to communicate *in writing* that he refuses to pay the debt and wishes the debt collector to cease further communications. The debt collector must comply, except

1. to advise the debtor that further collection efforts by the collector are being terminated;
2. to advise the debtor that the debt collector is going to use remedies which are normally used;
3. to advise the debtor that creditor or debt collector is going to invoke a special remedy.

The commentary extends the protection of this section to parties close to the consumer such as spouses, parents, guardians, executors, or administrators.

Section 806—Harassment and Abuse

This section sets forth some very special abuses which are not allowed. Whether a particular statement does or does not fall within the parameters of the listed abuses is purely a factual situation and will probably depend upon all the circumstances that affect the particular telephone call.

1. Use or threat of use of violence or other criminal means to harm the physical person, reputation, or property of the debtor.

2. Use of obscene or profane language or language which abuses the debtor, such as religious slurs, racial or sexual epithets, or calling the debtor a "liar" or "deadbeat."

3. Causing a telephone to ring or engaging in telephone conversations with a person repeatedly with intent to annoy, abuse, or harass. (The commentary lists six calls in one day as an example.)

4. Except as in Section 804 (Location Information) placing calls without disclosure of identity of the caller.

5. Under the commentary, leaving messages with many different neighbors is prohibited when the consumer's name and telephone number is known and the consumer can be reached

Section 807—False or Misleading Representations

The section starts with a general statement that no false, deceptive, or misleading representation may be made in connection with the collection of a debt. This creates a wide umbrella to protect the consumer. The debt collector must be honest and accurate in every statement made to the debtor. Any deviation may expose the debt collector to liability under the Act. This statement probably has made the strongest impact in curing the abuses of debt collection. The sixteen subdivisions should be examined very carefully as examples of what the Federal Trade Commission considers to be fraudulent. But even if the offending act is not expressly mentioned, but is false, deceptive, or fraudulent, a violation of the law may exist.

Affiliation with the Government: The first subdivision provides that representation of affiliation with any state or the United States is prohibited. Alleging employment by the FBI, the CIA, or local police department would fall under this category. This ploy is often used to locate a debtor who has left for parts unknown.

Amount or Status of Debt: The false representation of the character, amount, or legal status of any debt is prohibited. This would apply to a deliberate falsification of the balance due either by increasing the amount or by demanding an amount after the full balance has been paid. With respect to the status, sometimes debt collectors represented that the claim had already been forwarded to an attorney for suit when in fact it had not been referred.

Employed by Attorney: The representation that the telephone worker is an attorney or is employed by an attorney when in fact such is not the case is also a violation of the Act. Collectors with little respect for the law sometimes represent that they are an attorney or an employee of an attorney. In conjunction with the false statement, a threat of service of a summons and complaint was made, or other legal threats of action were used to intimidate the debtor. This approach is expressly prohibited.

Section 807(4)—Criminal Threat

A sequitur to the prior provision is the representation that nonpayment of a debt will result in arrest or imprisonment, seizure, garnishment, attachment, or sale of property unless the action is lawful and a judgment has been obtained. In most cases, the threat to garnishee a salary may come only after a suit and judgment have been rendered in a court of law. At this point, the creditor in most states has the right to garnish a salary, i.e., direct the employer to deduct a small percent of the wages (usually 10 percent) paid to the debtor and remit same to a sheriff for ultimate transfer to the creditor. Normally, a creditor needs a court order to seize or attach property. Since a collection agency and a creditor require an attorney to start suit, neither can threaten this action before suit is instituted or a judgment or order is obtained.

Debtor's prisons were a creature of the Middle Ages, but today we allow the debtor to file bankruptcy when his debts cannot be paid. Therefore, the threat of arrest or imprisonment for a civil debt cannot be used under any circumstances. Another subdivision states that a violation exists if there is an implication that the consumer has committed a crime by reason of the nonpayment of the debt. In short, civil actions are civil actions, and they carry no stigma of a criminal penalty.

Criminal Threat After Bounced Checks: In the 1930s a breed of confidence men would pass from small town to small town leaving behind a trail of rubber checks. In those days, the central banking system was not very efficient, and many innocent merchants in small communities were left holding worthless checks. By the time the merchants realized the checks were being returned for "insufficient funds," "closed account," or more often "no such named account," the confidence man was already in the next town passing a brand new set of checks. In order to deter these frauds, almost all states passed laws that essentially stated that such action constituted a crime and was punishable by a fine and imprisonment. Nevertheless, the necessary ingredient to support a conviction is "intent." The party delivering the check must intend to defraud the recipient of the check. This requirement eliminates the situation where the check is returned unintentionally. Some excuses which may refute an "intent to defraud" are as follows:

1. A check returned for uncollected funds is unintentional since the consumer did not know that his deposit made several days ago would not clear in time to clear the bank.

2. The check returned for insufficient funds is unintentional since the consumer forgot that his wife was going to make the deposit on Monday instead of last Friday.

3. The check returned because of a closed account is unintentional since the consumer forgot that his wife closed that account last week and reopened a new account in a new bank closer to home.

Therefore, in most cases "bounced" checks are issued without intent, and thus usually are not punishable as a crime under the laws of most states. This type of situation creates only a civil lawsuit with no criminal penalty. (See Appendix C for new laws affording double damages when checks are returned.)

Do not threaten any criminal action which cannot be taken since it would be a violation of the Act. Threatening criminal action because a check has "bounced" creates a serious risk of violating the Act unless a determination is made that the check was issued with "intent to defraud." This last phrase is very difficult to prove unless a set of circumstances is revealed disclosing that many checks are issued with the obvious purpose of obtaining money and property by fraudulent and deceptive means. You should consult with your attorney before any action is contemplated in this direction.

Warning—Time Frame: A creditor should not freely use threats of referral to a collection agency/attorney "within a week" or "within ten days" or even "immediately" unless the threatened act is done within the prescribed time. A threat to refer the claim in a week and then actually referring it three months later is a false and misleading representation if done intentionally. The commentary specifically refers to this in Section 807(4).

Warning—Statement of Possible Action: The commentary clearly delineates the circumstances under which the debt collector could state or imply that either the debt collector or any third person may take any action. First, the action must be legal. Second, at the time the statement is made, there is a reasonable likelihood of the action being taken. Third, the action should be frequently taken with respect to similar debts. Fourth, if the debt collector has reason to believe the action will not be taken, a threat of action would be misleading. Thus, a threat of legal action must be supported not only by the likelihood that legal action will be taken, but also the fact that similar legal action was taken against other consumers on other debts. A threat of imminent legal action may also be a misrepresentation where action is not taken immediately, or the prior history on other suits indicate that action is not taken immediately

Small Balances: The commentary then makes the following statement with respect to small balances: "Lack of intent may be inferred when the amount of the debt is so small as to make the action totally unfeasible or when the debt collector is unable to take the action because the creditor has not authorized him to do so." The commentary does say intent "may" be inferred as opposed to intent "is" inferred. The reader should be very wary of using this threat where it is not contemplated; and a thorough reading of the Act, the commentary, and the pertinent court decisions are in order; and of course, it is always wise to consult your attorney.

Threat to Sue or Take Legal Action: Communicating a threat to take legal action that cannot be taken or is not intended to be taken may be a violation of the Act. The problem is presented when the collection agency or the creditor states that if payment is not made, the matter will be referred to an attorney for suit. The use of the word *"will"* means that a suit *must be started unless the debtor becomes bankrupt, leaves for parts unknown, or circumstances suggest that a suit would be unproductive.* The question arises in the situations where debts are too small to warrant the expense of a suit. Is the creditor compelled to start suit, and if not, is the use of this statement a misrepresentation? A threat has been made that is not intended unless the creditor actually does intend to start suit.

May Sue or Will Sue: The next progression is using the word *"may"* instead of *"will"* on the theory that suits "may" be commenced as opposed to the fact that suits "will" be commenced. At one time the Federal Trade Commission took the position that the word "may" required that a certain percentage of the consumers be sued. The United States Court of Appeals, Ninth Circuit, struck down this concept in the case of Trans World Accounts, Inc., a California Corporation, and Floyd T. Watkins vs. Federal Trade Commission, 594 F. 2nd 212 (1979). (See Appendix.) The letters stated that legal action "may" be initiated against the debtor if payment is not made within a specified period. The case arose after the Federal Trade Commission had issued an order which said:

> Respondents should not state or imply that legal action may be taken unless they can demonstrate from their experience that suit is the ordinary response to nonpayment.... Suit in more than half the instances of nonpayment will suffice to substantiate a claim that legal action "may" be taken.

The quotes have been supplied by the author. The court responded to these sentences in the order with the following:

> We recognize that the FTC may order certain "fencing in" provisions. FTC vs. Mandel Bros. 359 U.S. 385, 3 L.Ed.2d 893 (1959), supra. Although we are certain that the FTC could draft an appropriate "fencing in" order, paragraph 3 is not such an order. It is not needed to prevent similar and related violations from occurring in the future: the very nub of the deception, in this case, was not whether appellant sued 50 percent of the time, 75 percent of the time, or 25 percent of the time. Rather, the deception arose from the fact that no decision regarding suit was made until 90 days following mailing of the last Trans-O-Gram, although appellant represented that such a decision was automatic.

This case was decided shortly before the enactment of the Debt Collection Practices Act, and the framers of the law discarded the FTC interpretation, and adopted the idea that suit may be threatened if it is intended by the creditor to start suit.

Intention to Sue: The more recent case of United States of America vs. ACB Sales and Service, Inc., et al., decided by the United States District Court of Arizona, 590 F. Supp. 561 (1984) (see Appendix) helped to explain the prior decision. In this case the government contended that legal action could not be intended unless authorization to sue was obtained from the creditor. The Court dismissed this requirement that the intent behind a representation be determined not by the party making the representation but by a home office several weeks later or by the creditor several weeks after the representation was made. The Court went on and stated that the only reasonable interpretation is that a violation occurs when the individual collector does not intend to bring legal action yet sends the letter to the debtor. It may also be true that a telephone call threatening legal action would be subject to the very same test.

The Court went further to interpret the meaning of "intent."

> Both section 807 (5) and paragraph 2 would retain some ambiguity if a distinction were not made between intending to sue and merely wanting to sue. Under both provisions, the intent to sue clearly rests with the collector who requests that the letter be sent to the debtor. The collector's intent to sue entails more than merely wanting to sue: it follows from the decision that legal action would be cost effective and, therefore, would likely be the final course of action if the debt is not paid. Absent this conscious decision by the collector prior to sending one of the letters, he would not have the requisite intention to take legal action.

The government argued that the collection agency did not have the requisite intent because the agency instituted no internal procedure to obtain authorization to sue, actually did not request authorization from the creditor, and did not file suit against any of the debtors. *The Court emphasized that it is the collector's intent when the letter was sent that determines the violation.* The Court then stated that "the *most probative evidence* is the fact that the collector did not initiate the internal procedure necessary to get authorization to sue the debtor after sending the letter." The collection agency was held to be in violation of the Act.

Whether the key to satisfying the law is to institute procedures to obtain authorization to sue is questionable. It seems that the words of the statute are controlling, i.e., not intended to be taken. The question of intent is a question of fact, and all the circumstances then and there prevailing will determine whether the creditor has the requisite intent.

If a good faith intent to sue exists, the circumstances will support it. If the intent is to evade the purpose of the law, the circumstances will reveal this deception.

In summary, a threat to sue the debtor may be used if there is at the time the threat is made an intent to fulfill said threat. Nevertheless, it appears that each situation will rest on the circumstances then and there prevailing; and if those circumstances indicate an intent to sue, the requisite intent will exist.

Catch 22—§807(10): The use of any false representation or any deceptive means to collect a debt or obtain information concerning a consumer is prohibited. This is the catch-all section which covers deception in general. The drafters recognized that some devious people spend all day and night concocting schemes to induce the consumers to part with their hard-earned money. The eternal hope is that misrepresentation and deception will be deterred to some degree

Warning—Sending a Note: Collection agencies sometimes mail a note to the debtor to call the collection agency right away. The commentary refers to this deceptive practice, and prohibits it unless there was prior contact between the parties and the debt collector is known to the consumer.

Section 807(12)—Threat to Sell Debt

The false implication that the transfer or sale of an interest in the debt will cause the consumer to lose any claim or defense to payment of the debt is also prohibited. Creditors advise a debtor that the debt will be sold to a finance company or bank, the implication being that the debtor will be unable to assert any defense to the debt since the bank or finance company will become the owner of the debt, free of any defenses of the debtor. This doctrine which permitted sellers to "negotiate" a debt to a purchaser, and thus cut off a defense or claim of the debtor, has been essentially abolished by the FTC Trade Regulation Rule on Preservation of Consumer's Claims and Defenses 16 C.F.R.433 (1978), a copy of which is in the Appendix. Accordingly, it is prohibited by the Act.

Section 808—Unfair Practices

This section prohibits using unfair or unconscionable means to collect a debt. What is unfair and unconscionable is difficult to determine even after one examines the dictionary. In my opinion, it means that if the collector is not acting in good faith to carry out the thrust and purpose of the law, the acts or act that are being conducted may be "unfair" or "unconscionable."

The commentary undertook the massive problem of defining what is "unfair and unconscionable." Unfortunately, the massive problem did not receive a massive solution. The commentary listed the following components of a definition of "unfair."

The injury to the consumer must be

a. substantial

b. not outweighed by countervailing benefits to consumers or competition

c. not reasonably avoidable

Frankly, the definition of "unfair" has now been further defined into such words as "substantial," "countervailing benefits," and "reasonably." Surely, a better definition or perhaps an example or two might have been helpful. Probably, the commission preferred to have a vague definition so that each situation could be treated on a case-by-case basis. Creditors and collection agencies would prefer a more black-and-white definition, but the law is not an exact science. To quote Justice Holmes in defining a scheme to defraud, he said, "The law does not define fraud. It needs no definition. It is as old-fashioned and as versatile as human ingenuity. It is the antithesis of the accepted moral standards, fair play and right dealing in the general, personal and business life of members of society." Certainly the definition of "unfair" is somewhat less than a "scheme to defraud."

Interest, Fees, and Charges: This subdivision deals with the collection of any amount including interest, fees, charges, or expenses unless such amount is authorized by the agreement creating the debt. Thus, handling charges, service charges, late charges, finance charges, and delinquency charges must be specified in the original contract, lease, loan agreement or purchase order unless state law specifically allows this practice. If not so specified, no charge can be made at a later date.

Frequently, a creditor waits until an account is 60 days past due and then advises the debtor that a 1 percent monthly finance charge will be added. This additional charge is prohibited under the Act unless it is set forth in the original agreement. Handling charges, shipping charges, and service charges must also be specified in advance in the original agreement.

Postdated Checks: Two subdivisions prohibit the acceptance of postdated checks except under certain conditions. First, the check must not be postdated more than five days unless the collector notifies the debtor in writing of the debt collector's intent to deposit the check not more than ten or less than three business days prior to deposit. The collector must not deposit or threaten to deposit a postdated check prior to the date on the check. Furthermore, solicitation of a postdated check for purposes of threatening criminal action is also a violation of the Act.

The obligation to notify the debtor if the check is postdated more than five days is a reasonable compromise to protect the debtor and permit the creditor to accept a postdated check.

The commentary particularly adds bad check handling charges (cost for redepositing the check) to the prohibited charges unless a retailer posts a sign allowing such charge and, in addition, can demonstrate that the consumer knew of the charge. Demonstrating the consumer knew of the charge may prove difficult.

Many creditors are strong believers in obtaining postdated checks, and there is no doubt that a series of checks are better than an oral promise to make payment. Nevertheless, the Act does place certain conditions on the solicitation of postdated checks. The other basic problem is that when the debtor's check is returned by reason of uncollected or insufficient funds, the balance of the debt represented by the remaining checks is not accelerated. In short, suit cannot be instituted on the other checks until they are deposited and returned unpaid. Of course, a check returned because the account is closed may produce a different result.

In any event, if the debtor is willing to deliver a series of postdated checks, the creditor should consider using a series of promissory notes with acceleration clauses that provide that when one note is not paid, the remaining notes immediately mature and become due. If the amount is large enough, we suggest you consult with your attorney to prepare the notes and then submit them to the debtor for signature. This device is far superior to obtaining postdated checks.

The FTC staff stated in the commentary that the provisions of the Act do not prohibit debt collectors from accepting postdated checks, but rather prohibits them from misusing such instruments.

Other Miscellaneous Sections to Be Aware of

Collect Telephone Calls—§808–(5): Using collect telephone calls and concealing their purpose so that the debtor will pay the cost of the telephone call is an unfair practice. Collect telegrams are also forbidden by the Act.

Validation of Debts—§809: This section deals with the initial communication to the debtor and the proscribed wording to be used in the letters by collection agencies. It should not apply to creditors since a creditor is representing itself.

Multiple Debts—§810: This merely provides that the debt collector must apply the payment to the debt designated by the debtor.

Legal Action by Debt Collector—§811: This sets forth limitations where a debt collector may sue.

Furnishing Deceptive Forms—§812: A creditor may become subject to the Act by virtue of the provisions of this section. The target is the user of collection form letters. It is unlawful to design, compile, and furnish any form knowing that such form would create a false belief in a consumer that a person other than the creditor is participating in the collection of the debt, when in fact, such person is not participating.

Creditors have discovered that consumers are more likely to pay a debt if they believe that the creditor has turned the debt over to a third party collection agency. However, creditors are very cost conscious and would prefer to purchase collection form letters than engage a third-party letter-writing agency. The creditor fills out the form, inserts it in the envelope, and then mails it. The name and address to whom to send the check is provided by the collection agency but the creditor receives and opens the mail. The net effect is that the debtor receives the impression that a third party debt collector is collecting the debt when in fact the creditor is controlling all the procedures and such third party just provides the forms.

This section creates proscribed conduct and penalties. In subdivision "a" the act is prohibited; and in subdivision "b" the creditor who violates the Act is liable to the same extent and in the same manner as a debt collector. Thus, when a creditor violates this subdivision, two things happen. The creditor becomes subject to the Act, and at the same time is in violation of the Act, a rather severe consequence. Another unanswered question is whether the creditor becomes subject to just this section, or the whole Act...and for how long. If the debtor removes the problem forms, is the Act no longer applicable to the creditor or does the creditor remain subject to the act indefinitely because of one indiscretion?

A telephone call made by a creditor communicating the false pretense that a third-party collection agency is calling would fall under Section 803 (6) which states that any creditor using a name other than his own to collect debts is subject to the Act. It seems logical that the creditor would not only be subject to the Act, but also would be in violation (the Act in the same manner as if the creditor were using letters under Section 812.

Civil Liability—§813: A debt collector is liable under this section for the following damages:

a. Actual damage sustained by the debtor.

b. In the case of an individual, any additional damages that the court may allow but not in excess of $1,000.

c. If a class action is started, such damages as are recoverable in subdivisions a and b and such other amounts as the Court may allow not to exceed $500,000 or 1 percent of the net worth of the debt collector.

d. If plaintiff is successful, attorney's fees.

If the defendant is successful and can prove the individual acted in bad faith and to harass the plaintiff, the defendant can recover attorney's fees. This, however, is not much help if the debtor cannot pay his bills.

In determining liability, frequency of noncompliance and the intent of the collection agency shall be considered by the Court. Of course, if the noncompliance was a bona fide error and not intentional, and adequate procedures were maintained, the debt collector should not be liable.

The remaining sections deal with administrative enforcement, reports, relation to state laws, exemption from state laws and the effective date. Nevertheless, the Act should be reviewed carefully with regard to its application to all aspects of the collection procedures. (See Appendix A.)

Procedure Manual: Any creditor who engages in substantial collection efforts should have a procedural manual setting forth the practices to be performed. This manual will help in training not only clerical help, but also supervisors. The manual will also be evidence of the creditor's efforts to comply with the Debt Collection Practices Act.

EMPLOYEE MONITORING

Employee monitoring has been authorized on a federal level since 1968 under Chapter 119 of the Wire Interception and Interception of Oral Communications (18 USCA 2510 et seq., see Appendix B). The use of live monitoring to enhance the performance of a telephone worker by a device installed by the telephone company is a use in the ordinary course of business, and thus would be permissible under the federal law. Nevertheless, many states have placed additional restrictions upon monitoring, such as beep tones, informed consent and consent of both parties. This means that the employer must arrange for an identifiable beep on the telephone before monitoring begins, and normally a beep should be played at the end of monitoring. Informed consent merely means that the employee must be advised that the telephone calls will be monitored, and that the employee consents to the monitoring. An agreement or letter in writing signed by the employee certainly would be advisable.

The use of such devices must be limited in time and scope and must not be used to spy upon your employees. Any such use will remove the monitoring from the exception and perhaps expose your company to liability.

The following suggestions are made in order to conform to the intent and purpose of the law:

1. Inform your employees of the program.
2. Limit the monitoring to random sampling at reasonable intervals.
3. Cease all monitoring once it is determined that the call is of a personal nature.
4. Do not use the system to spy on or to obtain other information about your employees.
5. Employ and utilize competent and responsible employees to comply with the above rules.
6. Utilize a training manual which incorporates the essential ingredients of the law and sets forth precisely the procedures to use as well as the prohibited practices. Be certain the employees performing the monitoring receive adequate training.

Use of Taping

An employer may tape the telephone calls of his telephone collectors for the purpose of reviewing the same at a later date with the consent of the employee. The law expressly states that a telephone call may be taped with the consent of only one party to the telephone call (18 U.S.C.A. Section 511 (c) (d)).

The above statute allows the respective states to pass more restrictive legislation to protect the rights of privacy to their telephone calls. The majority of the states follow the federal rule. Nevertheless, some states have exercised the option to pass more restrictive laws, the most prominent one being California's (California Penal Code Section 631–632). Thus, taping a telephone call without the prior consent of the recipient may result in criminal penalties in California (see Appendix B). Florida, Maryland, Delaware, Georgia, Illinois, Massachusetts, Michigan, Montana, New Hampshire, Pennsylvania, and Washington all have passed legislation on this subject.

THE LAW: STILL CHANGING

The creditor must realize that the law is changing on a daily basis. The growth of telemarketing has caused dynamic changes in taping telephone calls. Bills in the legislatures of many states are waiting to be passed. When and if said bills become law, they could radically change the laws that affect these subjects. California, New York, and Illinois are in the forefront of passing legislation to protect the consumer. Soon after legislation is passed in these states, many other states will adopt the laws in substantially the same form. Accordingly, a creditor is compelled to monitor the laws and decisions which may affect debt collection not only in his own state, but also in the state where the debtor resides or maintains his business.

EXEMPT PROPERTY

Both federal and state laws provide that certain property is exempt and not subject to the claims of creditors. At the federal level social security, veteran's benefits, employment retirement income (ERISA), civil service retirement benefits, railroad retirement annuities and pensions, and similar types of income can be totally or partially exempt. The Consumer Credit Protection Act, of which the Debt Collection Practices Act is a part, should also be reviewed.

At the state level the exemptions become even broader. Generally they include homestead, an exemption which may exclude a part of or the entire value of the consumer's place of residence. Pensions, both public and private, workman's compensation, unemployment benefits, alimony and child support, disability, damages for wrongful death, and certain life insurance proceeds may be partially or completely beyond the reach of creditors. Wedding rings, jewelry, household furnishings, household goods, wearing apparel, working tools, and books may be entirely exempt or may be exempt up to certain threshold values.

The meaning of these statutes is that caution must be used whenever any of these sources of money are mentioned or offered during a telephone conversation. Since the above items are exempt from being used to satisfy a money judgment, no threat should be made, implied, or inferred that the creditor will be able to reach this property or source of money to pay the debt due to the creditor. In short, the creditor cannot threaten to take any action that cannot be legally taken and that is not intended to be taken (Section 807 of the Debt Collection Practices Act). The Act should be reviewed for similar prohibitions.

It is strongly recommended that the creditor familiarize himself with the federal and state laws that are applicable to exemptions. When creditors cross state lines, the exemption laws of the state where the consumer resides would be applicable. Consultation with an attorney is recommended.

CHAPTER 10

Telephone Numbers

Obtaining an accurate telephone number is an art, and corporations expend a great deal of energy in order to procure a valid live telephone number. In this new electronic age, we have barely scratched the surface of the potential uses of telephones and tele-marketing. Video telephones are now a reality and the problems of economically producing and marketing these items will soon be solved. While it is said that computers are at the stage where airplanes were in 1908, telephones are probably at the stage where airplanes were at 1918. Communication by voice is far superior to any other form of transmission. When video communication is added, the possibilities are infinite. But before any of this technology can be used, an identification code must be used to make the communication, and this code is the telephone number.

A discussion of the best way to obtain a telephone number is inadequate without considering the cost of acquiring same. Both of these subjects will be covered in this chapter.

CREDIT APPLICATIONS AND ORDER FORMS

For Businesses

Credit Application: The best place to acquire a telephone number is on an application for credit. For those firms extending credit or loans, the credit application is usually no problem since most applications contain space for both the business and residential telephone numbers.

Order Form: Businesses are not quite that careful when extending credit or selling to other businesses. The seller may check credit and even verify the bank of the purchaser, but many times the seller will forget to record the telephone number of the business. A space for the business telephone number should be provided on the order form completed by the buyer. If the order is received over the telephone or obtained by a salesman, the seller should obtain the telephone number of the business In large businesses, the extension number should also be noted

For Consumers

Credit Application: Almost every financial institution secures the telephone number of the customer on the credit application. Many large firms that use credit applications also obtain the telephone number.

Order Form: If a credit application is not used, obtain the telephone number on the order form. The argument is made in the direct marketing industry that requesting a private telephone number will deter a customer from purchasing. Yet, many order forms in newspapers and magazines do request the telephone number of the consumer. Today, more and more marketers are finding that such a request does not inhibit sales; and with the advent of telemarketing, the telephone number becomes a very valuable commodity.

The other avenues to take to obtain the telephone number are all costly and time consuming; and in many instances, a telephone number of the consumer is never obtained. Thus, many times the creditor will never know why the debtor failed to pay and whether contact with the debtor would have resulted in payment.

OBTAINING HOME TELEPHONE NUMBERS

Telephone Number of Owner of Business

While the business telephone number is usually available in the telephone book, the private residence telephone number of the principal of the business is usually never acquired in business-to-business sales. The first impression of this statement is that such a request would be the equivalent of an invasion of privacy, and the owner of the business probably would decline such information. First, the owner does not wish to conduct business at his home. Second, the seller is dealing with a business, not an individual. Third, the owner might very well be insulted and take his business elsewhere.

Nevertheless, good reasons do exist for attempting to obtain the home telephone number of the owner or chief operating officer. To what extent the seller wishes to expend efforts in this direction is a function of many circumstances, including the size of the order, the size of the business, the past experience with the business, the nature of the business, the visible financial responsibility of the business, and whether such an action would offend the seller's counterpart. The most important factor is the calculated risk that such a request might change the purchaser from a buyer to a nonbuyer, and the further consideration that creating a nonbuyer may be in the best interest of the seller.

You may regard this suggestion as being ridiculous on the premise that very few firms, if any, engage in such a practice. Also, such procedures, if used at all, should be limited to very large and substantial orders. Yet, banks are very careful to procure the home addresses and telephone numbers of the principles of the businesses that borrow from the bank. Extending credit to a business is equivalent to granting a loan. Even in those instances where only one principal guarantees the loan to a bank, the telephone number of the principal officers who do not guarantee the loan are usually recorded on the loan application. This occurs even in small installment loans to businesses. Owners of buildings also use rather extensive credit applications. The basic premise of acquiring this information is that the creditor always can contact some officer with responsibility in the event of a default. Both sides will benefit, since communication in this event is essential. Lack of communication may result in precipitous action which would not have been taken had the parties had the opportunity to communicate.

When a business stops operating, the telephone number is disconnected and no contact can be made. At this point, information is necessary to make a decision as to what course of action is best suited for the situation. Contact with one of the officers of the corporation would certainly be helpful. Did the business file for bankruptcy? Was an assignment for the benefit of creditors filed with the likelihood of a substantial distribution? Did the sheriff sell the assets pursuant to a judgment? Did the bank repossess all the equipment subject to its lien? Did the Internal Revenue Service exercise its authority to recapture all the assets by reason of a tax lien? Did the debtor just leave for parts unknown? Each of these reasons warrant a different action by the creditor. Of course, the creditor will ultimately become aware of this information, but in the course of acquiring the information, substantial monies may have been spent on attorney's fees, accountant's fees, skip tracing efforts, litigation searches, and other types of investigatory reports, as well as the time spent on the telephone to initiate these procedures.

> **COLLECTION TIP: *Home Telephone Number of Owner.*** The above presentation may not persuade the reader to undertake what may be considered to be a serious departure from normal selling procedures. Nevertheless, while this may be true in most instances, I suggest that securing the home telephone number of the owner may not only be warranted, but may be essential on a case-by-case basis. Accordingly, I urge the reader to review the above with an open mind.

Unpublished Numbers

Unfortunately, unpublished numbers are increasing at a very substantial rate, to the extent that today in some areas the unpublished numbers represent almost 15 percent to 17 percent of the population, and in other areas, the percentage rises to 20 percent to 25 percent. The unpublished number is the strongest argument for obtaining the number of a consumer, and is also a persuasive argument for obtaining the telephone number of the owner of a business, due to the probability that his number might also be unpublished.

Inability to contact a debtor impacts heavily on the collection effort. The strength of direct voice-to-voice communication cannot be underestimated. A telephone number initially acquired is one that does not have to be located. Every businessman should strongly review his ability to procure a telephone number.

USING TELEPHONE DIRECTORIES

Telephone directories have acquired a brand-new attraction since the beginning of charges for information calls. Most employees would rather call information than use a telephone book, but now the employer has strong motivation to insist that the employees use telephone directories.

Usually telephone directories for the city or county can be obtained free of charge from the telephone company. But if telephone books are needed across county or state lines, the telephone companies charge for this service.

No magic is involved in looking for telephone numbers in a telephone directory. Tabs can be used for easier location of the alphabet, and, of course, hard covers are available. Magnifying glasses are helpful for older employees who must use glasses or bifocals. Rubber fingers assist in turning pages. Good lighting is absolutely necessary.

The library of telephone directories should include the areas involved in the collection effort. If a metropolitan area is the main marketing area, then all of the city plus its suburbs should be included. If the corporation sells nationally, the telephone directories of the major metropolitan areas of the country would be helpful, such as: Los Angeles, New York, Chicago, Miami, Dallas, San Francisco, Kansas City, St. Louis, Minneapolis, Cleveland, Boston, Baltimore, Washington, Atlanta, New Orleans, Denver, Salt Lake City, Phoenix, Philadelphia, Cleveland, Milwaukee, etc. The addition of other major cities would depend upon the customer list.

Since telephone books are listed alphabetically, the list of names to be worked should also be listed alphabetically. But before this alphabetical listing, a sorting should be made by the areas covered by the respective books. In some instances, this can be done by area code, but normally, the person sorting should be familiar with the geographical area.

USING DIRECTORY INFORMATION

Local directory information costs vary from state to state. For this reason, telephone directories should always be used first to obtain telephone numbers in local areas.

When contacting long distance information on a list of delinquent debtors, the debtors should be sorted by area code. AT&T will furnish up to two numbers for each information call. Thus, if two debtors exist in one area code, requesting both telephone numbers in one call saves money. Of course, if the telephone number is unlisted or not in service, a charge will still be made, but there is no charge for an unpublished number.

> **AT&T:** This is information. What city, please?
> **Cr:** I have two requests for St. Louis.
> **AT&T:** Please give them to me.

Area Code Maps

The telephone books provide maps listing the area codes. Unfortunately, area codes sometimes change to cover different geographical locations. If an incorrect area code is dialed, the operator will furnish the correct area code and there is no charge for this service. Unfortunately, this also consumes one request of the two available for a $.60 charge. The solution is to update the area code maps with the new information right away. The telephone company also publishes an area code manual which lists the major cities covered by the area codes. If many numbers are being sought all over the country, this manual is far superior to the maps in the telephone books.

HELPFUL HINTS: Make Evening Contact. Be sure that the communication with the operator is clear. Always try to furnish an address to the operator. Needless to say, night information calls are serviced faster, more easily, and more accurately than daytime calls since the information operators are not so busy.

Check the Number of Information Requests Available. While most states provide only two listings for each information call, some states, particularly California, at this time do allow three requests per information call. Accordingly, if you have three debtors in Los Angeles, your cost per debtor decreases from $.60 to $.20 per debtor.

Preventing a Disconnect. Operators from time to time have a nasty habit of hanging up before the telephone worker has time to make the second or third request. The suggestion is made that the telephone worker emphasize at the beginning of the first request that two or three requests are going to be submitted. Also, a request for a verbal listing as opposed to a computer listing will often prompt a quicker response.

AT&T: This is information. What city, please?

Cr: I have two requests for Cleveland.

AT&T: Go ahead.

Cr: The first request is for John Wilson at 235 Main Street, and the second request is for Robert Roosevelt at 58 Maple Avenue. Please give me a verbal listing. I do not want a computer listing.

COLLECTION TIP: Writing Telephone Numbers. Writing clearly is very important. The numbers most often confused are the 7s and 9s; the 3s and 8s; and the 6s and 0s. Crosses through the 7s and 0s are helpful, but only clarity will help the 3s and 8s.

COLLECTION TIP: WATS Line Information Call. Using a WATS line to call information is twice as expensive since a charge for the information call is being made as well as the time cost of the WATS line.

Multiple Requests

At the time this chapter was written, Illinois Bell provided a directory assistance operator to handle multiple requests. The charge is $33 per hour instead of $.50 per call. An appointment must be made with the operator and there is a $12.75 charge for this appointment.

Many of the other Bell systems are investigating new systems and procedures to service high-volume information callers. By the time this book is published high-volume users may be able to access the data base of AT&T or the regional companies in order to obtain telephone numbers. This would probably be the most efficient method for the high-volume user of information and also the most profitable for AT&T. Hopefully, AT&T and the regional companies will address this problem quickly.

MCI charges less than AT&T for each information call, but the cost is increased by the local call necessary to access MCI. This will change when MCI users have automatic access. The remaining long distance companies also may provide directory assistance, but must charge in a similar manner to AT&T and MCI. Contacting other companies for further information is advised.

Information Calls—Alternatives: Many heavy users of interstate directory assistance were devastated by this charge, and immediately sought other sources of telephone numbers. Initially, many enterprising individuals organized companies in Canada. The Canadian Bell system allowed Canadian users to call information in the United States without charge. Thus, a whole new industry sprouted. But as spring comes, so must winter. The Canadian government allowed the Bell System to charge the heavy users in almost the same way as their sister company does in the United States, and the no-charge information telephone call has practically disappeared from North America.

Data Banks

There are several large data banks available that will match names at a small fraction of the cost of an information call, but the recovery rate of telephone numbers is lower and a large number of names is required to make the minimum charge economical. Most of these data base services that match names with numbers are targeted at telemarketing companies, and thus would probably be unsuitable for a collection effort. Some of the regional telephone companies are now considering permitting firms that require large amounts of numbers to access their data banks. Again, this access may be more suitable to very large users, rather than those seeking the numbers for telephone collection calls. Nevertheless, as the computers become more sophisticated, perhaps adaptations for small users will be found.

WRONG NUMBERS

When contacting a party who asserts that the debtor is not there, an effort could be made to find out whether the correct number was dialed. The normal response is the following (Note: "Tp" refers to third party.):

Tp:	Hello.
Cr:	Is Mr. Monroe there?
Tp:	Who?
Cr:	John Monroe.
Tp:	You must have the wrong number. No such person here.
Cr:	Is this 420 Main Street, Boston, Massachusetts?
Tp:	No, this is 680 Parkway.
Cr:	Is this 617-555-1234?
Tp:	You have the wrong number.
Cr:	Thank you.

Comment on Dialogue: If the creditor would have asked the party "what number is this?" the third party would have been justified in refusing to divulge that information, and the party might have been antagonized enough to hang up the telephone before the creditor could confirm that the number was incorrect. The best approach is to ask whether the number dialed is the party's number. If the answer is negative, the creditor should politely thank the party and hang up.

HELPFUL HINT: When Wrong Number Is in Small Town. If the wrong number is in a very small town, an inquiry might be made of the party as follows:

Tp:	Hello.
Cr:	Is Mr. Monroe there?

Tp: Who?

Cr: John Monroe.

Tp: You must have the wrong number.

Cr: I want John Monroe of 420 Main Street, Four Corners.

Tp: No such person lives here.

Cr: Do you know John Monroe?

Tp: Yes, he lives at 240 Main Street.

Cr: Do you have his telephone number?

Tp: Yes, I have it here.

Cr: I would appreciate you giving it to me so I don't have to spend another sixty cents with the telephone company.

Tp: OK, here it is....

CHAPTER 11

The Business-to-Business Approach

When a business is the target of the telephone collection effort, the procedures set forth in the prior chapters of this book must be adapted to the type of indebtedness, the type of debtor, and the size of the business debtor. Whereas the approach for consumers is rather consistent, the approach to businesses may be very different depending upon a wide variety of circumstances.

The persuasion tactics used on General Motors are not necessarily the same as would be used on the local General Motors dealer. The electrician's vulnerability is somewhat different from the exposure of a major supermarket servicing the locality. Some businesses are more concerned with their public image than other businesses. Some businesses must defend a lawsuit for a few thousand dollars, since their survival might depend upon success, whereas other large businesses are in a position to settle rather than incur substantial legal fees to defend what is considered a minor problem.

A national chain would not allow the local store to settle disputes in certain areas, but the "mom and pop" debtor have the power to resolve all problems instantly. Today, most large corporations, either publicly owned or privately owned, maintain large legal departments.

These departments usually handle the routine collection suits instituted against the corporation. Accordingly, the threat of suit against the local manufacturing plant of a national stock exchange firm may not be very persuasive. A franchised restaurant normally does its bookkeeping through a central office, a distinct difficulty in dealing with this type of operation. The lesson is basic: different businesses require different collection techniques

---

COLLECTION TIP: *Dividing the Pie.* The creditor must acknowledge that the debtor has many other creditors. A debtor does not consciously select one debt not to pay—the creditor who is the easiest to stall is the last to be paid, and the creditor who delays suing will probably wait to be paid until all those who have sued have been paid in full. Therefore, the creditor is not competing against the debtor but against the other creditors. The debtor's assets are like a pie that is sliced into six pieces, but must serve ten guests. The job of the proficient collection manager is to be certain that his firm leaves with its piece of pie. The debtor tends to serve the guest who is the most persuasive, most persistent, and the most sophisticated. The singular purpose of this book is to enable you to be the most satisfied dinner guest.

TYPES OF BUSINESS DEBTORS

Retail Stores

Most retail stores operate on a cash or credit card basis. No credit is being extended to the customers, so retail stores do not have a problem with cash flow or accounts receivable. The credit card sales are usually paid rather quickly by Visa, Master Charge, and American Express. The general reason for delinquency is simply that the inventory turnover has slowed, or in more simple terms, sales have decreased to such a point that the owner is unable to meet his expenses.

The danger in dealing with retail stores is accepting payout promises which are never kept. Retail stores purchase on credit, and suits will certainly damage their credit rating. Therefore, payout plans should be monitored very carefully to be certain that other creditors have not already resorted to suit to recover their debts. Sometimes a litigation search is the proper procedure to determine whether any other creditors have already instituted suit. In most of the major cities there are firms which can provide this information. If the creditor knows there are suits against the debtor, the approach on the telephone might be somewhat different.

Here is an example where the creditor does not know if other creditors have started suit:

Cr: One hundred dollars a month sounds OK to me.

Dr: All right, I will send it to you in a few weeks.

Cr: No, a few weeks is too long. We must have the first payment by the first of May.

Dr: But that's only a few days away. I can't get the money together for at least a week.

Cr: Well, send me $50 on May 1st and the balance of the $100 on May 14; and then send me $100 on the first of every month.

Dr: Yeah, I think I can make that, at least I will try.

Cr: If you do, it will not be necessary to refer this matter to our attorney for suit. On the other hand, if we do not receive your check by the first of May, there will be no more telephone calls and this matter will be referred to our attorney. Be assured of that.

An example where the creditor knows that other creditors have already started suit against the debtor:

Cr: One hundred dollars a month sounds OK to me.

Dr: All right, I will send it to you in a few weeks.

Cr: That's no good. We must have weekly payments. Once an account is delinquent, our policy is to insist upon weekly payments.

Dr: That's a lot of paperwork. I'll send you one payment a month. I can't be writing checks every day.

Cr: We only need a check once a week. Perhaps you would like to sign a series of notes for $25 a week until the full amount is paid?

Dr: No notes.

Cr: Well, then we must have a payment each week. There is no alternative.

Dr: OK, I'll send you $25 per week.

Cr: That seems all right. But if one payment is not made, the matter will be referred to our attorney for suit. I am sure you do not want this, so please be certain that the checks are paid when we present them to your bank.

Comment on Dialogue: By arranging for weekly payments, the creditor will know within a week whether the debtor is experiencing further financial problems. Weekly payments are the tightest form of payment, but the creditor could also use a biweekly payout plan. Post-dated checks may be used providing there are no state laws restricting their use and the creditor complies with the Debt Collection Practices Act.

There is a problem if the aggressive creditor institutes legal action and the other creditors follow the lead and also institute suit. The end result may cause the retail store to cease to operate. Accordingly, the creditor is walking a thin line between working with the debtor and trying to keep him in business, as opposed to exerting such pressure that there is the possibility of forcing the retail store out of business. The size, financial stability, and number of years in business often will help the creditor to reach such a decision. The important aspect is that the creditor recognizes that a problem exists, and acts accordingly.

Hotels and Motels

Many hotels and motels are seasonal, and the telephone effort must be emphasized during that part of the season when the hotel is receiving its cash. Resort hotels are more subject to these problems than inner city businessmen's hotels. But even the business hotels are subject to fluctuations depending upon their convention, luncheon, and seminar business.

Summer camps, ski resorts, and country clubs fall into this classification also. If the camp owner cannot meet all of his bills from the current season, often the advances from next season will be used to discharge the old bills. Telephone calls to summer camps for children should be made during the preceding winter during current efforts to recruit new campers with accompanying deposits. At this point, the camp owner is most optimistic. A telephone call later in the spring may be too late, since new supplies have already been bought for the new season.

Private clubs usually charge their assessments and collect them during December and January. Dues are usually collected during the first few months of the year. If the club is active only during the summer months, collection efforts should be made from December to August, for efforts made during September to December may be totally useless.

Cr: This is the Brookfield Lumber Company. We still have not received payment for the lumber we shipped to you for outdoor benches and tables. We wrote you three letters, and have not received your check.

Dr: Well, the camp season was not so good. Two of the bungalows caught fire and the parents took their children home, and I was forced to refund their money. I am afraid you will have to wait until next year. As soon as I sign up some campers, I will send you the money. I usually start around December and January, so you can expect it by February. That's only four months from now.

Comment on Dialogue: A referral to an attorney may not accelerate payment. Unfortunately, the mistake was made in not pursuing the debt at the beginning of the camp season when the debtor had on deposit all the tuition that was paid in advance.

Not-for-Profit Associations

In most associations a new slate of officers are elected each year. If the association is small and relatively unknown, knowing the duration of the term of the officers may be very helpful. Once the new officers have been elected, difficulty in collecting debts may be encountered. The telephone call might take the following form:

Cr: We shipped the labels four months ago, and I spoke to Mr. Jones twice in the past two months. He said he would mail a check for the full amount each time.

Dr: Mr. Jones is no longer treasurer, and nobody knows anything about the labels. How can I pay for them?

Cr: Ask Mr. Jones. He knows about them.

Dr: Mr. Jones moved to Utah, and no one knows where he is.

Cr: Well, I will turn this claim of $750 over to our attorney for suit if we do not receive a check within ten days.

Dr: Go right ahead. The only judge in our town is also a vice-president of the association. Lots of luck.

Delay in collecting against associations, such as Girl Scouts; Boy Scouts; clubs, whether political or otherwise; fraternal groups; etc., is total disaster. The officers are volunteers and normally cannot wait until they relinquish their duties to the new slate of officers. The operation of a small association is quite informal, and in many instances, no formal books or records are kept.

The telephone procedure in these cases should be prompt and persistent, and referral to a collection agency/attorney should be considered early in the cycle. Of course, large nonprofit organizations with national or local exposure should be treated in the same manner as large business organizations.

Religious Organizations

The small religious organization presents distinct problems. Services are usually conducted on certain days during the week or weekend. During the rest of the week no one is present at the place of worship where the merchandise was shipped. Therefore, when contact cannot be made during business hours, telephone calls should be made at the time when it is most likely that someone is there to receive the call, even if the call has to be made on Friday evening, the weekend, or Sunday noon. Also, many religious organizations and places of worship employ just one person who operates from his or her own home. The organization is placed in the name of a religious entity which may have no assets or property. Thorough credit checking is in order.

The well-known religious organizations usually are available during the week, and efforts to reach them should be made during business hours.

Restaurants and Fast Food Establishments

To call a restaurant during lunch or dinner is the same as trying to sell an automobile to a fireman on his way to a fire. At these times, the manager or owner is preoccupied with serving the customers, and no amount of persuasion or threats will make an impact on him or her. A message will be forgotten as soon as the chef starts to complain. The best time to call is the mid-afternoon or morning, depending upon the restaurant's peak hours. It is doubtful whether a message left with waiters, waitresses, or even the cashier will be delivered. Problems might also arise as to whether the waiter or waitress has the authority to take a message.

Credit Cards

The collection of delinquent accounts of Master Charge and Visa credit cards are basically thought of as being similar to a consumer loan. Nevertheless, when an installment loan is delinquent, the debtor usually still has a bank account and a credit card in good standing. When a credit card becomes delinquent, rarely does the debtor still have a bank account. The credit card is usually the last line of credit available to the consumer. Thus, collection efforts should move faster. Another problem is that the credit cards are often promoted without financial information or a credit application.

Miscellaneous Professionals

Doctor, Dentist: Excluding medical coverage payments such as Blue Cross, Major Medical, Medicaid, and Medicare, medical practitioners are usually the last to be paid by the consumer. Most doctors have very substantial amounts outstanding in their accounts receivable. Nevertheless, most doctors are excellent credit risks and the reason for delinquency is often poor management.

While the doctor is treating patients, the discharge of his accounts payable are a low priority. An inquiry as to office hours will reveal those hours when the doctor is busy. A judgment should then be made as to whether to call before or after office hours. If he is a busy doctor, the office hours may extend later, and thus the best time for a telephone collection call would be before office hours. If the nurse takes the message, an inquiry should be made to ascertain if this particular nurse manages the books and records. If not, try to reach the nurse who does handle the books. Assuming the failure to pay is due to poor management, the collection effort should be relatively mild at first, for an excellent chance exists to retain the doctor as a customer. The major drug and medical equipment companies rely on the medical profession to market their products, and collection efforts are very diplomatic. Thus, doctors are not accustomed to strong telephone collection calls, and such efforts may very well produce a recalcitrant debtor. An opportunity to pay should be afforded before strong words are used.

> **Dr:** Dr. Joseph's Office. May I help you?
> **Cr:** This is Mr. McMann of the Easy Carpet Cleaners.
> **Dr:** Do you want an appointment?
> **Cr:** No. We cleaned your carpet three months ago, and our bill for $475 has not been paid.
> **Dr:** Oh, is it three months?
> **Cr:** Do you take care of the books and records?

Dr: No, Ms. Tyler does that, but she is not here.
Cr: When does she come in?
Dr: On Tuesdays and Thursdays between 9:00 and 12:00.
Cr: Well, will you tell her to call me at 555-1234?
Dr: I'll leave the message, Mr. McMann.
Cr: Thank you.

Here is another example:

Dr: Dr. Joseph's office. May I help you?
Cr: May I speak to Ms. Tyler?
Dr: Just a minute.
Cr: I'll wait.
Dr: This is Ms. Tyler.
Cr: I called last week about this bill to Easy Carpet Cleaners. I left a message.
Dr: I never got the message.
Cr: Well, the bill is past due three months.
Dr: How much is it for?
Cr: $475.
Dr: Did you send us an invoice?
Cr: At least three invoices. One each month.
Dr: I do remember the carpet being cleaned. Let me check the records to see if we mailed a check. In the meanwhile, could you send me another bill?
Cr: Shall I mail it to your attention?
Dr: Do that.
Cr: We would like to have payment by Monday, May 1. Will you be able to do that by then?
Dr: I don't know.
Cr: Well, I would appreciate you giving this your attention, since the bill is three months in arrears, and I don't want to have to refer this to a collection agency. I'll look for the check by Monday, May 1.
Dr: I will do my best.
Cr: Thank you.

Comment on Dialogue: The first telephone call omitted a message. Obviously, the creditor was trying very hard to retain the doctor as a customer. The creditor also asked the question, "Will you be able to do that by then?" and did not receive the answer he expected. Asking questions, in any case, is not recommended, although sometimes the situation not only suggests a question, but demands one. In this case, the creditor cured the mistake by again referring to the fact that a check will be expected on Monday, May 1. The creditor sent three invoices, but should have only sent one invoice, or two at the most.

Attorney, Accountant: The threat of suit may bring the response, "By all means, come play in my ball park." Suing an attorney may probably bring contested litigation since most attorneys delight in defending themselves. The attorney incurs no cost and speculates that the creditor will ultimately settle. The attorney is usually right, especially if the claim is relatively small and some justification rests for the dispute. The recommendation is to avoid the threat of suit and settle early rather than after suit is started. Using the standard statement that the claim will be referred to a collection agency or attorney only encourages the debtor attorney to become more stubborn, since a lawsuit does not present any problem for him. In short, the creditor is threatening to engage in the very business in which the attorney engages in on a day-to-day basis. Accountants may feel the same way, since they usually have a friend who is an attorney and will defend the case for no charge. Nevertheless, if all else fails, the threat of suit must be used, and in some instances, suit must be started.

Dr: Jones and Smith.
Cr: This is the ABC Copy Center. May I please speak to Mr. Smith?
Dr: What's this in reference to?
Cr: It's about the past due bill for $2,800.
Dr: Oh, just a moment.
Dr: Hello?
Cr: Mr. Smith?
Dr: Yes.
Cr: This is the ABC Copy Center. We have this bill for $2,800 which is over three months past due.
Dr: Yes, I know. Our client still has not paid us.
Cr: Well, that may be, but we extended credit to you.
Dr: Yes, I know. I will call the client now and see what I can do.
Cr: We must have payment within a week.
Dr: And if not, are you going to sue me?
Cr: Mr. Smith, I know you are an attorney and I know that if you want to, you can defend yourself.

Dr: Look, don't threaten me with suit. If you sue me, it will cost you more in legal fees than you will recover. Let me call the client and see if I can resolve this matter.

Cr: That is fine. But please understand that I must have payment within a week.

Dr: No way. Even if I could contact the client, it will take me two weeks.

Cr: OK. But please do your best. Otherwise, this will go to our attorney; and that is what we both don't want.

Dr: OK.

Service Businesses

This category covers a wide range of businesses such as plumbing, heating, air conditioning, exterminating, insurance brokerage, real estate brokerage, etc. Most of these businesses are either small businesses or one-person operations.

Some creditors will threaten suit and actually refer a small amount to an attorney for suit on the philosophy that the small businessman cannot afford an attorney to defend the case. The creditor surmises that when the small businessman receives the estimate from his attorney as to the cost of defending the action, an offer of settlement will be made. The creditor may fail to realize that the courts have adjusted to this problem by permitting the small businessman to defend himself in court without an attorney. Some states still require that a corporation be defended by an attorney, but even this concept is slowly changing. In short, when the individual debtor defends himself, the only one paying attorney's fees is the creditor, not the debtor. Therefore, suits based on this philosophy should receive very careful consideration. The creditor should also remember that if he does not intend to refer the claim for suit, he cannot threaten the debtor with suit. (See Chapter 9, "Legal Boundaries and Limitations.")

TYPES OF INDEBTEDNESS

Installment Debt

Banks, finance companies, department stores, and businesses extending revolving credit accounts are faced with the problem of collecting indebtedness on an installment basis.

Are the Records Available? The first basic step is to have all the records available for the telephone worker. Without the records, the time spent on the telephone is like time spent on a golf practice range without golf clubs. The dialogue might sound like this:

Cr: We have not received a payment in 60 days and your account is now three payments in arrears.

Dr: I made a double payment two months ago and the most I pay is one month, and that payment went out yesterday.

Cr: Well, I don't have all the records in front of me. I will have to check that double payment.

Dr: Well, you do that; and then I expect an apology the next time you call.

Payment History: The complete payment history must be in the file or on the computer screen. The telephone caller must know whether the records are current. If the entering of payments is several days or a week behind, the telephone worker must be aware of this condition so a proper judgment can be made. Thus, if the debtor claims a payment was made in the past few days, the telephone worker should try to verify this statement. On the other hand, if the debtor claims a payment was made several weeks ago, the telephone worker should firmly advise the debtor that no payment was made.

Dr: I sent you two payments over three weeks ago. There must be something wrong with your system.

Cr: Mr. Johnson, our records show no such payment. Perhaps you sent the payments to some other creditor.

Dr: No, I sent them to you.

Cr: Well, we never received them. Do you have canceled checks to show that we deposited the money?

Dr: I don't know. I haven't got my bank statement yet.

Cr: Well, our records show the account is in arrears over three months. The account is scheduled to be referred to our attorney for suit. I will do this for you. I will hold the account in abeyance for five days to give you a chance to check your records, or to call the bank. Nevertheless, if we do not hear from you by Monday, May 1st, either with a payment, or with copies of the checks, we will refer this to our attorney.

Is the Total Picture Available? An examination of the payment history will cue the telephone caller as to the general presentation based upon the number of delinquency occurrences and the pattern of delinquency compared to the pattern of payments. The collection letters mailed and the notations of prior telephone calls which produced payments must also be examined. This prior picture of the debtor presents the following very distinct advantages to the telephone caller:

1. The exact status of the account is available.
2. The frequency and spacing of defaults, payments, curing of defaults, and promises are evident.
3. The general reliability of promises are reflected.

All of these elements should be utilized in the collection effort.

Cr: Your account is three months in arrears.

Dr: I'll catch up. I'll send you a payment next week, and two payments the week after.

Cr: Mr. Carter, you have made many promises to bring your account up-to-date. Unfortunately, your track record is not very good. We don't need one payment, we need three payments.

Dr: Well, I've been having trouble lately I said I would pay

Cr: But you only pay after we make two or three telephone calls, and I don't intend to make three calls to obtain a payment

Dr: You won't have to. I said I will pay next week.

Cr: Well, if we do not receive all three payments within two weeks, by Monday, May 7, the installment loan will be referred to our attorney for institution of suit.

Dr: Don't get tough with me. I said I will pay.

Cr: Sir, I am not getting tough. I am only stating what will happen in the event the account is not brought up-to-date.

Comment on Dialogue: When the debtor mentioned he was having trouble lately, the proper approach would be to inquire as to the nature of the trouble. We will discuss that next.

Search for the Reason for Delinquency: An added ingredient to this type of telephone collection call is the inquiry as to the reason for the delinquency. While in most other creditor–debtor relationships, the reason for the delinquency normally will not change the content of the telephone call or the ultimate action to be taken, in this case, the reason might very well affect the reaction of the creditor because of the ongoing and continuous relationship between the creditor and the debtor. If the debtor professes a medical ailment as opposed to a strike or unemployment, the reaction of the creditor might be very different. The same approach applies to a business. A delinquency due to an inability to collect accounts receivable may produce a reaction far different than if the reason was due to a move to new quarters. Not only should an inquiry be made, but the creditor should explore the in-depth reasons for the delinquency in order to satisfy the creditor that the explanation seems reasonable, appears logical, and has at least some ring of truth to it.

Cr: We shipped you the fork lift over two months ago.

Dr: I know, but we just received our shipment of hemp. It was on one of those ships that was tied up in the St. Lawrence Seaway over four weeks.

Cr: I know, but I have to have payment.

Dr: Look, we are working all weekend to get this stuff out to our customers. I should be able to get some money to pay you within three or four weeks.

Cr: Why didn't you answer the letters that I wrote? Last week my controller called you and you did not call back.

Dr: Because I didn't know what to say. Until they fixed the locks on the river, my ship was stuck. I didn't know when the hemp would get here. Look, you're not the only one I am not paying. Now that I am shipping, I will be able to pay you.

Cr: Well, all right. But I want to hear from you in one week by telephone. If I do not get a call from you, I am going to refer this to our attorney. I'm sure you don't want that, and neither do I. But when I don't hear from you, I think the worst.

Dr: OK, I'll call you.

Based on the review of the file and the in-depth inquiry, the creditor finally must make a decision whether to grant a moratorium, extend the payment, renegotiate the amount of the payment, or possibly refinance the entire indebtedness. If the debtor is reluctant to make any proposal and merely pleads poverty, this may be one exception where the creditor must "bid against himself." The creditor should make some proposal to keep the debtor on a payout plan, no matter how nominal or insignificant the payments are. If security is available, communicate your option to exercise your rights. Otherwise, a debtor who shows an inclination to pay should be afforded every chance.

Dr: I just don't have any money.

Cr: How much is your rent?

Dr: I only pay $350 per month for two rooms.

Cr: How much is the telephone?

Dr: About $35.

Cr: Electricity?

Dr: About $30.

Cr: Well, could you pay $20 each month for the next three months, and then we will talk again?

Comment on Dialogue: The simple solution is closing the door and starting suit; but this simple solution is not always the best solution. Accepting reduced payments and changing due dates plus other adjustments sometimes will save a loan from ending up as an uncollected judgment.

Revolving Credit: The same rules that apply to installment loans are applicable to this type of indebtedness. Remember to provide all the records to the telephone worker before the call is made.

Time and Demand Loans

Banks usually grant this type of loan for large amounts. The telephone effort is somewhat similar to the installment loan except more emphasis is placed on the cause of the delinquency.

Although these loans are sometimes rolled over (refinanced for an additional period of from 30 days to 180 days) after a payment of interest and sometimes a part of the principal, the creditor often fails to obtain current financial statements, and for obvious reasons, the debtor never offers financial statements. If current financial statements were obtained, the creditor might not have permitted the loan to be rolled over. In all business-to-business situations, the status of the business and its current situation is most important and a telephone call should be directed to obtaining as much in-depth information as possible about the business and the security for the loan, if any.

Secured Loans

Although most promissory notes secured by mortgages to banks, lending institutions, mortgage lenders, and finance companies enable the lender to accelerate the balance due, threatening to foreclose the mortgage to compel payment sometimes only creates more problems for the lender. Most borrowers are aware that their loan can be accelerated and that their machinery and equipment, their automobile or their real estate, can be foreclosed and sold to satisfy the loan. A premature threat often ruins the relationship between the borrower and lender. The frightened borrower crawls into a shell and makes promises that he will never keep. The debtor slowly and surely retreats into a corner from which no escape exists except the inevitable foreclosure. Use the threat sparingly, and only when absolutely necessary. Exploiting this window of vulnerability may not lead to the orderly resumption of payments, which happens to be the singular aim of all lenders.

Dr: Good morning, R.W. Madison Insurance Agency.

Cr: Is Mr. Madison there?

Dr: Just a minute.

Cr: OK.

Dr: This is Mr. Madison.

Cr: This is Mr. Adams of the ABBC Mortgage Company. We have not received a payment for two months.

Dr: I know. I should be able to send both payments to you within ten days.

Cr: You know, your loan has continually been in arrears, sometimes as much as three months. What's the problem?

Dr: Well, with premiums jumping all over the place, and clients complaining, business is tough. Furthermore, in some instances our commissions have been reduced.

Cr: Well, maybe you should increase the first mortgage, and go out 20 years, so the payments will be a lot less.

Dr: I can't do that. I have a second mortgage.

Cr: I didn't know that. I don't have your records in front of me. How much is it for?

Dr: The maximum amount. You know, I have two kids in college. I don't have to tell you how much that costs.

Cr: I know. But that doesn't solve the problem. The loan committee is reviewing your loan next week. You know that you have a very low rate of interest, and they might call it due to force you into paying a higher rate of interest.

Dr: I can barely cover my expenses now. That would be a disaster, and also the additional expenses would be a burden.

Cr: Well, I don't know what to say, except try to get in the payments before the loan is reviewed, because with your track record, I can't promise you anything.

Dr: How much do I have to pay to be sure the loan is not called?

Comment on Dialogue: The creditor only threatened to accelerate the mortgage to increase the rate of interest. The word "foreclose"
is not used. The important impact is that the debtor recognized that
the delinquency was serious. This was achieved without any threats of
suit or foreclosure, and in fact, the normal closing statement of
referral to an attorney is deliberately omitted since it is not necessary.
This debtor is sophisticated enough to understand exactly what the
situation is. Also, note the embarrassment of the lender in admitting
that the records were not before him.

Rent, Telephone, and Utilities: The same rule that applies to
secured loans holds true for landlords. The tenant knows that eviction
is the ultimate leverage that rests in the hands of the owner of the real
property. The consumer realizes that the telephone company may
disconnect the telephone and the utilities company may disconnect the
gas and electric. The threat of such action is a powerful weapon, and
should not be used indiscriminately.

Some telephone workers representing these general types of
creditors immediately employ this crutch to drive home a "hard-core"
collection effort. Some use the threat before any effort is made to find
out why the debtor has not made the regular payment. The argument
is made that this is the only thing the debtor understands. This is not
necessarily true. The debtor should be afforded an opportunity to
evaluate the situation and respond to the situation. The threat should
be used as a gun is used: don't point it unless you intend to use it.

SIZE OF BUSINESS DEBTOR

The majority of telephone collection calls are directed at small
businesses, as opposed to large corporations, principally because
small businesses substantially exceed the number of large businesses
and large businesses are somewhat better financed. But instances do
exist where a large corporation does not pay its bills.

Handling Large Businesses: The major reason for delinquency
is usually a bona fide dispute, a lost shipment, a lost invoice, or no
purchase order. The key problem is finding the right department and
the right person. The first attempt should be made with the party who
placed the order. The collection effort should be directed at this

person. Do not permit him to divert you to another employee, or even another department. Impress upon the party that he ordered the merchandise and he should do whatever is necessary to arrange payment. The approach is similar to a call to a franchise.

Dr: I know I ordered it, but the accounts payable department takes care of paying the bills. You have to speak to them.

Cr: I'm not going to call them, I sold the merchandise to you, and I'm looking for payment from you. You can call them if you wish.

Dr: Look, it's in their ballpark. I approved the bill for payment. That's all I can do.

Cr: You can call them, and instruct them to send out a check.

Dr: They don't listen to me.

Cr: Will they listen if I approve this to be sent to our attorney for suit and you are served with a summons and complaint?

Dr: Look, don't threaten me. If you want to start suit, that's your business. We have plenty of attorneys.

Cr: I'm sure you have, but I will have no alternative but to do that since I do not seem to be able to get payment after you approved the bill.

Dr: OK, I will call them...

Unfortunately, sometimes this party has been transferred, discharged, or left for other employment. At this point, speaking to the correct party or correct department is most important. Persistence is the only recommendation to follow. Once the right person has been located and the problem explained, the proper documentation should be forwarded and hopefully payment should be received.

No Purchase Order: Where no purchase order is available, and the company refuses to pay stating that the party who ordered had no authority, counsel should be consulted to determine whether suit should be started. The question may depend upon whether the employee did or did not have apparent authority to order the merchandise, and this in turn, will depend upon many circumstances as well as the law that prevails in that particular state.

In the years of high inflation and high interest rates, many large corporations permitted their accounts payable to run 60, 90, and 120 days in arrears since borrowing was easier and cheaper from their suppliers, rather than borrowing from their banks. In these instances

suit was the only way to accelerate payments from certain corporations. During the low interest rates of the Reagan years, this problem
has improved but still exists, although to a lesser degree.

SIZE OF INDEBTEDNESS

When the size of the debt is substantial the same procedures still
apply, but more stress is placed on reaching an accommodation. The
telephone worker is the owner of the business or an officer and the
recipient of the collection call is probably the comptroller or treasurer.
Efforts to obtain information and settle should be thoroughly ex-
hausted before a threat of litigation is made. Yet, the contents of the
telephone call are essentially the same, for the simple reason that the
purpose of the telephone call is always essentially the same.

CHAPTER 12

Most Frequent
Business Excuses
and How to Handle Them

The business debtor over the years has developed a plethora of excuses to delay payment of a debt. Some of these excuses are easily recognized, and the creditor should be prepared with the proper response for them. But there are *some* business debtors who are quite sophisticated, and the technique of deferring payment on debts has become an art. The subject of this chapter is to alert the creditor to those devices most often used by the knowledgeable business debtor, and at the same time, set forth a few suggestions as to the proper rejoinder to this type of stratagem.

Just as the sophisticated consumer learns to deal with his creditors, the sophisticated businessman also develops a technique to delay and impede the creditor who is not going to be paid that month. The competent telephone worker must recognize these ploys for what they are, a stalling skill; and must react in the appropriate manner to ensure that the creditor eventually receives his money.

CHECK IN THE MAIL

How does the telephone worker respond to this statement made by the business debtor? This statement, in most instances, is a promise of payment, rather than a description of a past act. The creditor must acknowledge this fact, and treat the statement as if it was a promise of payment. Do not contradict the debtor since this serves no purpose and would probably antagonize the debtor. Such a contradiction merely infuriates the business debtor, and the debtor's first reaction is to contrive a response to evade payment. Thus, the proper response is to agree with the debtor, but use either a positive closing statement or a negative closing statement. Very often this approach will cause the debtor to sit down and send in the check.

Dr: Don't worry, my bookkeeper mailed the check out last week sometime. You know the mails are very slow during Christmas. You'll get it in a few days.

Cr: Well, we have not received it yet.

Dr: Look, if you don't get it by the end of the week, call me and I'll send another check.

Cr: Sir, the bill for the desk is 60 days old. This is my second telephone call to you. We will wait two more days, but if we do not receive the check, the matter will be referred to our attorney by Friday, May 12 with instructions to start suit. We will not call you again about this. If you mailed the check, we will receive it. If for some reason it was not mailed, we recommend that you put one in the mail immediately.

—or—

Dr: Roger's Computer Service Bureau.

Cr: May I speak to the comptroller, Mr. Nelson?

Dr: Just a minute.

Dr: Mr. Nelson speaking.

Cr: This is the Gramacy Machine Company. We have not received the balance of $3,500 due to us, and as you know, the printer was delivered over two months ago.

Dr: I approved that last week. A check is in the mail to you.

Cr: Well, we have not received it.

Dr: I am certain it was mailed.

Cr: Fine, so now it will not be necessary to send this claim to our attorney for institution of suit, since it was supposed to be mailed to the attorney on Monday.

Dr: Well, if you don't get the check on Monday, please call me.

Cr: Mr. Nelson, this is my third call to your firm. I have no control over this matter anymore. If you wish to call our firm Monday, fine; but the matter is out of my hands now and will go to an attorney on Monday, May 7, if the check is not received.

The response described above often will motivate the debtor to mail a check. In essence, a promise of payment is being converted to actual payment. Failure to use the closing statement will only encourage the debtor to delay payment.

Dr: I mailed the check yesterday. You should get it tomorrow.
Cr: Fine, I will look for it in the morning mail.

—or—

Dr: I sent two payments about an hour ago. I put them in the mailbox myself.
Cr: Great. That will make your loan current.

—or—

Dr: I saw the bookkeeper write the check and put it into an envelope. This was done yesterday about five in the afternoon.
Cr: Then I will receive it tomorrow, and your account will then be up-to-date.

The above statements followed by a "goodbye" will normally not produce a check. The debtor has succeeded in procrastinating, and the debtor will not write the check until he is prodded again by a letter or telephone call. The debtor now feels he has outwitted the creditor, and this will encourage him to attempt such a ploy again. Accordingly, the "check in mail" cliché requires a careful and considered reply together with a closing statement.

COLLECTION TIP: When the Check Is in the Mail. Always use a closing statement after the debtor states that the check is in the mail. While the closing statement should be a negative statement, the tone of voice should be firm. A weak negative closing statement will have little effect.

CHECK THE RECORDS

The debtor's assurance that he will check his records, since he has no recollection of the matter, is just another device to delay the inevitable. The debtor certainly knows that the bill or loan payment has not been made. Most businesses do not select one or two bills not to pay. If the firm is suffering financial problems, it may pay only the necessary bills and set aside those bills or debts that are not essential to the basic operation of the business. Such items as rent, telephone, electricity, gas, and payroll have priority. The priority of other bills depends on the business and the nature and character of the owner, manager, or president.

The foundation element of the telephone call should be repeated when reacting to an assurance that the records will be checked. The debtor should be reminded that several invoices were sent, several letters were mailed, and a prior telephone call was made. Do not accept this offer of cooperation. The debtor will not check his records if the excuse is accepted. The debtor will have achieved the purpose of delay, and will do nothing further until another letter or telephone call from the creditor is received. The telephone call has been wasted.

The proper response is that checking the records is unnecessary since the creditor has not received payment, and the matter is now ready to be forwarded to a collection agency or attorney. The debtor has had ample time to "check his records" and if payment is not received by a specific date, the matter will be referred to a collection agency or attorney.

Dr: General Sweet Candy Company.

Cr: May I speak to Frank?

Dr: Frank who?

Cr: The owner, Frank Elgot.

Dr: Just a minute.

Dr: This is Frank. Who is this?

Cr: This is Charlie from General Corn Syrup. Your outstanding balance with us is up to $53,000, and we haven't received a payment from you in over two months. We have sent you letters, and my accounts receivable clerk called you twice and you didn't call her back.

Dr: We've been very busy. We just got a big order from one of the chains.

Cr: I'm glad to hear that, but I'd be happier if I got paid.

Dr: I don't understand why you weren't paid. We paid all our bills on the 30th of last month, and I'm sure your bill was in there.

Cr: Well, we didn't receive any check.

Dr: Anyhow, I don't think we owe you that much.

Cr: My records show that you do.

Dr: Well, let me look into this and I will check our records. It may take me a day or two, but don't worry.

Cr: Look, Frank, this has gone too far. The comptroller says I must send it to our attorney if I don't get a payment of at least $10,000 by next Monday, May 7.

Dr: OK, I'll check it out.

Cr: You must understand that I don't have any choice now. I can only hold the account here until Monday, May 7.

Dr: I'll call you tomorrow and let you know what I can do.

Cr: OK, take my telephone number.

COLLECTION TIP: Blaming Third Party. A continuing relationship existed between the parties, and the debtor was slowly building up a balance. The creditor must be delicate in the approach if the customer is to be retained. Blaming a third party for the harsh action is the best technique, for this enables the contact person to maintain an ongoing relationship.

EMPLOYEE HAD NO AUTHORITY TO ORDER

A statement that the employee has no authority to order may have validity. If the creditor did business with the janitor, obviously a question arises as to whether the janitor has apparent authority to order industrial cleaning products, and perhaps building maintenance products such as piping, electrical wire, etc. The office manager has the apparent authority to order office supplies, and the purchasing department has the apparent authority to order all types of supplies. The purchasing department has the right to order for the entire firm, and usually relies on purchase orders. Any purchase that requires a written contract should bear the signature of an officer.

While the law may vary somewhat from state to state, the basic legal principle is that the employer is responsible if the employee had apparent authority to act on behalf of the business. This apparent authority may consist of the duties generally exercised by the employee who is a purchasing manager. The title of the employee, such as a "manager" or "officer," may in itself indicate apparent authority. Past dealings with the creditor where the employee has ordered merchandise in the past may also indicate apparent authority. In these cases, the creditor may be justified in relying upon the fact that the person ordering had the necessary authority to bind the employer to a contract.

Yet, each matter must be treated on a case-by-case basis since circumstances might exist which will clearly refute the "apparent" authority. For example, if the employer had already notified the vendor that all sales must be processed through the purchasing department and must carry a purchase order, a sale to the office manager for office supplies could be attacked on the grounds that the vendor was fully aware of the procedures of the purchasing firm.

Of course, the smaller the firm, the more authority each employee has and the more hats each employee wears. With a firm that employs 20 people, one person may be office manager, secretary, and purchasing officer. Actually, the creditor's position is much stronger if a salesman personally visited the debtor's place of business. In this instance, the salesman can attest to the apparent authority of the party who ordered the merchandise. Where the order is by mail, the signature and title should appear on the order form. The difficulty arises if the order is by telephone. Often, a firm does business on a regular basis with the debtor with no problems. An order is placed over the telephone. The debtor then encounters financial problems, and then says the employee had no authority to order in order to evade payment. Since the order was made over the telephone, the creditor may perceive his position as very weak, and not press too hard for payment.

Most employees who order have the authority to do so, and this should be the general position of the creditor. Practically speaking, an employee has no motivation to exceed his authority since no benefit accrues to the employee. Thus, this device is merely another stalling technique, and should be treated as such. The debtor firm should be told that the employee did have apparent authority, that the employer is thereby responsible, and if payment is not received the matter will be referred to a collection agency or attorney. This advice is always tempered by the fact that some validity may exist to this excuse, and the telephone worker should be aware of the legal principles and consequences of proceeding with suit. A well-documented file and careful inquiry should be made before a decision is made as to the proper avenue to take.

Another course of action is to accept a return of the merchandise or to settle, depending upon the inclination of both parties.

Dr: The law offices of Jones, Jones, and Green. May I help you?

Cr: This is the National Supplies Corporation.

Dr: With whom do you wish to speak?

Cr: Who does the ordering?

Dr: The office manager.

Cr: I will speak to her.

Dr: Ms. Miller speaking, may I help you?

Cr: We received an order for a coffee maker about three months ago, and we shipped it to you. We sent you two invoices and letter and have had no response.

Dr: Yes, I know. This was a catalog item.

Cr: Yes, it is.

Dr: Do you have an order?

Cr: Yes, we do.

Dr: Who signed it?

Cr: It appears to be Mary Monohan, or something like that.

Dr: Well, she had no authority to order the coffee maker. It is still here, unpacked.

Cr: She signed on behalf of the firm, and if she had no authority, that is your problem, not mine. We accepted the order in good faith and shipped.

Dr: Yes, I know, but we have no need for the machine and she really had no authority to order it. If you want, you can sue her and I will give her the machine.

Cr: I'm sorry, but we shipped to you, and unless we get payment by Monday, May 7, we will have to refer this to our collection agency/attorney. Of course, maybe we could discuss the matter a little and perhaps resolve our differences.

Dr: Maybe I could use it. Could you adjust the price?

Comment on Dialogue: The debtor is a law firm, and this fact must be considered. Suing a law firm is playing in the debtor's ballpark. A debtor in a different business might encourage the creditor to be more forceful in their approach. A settlement is probably the best result in this case.

EMPLOYEE NO LONGER EMPLOYED

Usually, the employer claims the merchandise was not received and that somehow the employee who left managed to remove the merchandise. This might be acceptable if the nature of the merchandise would warrant someone removing it from the office. Believability is stretched when the merchandise consists of four cartons of garbage bags. A direct question should be placed to the employer asking whether the merchandise is still in their possession. If the answer is positive, something exists which can be the subject negotiation. If the answer is negative, the employer must indirectly accuse the employee of stealing the merchandise. Most employers are reluctant to make this accusation, unless, of course, it is true.

The normal response should be the same as when the employer claims that the employee had no apparent authority. The debtor should be told that the employee had no apparent authority, the order was accepted, the merchandise or equipment was delivered, the money is due, and if payment is not made, the matter will be referred to a collection agency or attorney by a specific date. The status of the employee is totally immaterial and of no consequence. Only the ordering of the goods and the apparent authority of the employee to order are the essential ingredients for liability to attach to the employer.

The law may vary from state to state. When a situation of this nature is encountered, consultation with your attorney is recommended.

Dr: Sunny Valley Medical Group.

Cr: May I speak to the bookkeeping department?

Dr: Just a minute.

Dr: Mrs. Gruman speaking.

Cr: This is County Computer Supplies. We have an open bill of $153 for a business program. It was delivered to you over six weeks ago.

Dr: What was the program?

Cr: A program to handle taxes and other income.

Dr: I don't know anything about it.

Cr: It was picked up by a Jean Tyler.

Dr: She's no longer working here.

Cr: Well, that makes no difference.

Dr: It makes a world of difference. She was not authorized to order any office supplies. She was a nurse to one of the group's doctors. I'll be glad to give you her address.

Cr: What doctor did she work for?

Dr: That's not important.

Cr: Look, Mrs. Gruman. Ms. Tyler ordered the program while she was still employed and personally picked it up on behalf of the medical group. We delivered it, and I fully believe we are entitled to payment.

Dr: Not if she was not authorized.

Cr: Well, if she worked for the doctor as a nurse or receptionist, she certainly was authorized to order a program for his computer.

Dr: She was merely a medical assistant.

Cr: You originally said she was a nurse. Do you still have the program?

Dr: I told you I know nothing about it. I'll give you the address and telephone number of Ms. Tyler and you can speak to her.

Cr: She ordered for you. You know she is not going to pay, especially if she does not have the diskette.

Dr: Well, she may have the diskette.

Cr: Are you saying she took it with her?

Dr: I'm not saying anything.

Cr: Well, could you speak to the doctor.

Dr: It doesn't make any difference.

Cr: May I have the name of the doctor so I can speak to him?

Dr: That won't be necessary. I will speak to the doctor.

Cr: All right, find out if you still have the program.

Dr: I will speak to the doctor.

Cr: Will you please call me to let me know if the doctor has it?

Dr: I said I will speak to him.

Cr: Well, if I do not hear from you by Monday, May 7, I will be forced to refer this to our collection agency/attorney and I don't want to do that if we can resolve this matter. Please look into this, and be sure to call me before Monday, May 7.

Dr: Thank you and goodbye.

Comment on Dialogue: The creditor is dealing with a very sophisticated office manager who used every device possible to defer any decision on this matter. But the creditor was persistent and knew the legal validity of his claim, and thus was able to persuade the office manager to investigate the situation. Please note that after the creditor caught the office manager in a contradiction, he did not press it, but changed the subject. The creditor still wants to collect the money and negotiate a payment plan, if necessary. Pressing this mistake by the office manager would have achieved nothing but forcing her into a corner to defend herself. As a result, she would have been even less cooperative.

PURCHASE ORDER NEEDED

Many of the large corporations—and today even some of the small to medium firms—utilize purchase orders before a purchase is made. In some instances the only department authorized to issue the purchase order is naturally the purchasing department. Lack of a purchase order is often used to defer payment. Nevertheless, the creditor should examine the circumstances behind this excuse.

Perhaps the order emanated from a low-level employee and was actually unauthorized. In this instance, exerting pressure on the firm will produce only a negative response. The conditions and circumstances under which the order was obtained should be carefully scrutinized. Inquiry should be made as to whether the firm received the product and was using the product. If they did receive the merchandise, then with or without a purchase order, the firm is liable for immediate payment.

Furthermore, the firm is certainly liable if a person with authority ordered, even though no purchase order was issued. Again, the key is whether the firm received the merchandise. It is not important whether the firm used the merchandise as long as it was received. Evidence of receipt may range from the firm's oral acknowledgment to documented evidence of a common carrier receipt, Federal Express receipt, United Parcel receipt, or U.S. Postal Service receipt. If such evidence is available, impress upon the debtor that it is liable with or without a purchase order.

> **Cr:** Is this the accounts payable department?
> **Dr:** Yes, who is this?
> **Cr:** This is the Executive Cleaning Company.
> **Dr:** Yes.
> **Cr:** We have a bill for $1,100 which has been open since May. We have written several times and left a message once, but nothing has happenend.
> **Dr:** What's the purchase order?
> **Cr:** What do you mean purchase order?
> **Dr:** Without a purchase order, we do not pay any bills.

Cr: The order came from Mr. Harris for 50 mops, 20 buckets, and some other cleaning material.

Dr: Well, get Mr. Harris to submit the purchase order.

Cr: But I was just told that Mr. Harris left the firm about a month ago.

Dr: That is your problem. Speak to his successor and get me a purchase order.

Cr: I spoke to his successor, and he will not approve one since he was not here when the merchandise was ordered.

Dr: Well, I would like to help you, but there is nothing I can do.

Cr: Let me speak to the comptroller.

Dr: I am the comptroller.

Cr: Well, you received the merchandise and are using it now, so you should pay for it.

Dr: Not without a purchase order.

Cr: Look, you received the goods and you are using them. As far as I am concerned, you are liable for payment. Because you have an internal procedure requiring purchase orders and your employees do not comply with this procedure, this is not my fault, and no court will lay the blame at my feet. No one told me I needed a purchase order. If you do not pay the bill within seven days by May 7, I will refer the matter to my attorney to immediately institute suit. I am sorry, but I am not going to take a loss because your employee did not issue a purchase order.

Dr: Well....

Comment on Dialogue: A strong position was necessary, and it was used in response to an unreasonable excuse.

NEED PROOF OF DELIVERY

Proof of delivery should not be furnished to the debtor unless the creditor sincerely believes that the merchandise may not have arrived. If the telephone call is being made after several letters, and this is the first personal contact with the debtor, the question must be asked, "Why didn't the debtor respond to the letters with this claim of nondelivery?" Why did the debtor wait until the telephone call to raise the issue of nondelivery? The clear inference is that this allegation is just an excuse to ask for an extension of time. It should be treated in the same manner that is extended to any other request for an extension of time.

Cr: We wrote you several letters about this past due bill, and we still have not received payment.

Dr: Maybe we didn't receive it. Wait a minute. No. I find no record of having received it.

Cr: It was shipped over three months ago.

Dr: Why don't you send me proof of delivery, and then I may be able to trace it down?

Cr: We have proof of delivery, and we want payment now.

Dr: I said we never received it. If you have proof of delivery, send it to me.

Cr: Sir. We have proof of delivery from a common carrier, and it shows that Mr. Wiggins receipted the goods in January. Now, maybe you didn't receive it, but one of your employees with authority accepted it on your behalf. After that, it is your problem. I am not sending you the receipt because it would mean another two weeks without payment, but I will send the receipt after I receive payment. Either I receive your check within the next three days by Monday, May 7, or I will send this to a collection agency/attorney for immediate processing. Now, you know what that means.

Dr: OK, let me look into this....

Of course, if the request for proof of delivery is made after the first or second letter, the creditor should comply. Also, if the telephone call is the first effort to collect the debt or is made shortly after the first letter, compliance is in order.

BOOKKEEPER ON VACATION

Many variations of this tactic exist: the boss, my wife, the comptroller, the president, or just about anyone is either ill, in the hospital, out of town, on vacation, or confined to his bed with a rare tropical disease. The result is that the person who handles or approves payment is not available. In addition, this person is the only person who can arrange or approve payment. The flaw in this argument is that the business continues to operate in every other way, so why should only one operation of the business, i.e., paying bills, be discontinued? Payroll is being met, the telephone company is being paid, the electric and gas company are being paid, and certainly the rent is being paid. Accordingly, this stratagem should always be considered as an excuse for deferring payment.

Dr: I know about the arrearages on the loan, but I can't issue a check until the president returns, since he is the only one that signs checks.

Cr: When will he return?

Dr: He is visiting China, and he will be away three weeks.

Cr: We can't wait three weeks.

Dr: Well, I don't see what else I can do. I have to wait for the president to return.

Cr: Well, then wait for his return. In the meanwhile, I am referring this to our attorney to prepare a summons and complaint, so the president will have something else to read when he returns.

Dr: Don't be a wise guy. I said I would like to pay, but I can't.

Cr: I don't question your sincerity. You have to do what you must do, and I have to do what I must do. In plain terms, I cannot wait another three weeks. The loan is three months in arrears, and is scheduled for referral to an attorney.

Dr: Well, OK. I may speak to him long distance tomorrow....

Comment on Dialogue: The business appears to be operating in every other respect and checks are being issued, so there is no reason to accept a delay in payment because the president is away.

FINANCIAL TROUBLE

When the debtor admits that the reason for nonpayment is a lack of funds, the debtor is at this moment honest and sincere. This is the main reason for nonpayment, and all of the above excuses are only facades to cover the true reason. When the debtor chooses to be truthful, at least the creditor can proceed with a line of questioning to elicit more information concerning the debtor's financial position. At this point, the creditor is in a position to make a considered judgment as to whether the debtor is entitled to an extension of time. Converting the above excuses to the "real" reason should be the goal of the creditor. The real reason enables the creditor to obtain a fair picture of the chances of ultimately obtaining payment. This dismal picture may or may not be the catalyst for refinancing or reducing payments.

Dr: The bookkeeper is in the hospital.

Cr: I am sorry to hear that, but what is the real reason? Are you short of money?

—or—

Dr: The check is in the mail.

Cr: Look, this is the third time you promised that the check was in the mail. If you can't meet your bills, tell me the problem and maybe we can work this out.

—or—

Dr: I'll check my records.

Cr: Checking your records is not going to produce money. If you're having financial problems, let me know what they are. I understand that these things come up. But don't keep making promises that you break the next week. What's the real problem?

THE COMPUTER IS DOWN

The excuse usually sounds something like the following:

1. "The computer's down, and we don't know when they are going to fix it. As soon as it is fixed, you'll get your check. There's nothing I can do. You know what it is when computers take over your business."

2. "We just went off our parallel program with our new computer, and already we have a bug in the system. They've been working on it two days, and they still can't get it to work. One hundred thousand dollars down the drain and I can't even find out how much money is owed to me. It shouldn't be more than a day or two, and we should be back to normal. So be a little patient, and we will mail you the money as soon as it is fixed."

3. "I wish I was doing things by hand. At least I could operate my business. With a computer you are at the mercy of the programmer or service department. I've been calling for two days and I still haven't seen a repairman. I'm as anxious as you to repair this thing so I can send out my checks."

They all add up to a very deliberate and carefully orchestrated excuse to avoid making a payment for another week. The business is still operating. The rent was paid, the payroll was met, and the other basic expenses have all been paid. *There is no reason why a check could not be manually written.* The response to this scenario is to insist on payment, and use a closing statement.

Dr: The computer is down, but I've been assured it will be working by Monday. Give us a few days to run payroll and inventory, and by the end of next week, a check will be sent to you.

Cr: This payment is two months in arrears, and we must have a payment by Monday, May 7. I am sure you can write a check manually and mail it to me. We just cannot give you any further extension, with or without computer problems. Please be certain that we receive the check by Monday, May 7, for that is the very last day before your loan will be scheduled for further action.

CHAPTER 13

Special Legal Problems with Businesses

A wide variety of situations are encountered in a telephone collection call to a business. These range from the assertion of bankruptcy to being faced with a permanently disconnected telephone number. The telephone worker should have a basic knowledge of the bankruptcy law, since bankruptcy is a business "fact of life," and how to react to this depressing fact requires an elementary understanding of the bankruptcy law. Although this chapter primarily deals with a business bankruptcy, consumers also file for bankruptcy. This knowledge will be helpful when faced with consumer bankruptcy. Other laws affect businesses which do not affect consumers, and an attempt will be made to present these laws in an understandable form.

The second part of this chapter deals with the problems that may be encountered when dealing with special types of business debtors.

Bankruptcy laws are amended and repealed. State laws affecting businesses and the collection of debts vary from state to state, and also are amended and changed. Where appropriate and before any definitive action is taken, consultation with an attorney is recommended.

BANKRUPTCY

The word "bankruptcy" usually creates fear and anxiety in the hearts of creditors. Yet, the end of the world has not arrived. A very brief explanation of the Bankruptcy Reform Act is in order.

Four Ways for Bankruptcy to Be Legally Declared

The four principal chapters under which a person or business may file for bankruptcy are as follows:

Chapter 7—Straight Bankruptcy—Individual or Corporation—Liquidation.

Chapter 9—Adjustment of Debt of Municipalities.

Chapter 11—Reorganization—Applies to Corporations, Partnerships, or Individual.

Chapter 13—Wage Earner Plan—Individual only—Wage Earner or Individual Doing Business.

Under Chapter 7, an individual or a corporation may file a voluntary petition in bankruptcy, and merely must allege an inability to meet debts as they fall due. Involuntary petitions may be filed by creditors. Involuntary petitions are required to allege that the debtor is not paying his debts as they become due.

Under Chapter 11, a private or public corporation, a partnership, or an individual may file voluntarily if the bankrupt's debts cannot be met as they mature. An allegation of insolvency is not necessary. An involuntary petition may be filed by creditors under this Chapter.

Chapter 9 is restricted to municipalities, and thus does not affect businesses or consumers.

Under Chapter 13, a wage earner may file a petition and arrange to repay all or part of his obligations over a period of time. The Chapter allows noncorporate businesses, such as sole proprietorships or partnerships, to file under this Chapter. The unsecured debts cannot exceed $100,000 and the secured debts cannot exceed $350,000.

The duty of the trustee in the bankruptcy under Chapter 7 is to marshal and collect all the assets, sell the assets at the best possible price, and distribute the remaining funds to the creditors, after payment of expenses and the fees of the trustee.

In Chapter 11, the business continues to operate, generally under the supervision of the debtor in possession or trustee. The debtor submits a plan to the court to pay the creditors a percentage of the balance due over a period of time. In Chapter 13, the individual submits a similar plan to pay his creditors over a period of time.

Supervision of Court

The important ingredient of a bankruptcy is that all proceedings, including the sale of assets, payment of fees and expenses, dealing with secured creditors, and the amount distributed to the creditors are under the supervision of the bankruptcy court and require the approval of the judge presiding over the bankruptcy.

Stay of Action: The filing of a petition in bankruptcy by the debtor *"stays" all actions by creditors against debtors* (prohibits any further action against debtor except in bankruptcy court). This includes both collection efforts and lawsuits by creditors. The recourse of the creditor is to file a proof of claim with the bankruptcy court in which the petition is filed. The bankruptcy court notifies all the creditors of the debtor that a petition has been filed. Under Chapter 13, the filing of a petition will stay action against consumer guarantors, co-makers, and endorsers if the installment plan provides that the debts of the bankrupt ultimately will be paid in full. Generally, the filing of a petition in bankruptcy stays any and all lawsuits, foreclosure actions, and other proceedings to recover property. Specific creditors may, on application to the bankruptcy court, obtain relief from the stay.

Reaffirming a Debt: A promise, either orally or in writing, to repay a debt by a bankrupt after a petition in bankruptcy has been filed, is usually unenforceable if the debt has been listed in the schedules filed with the bankruptcy court. Reaffirmation of a debt obligates a debtor to repay an obligation, even after discharge. The approval by the bankruptcy court of any reaffirmation agreement is required to become legally binding.

Secured Creditors: Secured creditors, whether holding liens on real estate, automobiles, or computers, etc., may apply to the court to enforce the lien. The court may limit the rights of secured creditors, such as permitting the bankrupt to retain an automobile and pay the creditor the appraised value of the vehicle rather than the balance due upon the loan

Proof of Claim: A proof of claim is merely a statement by the creditor of the amount due to creditor, the date of the transaction, the nature of the transaction, the documents to support the transaction, such as a note, mortgage, invoice, or statement, and, of course, the name and address of the creditor. Forms may be provided by the bankruptcy court or may be obtained at the local stationery store. Creditors should file a proof of claim when they receive a notice of bankruptcy or notice of assignment for the benefit of creditors. Failure to file within the prescribed time may result in a forfeiture of the rights of the creditor to a distribution. Consultation with an attorney is suggested.

With this in mind, some suggestions are in order upon being informed that the debtor has filed a petition in bankruptcy.

1. Do not make any threat to enforce collection.
2. Obtain the date of filing, the court where the petition was filed, and the bankruptcy index or filing number.
3. If an attorney was used by the bankrupt, obtain the name, address, and telephone number of the attorney for the bankrupt.
4. If a trustee was appointed, obtain the name, address, and telephone number of the trustee.
5. If the creditor has a lien on property, attempt to obtain the location of the property securing the lien, and the present use of the property in the business.

Warning—No Notification of Bankruptcy: Even if the creditor has not yet received a notice of bankruptcy, and the creditor believes that no such petition has been filed, the creditor still should be very careful when a debtor alleges a bankruptcy petition has been filed. The failure to receive a bankruptcy notice is far from conclusive evidence that a bankruptcy has not been filed. Bankruptcy notices are sent by regular mail and the addresses are copied from the list of creditors contained in the petition prepared by the bankrupt. A mistake in copying by the court clerk, a failure in the post office to deliver, or delivery to another department of the creditor, may result in the creditor not knowing about the bankruptcy action. The creditor, however, is deemed to have notice after the clerk of the bankruptcy court files an affidavit of mailing. Accordingly, after being told about a bankruptcy proceeding, the creditor should check and verify care-

fully whether or not a petition has been filed. To proceed as if a
petition has not been filed may expose the creditor to liability if, in
fact, a petition actually was filed. Consultation with your attorney is
recommended.

Secured creditors should inquire deeply concerning the collateral. This information will be very helpful to their attorney in
deciding how to proceed before the bankruptcy court.

Dr: RB Machinery Company.

Cr: This is AC Machinery Company, Mr. Barlow. Is Harris there?

Dr: This is Harris.

Cr: I haven't received your check. You promised that I would receive
it this week, without fail. What are you doing to me?

Dr: We filed a Chapter 11 bankruptcy petition on Monday. That is the
only way I can stay in business.

Cr: What about the bill?

Dr: Well, I think we will be able to submit a plan to pay off a good
percentage of all our bills.

Cr: I'm not jumping with joy, but give me some information.

Dr: OK.

Cr: When did you do this?

Dr: May 7, Monday.

Cr: What Court?

Dr: Southern District, New York.

Cr: What is the bankruptcy number?

Dr: 5555/88.

Cr: Who is your attorney?

Dr: Fried and Fried, 555 Main Street. Their number is 555-1234.

Cr: Has a trustee been appointed?

Dr: I don't know. You better speak to my attorney.

Cr: What about the fork lift we sold you? Do you still have it?

Dr: Of course, we need it to operate.

Cr: We have a mortgage on that, and I think you are four payments
behind.

Dr: My attorney says I can continue to operate, and he will submit a
plan of repayment to the court. Look, Barlow, I'm trying to stay in
business.

Cr: I know.

Dr: Look, we need some new presses. You will continue to do business
with us?

Cr: I don't know. I will have to speak to our corporate counsel. I'm not going to give you credit. Maybe on a cash basis.

Dr: But you know that you become a preferred creditor in Chapter 11 if you extend credit after the filing of the petition.

Cr: I will have to discuss that with our attorney.

Dr: OK.

Cr: I wish you luck, Harris, and I'll be in touch.

Dr: OK.

HELPFUL HINT: Extension of Credit to Bankrupt. The extension of credit to a bankrupt in Chapter 11 is a decision which requires careful consideration and consultation with your attorney. While such an extension of credit does give you priority over general unsecured creditors created prior to the filing of the petition and certain other creditors, the repayment of the credit to the Chapter 11 creditor comes after certain trustee expenses and administrative expenses in Chapter 11 have been paid. If the petition is then converted to a Chapter 7 (where the bankrupt does not successfully enter a plan of repayment or discharge a plan of repayment and the court directs a liquidation of the business under Chapter 7), additional expenses in Chapter 7 may come before the creditor. Consultation with counsel is not only recommended but encouraged.

ASSIGNMENT FOR THE BENEFIT OF CREDITORS

Basically, an assignment for the benefit of creditors is the state equivalent of a federal bankruptcy. Each state has passed a law enabling a business to assign and transfer all of its assets to an assignee (trustee) whose main function is to sell all the assets at the best possible price and use the funds to pay all the expenses of the sale, and then distribute the remaining funds to the creditors on a pro rata basis. The statute provides for notice to all creditors. The assignee is entitled to a fee of about 5 percent of the total sale price of the assets.

The laws from state to state vary to a greater or lesser degree. The principal distinction is that some state laws provide no court procedure to examine or question the bankrupt to determine if fraud, deceit, or self-dealing occurred, while others do provide for this procedure.

The state proceeding also stays any action against the debtor, and the distribution to the creditors is in full satisfaction of the claims of the creditors.

The normal approach in response to an assignment for the benefit of creditors is somewhat similar to a bankruptcy. Obtain the index number, the court, and the date of filing, the name and address of the assignee, and the name and address of the attorney for the assignee, as well as the name and address of the attorney for the debtor. If security is involved, ascertain the location of the property. This information should be transmitted to your attorney, with whom you should consult.

BULK SALES BY BUSINESS DEBTOR

Most states have statutes which permit a creditor to sell the assets of a business for an amount less than its liabilities. The law provides that written notice of such a sale must be given to the creditors. This notice should be quickly forwarded to your attorney since prompt action may be required.

If the first notice of a bulk sale is received through a telephone collection call, a request should be made upon the debtor to forward a copy of the notice to the creditor. At the same time, basic information should be obtained, including the date of the sale, the place of the sale, the name and address of the debtor's attorney, the location of the property if it is security for a loan, and any other pertinent information. Of course, consult immediately with your attorney.

The debtor receives an amount for the sale of his assets, which is inadequate to pay all his creditors, and distributes this amount to the creditors. The creditor may take action with respect to the bulk sale if he feels that the debtor is not treating his creditors fairly. We recommend that you consult immediately with your attorney.

Dr: Hello.

Cr: Who is this?

Dr: This is Randy, who is this?

Cr: This is the telephone company, Mr. Cooper.

Dr: What can I do for you?

Cr: Is this Randolph Stewart, the president of Stewart Carpeting, Inc.?

Dr: That is correct.

Cr: Have you moved, since this is a new number?

Dr: No, but we are not operating anymore since we have arranged a bulk sale of our business.

Cr: You mean you have closed your doors?

Dr: I suggest you speak to my attorney.

Cr: Give me his name and address.

Dr: Day and Day, Main Street, telephone number 555-1214.

Cr: When is the sale to be held?

Dr: Next week. Didn't you receive notice of the sale?

Cr: No, can you send me the notice?

Dr: OK.

Cr: Why is the sale being held so quickly?

Dr: We gave the notice required by law.

Cr: What date?

Dr: May 7.

Cr: Is the sale being held at your store?

Dr: No, at the warehouse.

Cr: Where is that?

Dr: Across town, opposite the quarry.

Cr: Who is purchasing?

Dr: I suggest you speak to my attorney. He will give you all the information you need, and he will send you the legal notice.

Cr: Are you paying the creditors in full?

Dr: Speak to my attorney.

Cr: OK.

SHERIFF'S SALE OF DEBTOR'S ASSETS

This occurs when a sheriff or a marshal schedules a sale of some or all of the assets of a debtor to satisfy a judgment that a creditor has obtained. The sale of the assets pays off the judgment, and if any surplus is realized, the amount is returned to the debtor or used to pay off other judgment creditors which have asserted liens. Nevertheless, in most cases the proceeds of the sale of the assets are insufficient to pay off the judgment creditor who scheduled the sale, and rarely is there a surplus for other creditors.

A judgment creditor is a creditor who has sued the debtor and won his case either at trial or by default, and obtained a judgment. Obtaining the information concerning the sale, the date, the location of the sale, the name and address of the sheriff, the name and address of the purchaser (if one purchaser), and the name and address of the attorneys all may be helpful if future action is contemplated. Again, consult with counsel.

WHEN DEBTOR IS OUT OF BUSINESS

Questions should be propounded to the party answering the telephones as to his knowledge of the business debtor, and any of the principals. In most instances the responses will be negative, but at least the effort should be made.

Cr: This is the RX Company, and I would like to speak to the bookkeeper.

Dr: What about?

Cr: About $5,050 due to us since the beginning of the year.

Dr: This is the Center Valley Fertilizer Company, and we just got this telephone number a week ago.

Cr: Are you Green Ltd. at 555 Main Street?

Dr: No, this is State Street.

Cr: Oh! I'm sorry.

Dr: Green Ltd. must be out of business, because I've been getting quite a few calls like this.

Cr: Well, thanks anyway.

Dr: OK, goodbye.

Cr: Goodbye.

Comment on Dialogue: Most telephone companies do not reassign a telephone number until at least six months after the prior number was disconnected. If the new owner of the telephone number is receiving calls concerning the debtor, the creditor may assume that some very persistent creditors are searching for the debtor. Immediate steps are in order.

NEW OWNER

Often, the party answering will state that the business is under new management. New management may mean good news or bad news. If the new owner purchased the stock of the corporation, and was operating under the same corporate entity and the same name, the new owner is liable in the same manner as the old owner/debtor, for it is the same corporation. If the new owner organized a new corporation, and merely purchased all the assets of the old owner, but none of the liabilities, the recourse of the debtor lies with the old owner, i.e., the original corporate debtor. The creditor should inquire as to what took place, and if necessary, should contact the new owner's attorney. Usually, if your contact is with an employee, that employee may not know exactly what transpired, so an effort should be made to speak to the new owner. Of course, consult with your attorney.

Operating under a different corporate name indicates a purchase of assets and no liability for the prior owner's debts. Operating under the same corporate name indicates a purchase of stock and, thus, liability. But even operating under the same corporate name is not conclusive, and if liability is denied, consultation with an attorney is suggested.

Dr: Hello.

Cr: This is the Main Street Electrical Company, Mr. Robbins speaking.

Dr: Yes?

Cr: We wrote you several letters about your past due debt of $750 for some electrical work that we did about six months ago.

Dr: You did it six months ago?

Cr: Yes, we wired up some machinery.

Dr: Well, we just became the owner 60 days ago, so I suggest you contact the prior party.

Cr: What do you mean?

Dr: We bought the assets of the Argo Manufacturing Company and negotiated a new lease with the landlord. We are J & D Manufacturing Corporation.

Cr: How come you still have the same telephone number?

Dr: Because that was part of the agreement. You may contact our attorney.

Cr: Where is Mr. Wallace, the owner?

Dr: He left for Florida to retire.

Cr: Do you have his address?

Dr: No, but my attorney should have it, since we are sending him monthly payments.

Cr: Where in Florida?

Dr: I think Fort Lauderdale.

Cr: Did he buy a house?

Dr: I believe so.

Cr: Was there a bulk sale?

Dr: I don't know what that is. Please speak to my attorney.

Cr: Did you buy his accounts receivable also?

Dr: No, all we bought was the machinery and equipment. He kept the receivables and payables.

Cr: Give me the name and address of your attorney, please.

Comment on Dialogue: The creditor now knows that the principal has left for Fort Lauderdale, bought a house, and is receiving installment payments. The creditor also knows that the corporation with whom he did business still has accounts receivable and perhaps other assets. The next step is to furnish this information to your attorney, and follow your attorney's advice on the best method of collecting this debt.

REFERRAL TO ATTORNEY

An employee of the business who answers the telephone may refer the caller to an attorney and provide a telephone number. The creditor should use the number to contact the attorney. Often, the attorney will advise the creditor of a sale, assignment for benefit of creditors, a bankruptcy, or other information.

Occasionally, the creditor is unable to reach the attorney, and the attorney does not respond to the message that is left. The recommendation in this set of circumstances is to consult your own attorney, for he will be in a better position to obtain the information that you seek.

SKIP TRACING

Trying to locate a corporation that went out of business is more difficult than finding the secret of life. If a corporation is not receiving mail, does not have a telephone number, and no notice of bankruptcy, etc., has been received, and no fraud is apparent, with few exceptions the best course is to absorb the loss. Stories can be told of huge amounts recovered after being faced with the most bleak and dismal scenarios, but these are the exceptions to the rule. The lesson to be learned is that rules sometimes are to be broken, and that every delinquent account must be treated on a case-by-case basis.

On the other hand, sole proprietorships and partnerships are *people,* and people can be located. The telephone in the hands of a sophisticated telephone worker is the best device to use to locate people. Using the telephone for locating debtors who have skipped requires the ability to "ask." This ability to "ask" is a necessary characteristic of every successful business person, and certainly it is essential to any form of skip tracing by telephone. Of course, compliance with the Debt Collection Practices Act is recommended (Section 804) even though the act applies to consumer debts for "personal, family or household" purposes (Section 803).

For instance, if the new owner of the business answers the telephone, the questioning might go as follows:

Cr: Under what name do you operate?

Dr: Clark Corporation, same as the old owner.

Cr: Well, then you are still liable for this debt of $5,000 of Clark Corporation.

Dr: No, we only bought the machinery and equipment. My attorney said I am not liable for the debts.

Cr: But you are using the same name.

Dr: I know, but that is what my attorney said. Call him.

Cr: OK, give me his name and address.

Dr: John Smith, 435 Main Street.

Cr: By the way, do you know where the old owner is?

Dr: He moved to Springfield and is going into business there.

Cr: What kind of business?

Dr: Same as here, a letter shop.

Cr: Do you have his address?

Dr: No, but my attorney has since we have to give him some notices under our purchase agreement.

Comment on Dialogue: The contents of the next telephone call to the attorney is obvious. If the new owner is liable, the account will be paid since the new owner is operating a viable business. If the new owner is not liable, the creditor is on his way to locating the old owner.

In this example, the party answering the telephone responds that the debtor went out of business by virtue of a marshal's sale (same as sheriff's sale). The first question to ask is who is speaking. If it is the landlord, ask questions as to the date of the sale, the name of the attorney for the debtor, the name and address of the sheriff or auctioneer, and, of course, ask where the debtor is now.

Cr: Who is speaking?

Dr: This is the owner of the property. Who is this?

Cr: This is the National Bank. Isn't this AB Real Estate Agency?

Dr: No, there was a sheriff's sale two days ago, and all the desks, typewriters, and filing cabinets were sold.

Cr: Oh!!

Dr: They are out of business.

Cr: Do you have the name of the deputy from the sheriff's office who conducted the sale?

Dr: Yes, it was Herbert Jackson.

Cr: What was the date of the sale?

Dr: May 7, Wednesday.

Cr: Do you know who bought at the sale?

Dr: No.

Cr: What was the name of the attorney for the debtor?

Dr: I don't know, but the deputy should have that.

Cr: Do you know where Mr. Spartan is?

Dr: He was here yesterday and asked me to collect his mail for him.

Cr: Were you to send it somewhere?

Dr: No, he said he was going to pick it up.

Cr: Do you know where he lives?

Dr: No, except it's probably in Orange County because he said it takes him 20 minutes to drive north on Interstate 10 to his home.

Cr: Do you know if he is going into business again?

Dr: No, he didn't say anything.

Comment on Dialogue: The creditor asked many questions, and continued even though the answers were negative.

In this example, the third party (Tp) answering the telephone responds that the debtor has left the space and owes him a lot of money. The conversation might develop along the following lines:

Cr: When did the debtor leave?

Tp: Look, I only sublet space to him. I don't know when he left. One day he was here, the next day he was gone.

Cr: Do you know where he lived?

Tp: Yes, but I called there and the telephone was disconnected.

Cr: Could I have his address?

Tp: Sure, 425 Apple Lane.

Cr: Is he married?

Tp: Yes, she was a real nut.

Cr: What is her name?

Tp: Mary, but what difference does that make?

Cr: Did he have any partners?

Tp: No, he was a loner

Cr: How much does he owe you?

Tp: $1,500 for three months rent. He must have paid his telephone bill since it is still working.

Cr: Do you know what bank he dealt with?

Tp: The only bank is First National down the street, but that is a waste of time.

Cr: I know, but it's worthwhile checking.

Comment on Dialogue: The questions could continue depending upon the circumstances. The telephone worker has determined that his wife's name is Mary, and the name of his bank. If the debtor moved to another town, the telephone number may be listed under the name of the wife. The bank may have information on file as to addresses, officers, or the names of authorized signatories. This information may be helpful after an attorney has obtained a judgment, for a witness subpoena directed to the bank will compel them to disclose this information. Asking for information is most important. The information obtained may later become very useful for locating assets as opposed to locating the debtor. Sometimes, perfectly harmless information fits together neatly in a puzzle or later becomes important. As long as the party on the telephone is willing to talk and furnish information, either negative or positive, the rule is to continue to ask. Naturally, the efforts must be tempered by the amount involved. A $50 debt is not a $50,000 debt.

Information on a loan application, a credit application, or an application of any kind becomes important in the attempt to locate a debtor. Consider the following:

1. The landlord usually can furnish the apartment number and whether the rent is current.

2. The board of a condominium or cooperative has considerable information, but usually will refuse to furnish this information. Nevertheless, a diplomatic approach to the supervising employee might produce interesting information.

3. Some applications require the name and address of a relative or friend not living with the applicant.

4. Insurance companies and banks normally are not too cooperative in furnishing information concerning their insured or

their depositors, but verification of insurance and bank accounts usually can be obtained.

Public Records: Use of information filed in the county clerk's office sometimes will provide names and addresses of partnerships and sole proprietors. The examination of the partnership certificate will provide the home addresses of individual partners. An examination of a certificate of incorporation will usually provide the name of the attorney who did the incorporation and the name of the incorporator.

Warning—Sections 804 and 805 of the Debt Collection Practices Act and State Laws: In all instances where third parties are contacted, Sections 804 and 805 should be carefully reviewed. Section 804 deals with the acquisition of location information, and 805 deals with communications with third parties. While the Debt Collection Practices Act is concerned with consumers, and not with businesses, the creditor, in locating a debtor, is dealing with a consumer and an individual although it is in connection with a business debt. The better course of action would be to comply with the Act in every respect or face the possibility of a court deciding that the actions were subject to the Act. Review of state laws that affect collection is also recommended

SPECIAL BUSINESSES

Hospitals: Special care and special knowledge must be instilled in the telephone worker who is employed by a hospital. Knowledge of terms and conditions of reimbursement of the various medical plans is absolutely essential. Most debtors believe their insurance plan covers the entire charge for their hospital stay, whether in-patient or out-patient. The telephone worker must be familiar with the intricacies of Blue Cross, Blue Shield, Medicaid, and Medicare, as well as HIP and other group medical plans.

The telephone worker must take the time to explain why the balance is due. In many instances, the patient is still recovering from the illness and is not working, so appropriate post-dating may be in order so that another call is made four to eight weeks later, after the patient has recovered and has returned to employment.

Telephone calls from a hospital creditor produce distinct responses to avoid making payment. The following are the general categories:

Insurance: Most people carry some sort of medical insurance. The telephone worker must realize and emphasize that the hospital has no connection or relationship with the insurance carrier. The main ingredient of the hospital contract is that the hospital will provide medical services to the patient and the patient will pay. The patient, in turn, contracts with an insurance carrier to pay all or part of the bills of the patient. The patient accomplishes this by obtaining Blue Cross and Blue Shield coverage, Major Medical Insurance, or belongs to a Health Maintenance Organization (HMO). After payment to the hospital, the hospital will provide the necessary information to the patient so that the patient may obtain reimbursement from the insurance carrier.

Hospitals try to furnish the necessary information to the patient as quickly as possible and complete the necessary forms. The carrier then pays the hospital directly, and no problem of delinquency exists. The delinquency problems arise due to lapsed coverage, inadequate coverage, or no coverage.

An example of a telephone call is as follows:

Dr: I have Major Medical Insurance through my employer. Speak to the National Medical Insurance Company and they will pay you. All you have to do is fill out the forms.

Cr: We have not received payment. You are responsible for the bill. The hospital has no connection with the insurance company. You must pay your bill, and we will then help you to complete the necessary forms. If you send the forms with the check, we will provide you with the information to complete the form. Nevertheless, if we do not receive your check by Monday, May 7, we will have no alternative but to refer this to our collection agency/attorney.

Medicaid and Medicare: These claims are processed by the hospital, but the main problem is that the patient has not assisted the hospital in preparing these forms. Arrangements should be made for the patient to visit the hospital to complete the forms. The patient is still liable for the bill.

Bill Not Received: Some hospitals will furnish a new bill upon request, but because the bills are so lengthy, an additional amount is sometimes charged to the patient to reimburse the hospital for the expense of preparing a new bill.

Debtor Is a Minor: In almost all states the parents are legally liable for the necessities of their child. If a child requires emergency care, or at least immediate care, the parents are legally liable for the bills for medical services incurred by the child. While it may be advisable to explain the legal liability of the parents, a better approach might be to impress upon the parent the fact that the child required immediate care, and if the parent was present, the parent undoubtedly would have approved this care. The emphasis should be put on the welfare of the child, and the fact that the hospital responded to this need when the child required medical services.

Marital Difficulties: The husband is usually responsible for the necessities of his child until the divorce decree or separation agreement is final. After that time, his obligation is to make support payments to his wife. The husband is generally liable for the medical bills of his wife until the divorce decree is final.

Local Retail Stores: The local retail store, such as a hardware or pharmacy, have a peculiar problem in calling their customers to pay delinquent charge accounts. The owner of each store is friendly and familiar with the customer, for this is the only way the customer was able to delay payment. The best approach here is to have the bookkeeper or an employee not known to the customer make the telephone call. This approach converts a personal relationship to a business transaction.

Cr: This is Mrs. Hicks. Your bill has not been paid for four months.

Dr: Who is this?

Cr: This is the McKinley Pharmacy. You have made no payment on your charge account for four months.

Dr: Oh, tell John I will take care of that.

Cr: It is my responsibility. John has instructed me to call his customers on the telephone, and if I cannot arrange for immediate payment, I am to turn this over to our collection agency/attorney. Now, I don't want to do that since you have been a customer for many years, but we must have payment so we can continue to operate our business.

Dr: Well, you just speak to John.

Cr: Madam, John has already told me what to do. I am merely extending you the courtesy of advising you what the procedure is.

Dr: OK, I'll speak to John when I come in.

Cr: Please understand that this claim will be referred to a collection agency/attorney by Monday, May 7.

Dr: OK, don't get nasty.

Cr: Madam...

Dr: I'll take care of it.

Cr: Thank you. I'll post-date the file until Monday, May 7.

Service Trade: Air conditioning and heating service contracts, exterminator contracts, typewriter service agreements, computer service agreements, copy machine service agreements all present one unique problem. When the debtor needs service, the creditor usually arranges for the arrearages to be paid before the next service call.

What happens when the debtor is three or four months in arrears? In most instances, the debtor has already sought the services of another competing firm, and does not require the services of the creditor. No effort should be made to retain the debtor as a customer, for even if successful, the customer will either terminate again or delay payment again. The proper telephone effort should be firm and direct.

Department Stores: The key to an efficient collection effort is probably the improvement of the customer relations department. Customer relations is usually a function of the return policy and the manner in which complaints are handled as well as billing practices. The collection effort will fall into place much easier when the telephone worker does not have to deal with return problems or billing problems.

Direct Mail: The direct marketer located across the country is competing with the local merchant for the debtor's dollars. Also, the direct marketer must understand that other direct marketers are competing for the debtor's business. Therefore, the direct marketer must determine if any effort is to be made to retain the customer. The major problem is that the amount of the debt is small, and the consumer believes that the only action taken by a collection agency will be letters and telephone calls. For this reason, a firm effort by the creditor should be made.

Banks and Lending Institutions: This type of lending provides a loan application with a wealth of information. This information should be available during every telephone call, and should be used to its fullest extent. The status and payment history of the loan should always be in front of the telephone worker. A discussion of this appears in Chapter 3 and Chapter 11.

Mortgage and Secured Lenders: The threat of repossession is always a cloud over the debtor. The use of threats should be a last resort, for if the threat is made and not utilized, future threats of repossession are fruitless and will be totally ignored by the debtor.

Landlords: Landlords are similar to secured lenders. The tenant knows eviction looms in the background. Frequent threats of eviction only weaken the threat, and finally the tenant ignores the threat entirely.

Insurance Brokers: By the time a collection effort has been instituted, the policy has been canceled. Yet, insurance brokers very often engage in collection efforts to protect their commissions while the policy is still in force. This effort should be diplomatic and persuasive since the insured probably has paid substantial sums to keep the policy in force up to this moment. The loss of the policy is the loss of something of value, and emphasis should be placed on this aspect.

Electric Utilities and Telephone Companies: Again, the service can always be terminated (although with limitations in certain states and jurisdictions). But in this instance, the creditor knows that the debtor will probably become a customer again when the debtor returns to work or moves. This changes the collection effort somewhat so that the debtor does not develop a distaste for the creditor. Internal collection calls should be slanted towards encouraging the debtor to continue the service, or at least to renew the service as soon as monies become available.

Real Estate Contractors: In most states a vendor who performs services or furnishes material to improve real estate may file a lien (mechanic's lien) on the real estate. This lien is similar in some respects to a mortgage. If the contractor filed a mechanic's lien after performing services and delivering material (consultation with an attorney is recommended), the contractor is very much in the same status as a secured lender. But for those contractors that do not file a lien, the advantage is that usually the debtor is solvent since equity exists in the real estate. A soft approach should be made to allow the debtor to accumulate some money to meet the debt, for the real property remains as security. Nevertheless, if the property is not throwing off enough cash flow, no amount of time will produce payment. In this instance, filing suit is the only answer.

Professionals: Doctors, dentists, lawyers, and accountants maintain a special relationship with the client. The best recommendation is to have the secretary or bookkeeper make the telephone call, rather than the professional himself. Whether an effort should be made to retain the client is questionable, for retention will only cause the client to become delinquent again.

Cr: Your bill for $450 has been open for three months.

Dr: Well, we just started the business. Mike will have to wait a little.

Cr: The firm has waited over six months. The firm has expended money to file the certificate of incorporation and to purchase corporate books. We must insist upon payment.

Dr: Well, they're going to get business from us.

Cr: Well, we need payment now. So, unless we receive a check by Monday, May 7, we will have no alternative but to ....

HELPFUL HINT: Installment Payments—Get Them in Writing. Adjustments of the bill is within the discretion of the individual professional, but needless to say, many of the outstanding bills are resolved by allowing the consumer to make weekly or monthly installment payments. In these instances a strong effort to obtain a promise in writing should be made. The writing should be simple and to the point. For example:

The undersigned acknowledges that he is indebted to Dr. Dunlop for the sum of $550 and agrees to pay $50 a month on the first of each month until the full balance of $550 is paid. If there is a default, the entire balance becomes due without notice plus interest.

CHAPTER 14

Consumer Excuses: How to Tell If They Are Sincere

While the large majority of consumers sincerely desire to pay their bills, the small sophisticated minority which do not exhibit this desire must be recognized. Furthermore, the telephone approach must be reasonable with the sincere debtor, while the sophisticated debtor must be recognized and dealt with apppropriately. Each telephone call must elicit enough information upon which to base a decision.

Certain types of excuses seem to be offered more frequently than others. In this chapter are listed the excuses most often submitted by consumer debtors to delay or avoid payment of their debt.

We will try to separate the ingenuous consumer from the insincere consumer. Yet, this decision may rest less on the substance of the excuse than on the tone, attitude, and emotion of the human voice on the telephone. Therefore, the creditor must recognize that what may appear to be an unacceptable excuse based on substance may in reality be an unfeigned and true representation of the facts. Therefore, both the substance of the words and the overall impression projected by the consumer must be evaluated. What percentage of weight is assessed to each quality is difficult to define, but the well-trained and experienced telephone worker in most cases will be able to properly determine whether the consumer is honest and truthful.

MEDICAL TROUBLES

A brief illness or even an operation may not be reason to refer the matter to an attorney/collection agency. While illness of the debtor is an excuse for not paying, the thrust of the telephone call is to determine when the party will return to work so that payments can resume. An inquiry as to the type of sickness, the duration of the sickness, and the extent of medical insurance will enable the telephone worker to make an intelligent decision

Minor Illness

If, for example, the consumer has been in bed with the flu for a week or sprained his ankle while skiing in Vermont, the excuse of illness or injury in this instance is weak and not very persuasive. The response to this excuse is obvious if the debt is several months in arrears and not just a few weeks in arrears. Usually employees receive from five to ten paid sick days a year. Therefore, the consumer has suffered no loss of wages. The illness or injury is not serious enough to warrant a stay in a hospital. The suggested approach is to inquire as to the estimated date of returning to work, and arrange a payment to be made one week later, providing the length of time is not too long.

Cr: Your loan is two months in arrears.

Dr: I know, but I broke my leg two weeks ago and I'm on crutches now.

Cr: Have you returned to work yet?

Dr: No, I won't be able to get to work for at least another week and then only part time, because I won't travel to work in a car during the rush hour.

Cr: On May 7, your loan will be three payments behind, so we must have at least two payments by Monday, May 7.

Dr: That's impossible. I won't get paid until a week later. Don't you people have any compassion? I'm in my bed. I can't move around. What has to happen before the bank gives a little consideration?

Cr: Sir, you have not made a payment in two months. You say you had your injury two weeks ago. Obviously, your delinquency in paying and your injury have no connection at all. Furthermore, you probably have not lost any wages. In order to avoid a lawsuit, we must have a payment. I am sure you can arrange payment to prevent this loan being sent to our attorney for suit.

Dr: Boy, you people are tough! Can't you wait until I work for a month so I can accumulate some money to pay you? You know I have other bills to pay.

Cr: I'm sure you have, and I sincerely hope the other bills are not behind.

Dr: No, they are not in bad shape.

Cr: Well, then, I shall look forward to receiving two payments by Monday, May 7.

Dr: I don't know about two payments, but I'm sure I can get you one payment.

Comment on Dialogue: This appears to be a strong telephone call, but in fact, the proffered excuse is no excuse at all. The consumer's other bills are current at the expense of the bank loan. A firm dialogue is recommended.

Serious Illness

A serious illness of the debtor presents different problems. The emphasis should be in determining if other assets or other income are available to discharge the indebtedness. Recasting the loan is always a viable alternative. A suit will usually not create funds, but consideration must be given to the fact that funds are being secreted to withstand the future expenses of the serious illness. Only thorough inquiry will provide the facts necessary to resolve this problem.

A few suggested lines of inquiry are as follows:

1. Inquire as to other assets, such as bank accounts, etc., for a small immediate payment.

2. If return to work is imminent, arrange for a payment when the first paycheck is received.

3. Explore the refinancing or recasting of the loan.

4. If the inquiries indicate a suspicion that the illness is merely an excuse for delaying payment, a direct demand for payment should be made using the appropriate closing statement.

5. Inquire as to medical insurance coverage.

Cr: The Master Charge account has a balance of $1550, and we have not received a payment in three months.

Dr: My child was in the hospital and I had a lot of expenses and I just could not send you any money. If you give me another month, I will be able to send you something.

Cr: I'm sorry to hear that. What happened?

Dr: Oh, he had the flu, and the next thing I knew, it was pneumonia; then he went into the hospital for a week.

Cr: Has he recovered?

Dr: No, he is still home.

Cr: It must have been very serious, because a week is a long time in the hospital these days.

Dr: Not that serious, but it was pneumonia. Maybe it was only a few days, but it seemed like a week.

Cr: Well, at least your hospital bills were covered.

Dr: Well, no. They were only partially covered, but I had a lot of expenses that were not covered.

Cr: I understand. But we must have a payment on this account by Monday, May 7, or else it will be referred to our attorney.

Comment on Dialogue: The creditor inquired and was not satisfied that the excuse offered had any relationship to the delinquency.

Asking questions cannot be emphasized too much. An example of how a debtor *should not be handled* is illustrated as follows:

Cr: This is the State Bank. May I speak to Mr. Clark?

Dr: This is Mr. Clark.

Cr: We are calling in reference to the personal loan that was granted to you and which is now four payments in arrears.

Dr: Yes, I know and I am doing my best. My wife was in the hospital, and it has been very tough.

Cr: But you still must make payments on the loan.

Dr: What can I do? What do you want me to do?

Cr: Well, if we do not have payment within ten days, we will be forced to refer this to our attorney to institute suit.

Dr: I don't know what to tell you. My other creditors are going along with me.

Cr: We have no other choice.

Dr: OK, go ahead and sue. If I can do anything, I will.

Cr: Thank you.

Comment on Dialogue: No questions were asked. The question is whether this is the proper treatment of a medical problem. The argument made by the creditor is that suit will enable the creditor to be the first one to obtain judgment. Accordingly, the debtor's salary may be attached and the creditor will have priority. The debtor's claim is that a suit may precipitate other suits, and undue pressure will be brought to bear upon the debtor. The result may be filing bankruptcy, abandoning his job, or moving to parts unknown. In this call no information was obtained upon which to base an intelligent and reasoned decision.

Avoid Medical Histories

Sympathizing with the debtor is always suggested. Be sincere, but do not overdo it. I have had telephone calls turned into extensive medical reports and evaluations ranging from basic symptoms to a detailed explanation of how the surgical knife was manipulated. The telephone caller is not the doctor, the nurse, or the best friend of the debtor. A return to the subject at hand is in order.

Dr: I have been in such pain, and the aspirin did not help, so the doctor prescribed codeine, and all I did was sleep.

Cr: I know, and I am sorry to hear that, but there is still this matter of the debt...

Dr: I have been in bed for three weeks with mononucleosis, and you know how this effects you. My temperature was 101 and the headache was awful and...

Cr: I certainly hope you have a speedy recovery. But this debt is over three months in arrears, and we must arrange for an immediate payment.

FINANCIAL TROUBLES

We have said before that financial troubles, excluding disputed debts, are usually the only truthful excuse for nonpayment. When the debtor acknowledges this, it is a major step to resolution of the problem since the debtor is generally willing to promise payment or arrange for an installment payout.

The same rules apply to financial troubles as to medical troubles. Inquiry must be made by the telephone worker to render a decision. While the financial excuses may be a facade to enable the debtor to delay payment, asking the routine questions will reveal whether the debtor is sincere or just masquerading. Is habitual spending the problem, or does his income fluctuate from surplus income to no income for long periods of time? If the answer is the latter, such as is true for an artist or writer, a different approach is warranted. If overspending is the reason, then certainly strong action is recommended.

Determine Extent of Problem

Minor Financial Troubles: This is akin to a minor illness or injury. The consumer is not seeking sympathy of a personal kind, but is attempting to present a set of facts which will give a logical reason to defer payment. Usually, the plea consists of an unusual expenditure which is not recurring. In most instances a short extension will elicit a promise of payment. Exerting pressure in this case is probably not required or necessary.

Dr: I just loaned my brother some money to tide him over until he gets a new job, and I couldn't make the payment on time.

Cr: But the loan is now 60 days past due.

Dr: I know, but my brother just got a job, and he will repay me within two weeks. All I need is two more weeks.

Cr: All right, I will look for payment by Monday, May 7. Please do not disappoint me, because the loan is scheduled to be referred to our attorney on May 7, and neither you nor I want that to happen.

Dr: Don't worry, you will get your check.

Serious Financial Problems: The scenario is similar to a serious illness. In-depth questioning is necessary to find out how severe the problem actually is.

The excuse of financial trouble can produce some of the most outlandish and bizarre reasons for not paying. Here are some examples:

1. "My dog needed an operation."
2. "The plumber charged me over three hundred dollars for a job."
3. "I invested in a floating gambling casino which is docked three miles off the coast and is under contract to be sold next week. As soon as I get my money, you will get your money."
4. "I have four kids in college at the same time."

5. "I was mugged yesterday, and all my bankbooks were stolen. It will be at least three weeks before I can withdraw any money."

6. "The severe frost wiped me out."

7. "The van just disappeared. I did not report it to the police because I think my daughter took it, since she has disappeared also."

8. "The wash basin flooded the whole floor, and all your paper products were ruined."

9. "I picked up a hitchhiker and she rolled me."

10. "I had cash in a box in the basement, and there was an electrical fire; now all I have is ashes."

Here are some interesting telephone conversations, and how the caller should handle them:

Dr: My boyfriend left and took all my money.
Cr: I'm sorry to hear this. How much did he take?
Dr: He cleaned out our joint bank account for several thousand dollars.
Cr: That is too bad. How are you going to pay your rent?
Dr: Oh, I'm working. I'll just have to put in a little overtime.
Cr: Well, that's good. Did you have any other money?
Dr: Very little.
Cr: Well, about our debt...

Here is another example:

Cr: Is Mr. Lehrer there?
Dr: Just a minute.
Cr: OK.
Dr: Who is this?
Cr: This is Mr. Victor of Southern Mills, and I am calling about your debt to us of $4,700. I have called every week for the past four weeks, and I have sent you a letter each week. Your secretary keeps telling me you are out.
Dr: I know all about the debt.
Cr: Well, we must have payment. The bill is over six months in arrears. We have been very patient, but we cannot wait any longer.

Dr: Look, we know about the bill and you are getting to be a pain in the neck. You don't have to call every week and give my secretary a hard time. I know about the bill, and so does my partner.

Cr: Well, we must...

Dr: You must nothing. Now, you stop bothering me.

Cr: I will when you pay.

Dr: Look, each week my partner and I put all our bills in a hat, and then we select three bills. These three bills get paid. Now you may be the lucky creditor next week, but if you keep giving me a hard time, my partner and I will not even put your bills in the hat in the first place.

The list would certainly grow if my law partners and associates were asked to contribute their favorites. Certainly, some of these excuses were valid and deserved to be treated seriously, but others were blatant attempts to use the unusual and extraordinary as evidence of credibility. Inquiry and questioning are the only weapons available to the creditor to determine whether or not to accept the reason for nonpayment.

DEBTORS WITH LIMITED INCOMES

Welfare Recipient

The response to the welfare recipient is usually that the merchandise should not have been ordered. This response applies in all instances where the merchandise ordered is not a "necessity" item. Items of "necessity" usually consist of food, clothing, and medical and hygiene supplies. As a rule, most of these "necessity" items are supplied by local stores which receive payment in cash and food stamps. Usually, all other items are considered luxury items. The welfare recipient should be advised that the luxury item, such as a stereo, expensive radio, or office equipment purchased through a mail order catalog was not needed to subsist. The consumer is obligated to pay and the creditor should insist on payment.

Cr: This is Jean Russell. You purchased a kitchen clock for $39 from our catalog four months ago. We sent you three letters, and we have not heard from you nor have we received payment.

Dr: I know. It is a beautiful clock, but you know I am on welfare and I have no money to pay you.

Cr: Were you on welfare when you ordered the clock?

Dr: Oh yes, I've been on welfare for over two years now.

Cr: So you ordered the clock knowing that you could not pay for it.

Dr: Oh no. I thought I could pay for it since I had a few extra dollars, and I figured that by the time the bill came, I would have enough. You know you said in the order form that you would bill me, and I didn't have to send a check in with the order.

Cr: Well, the bill must be paid. If we don't receive payment, we will be forced to send this to our collection agency/attorney.

Dr: I was surprised when you filled the order. I have ordered from other mail order catalogs, and most of them want the money with the order. With those that say bill me, most times they turn down my order. You were nice and shipped the order.

Cr: We must insist on payments.

Dr: Well, maybe I can send a few dollars every now and then.

Cr: I shall expect $10 by the end of next week. Do you have the address?

Dr: I don't think I can send $10, but maybe I can send $5.

Comment on Dialogue: While the chances of the promise being kept are extremely slim, at least the creditor did everything possible to exact payment. A sophisticated debtor on welfare is the challenge of the century.

If the welfare debtor ordered a necessity, the challenge facing the creditor is even greater since it is an item that is necessary to subsist. The effort must be the same, for most welfare consumers do not want to pay. An extra motivation is if the consumer must return to you for future purchases. Refusing to extend him future credit may be very persuasive. (See "Exempt Property" in Chapter 9.)

Social Security Recipient

The approach to the social security recipient is not quite the same as the welfare recipient. Social security payments may be very substantial, and debtors may be receiving other income from pension and profit-sharing payments, investments, savings accounts, IRA accounts, trust accounts, annuities, insurance payments, and a wide variety of other types of income. The fundamental concept is that social security is a sign of old age but not a sign of poverty. Therefore, the approach should be the same as for any other consumer debtor. The debtor ordered it, the debtor received it, the debtor uses or used it. Ergo, the debtor is obligated to pay for it. (See "Exempt Property" in Chapter 9.)

The telephone call to the debtor who receives monthly checks should be timed so that the money is not already spent. Social security checks are usually mailed by the government around the beginning of the month (the third or fourth of the month), so contact should be made shortly after this date.

The consumer that claims social security is his only source of income presents a different problem. In this case, the approach is similar to that of a welfare recipient with a few exceptions. First, this consumer may actually be receiving other income, and the possibility is not necessarily remote. Second, the married consumer may be receiving two social security checks. Accordingly, the disposable income is greater since social security recipients usually are not burdened with the support of small or infant children.

POVERTY

This is the most difficult problem to deal with in collecting a debt. If, after a thorough series of questions have been asked, the debtor advises the creditor that there is no money available now or in the future to pay the debt, the creditor still has a few options open.

1. Complete the telephone call with a closing statement.
2. Use a credit checking agency to confirm the information furnished.
3. Investigate further in order to locate unrevealed assets.

How far the creditor proceeds is a function of the amount of the debt and how much money the creditor wants to spend. If a small amount is involved, the creditor, at this point, must make a decision whether or not to believe the debtor. Any other decision will require the expenditure of additional monies.

Warning—Mental Problem: If the debtor is believed to exhibit a mental problem, such as senility or retardation, be very gentle. Using an aggressive attitude may cause the debtor undue emotional upset which might expose the creditor to liability. Use of the closing statement should be tempered or even omitted where indicated. In short, this type of debtor should be handled very carefully and diplomatically, considering fully the mental disability.

Warning—Exempt Property. In Chapter 9 the federal and state laws involving exempt property were discussed. Special consideration must be given to this problem so that no threat is made, inferred, or implied to the debtor that the creditor will seek payment of his debt in any way from the exempt property. Social security, welfare, disability income, workman's compensation, and unemployment benefits are examples of what may be exempt property and may fall under this umbrella. The creditor should review carefully the federal laws as to exemption as well as the state laws, and not only the state where the creditor maintains his business but also the state where the consumer resides. Consultation with your attorney is recommended.

Unemployed Debtor

If the debtor is unemployed, the creditor must remember that the debtor will eventually return to work. During this unemployment period, the debtor is probably paying the bills which are necessary, but unfortunately not the creditor's bill. After determining the reason for unemployment, some questions to ask might be as follows:

1. Is the debtor receiving unemployment insurance?
2. How much is he receiving?
3. How long has he been receiving it?
4. Will he apply for extended unemployment insurance?
5. Is his wife or children working?
6. How is he paying for his rent, food, medical, etc.?
7. As a follow-up to the last question, what are the sources of other income?
8. What are the prospects for future employment?
9. Is the debtor registered with any employment agencies?
10. Is the debtor on welfare?

The list is long, for an unemployed debtor is a viable debtor. An effort should be made to extend payment or work out a monthly payment plan with token payments now and larger payments when the debtor returns to work.

The reason for unemployment should be explored thoroughly. If the plant closed down or was moved, retraining and financial assistance is probably available in a large firm. If a strike was the reason, financial aid may be available from the union or by way of a loan from a credit union. New York pays unemployment insurance during a strike. If the debtor quit his job in the hope of seeking a better paying position, the outlook is bright and can be handled with ease. A telephone call might take the following form:

Cr: This is the Neighborly Finance Company, and your loan is three months in arrears.

Dr: Yes, I know, but I lost my job.

Cr: When did you lose your job?

Dr: About a month and a half ago, just when I was going to make up that last payment I missed.

Cr: What happened?

Dr: Business was bad, and they started cutting all over the place, and I got cut like 40 other lucky ones.

Cr: Did you apply for unemployment insurance?

Dr: Yeah, I get a lousy $125 a week.

Cr: Do you get anything from your union?

Dr: No, there was no union.

Cr: How are you managing on $125 a week?

Dr: With great difficulty. I saved a few bucks, but it is going fast.

Cr: Well, something must be done about this loan. I understand your problems. How do you suggest we handle this loan?

Dr: If you understand my problem, you know there is nothing I can do about the loan. You will just have to wait. My family comes first and we can barely survive. If I don't get a job quickly, I will be forced to go on welfare.

Cr: I do understand your problems, but we insist that something be done about this loan. We must have an interim payment.

Dr: Are you kidding? Where is it coming from? I need every dime I have.

Cr: Well, if you don't pay, the matter will be referred to an attorney for suit and you will have to pay the costs and disbursements of suit as well as attorneys fees (if provided for in the note). I know you will get another job quickly, so why don't you make one payment now and we will take one step at a time.

Dr: Forget it.

Cr: You don't want me to forward this to an attorney now. I am sure you can arrange a small payment to defer this action and buy a little time until you get a new job, which I am sure you will do.

Dr: How much time will I buy?

Cr: At least a month, maybe more.

Dr: OK, suppose I send you $50?

Cr: Well, the payment is $125. How about the full monthly payment and then we will carry your loan two months in arrears.

Dr: The most I can send is $75.

Cr: Well, OK, but be certain that it is in my office by Monday, May 7, for that is the day this loan is scheduled for referral to our attorney.

Dr: All right, it will be there.

Cr: Fine, and when I receive it, I will remove it from the scheduling and we will speak again in 30 days.

Dr: OK.

Cr: Good luck, and I know you will get another job quickly.

Dr: Thanks.

Comment on Dialogue: The telephone caller adhered to the four elements of the telephone call—Identification, Foundation (three months in arrears), Demand for Payment (insisting on payment), and Closing Statement (referral to our attorney). In addition, a thorough inquiry was made to determine the extent of the problem. Then, the extent of the pressure to exert was decided upon and applied gently to obtain the best results.

DOMESTIC OR FAMILY TROUBLE

"My son was just busted by the police for selling cocaine; my daughter is in the hospital bleeding to death after an abortion; and my husband just left for the Caribbean with his secretary and all the money; and you are calling me to make a payment on a loan." The script may read like a soap opera, but soap operas do reflect a page of life, and these problems are very often the excuses for nonpayment of a debt or loan.

Normally, the excuses are more mundane, such as a pending divorce, an upcoming wedding, a move to another state, a casualty such as a fire or flood, overstretching the budget around Christmas, or the death of a loved one. The list is endless, but the important point is that almost all domestic or family problems are temporary and will be solved shortly. The impact on the family finances may be substantial, such as a fire where insurance has lapsed, but answers will be quickly found for these difficult problems.

Again, questions are to be used to determine the extent of the problem and to seek the opening to insist upon payment of the obligation.

Cr: Your Master Card has reached its limit and we have not received any payments for over three months.

Dr: My mother died, and she had no money. I had to pay the balances due to the nurses, doctor, and hospital. Then there was the funeral, at a cost of over $2,000. I can't pay everybody at once.

Cr: But no payment has been made in three months.

Dr: I know, but understand my problems.

Cr: We do understand, but your agreement calls for payments every month; we haven't received a payment in three months.

Dr: Well, maybe next month.

Cr: Next month will be too late. We need a payment now, or else we will be forced to refer this to our attorney to institute suit. I am sure you do not want that.

Dr: No, I guess not....

DIVORCE

The most common response is that the couple is divorced and that one of the spouses has moved from the premises. Somehow, the one who moved out is always the one who is supposed to pay bills.

In most states a husband is generally responsible for the necessities of his wife during the marriage. These necessities are such things as food, rent, clothing, and medical supplies. This obligation is applicable both before and after separation. If the wife used a joint credit card, he is also responsible for any charges she made. With regard to luxury items, the husband may also be responsible for all the items purchased while the couple were living together. After the couple separates, usually a husband is not responsible for debts incurred for luxury items. Sometimes the husband will send letters to creditors or place an advertisement in the newspaper notifying the creditors and the business world in general that he is no longer obligated for his wife's debts. In some states receipt of such a notice is sufficient to relieve the husband from liability. The legal consequences of each of these actions may vary somewhat from state to state, and the creditor should be fully informed about its rights and consult with an attorney concerning the specific state law that covers the problem.

Of course, the wife is jointly liable for payment when she makes the purchase. If the wife is alleging that her attorney said her husband is to pay the bills, the response should be that the wife ordered it, she received it, and the wife either is using it or used it. Therefore, she is obligated to pay. As to loans, if the wife signed the note, she is responsible. Of course, if merchandise was ordered by the husband, delivered to the wife, but the husband has possession of the property (for example, a tennis racket), then the husband is probably liable and not the wife.

Dr: Hello.

Cr: This is National Department Stores. Mr. Henry speaking. Is this Mrs. Jackson?

Dr: Yes.

Cr: We have a charge account for you with a balance of $700 for two dresses from our fashion salon. These purchases were made over two months ago, and we have sent several notices, all to no avail

Dr: My husband and I are getting a divorce.

Cr: I'm sorry to hear that.

Dr: Thank you, I suggest you contact him.

Cr: Mrs. Jackson, you purchased the dresses, and I am afraid we must insist upon you paying for them.

Dr: Well, I don't have the money. Do you want to speak to my attorney?

Cr: No. Your attorney cannot help. The purchase was made by you, you are wearing the dresses, and you are obligated to pay for them. If payment is not received by Monday, May 7, we will have no alternative but to refer this to our attorney.

Dr: Well, I can't pay since I do not have the money. I will call my attorney. Maybe he can get you the money.

Cr: Well, I certainly hope so, because we do not want to refer this to our attorney.

Dr: I understand.

Cr: Please tell your attorney the bill must be paid by Monday, May 7.

Dr: OK, I'll call him.

Cr: Thank you, goodbye.

Comment on Dialogue: At least the wheels are turning, and the husband will know that his wife is pressed for payment of bills. Notice that the creditor did not accept the offer to call the consumer's attorney. Usually, telephone calls to an attorney in this situation do not produce substantive results. Nevertheless, when the client calls her own attorney, she may persuade her attorney to act. See Debt Collection Practices Act, Section 805 (a)(2).

SKIP TRACING THE INDIVIDUAL

Locating individuals who have left for parts unknown over the telephone is an art. The subject is covered in Chapter 13, "Special Legal Problems with Businesses." Nevertheless, there are a few procedures used to locate individuals which should be mentioned here:

1. Use the post office to send a certified or registered letter requesting a return receipt, showing address where delivered.

Another device is to send $1.00 to the post office requesting the forwarding address of a debtor. A form of a letter might be as follows:

General Post Office
County of _____,
New York

Gentlemen:

Enclosed is a check for $1.00. Kindly furnish me with the present address of the following named person: John Jones.

The previous address of this person was:
100 Main Street
Centerville, New York 10000

                                        Very truly yours,

---

2. If the party's social security number is available, the creditor may determine the state where the social security number was issued, since the first three numbers of each social security number indicate the state.

When a debtor has left a major city due to financial problems, it is not unreasonable to suspect that he has returned to the state where he lived when he was a child, which is usually where the social security number was issued. Using telephone information in the major cities of that state or requesting a motor vehicle bureau search in that state might very well locate the debtor.

3. Some creditors will run motor vehicle bureau searches in the states where a debtor will most likely relocate, i.e., Florida, California, or Arizona. An information call will produce a telephone number of the motor vehicle bureau, and a telephone call will produce the fee for the search and the address to which a letter may be sent.

4. If certain applications on file contain prior addresses or addresses of friends or relatives in distant cities or states, information calls to the city seeking a new number for the debtor might be rewarding. Of course, efforts to locate the debtor may also be made by calling relatives or friends (such calls are regulated by the Debt Collection Practices Act).

5. When contacting former employers, be certain you inquire whether the former employer received a request for a reference. This may reveal where the new job is located. Also, try to determine to what address the W–2 Form was forwarded. The debtor needs this W–2 Form, and the former employer usually is provided by the debtor with a new address if the debtor has moved.

6. If the debtor skipped and recently sold his house, searching the real estate records of the county at the debtor's former address should reveal the new owner of the house. Sometimes the new owner executed a second mortgage to the debtor as part of the purchase price. The new owner may be mailing payments to the debtor. An inquiry may be fruitful even if the new owner is not mailing payments to the debtor.

7. Credit reporting agencies such as Dun and Bradstreet, TRW, and Hooper Holmes will furnish additional information.

8. Use of reverse telephone directories will provide the name and telephone numbers of other tenants in the same building where the debtor resides.

9. There are skip tracing agencies whose sole business is to locate persons and who perform this service for a fee.

Warning: Any contact with third parties is regulated by the Debt Collection Practices Act. The creditor should comply. Remember, in all instances, comply with the appropriate sections of the Debt

Collection Practices Act, and particularly the sections dealing with locating the debtor by communicating with third parties (Sections 804 and 805) in Appendix A.

DEBTORS WHO ARE IN THE ARMED SERVICES

Soldiers' and Sailors' Civil Relief Act: The creditor should be aware of the Soldiers' and Sailors' Civil Relief Act (SSCRA) 50 U.S.C. 500–548 (1976). Many believe that this Act prohibits all civil suits and actions against servicemen, and prevents execution of any judgment. While the Act may stay civil suits or actions, and may prevent execution of judgments, situations do exist where civil actions can proceed and judgments may be executed. The purpose of the law is to protect servicemen's rights during such litigation and any inequities which may result by reason of military service by insuring the serviceman's right to present all meritorious claims and defenses. The statute provides for a stay unless the ability of the debtor to defend is not *materially affected* by reason of military service.

Before a creditor abandons a claim against a serviceman, consultation with an attorney is strongly recommended.

CHAPTER 15

Types of Consumer Debtors

The consumer debtor is the average ordinary citizen, our neighbor, our fellow employee, our relative, the nurse, the police officer, the counter clerk, the local politician and, of course, ourself. But certain distinctions must be made when dealing with the consumer, depending upon those characteristics which distinguish one person from another. While we are all alike in some respects, we are also quite different, too. How these distinctions come into play to affect the collection process over the telephone is the subject of this chapter.

SIZE OF DEBTS

Large Debts

If a large balance is involved, the number of telephone calls to be made is dictated entirely by the response of the debtor. The larger the debt, the greater the attention. The number of telephone calls is dictated solely by the circumstances and the progress being made. Any indication of a good faith intention to repay should be followed by continual telephone calls as long as some payments are being received.

The total overall impression to be made on the consumer is that this is the only account that is being handled by the collector and that the progress of payments is being monitored on a day-to-day or week-to-week basis.

Remember to follow up each telephone call with a letter if the calls are spaced more than one or two weeks apart. Of course, if contact is being made on a more frequent basis, letters would be oppressive and might affect the progress between the parties. Be certain not to violate The Debt Collection Practices Act and the commentary to the Act dealing with frequency of telephone calls.

Small Debts

If the debt is small, then the number of telephone calls that can economically be made is somewhat limited. Thus, everything that "must be done" must be done in the very first telephone call. Therefore, with small balances, a specially prepared script might be the answer.

INSTALLMENT PAYMENTS

Installment payments are treated in Chapter 2 ("Four Golden Keys to an Effective Telephone Conversation"), but there are a few items to be considered when dealing with the consumer. You must consider the ability of the consumer to meet the obligation. A promise to pay with no visible means of making payment will only produce a default. In this instance, a careful questioning period must be performed to determine the extent of the personal or financial problem. The source of the funds is very important, and the telephone worker must consider all the essential expenses of the consumer. Remember that the essential expenses will always be paid before the installment payment. A realistic approach must supersede the goal of obtaining a promise of payment.

Cr: There is a balance due of $4,700 for the extra room and bath we added to your house.

Dr: I know, but I've had a few setbacks and you are going to have to wait a while for payment.

Cr: But it is almost four months now.

Dr: Well, maybe I can send you something in a month.

Cr: Mr. Schultz, I must have payment in full, or at least a certain amount every month. Otherwise, I am going to give this to my attorney. In any event, you know I already have filed a mechanic's lien on your property.

Dr: Yes, I received your notice of lien. It really wasn't necessary. You know I am going to pay you.

Dr: Yes, but when?

Dr: How about $300 a month?

Cr: That is far too little. How about $750?

Dr: Look, my wife lost her job and we are barely able to make it.

Cr: You are an accountant with a big accounting firm. You must have a substantial salary.

Dr: Look, it isn't that much.

Cr: Well, how much do you earn?

Dr: That's none of your business.

Cr: It is when you are asking me to extend you time to repay a debt owed to me. How can I make a decision without knowing what your financial position is?

Dr: All right, I make $50,000 a year, which nets out to about $37,000. I have three high school children. Why do you think my wife was working?

Cr: How big is your mortgage?

Dr: I have $110,000 mortgage on the house.

Cr: Well, when will your wife return to work?

Dr: I hope in the next couple of weeks.

Cr: OK. Send me $300 a month, and two months after your wife returns to work, send me $500 a month.

Comment on Dialogue: The creditor is realistic, and accepted the first offer of payment.

HOMEOWNERS VERSUS APARTMENT DWELLERS

Apartment Tenant

The rent is a high priority debt, and basically, the tenant recognizes the absolute necessity of paying the rent. Most landlords have one or two months' security, and probably will not commence eviction proceedings until the rent is one or two months in arrears.

Telephone calls should be made 10 days after the first notice of delinquency in order to identify the problem. Many tenants are just not attuned to the fact that rent is due on the first of the month.

Landlords tend to use their own timetables which range from strict to lenient. In either instance, a telephone call is most important at an early stage to determine what the circumstances are that are causing the delay.

Homeowners

Whatever is applicable to tenants is also applicable to the mortgage borrower, only more so. The homeowner who fails to pay the mortgage is not only faced with eviction, but also with the possibility of losing his life savings in the equity of his home.

Each state in the union has enacted laws to protect the homeowner from the unscrupulous mortgagee. But that predicament does not exist in today's environment. Now, the foreclosure process in most states can take between four and six months or much longer. For this reason, an effort should be made by telephone to inquire as to why a mortgage payment has not been made. The timing of this call depends upon the procedures of the mortgagee, but we believe it should be made early rather than late. The purpose of the call is to ferret out the problem, and provide enough information so that an intelligent decision can be made. Once the problem is known, the solution becomes evident.

CLIENTS OF ATTORNEYS AND ACCOUNTANTS

For accountants and lawyers, the problems are similar to those of other professionals. The attorney who telephones his client to remind him to pay the bill is either too friendly or too harsh. This is one situation where it is recommended that the attorney use his secretary or bookkeeper to make the telephone call. After several calls are made, the best suggestion is to refer the matter to another attorney for collection.

SERVICE BUSINESSES

There is really nothing unusual in the efforts of service businesses, such as painters, exterminators, electricians, heating and air conditioning services, etc., to try to collect a bill from the consumer, except that sometimes a personal relationship has developed between the user and the provider of the service. The best approach is to have someone other than the direct provider make the telephone collection call. This may be the office manager, the bookkeeper, or an officer, as long as it is not the one who has direct contact with the customer. The call must be made on a businesslike basis. When the customer responds that he will speak to "Joe" about the bill, the reply should be a terse and conclusive statement that "Joe" is not involved in the preparation of the bill nor the billing process. An effort should be made to convince the debtor that billing is an automatic process, and not subject to the discretion of the individual who performed the service.

CHILDREN AS DEBTORS

When the debtor is a child under the age of 18 years (the age varies from state to state), the law in most states is that generally a child can disavow a debt or contract. Accordingly, a request for payment should be made but no other threat is appropriate. Of course, if the minor is conducting a business, the business is liable for the debt.

Under 18: The first indication that the debtor is a child or minor should come from the first telephone call. The simplistic approach is to ask the party "How old are you?" if you suspect he is underage. In almost all cases, the child will respond with his age. In most states a minor is not responsible for his debts; but if the minor is over the legal age, he is responsible, providing the transaction creating the debt occurred after the legal age was reached. If the transaction occurred before reaching the legal age, and collection efforts are being made after reaching the legal age, the child is not responsible.

Parents: If the debtor is a minor, an effort should be made to speak to the parents. In most states the parents are usually responsible for the necessitites provided to their children, but not for all items. Accordingly, threats to refer the matter to a collection agency/attorney must be handled very carefully. Reference to the state law is necessary and consultation with your attorney is recommended.

Under 13–14: If the child is under 13 or 14 years of age, no collection effort should be utilized. The telephone worker should immediately request to speak to the parents. Even between 14 and 18 the presentation should be limited.

Cr: May I speak to Helen Smith?
Dr: That's me.
Cr: (Recognizing a young voice). How old are you?
Dr: Ten.
Cr: May I please speak to your parents?
Dr: They are not home.
Cr: I will call back.

It is strongly recommended that in the above situation no message of any kind be left. Another example follows:

Cr: How old are you?
Dr: I am 17 years old.
Cr: I am calling about the record albums you ordered by mail over four months ago for $29.95. We have written you several letters.
Dr: Oh yeah.
Cr: Well, we would like to have payment.
Dr: I don't have any money now. My father grounded me after I wasted his Porsche.
Cr: Can you make a partial payment of a few dollars?
Dr: I told you I'm broke.
Cr: May I please speak to your parents?
Dr: They're not home.
Cr: All right. Thank you very much.

Comment on Dialogue: If another call is to be made, the telephone worker should speak to the parents.

Child Answering the Telephone: When a child under 18 answers the telephone, the creditor should be very careful that the message left contains only the name of the firm and the telephone number. No indication that the caller is a creditor should be furnished. Consumers are very sensitive about their children knowing that they are in debt, and rightly so. For children under the age of 18, it is recommended that no message be left and another call be made. (See the Debt Collection Practices Act).

Of course, you must determine the age of the child. If the child refuses to tell his age, treat the child as being under the age of 18.

Nurse: The same rules apply to a nurse or nurse's aide as apply to a baby sitter.

Baby sitter: Do not leave a message with a baby sitter, for he or she is a third party. Furthermore, the baby sitter may be under the age of 18 years.

WHEN DEBTOR IS DECEASED

If the party answering the telephone tells you that the debtor is deceased, the very first response should be an expression of your sympathies. One should then inquire where and when it happened. If it is a large debt, this information may be helpful later. The next inquiry is to determine who is the attorney for the estate of the deceased, and make the assumption that an estate does exists. Obtain the name and address of the attorney or the administrator of the estate and then ask for the name and address of the party furnishing you with this information. Also try to obtain the place of death.

When you are asked, "Who are you and why do you want this information?" identification is in order and furnish whatever information is requested.

The telephone call might sound like this:

Cr: This is the Jones Department Store. May I speak to Mrs. Smith.

Dr: Mrs. Smith died three days ago.

Cr: Oh! I am sorry to hear that. Please accept my sincere sympathies.

Dr: That is all right. What can I do for you?

Cr: What happened that caused her demise?

Dr: She died of a heart attack. What do you want?

Cr: My name is Mr. Clark and I am from the credit department of Jones Department Store. I am calling about a revolving balance that is in arrears three months.

Dr: Well, she is not going to use it anymore.

Cr: Did she die at home?

Dr: No, she was on vacation in Atlantic City. I can't really help you since she lived alone.

Cr: Well, can you give me the name and address of the attorney who will be handling the estate?

Dr: I don't know if she has an estate or who the attorney will be.

Cr: With whom am I speaking?

Dr: I am her daughter.

Cr: Well, can I call you in a week or two after this difficult time has passed?

PATIENTS OF DOCTORS AND DENTISTS

Although most of the population may agree that doctors and dentists undergo rigorous training and reap substantial financial rewards, an established fact is that the same doctors and dentists have some of the highest rates of delinquencies in collecting their bills. The personal relationship between doctor and patient may very well encourage the patient to place the doctor's bill at the very bottom of the pile of bills to be paid.

Doctors' collection efforts require a certain amount of tact and diplomacy. The affluent patient should be enlightened as to the expenses of operating an office, and the fact that the doctor must pay his rent and malpractice insurance as well as meet his payroll for the nurse and receptionist. To the impoverished patient, the emphasis should be on the services rendered to the patient and the fact that the patient is now well and healthy. A complaint that the bill is exorbitant should be met with the statement that this is the normal charge for the services to other patients, and the outcome of the diagnosis or treatment is what really counts. Threats to refuse further treatment should not be made. Many of the other issues connected with doctors are covered in Chapter 14, "Consumer Excuses."

Cr: The balance of $550 for your operation is over five months past due, Mrs. Lombardo.

Dr: I know, but I only returned to work three months ago, and I'm just beginning to catch up.

Cr: I am glad you have recovered so well. But we must insist upon payment.

Dr: That bill was pretty high. I thought Blue Cross and Blue Shield would cover the bill. I think the doctor ought to reduce the bill.

Cr: Mrs. Lombardo, the doctor doesn't receive the full amount. He must pay rent, salaries to his nurse and secretary, electricity, medical supplies, and a lot of other expenses before any money goes into his pocket.

Dr: Well, at those fees, he can afford all those expenses.

Cr: Well, the important thing is that you are well and healthy. Is there a price on that?

Dr: Well, maybe not, but...

Cr: Perhaps we can enter into a plan whereby you pay a fixed amount each month.

Appendices

The purpose in providing these Appendices is to acquaint the reader with some of the laws that affect collection practices. We have provided the principal federal laws affecting collection, but the Debt Collection Practices Act is by far the most important for collection efforts and has the most impact on these efforts. Although the law does not technically apply to the creditor collecting its own account, the law has set the standards and customs in the industry; creditors who violate the law because the law does not cover a creditor collecting its own account will probably find that a law exists in the state that prohibits the same action.

For this reason, the laws of four states which affect the collection of debts have been included. Almost every state has some form of law regulating the collection of debts. There are listed three major industrial states and one rural state: Massachusetts, Illinois, New York, and New Hampshire. A law passed by a major city, New York, which is much more comprehensive than the law of the state of New York, is also provided. Actually, the New York City law is a mirror image of the Debt Collection Practices Act with very few changes.

The Federal Trade Commission Statement of General Policy and Interpretation with regard to the Fair Debt Collection Practices Act is a proposed commentary, and the commission held public hearings during 1986, concerning these proposed commentaries and interpretations. We suggest that the Federal Trade Commission be monitored with respect to final commentaries and interpretations which will be issued by the Commission.

For those that monitor and tape phone calls, the two major federal sections are set forth as well, as laws concerning this procedure of one of the more restrictive states, California. California requires the consent of both parties to tape a telephone call, which is more restrictive than the federal law which requires only the consent of one party. A few states follow California, but most follow the federal law.

Some examples of the laws affecting dishonored checks are also presented as well as some other general information which will be helpful in the collection effort.

Some of the laws and statutes set forth are not complete and are excerpts, due to space. Laws and statutes are continually amended, revised, and repealed. Furthermore, laws and statutes are continually interpreted not only by the federal agencies, such as the Federal Trade Commission, but, more significantly, by the state and federal courts.

Therefore, the laws, statutes, and decisions contained in this appendix and reference to laws in the book should be monitored on a continual basis and should be relied upon only to provide an overview of the basic considerations of a particular problem. Furthermore, the opinion and analysis of the author with regard to the meaning of the law, statutes, and decisions could radically change in view of new interpretations by Congress, the Federal Trade Commission, the legislatures of the states, or the decisions issued by both the state and federal courts.

Consultation with an experienced attorney is not only recommended but encouraged.

APPENDIX A

Federal Laws
Affecting Collection

1. CONSUMER PROTECTION ACT, AMENDMENTS

Public Law 95-109

91 STAT. 874   95th Congress

An Act

Sept. 20, 1977
[H.R. 5294]

To amend the Consumer Credit Protection Act to prohibit abusive practices by debt collectors.

Consumer Credit
Protection Act,
amendments.

Be it enacted by the Senate and House of Representatives of the United States of America in Congress assembled, that the Consumer Credit Protection Act (15 U.S.C. 1601 et seq.) is amended by adding at the end thereof the following new title:

Fair Debt Collection
Practices Act.

TITLE VIII—DEBT COLLECTION PRACTICES

15 USC 1601 note.

§801. Short title

"This title may be cited as the 'Fair Debt Collection Practices Act.'

15 USC 1692.

"§802. Findings and purpose

"(a) There is abundant evidence of the use of abusive, deceptive, and unfair debt collection practices by many debt collectors. Abusive debt collection practices contribute to the number of personal bankruptcies, to marital instability, to the loss of jobs, and to invasions of individual privacy.

"(b) Existing laws and procedures for redressing these injuries are inadequate to protect consumers.

"(c) Means other than misrepresentation or other abusive debt collection practices are available for the effective collection of debts.

"(d) Abusive debt collection practices are carried on to a substantial extent in interstate commerce and through means and instrumentalities of such commerce. Even where abusive debt collection practices are purely intrastate in character, they nevertheless directly affect interstate commerce.

"(e) It is the purpose of this title to eliminate abusive debt collection practices by debt collectors, to insure that those debt collectors who refrain from using abusive debt collection practices are not competitively disadvantaged, and to promote consistent State action to protect consumers against debt collection abuses.

15 USC 1692a.

"§803. Definitions

"As used in this title—

"(1) The term 'Commission' means the Federal Trade Commission.

"(2) The term 'communication' means the conveying of information regarding a debt directly or indirectly to any person through any medium.

"(3) The term 'consumer' means any natural person obligated or allegedly obligated to pay any debt.

"(4) The term 'creditor' means any person who offers or extends credit creating a debt or to whom a debt is owed, but such term does not include any person to the extent that he receives an assignment or transfer of a debt in default solely for the purpose of facilitating collection of such debt for another.

"(5) The term 'debt' means any obligation or alleged obligation of a consumer to pay money arising out of a transaction in which the money, property, insurance, or services which are the subject of the transaction are primarily for personal, family, or household purposes, whether or not such obligation has been reduced to judgment.

"(6) The term 'debt collector' means any person who uses any instrumentality of interstate commerce or the mails in any business the principal purpose of which is the collection of any debts, or who regularly collects or attempts to collect, directly or indirectly, debts owed or due or asserted to be owed or due another. Notwithstanding the exclusion provided by clause (G) of the last sentence of this paragraph, the term includes any creditor who, in the process of collecting his own debts, uses any name other than his own which would indicate that a third person is collecting or attempting to collect such debts. For the purpose of section 808(6), such term also includes any person who uses any instrumentality of interstate commerce or the mails in any business the principal purpose of which is the enforcement of security interests. The term does not include—

"(A) any officer or employee of a creditor while, in the name of the creditor, collecting debts for such creditor;

"(B) any person while acting as a debt collector for another person, both of whom are related by common ownership or affiliated by corporate control, if the person acting as a debt collector does so only for persons to whom it is so related or affiliated and if the principal business of such person is not the collection of debts;

"(C) any officer or employee of the United States or any State to the extent that collecting or attempting to collect any debt is in the performance of his official duties;

"(D) any person while serving or attempting to serve legal process on any other person in connection with the judicial enforcement of any debt;

"(E) any nonprofit organization which, at the request of consumers, performs bona fide consumer credit counseling and assists consumers in the liquidation of their debts by receiving payments from such consumers and distributing such amounts to creditors;

"(F) any attorney-at-law collecting a debt as an attorney on behalf of and in the name of a client; and

"(G) any person collecting or attempting to collect any debt owed or due or asserted to be owed or due another to the extent such activity (i) is incidental to a bona fide fiduciary obligation or a bona fide escrow arrangement; (ii) concerns a debt which was originated by such person; (iii) concerns a debt which was not in default at the time it was obtained by such person; or (iv) concerns a debt obtained by such person as a secured party in a commercial credit transaction involving the creditor.

"(7) The term 'location information' means a consumer's place of abode and his telephone number at such place, or his place of employment.

"(8) The term 'State' means any State, territory, or possession of the United States, the District of Columbia, the Commonwealth of Puerto Rico, or any political subdivision of any of the foregoing.

15 USC 1692b.

§804. Acquisition of location information

"Any debt collector communicating with any person other than the consumer for the purpose of acquiring location information about the consumer shall—

"(1) identify himself, state that he is confirming or correcting location information concerning the consumer, and, only if expressly requested, identify his employer;

"(2) not state that such consumer owes any debt;

"(3) not communicate with any such person more than once unless requested to do so by such person or unless the debt collector reasonably believes that the earlier response of such person is erroneous or incomplete and that such person now has correct or complete location information;

"(4) not communicate by post card;

"(5) not use any language or symbol on any envelope or in the contents of any communication effected by the mails or telegram that indicates that the debt collector is in the debt collection business or that the communication relates to the collection of a debt; and

"(6) after the debt collector knows the consumer is represented by an attorney with regard to the subject debt and has knowledge of, or can readily ascertain, such attorney's name and address, not communicate with any person other than that attorney, unless the attorney fails to respond within a reasonable period of time to communication from the debt collector.

15 USC 1692c.

"§805. Communication in connection with debt collection

"(a) COMMUNICATION WITH THE CONSUMER GENERALLY.—Without the prior consent of the consumer given directly to the debt collector or the express permission of a court of competent jurisdiction, a debt collector may not communicate with a consumer in connection with the collection of any debt—

"(1) at any unusual time or place or a time or place known or which should be known to be inconvenient to the consumer. In the absence of knowledge of circumstances to the contrary, a debt collector shall assume that the convenient time for communicating with a consumer is after 8 o'clock antimeridian and before 9 o'clock postmeridian, local time at the consumer's location;

"(2) if the debt collector knows the consumer is represented by an attorney with respect to such debt and has knowledge of, or can readily ascertain, such attorney's name and address, unless the attorney fails to respond within a reasonable period of time to a communication from the debt collector or unless the attorney consents to direct communication with the consumer; or

"(3) at the consumer's place of employment if the debt collector knows or has reason to know that the consumer's employer prohibits the consumer from receiving such communication.

"(b) COMMUNICATION WITH THIRD PARTIES.—Except as provided in section 804, without the prior consent of the consumer given directly to the debt collector, or the express permission of a court of competent jurisdiction, or as reasonably necessary to effectuate a postjudgment judicial remedy, a debt collector may not communicate, in connection with the collection of any debt, with any person other than the consumer, his attorney, a consumer reporting agency if otherwise permitted by law, the creditor, the attorney of the creditor, or the attorney of the debt collector.

"(c) CEASING COMMUNICATION.—If a consumer notifies a debt collector in writing that the consumer refuses to pay a debt or that the consumer wishes the debt collector to cease further communication with the consumer, the debt collector shall not communicate further with the consumer with respect to such debt, except—

　"(1) to advise the consumer that the debt collector's further efforts are being terminated;

　"(2) to notify the consumer that the debt collector or creditor may invoke specified remedies which are ordinarily invoked by such debt collector or creditor; or

　"(3) where applicable, to notify the consumer that the debt collector or creditor intends to invoke a specified remedy.

If such notice from the consumer is made by mail, notification shall be complete upon receipt.

"(d) For the purpose of this section, the term 'consumer' includes the consumer's spouse, parent (if the consumer is a minor), guardian, executor, or administrator.

15 USC 1692d.

"§806. Harassment or abuse

"A debt collector may not engage in any conduct the natural consequence of which is to harass, oppress, or abuse any person in connection with the collection of a debt. Without limiting the general application of the foregoing, the following conduct is a violation of this section:

　"(1) The use or threat of use of violence or other criminal means to harm the physical person, reputation, or property of any person.

　"(2) The use of obscene or profane language or language the natural consequence of which is to abuse the hearer or reader.

　"(3) The publication of a list of consumers who allegedly refuse to pay debts, except to a consumer reporting agency or to persons meeting the requirements of section 603(f) or 604(3) of this Act.

15 USC 1681a, 1681b.

(4) The advertisement for sale of any debt to coerce payment of the debt.

"(5) Causing a telephone to ring or engaging any person in telephone conversation repeatedly or continuously with intent to annoy, abuse, or harass any person at the called number.

"(6) Except as provided in section 804, the placement of telephone calls without meaningful disclosure of the caller's identity.

15 USC 1692e.

"§807. False or misleading representations

"A debt collector may not use any false, deceptive, or misleading representation or means in connection with the collection of any debt.

Without limiting the general application of the foregoing, the following conduct is a violation of this section:

"(1) The false representation or implication that the debt collector is vouched for, bonded by, or affiliated with the United States or any State, including the use of any badge, uniform, or facsimile thereof.

"(2) The false representation of—

"(A) the character, amount, or legal status of any debt; or,

"(B) any services rendered or compensation which may be lawfully received by any debt collector for the collection of a debt.

"(3) The false representation or implication that any individual is an attorney or that any communication is from an attorney.

"(4) The representation or implication that nonpayment of any debt will result in the arrest or imprisonment of any person or the seizure, garnishment, attachment, or sale of any property or wages of any person unless such action is lawful and the debt collector or creditor intends to take such action.

"(5) The threat to take any action that cannot legally be taken or that is not intended to be taken.

"(6) The false representation or implication that a sale, referral, or other transfer of any interest in a debt shall cause the consumer to—

"(A) lose any claim or defense to payment of the debt; or

"(B) become subject to any practice prohibited by this title.

"(7) The false representation or implication that the consumer committed any crime or other conduct in order to disgrace the consumer.

"(8) Communicating or threatening to communicate to any person credit information which is known or which should be known to be false, including the failure to communicate that a disputed debt is disputed.

"(9) The use or distribution of any written communication which simulates or is falsely represented to be a document authorized, issued, or approved by any court, official, or agency of the United States or any State, or which creates a false impression as to its source, authorization, or approval.

"(10) The use of any false representation or deceptive means to collect or attempt to collect any debt or to obtain information concerning a consumer.

"(11) Except as otherwise provided for communications to acquire location information under section 804, the failure to disclose clearly in all communications made to collect a debt or to obtain information about a consumer, that the debt collector is attempting to collect a debt and that any information obtained will be used for that purpose.

"(12) The false representation or implication that accounts have been turned over to innocent purchasers for value.

"(13) The false representation or implication that documents are legal process.

"(14) The use of any business, company, or organization name other than the true name of the debt collector's business, company, or organization.

"(15) The false representation or implication that documents are not legal process forms or do not require action by the consumer.

"(16) The false representation or implication that a debt collector operates or is employed by a consumer reporting agency as defined by section 603(f) of this Act.

15 USC 1681.

15 USC 1692f.

"§808. Unfair practices

"A debt collector may not use unfair or unconsciona-ble means to collect or attempt to collect any debt. Without limiting the general application of the foregoing, the following conduct is a violation of this section:

"(1) The collection of any amount (including any interest, fee, charge, or expense incidental to the principal obligation) unless such amount is expressly authorized by the agreement creating the debt or permitted by law.

"(2) The acceptance by a debt collector from any person of a check or other payment instrument postdated by more than five days unless such person is notified in writing of the debt collector's intent to deposit such check or instrument not more than ten nor less than three business days prior to such deposit.

"(3) The solicitation by a debt collector of any postdated check or other postdated payment instru-ment for the purpose of threatening or instituting criminal prosecution.

"(4) Depositing or threatening to deposit any postdated check or other postdated payment instru-ment prior to the date on such check or instrument.

"(5) Causing charges to be made to any person for communications by concealment of the true pur-pose of the communication. Such charges include, but are not limited to, collect telephone calls and telegram fees.

"(6) Taking or threatening to take any non-judicial action to effect dispossession or disablement of property if—

"(A) there is no present right to possession of the property claimed as collateral through an enforceable security interest;

"(B) there is no present intention to take possession of the property; or

"(C) the property is exempt by law from such dispossession or disablement.

"(7) Communicating with a consumer regard-ing a debt by post card.

"(8) Using any language or symbol, other than the debt collector's address, on any envelope when communicating with a consumer by use of the mails or by telegram, except that a debt collector may use his business name if such name does not indicate that he is in the debt collection business.

15 USC 1692g.   **"§809. Validation of debts**

"(a) Within five days after the initial communication with a consumer in connection with the collection of any debt, a debt collector shall, unless the following information is contained in the initial communication or the consumer has paid the debt, send the consumer a written notice containing—

"(1) the amount of the debt;

"(2) the name of the creditor to whom the debt is owed;

"(3) a statement that unless the consumer, within thirty days after receipt of the notice, disputes the validity of the debt, or any portion thereof, the debt will be assumed to be valid by the debt collector;

"(4) a statement that if the consumer notifies the debt collector in writing within the thirty-day period that the debt, or any portion thereof, is disputed, the debt collector will obtain verification of the debt or a copy of a judgment against the consumer and a copy of such verification or judgment will be mailed to the consumer by the debt collector; and

"(5) a statement that, upon the consumer's written request within the thirty-day period, the debt collector will provide the consumer with the name and address of the original creditor, if different from the current creditor.

"(b) If the consumer notifies the debt collector in writing within the thirty-day period described in subsection (a) that the debt, or any portion thereof, is disputed, or that the consumer requests the name and address of the original creditor, the debt collector shall cease collection of the debt, or any disputed portion thereof, until the debt collector obtains verification of the debt or a copy of a judgment, or the name and address of the original creditor, and a copy of such verification or judgment, or name and address of the original creditor, is mailed to the consumer by the debt collector.

"(c) The failure of a consumer to dispute the validity of a debt under this section may not be construed by any court as an admission of liability by the consumer.

15 USC 1692h.

"§810. Multiple debts

"If any consumer owes multiple debts and makes any single payment to any debt collector with respect to such debts, such debt collector may not apply such payment to any debt which is disputed by the consumer and, where applicable, shall apply such payment in accordance with the consumer's directions.

15 USC 1692i.

"§811. Legal actions by debt collectors

"(a) Any debt collector who brings any legal action on a debt against any consumer shall—

"(1) in the case of an action to enforce an interest in real property securing the consumer's obligation, bring such action only in a judicial district or similar legal entity in which such real property is located; or

"(2) in the case of an action not described in paragraph (1), bring such action only in the judicial district or similar legal entity—

"(A) in which such consumer signed the contract sued upon; or

"(B) in which such consumer resides at the commencement of the action.

"(b) Nothing in this title shall be construed to authorize the bringing of legal actions by debt collectors.

15 USC 1692j.

"§812. Furnishing certain deceptive forms

"(a) It is unlawful to design, compile, and furnish any form knowing that such form would be used to create the false belief in a consumer that a person other than the creditor of such consumer is participating in the collection of or in an attempt to collect a debt such consumer allegedly owes such creditor, when in fact such person is not so participating.

"(b) Any person who violates this section shall be liable to the same extent and in the same manner as a debt collector is liable under section 813 for failure to comply with a provision of this title.

"§813. Civil liability

"(a) Except as otherwise provided by this section, any debt collector who fails to comply with any provision of this title with respect to any person is liable to such person in an amount equal to the sum of—

"(1) any actual damage sustained by such person as a result of such failure;

"(2) (A) in the case of any action by an individual, such additional damages as the court may allow, but not exceeding $1,000; or

"(B) in the case of a class action, (i) such amount for each named plaintiff as could be recovered under subparagraph (A), and (ii) such amount as the court may allow for all other class members, without regard to a minimum individual recovery, not to exceed the lesser or $500,000 or 1 per centum of the net worth of the debt collector; and

"(3) in the case of any successful action to enforce the foregoing liability, the costs of the action, together with a reasonable attorney's fee as determined by the court. On a finding by the court that an action under this section was brought in bad faith and for the purpose of harassment, the court may award to the defendant attorney's fees reasonable in relation to the work expended and costs.

"(b) In determining the amount of liability in any action under subsection (a), the court shall consider, among other relevant factors—

"(1) in any individual action under subsection (a)(2)(A), the frequency and persistence of noncompliance by the debt collector, the nature of such noncompliance, and the extent to which such noncompliance was intentional; or

"(2) in any class action under subsection (a)(2)(B), the frequency and persistence of noncompliance by the debt collector, the nature of such noncompliance, the resources of the debt collector, the number of persons adversely affected, and the extent to which the debt collector's noncompliance was intentional.

"(c) A debt collector may not be held liable in any action brought under this title if the debt collector shows by a preponderance of evidence that the violation was not intentional and resulted from a bona fide error notwithstanding the maintenance of procedures reasonably adapted to avoid any such error.

Jurisdiction

"(d) An action to enforce any liability created by this title may be brought in any appropriate United States district court without regard to the amount in controversy, or in any other court of competent jurisdiction, within one year from the date on which the violation occurs.

"(e) No provision of this section imposing any liability shall apply to any act done or omitted in good faith in conformity with any advisory opinion of the Commission, notwithstanding that after such act or omission has occurred, such opinion is amended, rescinded, or determined by judicial or other authority to be invalid for any reason.

15 USC 1692l.

"§814. Administrative enforcement

"(a) Compliance with this title shall be enforced by the Commission, except to the extent that enforcement of the requirements imposed under this title is specifically committed to another agency under subsection (b). For purpose of the exercise by the Commission of its functions and powers under the Federal Trade Commission Act, a violation of this title shall be deemed an unfair or deceptive act or practice in violation of that Act. All of the functions and powers of the Commission under the Federal Trade Commission Act are available to the Commission to enforce compliance by any person with this title, irrespective of whether that person is engaged in commerce or meets any other jurisdictional tests in the Federal Trade Commission Act, including the power to enforce the provisions of this title in the same manner as if the violation had been a violation of a Federal Trade Commission trade regulation rule.

15 USC 58.

"(b) Compliance with any requirements imposed under this title shall be enforced under—

"(1) section 8 of the Federal Deposit Insurance Act, in the case of—

12 USC 1818.

"(A) national banks, by the Comptroller of the Currency;

"(B) member banks of the Federal Reserve System (other than national banks), by the Federal Reserve Board; and

"(C) banks the deposits or accounts of which are insured by the Federal Deposit Insurance Corporation (other than members of the Federal Reserve System), by the Board of Directors of the Federal Deposit Insurance Corporation;

12 USC 1464.

12 USC 1730.

12 USC 1426, 1437.

12 USC 1751.

"(2) section 5(d) of the Home Owners Loan Act of 1933, section 407 of the National Housing Act, and sections 6(i) and 17 of the Federal Home Loan Bank Act, by the Federal Home Loan Bank Board (acting directly or through the Federal Savings and Loan Insurance Corporation), in the case of any institution subject to any of those provisions;

"(3) the Federal Credit Union Act, by the Administrator of the National Credit Union Administration with respect to any Federal credit union:

"(4) the Acts to regulate commerce by the Interstate Commerce Commission with respect to any common carrier subject to those Acts;

49 USC 1301 note.

"(5) the Federal Aviation Act of 1958, by the Civil Aeronautics Board with respect to any air carrier or any foreign air carrier subject to that Act; and

7 USC 181.

7 USC 226, 227

"(6) the Packers and Stockyards Act, 1921 (except as provided in section 406 of that Act), by the Secretary of Agriculture with respect to any activities subject to that Act.

"(c) For the purpose of the exercise by any agency referred to in subsection (b) of its powers under any Act referred to in that subsection, a violation of any requirement imposed under this title shall be deemed to be a violation of a requirement imposed under that Act. In addition to its powers under any provision of law specifically referred to in subsection (b), each of the agencies referred to in that subsection may exercise, for the purpose of enforcing compliance with any requirement imposed under this title any other authority conferred on it by law, except as provided in subsection (d).

"(d) Neither the Commission nor any other agency referred to in subsection (b) may promulgate trade regulation rules or other regulations with respect to the collection of debts by debt collectors as defined in this title

15 USC 1692m.

"§815. Reports to Congress by the Commission

"(a) Not later than one year after the effective date of this title and at one-year intervals thereafter, the Commission shall make reports to the Congress concerning the administration of its functions under this title, including such recommendations as the Commission deems necessary or appropriate. In addition, each report of the Commission shall include its assessment of the extent to which compliance with this title is being achieved and a summary of the enforcement actions taken by the Commission under section 814 of this title.

"(b) In the exercise of its functions under this title, the Commission may obtain upon request the views of any other Federal agency which exercises enforcement functions under section 814 of this title.

15 USC 1692n.

"§816. Relation to State laws

"This title does not annul, alter, or affect, or exempt any person subject to the provisions of this title from complying with the laws of any State with respect to debt collection practices, except to the extent that those laws are inconsistent with any provision of this title, and then only to the extent of the inconsistency. For purposes of this section, a State law is not inconsistent with this title if the protection such law affords any consumer is greater than the protection provided by this title.

15 USC 1692o.

"§817. Exemption for State regulation

"The Commission shall by regulation exempt from the requirements of this title any class of debt collection practices within any State if the Commission determines that under the law of that State that class of debt collection practices is subject to requirements substantially similar to those imposed by this title, and that there is adequate provision for enforcement.

15 USC 1692 note.

"§818. Effective date

"This title takes effect upon the expiration of six months after the date of its enactment, but section 809 shall apply only with respect to debts for which the initial attempt to collect occurs after such effective date."

Approved September 20, 1977.

LEGISLATIVE HISTORY:

HOUSE REPORT No. 95-131 (Comm. on Banking, Finance, and Urban Affairs).
SENATE REPORT No. 95-382 (Comm. on Banking, Housing, and Urban Affairs).
CONGRESSIONAL RECORD, Vol. 123 (1977):
        Apr. 4, considered and passed House.
        Aug. 5, considered and passed Senate, amended.
        Sept. 8, House agreed to Senate amendment.
WEEKLY COMPILATION OF PRESIDENTIAL DOCU-MENTS, Vol. 13, No. 39:
        Sept. 20, Presidential statement.

2. EXPLANATION FROM FEDERAL TRADE COMMISSION ON THE FAIR DEBT COLLECTION PRACTICES ACT

ABUSIVE DEBT COLLECTION PRACTICES PROHIBITED

As of March 20, 1978, federal law prohibits abusive, deceptive, and unfair debt collection practices by debt collectors. What does this mean to the consumer? What is the law designed to do? Its purpose is to see that people are treated fairly by debt collectors. The law will not permit debt collectors to use unjust means while attempting to collect a debt. But, the law does not cancel genuine debts which consumers owe.

Many people never come in contact with a debt collector. For those who do, under the new law, you have new rights. This pamphlet is written to let you know your rights.

What Debts Are Covered?

Personal, family, and household debts are covered, like money owed for the purchase of a car, for medical care, or for charge accounts.

Who Is a Debt Collector?

A debt collector is anyone, other than the creditor or his attorney, who regularly collects debts for others.

How May a Debt Collector Contact You?

A debt collector may contact you in person, by mail, telephone, or telegram. However, it can't be at inconvenient or unusual times or places, such as before 8:00 a.m. or after 9:00 p.m., unless you agree.

A debt collector may **not** contact you at work, if your employer disapproves.

Can You Stop a Debt Collector from Contacting You?

Yes, you may stop a debt collector from contacting you by saying so in writing. Once you tell a debt collector not to contact you, the debt collector

can no longer do so, **except** to tell you that there will be no further contact
Also, the debt collector may notify you that some specific action may be taken,
but only if the debt collector or the creditor usually takes such action.

May a Debt Collector Contact Any Other Person Concerning Your Debt?

A debt collector may contact any person to locate you.

However, the debt collector must:

Only tell people that the purpose is to try to contact you.
Only contact your attorney if you have an attorney.

The debt collector must not:

Tell anybody else that you owe money.
In most cases, talk to any person more than once.
Use a post card.
Put anything on an envelope or in a letter that identifies the writer as a
debt collector.

What Is the Debt Collector Required to Tell You About the Debt?

Within five days after you are first contacted, the debt collector must send
you a **written notice** telling you—

- the amount of money you owe;
- the name of the creditor to whom you owe the money; and
- what to do if you feel you do not owe the money.

If You Feel You Do Not Owe the Money, May a Debt Collector Continue to Contact You?

The debt collector must not contact you if you send a letter within thirty
days after you are first contacted saying you do not owe the money. However,
a debt collector can begin collection activities again if you are sent proof of
the debt, such as a copy of the bill.

What Types of Debt Collection Practices Are Prohibited?

A debt collector may not **harass, oppress,** or **abuse** any person. For
example, a debt collector cannot:

Use threats of violence to harm anyone or anyone's property or
reputation.
Publish a list of consumers which says you refuse to pay your debts
(except to a credit bureau).
Use obscene or profane language.

Repeatedly use the telephone to annoy anyone.

Telephone any person without identifying the caller.

Advertise your debt.

A debt collector may **not** use any **false** statements when collecting any debt. For example, the debt collector cannot:

Falsely imply that the debt collector represents the United States government or any state government.

Falsely imply that the debt collector is an attorney.

Falsely imply that **you** committed any crime.

Falsely represent that the debt collector operates or works for a credit bureau.

Misrepresent the amount of the debt.

Represent that papers being sent are legal forms, such as a summons, when they are not.

Represent that papers being sent are **not** legal forms when they **are**. Also, a debt collector may not say:

- That you will be arrested or imprisoned if you do not pay your debt.

- That he will **seize, garnish, attach,** or **sell your property** or **wages, unless** the debt collector or the creditor intends to do so and it is legal.

- That any **action** will be taken against you which **cannot legally** be taken.

A debt collector may not:

- Give false **credit information** about you to anyone.

- Send you anything that looks like an **official** document which might be sent by any **court** or **agency** of the **United States** or any **state** or **local** government.

- Use any false name.

A debt collector must not be **unfair** in attempting to collect any debt. For example, the debt collector cannot:

- Collect any amount greater than the amount of your debt, unless allowed by law.

- Deposit any postdated check before the date on that check.

- Make you accept collect calls or pay for telegrams.

- Take or threaten to take your property unless there is a present right to do so.

- Contact you by post card.

- Put anything on an envelope other than the debt collector's address and name. Even the name cannot be used if it shows that the communication is about the collection of a debt.

What Control Do You Have over Specific Debts?

If you owe several debts, any payment you make must be applied as you choose. And, a debt collector cannot apply a payment to any debt you feel you do not owe.

What Can You Do If the Debt Collector Breaks the Law?

You have the right to sue a debt collector in a state or federal court within 1 year from the date the law was violated. You may recover money for the damage you suffered. Court costs and attorney's fees can also be recovered.

A group of persons may sue a debt collector and recover money for damages up to $500,000.

Who Can You Tell If the Debt Collector Breaks the Law?

You should contact the proper federal government enforcement agency. The agencies use complaints to decide which companies to investigate. Many states also have debt collection laws of their own. Check with your state Attorney General's office to determine your rights under state law

Where Should You Send Complaints and Questions?

Unless your complaint is about collection practices by banks and other financial institutions, write to:

Federal Trade Commission, Debt Collection Practices, Washington, D.C. 20580 or one of the FTC Regional Offices listed below:

Atlantic Regional Office, 1718 Peachtree Street, N.W., Suite 1000, Atlanta, Georgia 30309 • **Boston Regional Office,** 1301 Analex Building, 150 Causeway, Boston, Massachusetts 02114 • **Chicago Regional Office**, Suite 1437, 55 East Monroe Street, Chicago, Illinois 60603 • **Cleveland Regional Office,** Suite 500, The Mall Bldg., 118 Saint Clair, Cleveland, Ohio 44114 • **San Francisco Regional Office,** 450 Golden Gate Avenue, Box 36005, San Francisco, California 94102 • **Dallas Regional Office,** 2001 Bryan Street, Suite 2665, Dallas, Texas 75201 • **Denver Regional Office,** Suite 2900, 1405 Curtis Street, Denver, Colorado 80202 • **Los Angeles Regional Office,** 11000 Wilshire Blvd., Room 13209, Los Angeles, California 90024 • **New York Regional Office,** 22nd Floor, Federal Bldg., 26 Federal Plaza, New York, New York 10007 • **Seattle Regional Office,** 28th Floor, Federal Bldg., 915 Second Ave., Seattle, Washington 98174

If a bank is involved, write to one of the agencies listed below:

- If the bank is nationally chartered ("National" or "N.A." will appear in the bank's name), write to:

Comptroller of the Currency, Consumer Affairs Division, Washington, D.C. 20219.

- If the bank is state chartered and is a member of the Federal Reserve System, write to:
  Board of Governors of the Federal Reserve System, Director, Division of Consumer Affairs, Washington, D.C. 20551.

- If the bank is state chartered and is insured by the Federal Deposit Insurance Corporation (FDIC) but is not a member of the Federal Reserve System, write to:
  Federal Deposit Insurance Corporation, Office of Bank Customer Affairs, Washington, D.C. 20429.

- If a federally-chartered or federally-insured Savings and Loan Association is involved, write to:
  Federal Home Loan Bank Board, Washington, D.C. 20552.

- If a federally chartered Credit Union is involved, write to:
  Federal Credit Union Administration, Division of Consumer Affairs, Washington, D.C. 20456.

To Find Out More

If you have any general questions about the Fair Debt Collection Practices Act that are not answered by this pamphlet, or you wish to complain about collection practices by creditors, write to the Federal Trade Commission, Debt Collection Practices, Washington, D.C. 20580 or to one of its regional offices.

3. FEDERAL TRADE COMMISSION STATEMENTS OF GENERAL POLICY OR INTERPRETATION ON THE DEBT COLLECTION PRACTICES ACT

AGENCY: Federal Trade Commission

ACTION;   Proposed Official Staff Commentary

SUMMARY: The Commission staff is seeking comment on its proposal for a commentary on the Fair Debt Collection Practices Act that will supersede all previously issued staff interpretations of the Act. The purpose of the commentary is to clarify and codify these interpretations.

DATE: The Commission staff is requesting public comment on the proposed official staff commentary until *(60 days after publication)*.

ADDRESS: Comments on the commentary should be sent to
Secretary, Federal Trade Commission
Attention: FDCPA Commentary
Washington, D.C. 20580

FOR FURTHER INFORMATION CONTACT:
Clarke Brinckerhoff, Attorney
John F. LeFevre, Program Advisor, General Credit Program
Division of Credit Practices
Federal Trade Commission
Washington, D.C. 20580
(202) 326-2000

SUPPLEMENTARY INFORMATION

Background

The Fair Debt Collection Practices Act [15 USC 1692 et seq.] was enacted on September 20, 1977, and became effective on March 20, 1978. The Act regulates the collection activities of independent debt collectors and specifically proscribes certain practices found by Congress to be deceptive, unfair, or abusive to consumers. It also requires debt collectors to disclose

310

certain information to consumers about the debts being collected, as well as about consumers' rights to dispute and obtain verification of their debts. Finally, it requires debt collectors to abide by consumers' written requests to cease all further communication about their debts.

Section 814 [15 USC 1692 (1)] gives the Federal Trade Commission primary responsibility for the Act's administration and enforcement, using all the functions and powers that it has under the Federal Trade Commission Act. Although the Commission has initiated a number of formal actions against debt collectors in the eight years since the Fair Debt Collection Practices Act became effective, a significant part of its activity has involved informal staff interpretations issued by the staff of the Bureau of Consumer Protection's Division of Credit Practices in response to hundreds of requests from consumers and industry. There are now approximately 210 interpretations totaling more than 1,000 pages.

Although many interpretations have been published in three volumes as official staff interpretations, they are inadequately indexed and are only occasionally cross-referenced. Some have been superseded or overruled by court opinions, by subsequent interpretations, or by consent judgments obtained in the Commission's enforcement program. Others reflect a reading of the statute that is either inconsistent with the Act's language or purpose, or is inappropriate in light of subsequent experiences. As a result, these informal staff letters appear to be of little assistance to debt collectors, consumers, or their respective counsel, in interpreting the Act.

The Bureau of Consumer Protection staff believes that this system of interpreting the Act needs to be streamlined and brought up-to-date. For this reason, the staff has prepared a "commentary" on the Act. The staff reviewed all the interpretations, resolved inconsistencies, and discarded those that it believes are not supported by the Act or that merely paraphrase the Act without clarifying its meaning. The Consumer Protection staff summarized the remaining interpretations that the staff believes need clarification in one document that comments upon each provision of the statute that has given rise to questions.

Changing the current system will offer three benefits. First, modifying and simplifying the format of the staff interpretations will make it easier for interested parties to find answers to their questions. Currently, the interpretations are voluminous and difficult to handle and, in their present format, cannot effectively communicate staff's views about the Act to the public.

Second, the commentary will present a more comprehensive view of the statute. Previously, a particular interpretation might have been useful only for parties whose specific problems were similar to the factual situation addressed in the interpretation, since the interpretations did not provide a rationale that could be more generally applied, when appropriate, to a larger number of factually related cases. Additionally, there are portions of the statute that may need clarification, but have not been interpreted at all. The staff has addressed these problems in the proposed commentary by (1) expanding the discussion of certain portions of the statute, where appropriate, and (2) providing views on some portions of the statute that have not been the subject of previous interpretations.

Third, the commentary's pre-emption of inconsistent and inaccurate advice in some prior interpretations should increase compliance with the Act. Members of the debt collection industry are more likely to rely on staff interpretations for guidance if the interpretations consistently offer sound advice.

The proposed commentary presents the most helpful of the existing interpretations and interprets other portions of the statute, where needed, in a clear and comprehensible format. Some previous interpretations have been eliminated, some have been recast, and some remain as originally published. All have been drafted to include only the essential elements of the principle involved to make them easy to understand. Since they are only interpretations, however, they are not trade regulation rules or regulations, and therefore have no binding effect on the Commission or the public.

The following paragraphs highlight some subjects where the views expressed in the commentary are different either in substance or emphasis from those expressed in prior informal staff interpretations. This list is not all-inclusive.

1. *Inclusion of Taxes and Fines in the Definition of "Debt"* [§803(5)]. The commentary overrules interpretations that taxes and fines may be "debts" within the meaning of the Act, because they do not result from a transaction involving purchase of a property or service. It is in accord with the well-reasoned opinion of the Court of Appeals in *Staub v. Harris*, 626 F.2d 275 (3d Cir. 1980), which specifically rejected the prior staff opinions that taxes are debts.

2. *Scope of the Exemption for Attorneys* [§803 (6) (F)]. The meaning of the phrase "collecting a debt as an attorney on behalf of and in the name of a client" has been the subject of much discussion and confusion. The commentary eliminates all previous interpretations and substitutes the standards outlined in the Commission's statement accompanying its recent consent judgment in *United States v. Shaffner*, Civil Action No. 83-C-3130 (N.D. Ill. 1983). It includes within the exemption attorneys conducting professional legal services, but excludes attorneys operating traditional debt collection agencies.

3. *Calls at Inconvenient Times* [§805 (a) (1)]. Some previous staff interpretations stated that Sunday calls by a collector to a consumer are illegal *per se*. The commentary overrules these opinions, which are inconsistent with the Act's flexible treatment of this issue.

4. *Incidental Contacts with Telephone Operators* [§805 (b)]. Previously issued interpretations considered certain incidental collection contacts with telephone operators, which occurred in the course of calling a consumer, to be illegal third-party contacts. The commentary overrules these opinions, and states that there is no violation where the sole purpose of the contact with an operator (or telegraph clerk) is transmission of a message, and the information conveyed is limited to that necessary to enable the debt collector to make contact with the consumer. It is staff's view that the communication is with the consumer, not the operator, and that this section was not intended to prohibit incidental contacts with intermediaries who are assisting a debt collector to communicate with the consumer.

5. *Reference to "Copy of a Judgment" in Validation Notice* [§§807 (2) (A) ; 809 (a) (4)]. Previous staff interpretations stated that there must be a judgment in existence if the words "copy of a judgment" are included in the validation notice sent out by a debt collector to comply with §809 (a) (4), or the notice including this phrase would violate §807 (2) (A) by misleading the consumer as to the legal status of the debt. Because the practical effect of these interpretations has made compliance with one section of the Act [§809 (a) (4)] a violation of another [§807 (2) (A)], the commentary overrules this position and states that the phrase may be used in the notice, whether or not a judgment in fact exists. The staff's current position is in accord with the decision in *Blackwell v. Professional Business Services of Georgia, Inc.*, 526 F. Supp. 535 (N.D. Ga. 1981), which specifically rejected the staff opinions to the contrary.

6. *Reference to Impending Action* [§807 (5)]. A number of previous interpretations imposed differing, and sometimes inconsistent, standards concerning the circumstances under which a debt collector is permitted to represent that legal action or other action may or will occur. The commentary supersedes these interpretations and substitutes the more uniform standards imposed in the Commission's most recent consent judgments concerning this issue.

7. *Required Disclosures in Collection Communications* [§807 (11)]. Some courts have required the designated disclosures in every single written and oral collection communication to the consumer and third parties. The commentary interprets the subsection less strictly, taking into account situations where the disclosures do not appear necessary, in accordance with the Commission's Sixth and Seventh Annual Reports to Congress and with the most recent Court of Appeals decision in *Pressley v. Capital Credit and Collection Service, Inc.*, 760 F.2d 922 (9th Cir. 1985).

8. *General Elements of Unfairness* [§808]. Previous staff interpretations have not addressed what criteria will be used in determining whether an act or

practice violates the basic requirements of §808. The commentary addresses these issues, stating that an act by a debt collector will be deemed "unfair" if it causes injury to a consumer that is substantial, not reasonably avoidable, and is not outweighed by countervailing benefits.

9. *Surcharges* [§808 (1)]. A number of early interpretations have attempted to prescribe varying standards concerning (1) when a "surcharge" is permitted and (2) how much it should be. The commentary overrules these interpretations and establishes that state law will determine the result, because this approach is consistent with the specific language of the Act.

10. *Form of Validation Notice* [§809 (a)]. Several staff interpretations have indicated that the statement of consumer rights required by §809 (a) (3-5) may be on a separate piece of paper from (or the reverse side of) the disclosure of the debt required by §809 (a) (1-2) only if there is clear notice on the first piece (or in front of) the disclosure. The commentary overrules these opinions, because the Act contains no requirements as to particular form, sequence, or location for such a statement.

Requests for Information

The staff of the Bureau of Consumer Protection's Division of Credit Practices will accept written comments on the proposed staff commentary for a period of 60 days. The Commission staff is interested in receiving comments to aid in its consideration of the commentary, because it recognizes that it may have a substantial impact on the debt collection industry and the consuming public. Comments may be addressed to any aspect of the commentary, including the following:

1. Is a commentary an acceptable format in which to communicate staff views on the FDCPA? Are members of the public (including the debt collection industry, consumers, and others) more likely to rely on the commentary than on existing staff interpretations of the Act? Why or why not?

2. The proposed commentary (a) eliminates interpretations that are considered to be relatively unimportant, (b) recasts or overrules other interpretations that appear inaccurate, or inconsistent with other more recent interpretations, and (c) restates the remaining interpretations in a more understandable format. Are the modifications made by the proposed commentary beneficial to the industry and members of the public?

3. Are there any changes from prior staff interpretations reflected in the commentary that you think are particularly valuable? If so, which one(s) and why?

4. Will any part of the commentary as presently drafted impose unnecessary burdens on industry or cause unnecessary injury to consumers?

By direction of the Commission.

Emily H. Rock

Secretary

4. FEDERAL TRADE COMMISSION STAFF COMMENTARY ON THE FAIR DEBT COLLECTION PRACTICES ACT

INTRODUCTION

This Commentary is the vehicle by which the staff of the Bureau of Consumer Protection publishes its interpetations of the Fair Debt Collection Practices Act (FDCPA). It is a guideline intended to clarify the staff interpretations of the statute, but does not have the force or effect of statutory provisions. It is not a formal trade regulation rule or advisory opinion of the Commission, and thus is not binding on the Commission or the public.

The Commentary is based primarily on issues discussed in informal staff letters responding to public requests for interpretations and on the Commission's enforcement program, subsequent to the FDCPA's enactment. It is intended to synthesize staff views on important issues and to give clear advice where inconsistencies have been discovered among staff letters. In some cases, reflection on the issues posed or relevant court decisions have resulted in a different interpretation from that expressed by staff in those informal letters. Therefore, the Commentary supersedes the staff views expressed in such correspondence. However, the Bureau of Consumer Protection staff will not recommend an enforcement action for prior conduct in reliance upon previous staff advice that we now overrule or otherwise modify.

In many cases, several different sections or subsections of the FDCPA may apply to a given factual situation. This results from the effort by Congress in drafting the FDCPA to be both explicit and comprehensive, in order to limit the opportunities for debt collectors to evade the underlying legislative intention. Although it may be of only technical interest whether a given act violates one, two, or three sections of the FDCPA, the staff has attempted to refer to all applicable sections so that the Commentary may serve as a comprehensive reference for its users. The Commentary contains discussions of the most common overlapping references (usually under the heading "Relation to other sections"), and deals with issues raised by each factual situation under the section or subsection that staff deems most directly applicable to it.

The Commentary will be revised and updated by the staff as needed, based on the experience of the Commission in responding to public inquiries about, and enforcing, the FDCPA. The Commission welcomes input from interested industry, consumer, and other public parties on the Commentary and on issues discussed in it.

Staff will continue to respond to requests for informal interpretations. Updates of the Commentary will consider and, where appropriate, incorporate issues raised in correspondence and other public contacts, as well as the Commission's enforcement efforts. Therefore, a party who is interested in raising an issue for inclusion in future editions of the Commentary does not need to make any formal submission or request to that effect. However, requests for formal advisory opinions of the Commission must still be made in accord with Commission rules [16 C.F.R. 1.2].

The Commentary should be used in conjunction with the statute. The abbreviated description of each section or subsection in the Commentary is designed only as a preamble to discussion of issues pertaining to each section, and is not intended as a substitute for the statutory text.

The Commentary should not be considered as a reflection of all court rulings under the FDCPA. Indeed, the staff's enforcement position may not be in accord with some judicial interpretations of the statute, particularly on issues that have been addressed only by lower courts or that have been addressed by the courts in ways that are not consistent with one another.

§801—Short Titles

Section 801 names the statute the "Fair Debt Collection Practices Act."

The Fair Debt Collection Practices Act (FDCPA) is Title VIII of the Consumer Credit Protection Act, which also includes other federal statutes relating to consumer credit, such as the Truth in Lending Act (Title I), the Fair Credit Reporting Act (Title VI), and the Equal Credit Opportunity Act (Title VII).

§802—Findings and Purpose

Section 802 recites the Congressional findings that serve as the basis for the legislation.

§803—Definitions

Section 803 (1) defines "Commission" as the Federal Trade Commission.

  1. *General.* The definition includes only the Federal Trade Commission, not necessarily the staff acting on its behalf.

Section 803 (2) defines "communication" as the "conveying of information regarding a debt directly or indirectly to any person through any medium."

1. *General.* The definition includes oral and written transmission of messages which refer to a debt.

2. *Exclusions.* The term does not include situations where the debt collector does not convey information regarding the debt, such as:

   - A request to a third party for a consumer to return a telephone call to the debt collector, if the debt collector does not refer to the debt or the caller's status as (or affiliation with) a debt collector.

   - A request to a third party for information about the consumer's assets, if the debt collector does not reveal the existence of a debt.

Section 803 (3) defines "consumer" as "any natural person obligated or allegedly obligated to pay any debt."

1. *General.* The definition includes only a "natural person" and not an artificial person such as a corporation or other entity created by statute.

Section 803 (4) defines "creditor" as "any person who offers or extends credit creating a debt or to whom a debt is owed." However, the definition excludes a party who "receives an assignment or transfer of a debt in default solely for the purpose of facilitating collection of such debt for another."

1. *General.* The definition includes the party that actually extended credit or became the obligee on an account in the normal course of business, and excludes a party that was assigned the debt only for collection purposes.

Section 803 (5) defines "debt" as a consumer's monetary obligation "arising out of a transaction in which the money, property, insurance, or services (being purchased) are primarily for person, family, or household purposes...."

1. *Examples.* The term includes:
   - Overdue obligations such as medical bills that were originally payable in full within a certain time period (e.g., 30 days).

   - A dishonored check that was tendered in payment for goods or services acquired or used primarily for personal, family, or household purposes.

2. *Exclusions.* The term does not include:
   - Unpaid taxes and fines, because they are not debts incurred from a "transaction (involving purchases of) property...or services...for personal, family, or household purposes."

- A credit card that a cardholder retains after the card issuer has demanded its return. The cardholder's account balance is the debt.

Section 803 (6) defines "debt collector" as a party "who uses any instrumentality of interstate commerce or the mails in [connection with]...any debt owed...another."

1. *Examples.* The term includes:
   - Employees of a debt collection business, including a corporation, partnership, or other entity whose business is the collection of debts owed another.

   - A management firm that regularly collects overdue rent on behalf of real estate owners, because it "regularly collects...debts owed or due another."

   - A party based in the United States who collects debts owed by consumers residing outside the United States, because he "uses...the mails" in a collection business. The residence of the debtor is irrelevant.

   - A firm that collects debts for a creditor solely by mechanical techniques, such as (1) placing phone calls with prerecorded messages and recording consumer responses, or (2) making computer-generated mailings.

2. *Exclusions.* The term does not include:
   - Any person who collects debts (or attempts to do so) only in isolated instances, because the definition includes only those who "regularly" collect debts.

   - A credit card issuer that collects its cardholder's account, even when the account is based upon purchases from participating merchants, because the issuer is collecting its own debts, not those "owed or due another."

3. *Application of definition to creditor using another name.* Creditors are generally excluded from the definition of "debt collector" to the extent that they collect their own debts in their own name. However, the term specifically applies to "any creditor who, in the process of collecting his own debts, uses any name other than his own which would indicate that a third person is involved in the collection."

   A creditor is a debt collector for purposes of this Act if:

   - He uses a name other than his own to collect his debts, including a fictitious name.

   - His salaried attorney employees who collect debts use stationery that indicates the attorneys are employed by someone other than the creditor or are independent or separate from the creditor.

- He regularly collects debts for another creditor; however, he is a debt collector only for purposes of collecting these debts, not when he collects his own debt in his own name.

- The creditor's collection division is not clearly designated as being affiliated with the creditor; however, the creditor is not a debt collector if the creditor's correspondence is clearly labeled as being from the "collection unit of the (creditor's name)," since the creditor is not using a "name other than his own" in that instance.

Relation to other sections. A creditor who is covered by the FDCPA because he uses a "name other than his own" also may violate §807 (14), which prohibits using a false business name. When he uses an attorney's name, he violates §807(3).

4. *Specific exemptions from definition of debt collector.*

(a) *Creditor employees.* Section 803 (6) (A) provides that "debt collector" does not include "any officer or employee of a creditor while, in the name of the creditor, collecting debts for such creditor."

The exemption includes a collection agency employee, who works for a creditor to collect in the creditor's name at the creditor's office under the creditor's supervision, because he has become the *de facto* employee of the creditor.

The exemption does not include a creditor's former employee who continues to collect accounts on the creditor's behalf, if he acts under his own name rather than the creditor's.

(b) *Creditor-controlled collector.* Section 803(6) (B) provides that "debt collector" does not include a party collecting for another, where they are both "related by common ownership or affiliated by corporate control, if the (party collects) only for persons to whom it is so related or affiliated and if the principal business of such person is not the collection of debts."

The exemption applies where the collector and creditor have "common ownership or…corporate control." For example, a company is exempt when it attempts to collect debts of another company after the two entities have merged.

The exemption does not apply to an entity whose principal activity is debt collection, even if it is under common ownership with a differently-named creditor and collects debts only for that party.

The exemption does not apply to a party related to a creditor if it also collects debts for others in addition to the related creditors.

(c) State and federal officials. Section 803 (6) (C) provides that "debt collector" does not include any state or federal employee "to the extent that collecting or attempting to collect any debt is in the performance of his official duties."

The exemption applies only to such governmental employees in the performance of their "official duties" and, therefore, does not apply to an attorney employed by a county government who also collects bad checks for local merchants where that activity is outside his official duties.

(d) *Process servers.* Section 803 (6) (D) provides that "debt collector" does not include "any person while serving or attempting to serve legal process on any other person in connection with the judicial enforcement of any debt."

The exemption covers marshals, sheriffs, and any other process servers while conducting their normal duties relating to serving legal papers.

(e) *Nonprofit counselors.* Section 803 (6) (E) provides that "debt collector" does not include "any nonprofit organization which, at the request of consumers, performs bona fide consumer credit counseling and assists consumers in the liquidation of their debts by receiving payments from such consumers and distributing such amounts to creditors."

This exemption applies only to nonprofit organizations; it does not apply to for-profit credit counseling services that accept fees from debtors and regularly transmit such funds to creditors.

(f) *Attorneys.* Section 803 (6) (F) provides that "debt collector" does not include "any attorney-at-law collecting a debt as an attorney on behalf of and in the name of a client."

The exemption includes attorneys who collect debts in the course of providing professional legal services to either a creditor or debt collector.

The exemption includes an attorney's nonattorney employees only when they are participating in the provision of legal services by attorneys.

The exemption includes firms that are engaged primarily in the provision of professional legal services. For example, it includes a firm whose clientele includes merchants who expect their attorneys to handle delinquent accounts, among other legal chores (e.g., leases, licenses, contract negotiations).

The exemption does not include firms that are engaged primarily in the collection of debts rather than the provision of professional legal services, even if they are owned by attorneys. For example, firms that primarily collect debts and typically delegate primary or exclusive responsibility to their nonattorney employees to handle all aspects of collection work, such as evaluating consumer files, handling mail and telephone contacts, negotiating settlements, making payment arrangements and the like, are not within the exemption.

Whether or not an attorney or law firm is providing professional legal services to a creditor is a question of fact that will turn on a number of factors, including the nature of the attorney-creditor relationship, the type and variety of legal work done by the attorney for the creditor, and the degree to which such work requires the unique expertise, training, and background of an attorney.

(g) *Miscellaneous*. Section 803 (6) (G) provides that "debt collector" does not include collection activity by a party about a debt that "(i) is incidental to a bona fide fiduciary obligation or...escrow arrangements; (ii)...was originated by such person; (iii)...was not in default at the time it was obtained by such person; or (iv) (was) obtained by such person as a secured party in a commercial credit transaction involving the creditor."

The exemption (i) for bona fide fiduciary obligations or escrow arrangements applies to entities such as trust departments of banks, and escrow companies.

The exemption (ii) for a party that originated the debt applies to the original creditor collecting his own debts in his own name. It also applies when a creditor assigns a debt originally owed to him, but retains the authority to collect the obligation on behalf of the assignee to whom the debt becomes owed. For example, the exemption applies to a creditor who makes a mortgage or school loan and continues to handle the account after assigning it to a third party. However, it does not apply to a party that takes assignment of retail installment contracts from the original creditor and then reassigns them to another creditor but continues to collect the debt arising from the contracts, because the debt was not "originated by" the collector/first assignee.

The exception (iii) for debts not in default when obtained applies to parties such as mortgage service companies whose business is servicing current accounts.

The exemption (iv) for a secured party in a commercial transaction applies to a commercial lender who acquires a consumer account that was used as collateral, following default on a loan from the commercial lender to the original creditor.

Section 803 (7) defines "location information" as "a consumer's place of abode and his telephone number at such place, or his place of employment."

This definition includes only residence, home phone number, and place of employment. It does not cover work phone numbers, names of supervisors and their telephone numbers, salaries or dates of paydays.

Section 803 (8) defines "state" as "any State territory, or possession of the United States, the District of Columbia, the Commonwealth of Puerto Rico, or any political subdivision of any of the foregoing."

§804—Acquisition of Location Information

Section 804 requires a debt collector, when communicating with third parties for the purpose of acquiring information about the consumer's location to "(1) identify himself, state that he is confirming or correcting location information concerning the consumer, and, only if expressly requested identify his employer," (2) not refer to the debt, (3) usually make only a single contact with each third party, (4) not communicate by post card, (5) not indicate the collection nature of his business purpose in any written communication, and (6) normally limit communications to the consumer's attorney, where the collector knows of the attorney.

1. *General.* Although the FDCPA generally protects the consumer's privacy by limiting debt collector communications about personal affairs to third parties, it recognizes the need for some third party contact by collectors to seek the whereabouts of the consumer.

2. *Identification of debt collector [§804 (1)].* An individual employed by a debt collector seeking location information must identify himself, but must not identify his employer unless asked. When asked, however, he must give the true and full name of the employer, to comply with this provision and avoid a violation of §807 (14).

An individual debt collector may use an alias if it is used consistently and if it does not interfere with another party's ability to identify him (e.g., the true identity can be ascertained from the employer).

3. *Referral to debt [§804 (2)].* A debt collector may not refer to the consumer's debt in any third party communication seeking location information, including those with other creditors.

4. *Reference to debt collector's business [§804 (5)].* A debt collector may not use his actual name in his letterhead or elsewhere in a written communication seeking location information, if the name indicates collection activity, such as a name containing the word "debt", "collector", or "collection."

5. *Communication with consumer's attorney [§804 (6)].* Once a debt collector learns a consumer is represented by an attorney, he must limit his request for location information to the attorney. [See also comments on §805 (a) (2).]

§805—Communication in Connection with Debt Collection

Section 805 (a)—Communication with the consumer. Unless the consumer has consented or a court order permits, a debt collector may not

communicate with a consumer to collect a debt (1) at any time or place which is unusual or known to be inconvenient to the consumer (8AM-9PM is presumed to be convenient), (2) where he knows the consumer is represented by an attorney with respect to the debt, or (3) at work if he knows the consumer's employer prohibits such contacts.

1. *Scope.* For purposes of this section, the term "communicate" is given its commonly accepted meaning. Thus, the section applies to contacts with the consumer related to the collection of the debt, whether or not the debt is specifically mentioned.

2. *Inconvenient or unusual times or places [§805 (a) (1)].* A debt collector may not call the consumer at any time, or on any particular day, if he has credible information (from the consumer or elsewhere) that it is inconvenient. If the debt collector does not have such information, a call on Sunday is not *per se* illegal.

3. *Consumer represented by attorney [§805 (a) (2)].* If a debt collector learns that a consumer is represented by an attorney, even if not formally notified of this fact, the debt collector must contact only the attorney and must not contact the consumer.

A debt collector who knows a consumer is represented by an attorney with respect to a debt is not required to assume similar representation on other debts; however, if a consumer notifies the debt collector that the attorney has been retained to represent him for all current and future debts that may be placed with the debt collector, the debt collector must deal only with that attorney.

The creditor's knowledge that the consumer has an attorney is not automatically imputed to the debt collector.

4. *Calls at work [§805 (a) (3)].* A debt collector may not call the consumer at work if he has reason to know the employer forbids such communication.

Section §805 (b)—Communication with third parties. Unless the consumer consents, or a court order or §804 permits, "or as reasonably necessary to effectuate a postjudgment judicial remedy," a debt collector "may not communicate, in connection with the collection of any debt, with any person other than the consumer, his attorney, a consumer reporting agency if otherwise permitted by law, the creditor, the attorney of the creditor, or the attorney of the debt collector."

1. *Consumer consent to the third party contact.* The consumer's consent need not be in writing. It may be presumed from circumstances, such as if a third party volunteers that a consumer has authorized him to pay

the consumer's account. However, consent may not be inferred only from a consumer's reaction when the debt collector requests such consent.

2. *Location information.* Although a debt collector's search for information concerning the consumer's location (provided for in §804) is expressly excepted from the ban on third party contacts, a debt collector may not call third parties under the pretense of gaining information already in his possession.

3. *Incidental contacts with telephone operator or telegraph clerk.* A debt collector may contact an employee of a telephone or telegraph company in order to contact the consumer, without violating the prohibition on communication to third parties, if the only information given is that necessary to enable the collector to transmit the message to, or make the contact with, the consumer.

4. *Accessibility by third party.* A debt collector may not send a written message that is easily accessible to third parties. For example, he may not use a computerized billing statement that can be seen on the envelope itself.

A debt collector may use an "in care of" letter only if the consumer lives at, or accepts mail at, the other party's address.

A debt collector does not violate this provision when an eavesdropper overhears a conversation with the consumer, unless the debt collector has reason to anticipate the conversation will be overheard.

5. *Non-excepted parties.* A debt collector may contact only the parties specified in this section (consumer, creditor, a party's attorney, or credit bureau). For example, a collector may not contact a bank about a dishonored check, or (without the consumer's consent) make a report on a consumer to a nonprofit counseling service.

6. *Judicial remedy.* The words "as reasonably necessary to effectuate a postjudgment judicial remedy" mean a communication necessary for execution or enforcement of the remedy. A debt collector may not send a copy of the judgment to an employer, except as part of a formal service of papers to achieve a garnishment or other remedy.

7. *Audits or inquiries.* A debt collector may disclose his files to a government official or an auditor, to respond to an inquiry or conduct an audit, because the disclosure would not be "in connection with the collection of any debt."

8. *Receipt to third party.* A debt collector does not violate this section when he gives a receipt to a consumer's friend or relative who makes a payment on a debt, as long as the collector does not convey information about the details of the debt to the payer.

Section 805 (c)—Ceasing communication. **Once a debt collector receives written notice from a consumer that he or she refuses to pay the debt or wants the collector to stop further collection efforts, the debt collector must cease any further communication with the consumer except "(1) to advise the consumer that the debt collector's further efforts are being terminated; (2) to notify the consumer that the debt collector or creditor may invoke specified remedies which are ordinarily invoked by such debt collector or creditor; or (3) where applicable, to notify the consumer that the debt collector or creditor intends to invoke a specified remedy."**

1. *Scope.* For purposes of this section, the term "communicate" is given its commonly accepted meaning. Thus, the section applies to any contact with the consumer related to the collection of the debt, whether or not the debt is specifically mentioned.

2. *Request for payment.* A debt collector's response to a "cease communication" notice from the consumer may not include a demand for payment, but is limited to the three statutory exceptions.

Section 805 (d)—"consumer" definition. **For Section 805 purposes, the term "consumer" includes the "consumer's spouse, parent (if the consumer is a minor), guardian, executor, or administrator."**

1. *Broad "consumer" definition.* Because of the broad statutory definition of "consumer" for the purposes of this section, many of its protections extend to parties close to the consumer. For example, the debt collector may not call the consumer's spouse at work, or a time known to be an inconvenient time. Conversely, he may call the spouse (guardian, executor, etc.) whenever he could call the consumer.

§806—Harassment or Abuse

Section 806 prohibits a debt collector from any conduct that would **"harass, oppress, or abuse any person in connection with the collection of a debt." It provides six examples of harassment or abuse.**

1. *Scope.* Prohibited actions are not limited to the six subsections listed as examples of activities that violate this provision.

2. *Unnecessary calls to third parties.* A debt collector may not leave telephone messages with many different neighbors when the debt collector knows the consumer's name and telephone number and could have reached him directly.

3. *Multiple contacts with consumer.* A debt collector may not engage in repeated personal contacts with a consumer with such frequency as to harass him. For example, the debt collector may not follow the consumer, or contact him six times in one day. Subsection (5) deals specifically with harassment by multiple phone calls.

4. *Abusive conduct.* A debt collector may not pose a lengthy series of questions or comments to the consumer without giving the consumer a chance to reply. Subsection (2) deals specifically with harassment involving obscene, profane, or abusive language.

Section 806 (1) prohibits "the use or threat of use of violence or other criminal means to harm...any person."

1. *Implied threat.* A debt collector may violate this section by an implied threat of violence. For example, a debt collector may not pressure a consumer with statements such as "We're not playing around here—we can play tough" or "We're going to send somebody to collect for us one way or the other."

Section 806 (2) prohibits the use of obscene, profane, or abusive language.

1. *Abusive language.* Abusive language includes religious slurs, profanity, obscenity, calling the consumer a liar or a deadbeat, and the use of racial or sexual epithets.

Section 806 (3) prohibits "the publication of a list of consumers who allegedly refuse to pay debts," except to report the items to a "consumer reporting agency." as defined in the Fair Credit Reporting Act.

Section 806 (4) prohibits "the advertisement for sale of any debt to coerce payment of the debt."

1. *Shaming prohibited.* These provisions are designed to prohibit debt collectors from "shaming" a customer into payment, by publicizing the debt.

2. *Exchange of lists.* Debt collectors may not exchange lists of consumers who allegedly refuse to pay their debts.

3. *Information to creditor subscribers.* A debt collector may not distribute a list of alleged debtors to its creditor subscribers, because the statute permits it to provide such information only to consumer reporting agencies.

Section 806 (5) prohibits contacting the consumer by telephone "repeatedly or continuously with intent to annoy, abuse, or harass any person at the called number."

1. *Multiple phone calls.* "Continuously" means making a series of telephone calls, one right after the other. "Repeatedly" means calling with excessive frequency, such as six phone calls in an hour.

Section 806 (6) prohibits, except where §804 applies, "the placement of telephone calls without meaningful disclosure of the caller's identity."

1. *Aliases.* A debt collector employee's use of an alias that permits identification of the debt collector (i.e., where he uses the alias consistently, and his true identity can be ascertained by contact with the employer) constitutes a "meaningful disclosure of the caller's identity."

2. *Identification of caller.* An individual debt collector must disclose his employer's identity, when contacting consumers or third parties permitted by §805 (b).

3. *Relation to other sections.* A debt collector who uses a false business name in a phone call to conceal his identity violates §807 (14), as well as this section.

§807—False or Misleading Representations

Section 807 prohibits a debt collector from using any "false, deceptive, or misleading representation or means in connection with the collection of any debt." It provides sixteen examples of false or misleading representations.

1. *Scope.* Prohibited actions are not limited to the sixteen subsections listed as examples of activities that violate this provision. In addition, §807 (10), which prohibits the "use of any false representation or deceptive means" by a debt collector, is particularly broad and encompasses virtually every violation, including those not covered by the other subsections.

Section 807 (1) prohibits "the false representation or implication that the debt collector is vouched for, bonded by, or affiliated with the United States or any State..."

1. *Symbol on dunning notice.* A debt collector may not use a symbol in correspondence that makes him appear to be a government official. For example, a collection letter depicting a police badge, a judge, or the scales of justice, violates this section.

Section 807 (2) prohibits falsely representing either "(A) the character, amount, or legal status of any debt; or (B) any services rendered or compensation which may be lawfully received by" the collector.

1. *Legal status of debt.* A debt collector may not falsely imply that legal action has begun.

2. *Amount of debt.* A debt collector may not claim an amount more than actually owed, or falsely assert that the debt has matured or that it is immediately due and payable, when it is not.

3. *Judgment.* When a debt collector provides the validation notice required by §809 (a) (4), the notice may include the words "copy of a judgment" whether or not a judgment exists, because §809 (a) (4)

provides for a statement including these words. This information avoids making compliance with §809 (a)(4) a violation of §807 (2)(A).

Section 807 (3) prohibits falsely representing or implying that "any individual is an attorney or that any communication is from an attorney."

1. *Form of legal correspondence.* A debt collector may not send a collection letter from a "Pre-Legal Department," where no legal department exists. An attorney may use a computer service to send letters on his own behalf, but a debt collector may not send a computer-generated letter using an attorney's name.

2. *Named individual.* A debt collector may not falsely represent that a person named in a letter is his attorney.

3. *Relation to other sections.* If a creditor uses an attorney's name rather than his own in his collection communications, he both loses his exemption from the FDCPA's definition of "debt collector" [Section 803 (6)] and violates this provision.

Section 807 (4) prohibits falsely representing or implying to the consumer that nonpayment "will result in the arrest or imprisonment of any person or the seizure, garnishment, attachment, or sale of any property or wages of any person..."

Section 807 (5) prohibits "the threat to take any action that cannot legally be taken or that is not intended to be taken."

1. *Debt collector's statement of his own definite action.* A debt collector may not state that he will take any action unless he intends to take the action when the statement was made, or ordinarily takes the action in similar circumstances.

2. *Debt collector's statement of definite action by third party.* A debt collector may not state that a third party will take any action unless he has reason to believe, at the time the statement is made, that such action will be taken.

3. *Statement of possible action.* A debt collector may not state or imply that he or any third party may take any action unless such action is legal and there is a reasonable likelihood, at the time the statement is made, that such action will be taken. A debt collector may state that certain action is possible, if it is true that such action is legal and is frequently taken by the collector or creditor with respect to similar debts; however, if the creditor has reason to know there are facts that make the action unlikely in the particular case, a statement the action was possible would be misleading.

4. *Threat of criminal action.* A debt collector may not threaten to report a dishonored check or other fact to the police, unless he actually intends to take this action.

5. *Threat of attachment.* A debt collector may not threaten to attach a consumer's tax refund, when he has no authority to do so.

6. *Threat of legal or other action.* Section 807 (5) refers not only to a false threat of legal action, but also a false threat by a debt collector that he will report a debt to a credit bureau, assess a collection fee, or undertake any other action if the debt is not paid. A debt collector may also not misrepresent the imminence of such action.

A debt collector's implication, as well as a direct statement, of planned legal action may be an unlawful deception. For example, reference to an attorney or to legal proceedings may mislead the debtor as to the likelihood or imminence of legal action.

A debt collector's statement that legal action has been recommended is a representation that legal action may be taken, since such a recommendation implies that the creditor will act on it at least some of the time.

Lack of intent may be inferred when the amount of the debt is so small as to make the action totally unfeasible or when the debt collector is unable to take the action because the creditor has not authorized him to do so.

7. *Illegality of threatened act.* A debt collector may not threaten that he will illegally contact an employer, or other third party, or take some other "action that cannot legally be taken" (such as advising the creditor to sue where such advice would violate state rules governing the unauthorized practice of law). If state law forbids a debt collector from suing in his own name (or from doing so without first obtaining a formal assignment and that has not been done), the debt collector may not represent that he will sue in that state.

Section 807 (6) prohibits falsely representing or implying that a transfer of the debt will cause the consumer to (A) lose any claim or defense, or (B) become subject to any practice prohibited by the FDCPA.

1. *Referral to creditor.* A debt collector may not falsely state that the consumer's account will be referred back to the original creditor, who would not be bound by the FDCPA.

Section 807 (7) prohibits falsely representing or implying that the "consumer committed any crime or other (disgraceful) conduct."

1. *False allegation of fraud.* A debt collector may not falsely allege that the consumer has committed fraud.

2. *Misrepresentation of criminal law.* A debt collector may not make a misleading statement of law, falsely implying that the consumer has committed a crime, or mischaracterize what constitutes an offense by

misstating or omitting significant elements of the offense. For example, a debt collector may not tell the consumer that he has committed a crime by issuing a check that is dishonored, when the statute applies only where there is a "scheme to defraud."

Section 807 (8) prohibits "communicating or threatening to communicate to any person (false) credit information…, including the failure to communicate that a disputed debt is disputed."

1. *Disputed debt.* If a debt collector knows that a debt is disputed by the consumer, either from receipt of written notice (§809) or other means, and reports it to a credit bureau, he must report it as disputed.

2. *Post-report dispute.* When a debt collector learns of a dispute after reporting the debt to a credit bureau, the dispute need not also be reported.

Section 807 (9) prohibits "the use of any document designed to falsely imply that it issued from a state or federal source."

1. *Relation to other sections.* Most of the violations of this section involve simulated legal process, which is more specifically covered by §807 (13). However, this subsection is broader in that it also covers documents that fraudulently appear to be official government documents.

Section 807 (10) prohibits "the use of any false representation or deceptive means to collect or attempt to collect any debt or to obtain information concerning a consumer."

1. *Relation to other sections.* The prohibition is so comprehensive that violation of any part of §807 will usually also violate subsection (10). Actions that violate more specific provisions are discussed in those sections.

2. *Communication format.* A debt collector may not communicate by a format or envelope that misrepresents the nature, purpose, or urgency of the message. It is a violation to send any communication that conveys to the consumer a false sense of urgency. However, it is usually permissible to send a letter generated by a machine, such as a computer or other printing device. A bona fide contest entry form, which provides a clearly optional location to enter employment information, enclosed with a request for payment, is not deceptive.

3. *False statement or implications.* A debt collector may not falsely state or imply that a consumer is required to assign his wages to his creditor when he is not, that the debt collector has counseled the creditor to sue when he has not, that adverse credit information has been entered on the consumer's credit record when it has not, that the

entire amount is due when there is no acceleration clause, or that he cannot accept partial payments when in fact he is authorized to accept them.

4. *Misrepresentation of law.* A debt collector may not mislead the consumer as to the legal consequences of the consumer's actions (e.g., by implying that a failure to respond is an admission of liability).

A debt collector may not state that federal law requires a notice of the debt collector's intent to contact third parties.

5. *Misleading letterhead.* A debt collector's employee who is an attorney may not use "attorney-at-law" stationery without referring to his employer, so as to falsely imply to the consumer that the debt collector had retained a private attorney to bring suit on the account.

Section 807 (11) requires the debt collector to "disclose clearly in all communications made to collect a debt or to obtain information about a consumer, that the debt collector is attempting to collect a debt and that any information obtained will be used for that purpose," except where §804 provides otherwise.

1. *Oral communications.* A debt collector must make the required disclosures in both oral and written communications.

2. *Disclosure to consumers.* When a debt collector contacts a consumer and clearly discloses that he is seeking payment of a debt, he need not state that all information will be used to collect a debt, since that should be apparent to the consumer. The debt collector need not repeat the required disclosure in subsequent contacts.

A debt collector may not send the consumer a note saying only "please call me right away" unless there has been prior contact between the parties and the collector is thus known to the consumer.

3. *Disclosures to third parties.* The debt collector must state in his first communication with a third party that he is attempting to collect the debt and that information will be used for that purpose, but need not do so in subsequent communications with that party.

Section 807 (12) prohibits falsely representing or implying that "accounts have been turned over to innocent purchasers for value."

1. *Relation to other sections.* Section 807 (6) (A) prohibits threatening to affect the consumer's rights by transferring the account; this subsection forbids falsely stating or implying that this has been done.

Section 807 (13) prohibits falsely representing or implying that "documents are legal process."

1. *Simulated legal process.* A debt collector may not send written communication that deceptively resemble legal process forms. He may

not send a form or a dunning letter that, taken as a whole, appears to simulate legal process. However, one legal phrase (such as "notice of legal action" or "show just cause why") alone will not result in a violation of this section unless it contributes to an erroneous impression that the document is a legal form.

Section 807 (14) prohibits "the use of any business, company, or organization name other than the (collector's) true name."

1. *Permissible business name.* A debt collector may use a name that does not misrepresent his identity or deceive the consumer. Thus, a collector may use its full business name, the name under which it usually transacts business, or a commonly used acronym. When the collector uses multiple names in its various affairs, it does not violate this subsection if it consistently uses the same name when dealing with a particular consumer.

2. *Creditor misrepresentation of identity.* A creditor may not use any name that would falsely imply that a third party is involved in the collection. The in-house collection unit of "ABC Corp." may use the name "ABC Collection Division," but not the name "XYZ Collection Agency" or some other unrelated name.

A creditor violates this section if he uses the name of a collection bureau as a conduit for a collection process that the creditor controls in collecting his own accounts. Similarly, a creditor may not use a fictitious name or letterhead, or a "post office box address" name that implies someone else is collecting his debts.

A creditor does not violate this provision where an affiliated (and differently named) debt collector undertakes collection activity, if the debt collector does business separately from the creditor (e.g., where the debt collector in fact has other clients that he treats similarly to the creditor, has his own employees, deals at arms length with the creditor, and controls the process himself).

3. *All collection activities covered.* A debt collection business must use its real business name, commonly used name, or acronym in both written and oral communications.

4. *Relation to other sections.* If a creditor uses a false business name, he both loses his exemption from the FDCPA's definition of "debt collector" [§803(6)] and violates this provision. If a debt collector falsely uses the name of an attorney rather than his true business name, he violates §807 (3) as well as this section. When a debt collector uses a false business name in a phone call, he violates §806 (6) as well as this section.

When using the mails to obtain location information, a debt collector may not use a name that indicates he is in the debt collection business, or he will violate §804 (5). When a debt collector's employee who is seeking location information replies to an inquiry about his employer's identity under §804 (1), he must give the true name of his employer.

Section 807 (15) prohibits falsely representing or implying that documents are not legal process forms or do not require action by the consumer.

1. *Disguised legal process.* A debt collector may not deceive a consumer into failing to respond to legal process by concealing the import of the papers, thereby subjecting the consumer to a default judgment.

Section 807 (16) prohibits falsely representing or implying that a debt collector operates or is employed by a "consumer reporting agency," as defined in the Fair Credit Reporting Act.

1. *Dual agencies.* The FDCPA does not prohibit a debt collector from operating a consumer reporting agency.

2. *Misleading names.* Only a bona fide consumer reporting agency may use names such as "Credit Bureau," "Credit Bureau Collection Agency," "General Credit Control," "Credit Bureau Rating, Inc.," or "National Debtors Rating." A debt collector's disclaimer in the text of a letter that the debt collector is not affiliated with (or employed by) a consumer reporting agency, will not necessarily avoid a violation if the collector uses a name that indicates otherwise.

3. *Factual issue.* Whether a debt collector that has called itself a credit bureau actually qualifies as such is a factual issue, to be decided according to the debt collector's actual operation.

§808—Unfair Practices

Section 808 prohibits a debt collector from using "unfair or unconscionable means" in his debt collection activity. It provides eight examples of unfair practices.

1. *Scope.* Prohibited actions are not limited to the eight subsections listed as examples of activities that violate this provision.

2. *Elements of unfairness.* A debt collector's act in collecting a debt is "unfair" if it causes injury to the consumer that is (1) substantial, (2) not outweighed by countervailing benefits to consumers or competition, and (3) not reasonably avoidable.

Section 808 (1) prohibits collecting any amount unless the amount is expressly authorized by the agreement creating the debt or is permitted by law.

1. *Kinds of amounts covered.* For purposes of this section, "amount" includes not only the debt, but also any incidental charges, such as collection charges, interest, service charges, late fees, and bad check handling charges.

2. *Legality of charges.* A debt collector may attempt to collect a fee or charge in addition to the debt if either (A) the charge is expressly provided for in the contract creating the debt and the charge is not prohibited by state law, or (B) the contract is silent but the charge is otherwise expressly permitted by state law. Conversely, a debt collector may not collect an additional amount if either (A) state law expressly prohibits collection of the amount or (B) the contract does not provide for collection of the amount and state law is silent.

3. *Legality of fee under state law.* If state law permits collection of reasonable fees, the reasonableness and consequential legality of these fees is determined by state law.

4. *Agreement not in writing.* A debt collector may establish an "agreement" without a written contract. For example, he may collect a service charge on a dishonored check based on a posted sign on the merchant's premises allowing such a charge, if he can demonstrate that the consumer knew of the charge.

Section 808 (2) prohibits accepting a check postdated by more than five days unless timely written notice is given to the consumer prior to deposit.

Section 808 (3) prohibits soliciting any postdated check for purposes of threatening or instituting criminal prosecution.

Section 808 (4) prohibits depositing a postdated check prior to its date.

1. *Postdated checks.* These provisions do not totally prohibit debt collectors from accepting postdated checks from consumers, but rather prohibit debt collectors from misusing such instruments.

Section 808 (5) prohibits causing any person to incur telephone or telegram charges by concealing the true purpose of the communication.

1. *Long distance calls to the debt collector.* A debt collector may not ask a consumer to call him long distance without disclosing the debt collector's identity and the communication's purpose.

2. *Relation to other section.* A debt collector who conceals his purpose in asking consumers to call long distance may also violate §807 (11), which requires the debt collector to disclose his purpose in some communications.

Section 808 (6) prohibits enforcing a security interest on property, or threatening to do so, where (A) there is no present right to the collateral, (B) there is no present intent to exercise such rights, or (C) the property is exempt by law.

1. *Security enforcers.* Because the FDCPA's definition of "debt collector" includes parties whose principal business is enforcing security interests only for §808 (6) purposes, such parties are subject only to this provision and not to the rest of the FDCPA.

Section 808 (7) prohibits "Communicating with a consumer regarding a debt by post card."

1. *Debt.* A debt collector does not violate this section if he sends a postcard to a consumer that does not communicate the existence of the debt. However, if he had not previously disclosed that he is attempting to collect a debt, he would violate Section 807 (11), which requires this disclosure.

Section 808 (8) prohibits showing anything other than the debt collector's address, on any envelope in any written communication to the consumer, except that a debt collector may use his business name if it does not indicate that he is in the debt collection business.

1. *Business names prohibited on envelopes.* A debt collector may not put on his envelope any business name with "debt" or "collector" in it, or any other name that indicates he is in the debt collection business. A debt collector may not use the American Collectors Association logo on an envelope.

2. *Collector's name.* Whether a debt collector/consumer reporting agency's use of his own "credit bureau" or other name indicates that he is in the collection business, and thus violates the section, is a factual issue to be determined in each individual case.

3. *Telegrams.* A debt collector does not violate this section by using an actual telegram or similar service, notwithstanding a Western Union (or other provider) logo and the word "telegram" (or similar word) on the envelope.

4. *Transparent envelopes.* A debt collector may not use a transparent envelope, which reveals language or symbols indicating his debt collection business, because it is the equivalent of putting information on an envelope.

§809—Validation of Debts

Section 809 (a) requires a collector, within 5 days of the first communication, to send the consumer a written notice containing (1) the amount of the debt and (2) the name of the creditor, along with a statement

that he will (3) assume the debt's validity unless the consumer disputes it within 30 days, (4) send a verification or copy of the judgment if the consumer timely disputes the debt, and (5) identify the original creditor upon written request.

1. *Who must send notice.* If the employer debt collection agency sends the required notice, employee debt collectors need not also send it. A debt collector's agent may send the notice, as long as it is clear that the information is being sent on behalf of the debt collector.

2. *Single notice required.* The debt collector is required to send only one notice for each debt. A notice need not offer to identify the original creditor unless the name and address of the original creditor are different from the current creditor.

3. *Form of notices.* The FDCPA imposes no requirements as to the form, sequence, location, or typesize of the notice. However, an illegible notice does not comply with this provision.

4. *Alternate terminology.* A debt collector may condense and combine the required disclosures, as long as he provides all required information.

5. *Oral notice.* If a debt collector's first communication with the consumer is oral, he may make the disclosures orally at that time in which case he need not send a written notice.

6. *Legal action.* A debt collector's institution of formal legal action against a consumer is not a "communication in connection with collection of any debt," and thus does not confer §809 notice-and-validation rights on the consumer.

Section 809 (b) requires that, if the consumer disputes the debt or requests identification of the original creditor in writing, the collector must cease collection efforts until he verifies the debt and mails a response. Section 809 (c) states that a consumer's failure to dispute the validity of a debt under this section is not an admission of liability.

1. *Pre-notice collection.* A debt collector need not cease normal collection activities within the consumer's 30-day period to give notice of a dispute until he receives a notice from the consumer.

A debt collector may report a debt to a credit bureau within the 30-day notice period, before he receives a request for validation or a dispute notice from the consumer.

§810—Multiple Debts

Section 810 provides that when a debt collector is collecting multiple debts and the consumer directs that a payment be applied to a certain debt or debts, the debt collector must honor those directions. A debt collector

may not apply a payment to a disputed debt even if the consumer gives no direction in this regard.

§811—Legal Actions by Debt Collectors

Section 811 provides that a debt collector may sue a consumer only in the judicial district where the consumer resides or signed the contract sued upon, except that an action to enforce a security interest in real property which secures the obligation must be brought where the property is located.

1. *Waiver.* Any waiver by the consumer must be provided to the debt collector, because the forum restriction applies to actions initiated by the party.

2. *Multiple defendants.* Since a debt collector may sue only where the consumer (1) lives or (2) signed the contract, the collector may not join an ex-husband as a defendant to a suit against the ex-wife in the district of her residence, unless he also lived there or signed the contract there. The existence of community property at her residence that is available to pay his debts does not alter the forum limitations on individual consumers.

3. *Real estate security.* A debt collector may sue based on the location of a consumer's real property only when he seeks to enforce an interest in such property that secures the debts.

4. *Services without written contract.* Where services were provided pursuant to an oral agreement, the debt collector may sue only where the consumer resides. He may not sue where services were performed (if that is different from the consumer's residence), because that is not included as a permissible forum location by this provision.

§812—Furnishing Certain Deceptive Forms

Section 812 (a) prohibits any party from designing and furnishing forms, knowing they are or will be used to deceive a consumer to believe that someone other than his creditor is collecting the debt, and imposes FDCPA civil liability on parties who supply such forms.

1. *Practice prohibited.* This section prohibits the practice of selling to creditors dunning letters that falsely imply that a debt collector is collecting the debt, when in fact only the creditor is collecting.

2. *Coverage.* This section applies to anyone who designs, compiles, or furnishes the forms prohibited by this section.

3. *Precollection letters.* A form seller may not furnish a creditor with (1) a letter on a collector's letterhead to be used when the collector is not

involved in collecting the creditor's debts, or (2) a letter indicating "copy to (the collector)" if the collector is not participating in collecting the creditor's debt. A form seller may not avoid liability by including a statement in the text of a form letter that the sender has not yet been assigned the account for collection, if the communication as a whole, using the collector's letterhead, represents otherwise.

4. *Knowledge required.* A party does not violate this provision unless he has knowledge that his form letter will be used to mislead consumers into believing that someone other than the creditor is involved in collecting the debt.

5. *Participation by debt collector.* A debt collector that uses letters as his only collection tool does not violate this section, merely because he charges a flat rate per letter, if he is meaningfully "participating in the collection of a debt." The consumer is not misled in such cases, as he would be in the case of a party who supplied the creditor with form letters and provided little or no additional service in the collection process. The performance of other tasks associated with collection (e.g., handling verification requests, negotiating payment arrangements, keeping individual records) is evidence that such a party is "participating in the collection."

§813—Civil Liability

Section 813 (A) imposes civil liability in the form of (1) actual damages, (2) discretionary penalties, and (3) costs and attorney's fees, (B) discusses relevant factors a court should consider in assessing damages, (C) exculpates a collector who maintains reasonable procedures from liability for an unintentional error, (D) permits actions to be brought in federal or state courts within one year from the violation, and (E) shields a defendant who relies on an advisory opinion of the Commission.

1. *Employee liability.* Since the employees of a debt collection agency are "debt collectors," they are liable for violations to the same extent as the agency.

2. *Damages.* The courts have awarded "actual damages" for FDCPA violations that were not just out-of-pocket expenses, but included damages for personal humiliation, embarrassment, mental anguish, or emotional distress.

3. *Application of statute of limitation period.* The section's one year statute of limitations applies only to private lawsuits, not to actions brought by a government agency.

4. *Advisory opinions.* A party may act in reliance on a formal advisory opinion of the Commission pursuant to 16 CFR §§1.1-1.4,

without risk of civil liability. This protection does not extend to reliance on this Commentary or other informal staff interpretations.

§814—Administrative Enforcement

Section 814 provides that the principal federal enforcement agency for the FDCPA is the Federal Trade Commission, but assigns that power to other authorities empowered by certain federal statutes to regulate financial, agricultural, and transportation activities, where FDCPA violations relate to acts subject to those laws.

§815—Reports to Congress by Commission

Section 815 requires the Commission to submit an annual report to Congress which discusses its enforcement and other activities administering the FDCPA, assesses the degree of compliance, and makes recommendations.

§816—Relation to State Laws

Section 816 provides that the FDCPA pre-empts state laws only to the extent that those laws are inconsistent with any provision of the FDCPA, and then only to the extent of the inconsistency. A State law is not inconsistent if it gives consumers greater protection than the FDCPA.

1. *Inconsistent laws.* Where a state law provides protection to the consumer equal to, or greater than, the FDCPA, it is not pre-empted by the federal statute.

§817—Exemption for State Regulation

Section 817 orders the Commission to exempt any class of debt collection practices from the FDCPA within any State if it determines that State laws regulating those practices are substantially similar to the FDCPA, and contain adequate provision for enforcement.

1. *State exemptions.* A state with a debt collection law may apply to the Commission for an exemption. The Commission must grant the exemption if the state's law is substantially similar to the FDCPA, and there is adequate provision for enforcement. The Commission has published procedures for processsing such applications (16 C.F.R. §901).

§818—Effective Date

Section 818 provides that the FDCPA took effect six months from the date of its enactment.

1. *Key dates.* The FDCPA was approved September 20, 1977, and became effective March 20, 1978.

5. EXCERPTS OF TWO COURT DECISIONS INTERPRETING THE FAIR DEBT COLLECTION PRACTICES ACT

A. *Trans World Accounts; appellant v. Federal Trade Commission; appellee. 594 f.2d 212 (1979) at page 216 United States Court of Appeals, Ninth Circuit. (March 29, 1979)*

CONTENT OF THE LETTERS (PARAGRAPH 3)

[7] The Commission found that the letters sent by Trans World were deceptive in that they threatened imminent legal action when no such action was contemplated: even when the letter series had been completed, legal action would not be taken until an evaluation of the individual file had been made. This factual finding will not be overturned if there is substantial evidence supporting it. Ash Grove Cement Co., supra. *(Ash Grove Cement Co., v. FTC,* 577 F.2d 1368, 1378 [9th Cir. 1978]). Upon reviewing the evidence here, we find that there is substantial evidence to support the Commission's findings.[1] Nonetheless, we remand paragraph 3 of the FTC order for further consideration because it is overbroad and vague.

Paragraph 3 of the order prohibits appellants from "[m]isrepresenting directly or by implication, that legal action with respect to an alleged delinquent debt has been, is about to be, or may be initiated, or otherwise misrepresenting in any manner the likelihood or imminency of legal action." In delineating the parameters of the order, the Commission stated:

> Respondents should not state or imply that legal action may be taken unless they can demonstrate from their experience that suit is the ordinary response to nonpayment.... Suit in more than half the instances of nonpayment will suffice under this order to substantiate a claim that legal action may be taken.

FTC Decision and Order at 12. This interpretation of the meaning of the word "may" is overly restrictive because it attributes to the word a statistical meaning counter to common sense and usage.

[8, 9] Thus, although appellant's communications have been found to be deceptive, and although that factual finding is supported by substantial evidence, cease-and-desist orders must be sufficiently "clear and precise to

avoid raising serious questions as to their meaning and application." *FTC v. Henry Broch & Co.*, 368 U.S. 360, 367-8 82 S.Ct. 431, 436, 7 L.Ed.2d 353 (1962). The Federal Trade Commission's power to fashion remedies for deceptive practices does not carry with it the concomitant power to be deceptive or ambiguous in dealing with persons and businesses subject to its jurisdiction. Here, appellant acts at its peril if its common-sense definition of the word "may" fails to comport with the statistical interpretation which the FTC urges.

We recognize that the FTC may order certain "fencing in" provisions. *FTC v. Mandel Bros.*, supra. (359 U.S. 385, 79 S.Ct. 818, 824, 3 L.Ed.2d 893 [1959]). Although we are certain that the FTC could draft an appropriate "fencing in" order, paragraph 3 is not such an order. It is not needed to prevent similar and related violations from occurring in the future: the very nub of the deception, in this case, was not whether appellant sued 50 percent of the time, 75 percent of the time, or 25 percent of the time. Rather, the deception arose from the fact that *no* decision regarding suit was made until 90 days following mailing of the last Trans-O-Gram, although appellant represented that such a decision was automatic.

To conclude, paragraph 3, as presently drafted, is overbroad and vague. Accordingly, we remand that portion of the order for further clarification by the Commission.

The order of the Federal Trade Commission is affirmed in part, and reversed and remanded in part for further proceedings in accordance with this Opinion. Pursuant to F.R.App.P., Rule 19, the Commission shall serve and file a proposed judgment in conformity with this Opinion.

Footnote

1. By way of example, the following three paragraphs were contained in three of the letters in the letter series which Trans World sent:

   1. "Urgent—Appear at Claimant's Office within four days to pay above claim or protest liability. Failure to appear in person or have legal counsel represent you may result in immediate litigation by our client with ultimate seizure of property, auto, bank accounts, and other personal assets if judgment is obtained."

   2. "You are hereby directed to appear at our client's office at 9:00 A.M. next Tuesday to protest liability of the above claim. Failure to comply may result in immediate commencement of litigation by our client. If judgment is granted, property, including monies, automobile, credits, and bank deposits now in your possession could be attached. If our client receives payment in full prior to the time of protest as scheduled, your appearance will not be required."

3. "Urgent—Immediately contact our client and make arrangements for payment. Imperative to avoid further action which may be taken against you under provisions of state statutes. If settlement is not made within 5 days after receipt of this telegram, you may wish to consult your attorney regarding your legal liability."

EXCERPT OF DECISION

B. United States of America; plaintiff v. ACB Sales and Service, Inc., et al; defendant; 590 Fed. Supp. 561 (1984) at page 570 United States District Court, District of Arizona.

Violations by Individual Collectors

A. *Letter Violations*

The government alleges that the three form letters 003, 005, and 006 threaten legal action and the ACB Companies mailed these letters to debtors without intending to bring any legal action against them. The government concludes that the ACB Companies violated the second paragraph of the Order, which prohibits the respondents from "[r]epresenting directly or by implication, orally or in writing, contrary to fact, that legal action has been, is being or will be taken against the debtor" and violated section 807(5) of the FDCPA, 15 U.S.C. § 1692e(5), which prohibits "[t]he threat to take any action that cannot legally be taken or that is not intended to be taken."

The first inquiry is what each of these prohibitions means. There is little, if any, ambiguity in section 807 (5). This provision is violated if, when the threat of legal action is made, the speaker does not intend to carry out his threat. Although the wording of paragraph 2 is different, I interpret this provision similarly.

Paragraph 2 prohibits representation that legal action will be taken when "contrary to fact." In oral argument, the government contended that legal action would not be intended unless, after sending the letter, ACB Sales & Service requests authorization to sue from the creditor. I find the government's interpretation untenable. It is unreasonable to suggest that the intent behind a representation be determined by a decision made not by the collector who sends the letter, but by the home office, perhaps weeks after the representation was made. The only reasonable interpretation of paragraph 2 is that offered by the defendants, which is that a violation occurs when the individual collector does not intend to bring a legal action, yet sends the letter to the debtor.

Both section 807 (5) and paragraph 2 would retain some ambiguity if a distinction were not made between intending to sue and merely wanting to sue. Under both provisions, the intent to sue clearly rests with the collector who requests that the letter be sent to the debtor. The collector's intent to sue entails more than merely wanting to sue; it follows from the decision that legal action would be cost effective and, therefore, would likely be the final course of action if the debt is not paid. Absent this conscious decision by the collector prior to sending one of the letters, he would not have the requisite intention to take legal action.

The second inquiry is whether the collector's conduct violated section 807(5) and paragraph 2 of the Order. Specifically, two issues must be resolved in this inquiry: First, do the form letters threaten legal action and, second, did the collector who sent the letter intend to take legal action against the debtor?

1. *The Meaning of the Form Letters*

[6] The question of what each of these form letters means is clearly a question of fact, but it is a question of ultimate fact. There is no dispute concerning the underlying evidentiary facts necessary to make the determination of what the letters mean. The defendants have not offered by affidavit or transcript any competent evidence that would assist in the interpretation of the letters.[2] Full trial on this issue, therefore, would not serve any purpose other than to formalize evidence concerning facts which are undisputed in this motion for summary judgment. Accordingly, I conclude that this issue may be resolved in this motion for summary judgment.

Letter 003 clearly threatens legal action against the debtor. This threat is communicated both by the form of the letter, a 48-hour notice telling the debtor that he must act immediately, and the statement that the ACB agency is "authorized to proceed with any necessary lawful action." The defendants object to this interpretation, noting that the message threatens any necessary "lawful action" rather than "legal action." Because of the context of the notice, however, this distinction would not be apparent to the average debtor. The clear impression of the notice is that the agency will file a lawsuit if the debt is not paid within 48 hours.

Even though there is no express threat of legal action, Letter 005 implies that legal action will be taken against the debtor if the debt is not paid. The implication that a suit will be filed is found in the letter's reference to the fact that lawsuits are filed in an unspecified "percentage of cases" and that, if suit were filed against the debtor, costs well beyond the amount of the debt might result. These references might be interpreted only as a statement of the legal rights of the creditor were it not for the penultimate paragraph of the letter. This paragraph disclaims that legal action "has been or is being taken" against the debtor. By omitting any expression as to his future intentions, the collector implies that a lawsuit is in the contemplated course of action if the debt remains unpaid.

[7] Letter 006 cures the deficiency of Letter 005. The penultimate paragraph is modified to state that the letter does not "represent directly or indirectly that legal action has been, is being, or will be taken against [the debtor]." Also the paragraph concludes with the comment that the agency "would prefer that the money which is due to be paid without necessity of further processing." This disclaimer that the collector implies any intent to bring suit strikes a proper balance to the earlier portion of the letter describing the creditor's legal rights. I conclude that in light of the disclaimer the average debtor could not reasonably interpret the letter as threatening suit. Letter 006, therefore, cannot serve as the basis for a violation of section 807 (5) or paragraph 2 of the Order.

2. *The Intention of the Collector*

The government argues that three types of evidence establish as an undisputed fact that the collector did not intend to bring legal action against the debtors who received one of the form letters. First, the individual collector, after sending the letter, did not initiate the internal procedure to procure authorization to sue by recommending to his office manager that suit be brought against the debtor. Second, the ACB Companies did not request authorization from the creditors to sue these debtors. Indeed, as to those debtors of LaSalle Extension University, International Correspondence School, and Northridge Hospital, the debtor jacket instructed the individual collector that legal action could not be threatened or brought against the debtor. Finally, the ACB Companies did not file suit against any of the debtors who received the letters.

[8] Because it is the collector's intent when the letter was sent that determines the violation, the most probative evidence is the fact that the collector did not initiate the internal procedure necessary to get authorization to sue the debtor after sending the letter. There is no reason to believe that a collector considered legal action to be both feasible and the ultimate course of action if he never recommended to his office manager that suit be brought. With the exception of only a few isolated mailings, the defendants have failed to challenge this evidence and failed to produce any rebutting evidence concerning the collector's intent.[3] I conclude, therefore, that with respect to most of the mailings of form letters 003 and 005 it is an undisputed fact that the collectors did not intend to bring legal action when the letters were sent to the debtors. These mailings, consequently, violated paragraph 2 of the Order and section 807(5) of the FDCPA.[4]

Footnotes

Footnotes 2, 3, and 4 are not cited here as they are not relevant.

6. FAIR CREDIT BILLING ACT

Public Law 93-495

88. STAT 1511.   93rd Congress, H. R. 11221

October 28, 1974

TITLE III—FAIR CREDIT BILLING

§301. Short Title

This title may be cited as the "Fair Credit Billing Act."

Fair Credit Billing Act.
15 USC 1601 note.

§302. Declaration of Purpose

The last sentence of section 102 of the Truth in Lending Act (15 U.S.C. 1601) is amended by striking out the period and inserting in lieu thereof a comma and the following: "and to protect the consumer against inaccurate and unfair credit billing and credit card practices."

§303. Definitions of Creditor and Open End Credit Plan

Post, p. 1512. *Infra,* 15 USC 1637.

The first sentence of section 103(f), of the Truth in Lending Act (15 U.S.C. 1602(f)) is amended to read as follows: "The term 'creditor' refers only to creditors who regularly extend, or arrange for the extension of, credit which is payable by agreement in more than four installments or for which the payment of a finance charge is or may be required, whether in connection with loans, sales of property or services, or otherwise. For the purposes of the requirements imposed under Chapter 4 and sections 127(a)(6), 127(a)(7), 127(a)(8), 127(b)(1), 127(b)(2), 127(b)(3), 127(b)(9), and 127(b)(11) of Chapter 2 of this Title, the term 'creditor' shall also include card issuers whether or not the amount due is payable by agreement in more than four installments or the payment of a finance charge is or may be required, and the Board shall, by regulation, apply these requirement to such card issuers, to the extent appropriate, even though the requirements are by their terms applicable only to creditors offering open end credit plans.

§304. Disclosure of Fair Credit Billing Rights

(a) Section 127(a) of the Truth in Lending Act (15 U.S.C. 1637 (a)) is amended by adding at the end thereof a new paragraph as follows:

Post, pp. 1512, 1515.

"(8) A statement, in a form prescribed by regulations of the Board of the protection provided by sections 161 and 170 to an obligor and the creditor's responsibilities under sections 162 and 170. With respect to each of two billing cycles per year, at semi-annual intervals, the creditor shall transmit such statement to each obligor to whom the creditor is required to transmit a statement pursuant to section 127(b) for such billing cycle."

(b) Section 127(c) of such Act (15 U.S.C. 1637(c)) is amended to read:

"(c) In the case of any existing account under an open end consumer credit plan having an outstanding balance of more than $1 at or after the close of the creditor's first full billing cycle under the plan after the effective date of subsection (a) or any amendments thereto, the items described in subsection (a), to the extent applicable and not previously disclosed, shall be disclosed in a notice mailed or delivered to the obligor not later than the time of mailing the next statement required by subsection (b)."

§305. Disclosure of Billing Contact

Section 127(b) of the Truth in Lending Act (15 U.S.C. 1637(b)) is amended by adding at the end thereof a new paragraph as follows:

88 STAT. 1512

"(11) The address to be used by the creditor for the purpose of receiving billing inquiries from the obligor."

§306. Billing Practices

The Truth in Lending Act (15 U.S.C. 1601-1665) is amended by adding at the end thereof a new chapter as follows:

Chapter 4—CREDIT BILLING

"Sec.
"161. Correction of billing errors.

15 USC 1666.

Ante, p. 1511.

Ante, p. 1511.

§161. Correction of Billing Errors

"(a) If a creditor, within sixty days after having transmitted to an obligor a statement of the obligor's account in connection with an extension of consumer credit, receives at the address disclosed under section 127(b)(11) a written notice (other than notice on a payment stub or other payment medium supplied by the creditor if the creditor so stipulates with the disclosure required under section 127(a)(8)) from the obligor in which the obligor—

"(1) sets forth or otherwise enables the creditor to identify the name and account number (if any) of the obligor,

"(2) indicates the obligor's belief that the statement contains a billing error and the amount of such billing error, and

"(3) sets forth the reasons for the obligor's belief (to the extent applicable) that the statement contains a billing error,

the creditor shall, unless the obligor has, after giving such written notice and before the expiration of the time limits herein specified, agreed that the statement was correct—

"(A) not later than thirty days after the receipt of the notice, send a written acknowledgement thereof to the obligor, unless the action required in subparagraph (B) is taken within such thirty-day period, and

"(B) not later than two complete billing cycles of the creditor (in no event later than ninety days) after the receipt of the notice and prior to taking any action to collect the amount, or any part thereof, indicated by the obligor under paragraph (2) either—

"(i) make appropriate corrections in the account of the obligor, including the crediting of any finance charges on amounts erroneously billed, and transmit to the obligor a notification of such corrections and the creditor's explanation of any change in the amount indicated by the obligor under paragraph (2) and, if any such change is made and the obligor so requests, copies of documentary evidence of the obligor's indebtedness; or

"(ii) send a written explanation or clarification to the obligor, after having conducted an investigation, setting forth to the extent applicable the reasons why the creditor believes the account of the obligor was correctly shown in the statement and, upon request of the obligor, provide copies of documentary evidence of the obligor's indebtedness. In the case of a billing error where the obligor alleges that the creditor's billing statement reflects goods not delivered to the obligor or his designee in accordance with the agreement made at the time of the transaction, a creditor may not construe such amount to be correctly shown unless he determines that such goods were actually delivered, mailed, or otherwise sent to the obligor and provides the obligor with a statement of such determination.

88 STAT. 1513

Definitions.

"After complying with the provisions of this subsection with respect to an alleged billing error, a creditor has no further responsibility under this section if the obligor continues to make substantially the same allegation with respect to such error.

"(b) For the purpose of this section, a 'billing error' consists of any of the following:

"(1) A reflection on a statement of an extension of credit which was not made to the obligor, or, if made, was not in the amount reflected on such statement.

"(2) A reflection on a statement of an extension of credit for which the obligor requests additional clarification including documentary evidence thereof.

"(3) A reflection on a statement of goods or services not accepted by the obligor or his designee or not delivered to the obligor or his designee in accordance with the agreement made at the time of a transaction.

"(4) The creditor's failure to reflect properly on a statement a payment made by the obligor or a credit issued to the obligor.

"(5) A computation error or similar error of an accounting nature of the creditor on a statement.

"(6) Any other error described in regulations of the Board.

"(c) For the purposes of this section, 'action to collect the amount, or any part thereof, indicated by an obligor under paragraph (2)' does not include the sending of statements of account to the obligor following written notice from the obligor as specified under subsection (a), if—

"(1) the obligor's account is not restricted or closed because of the failure of the obligor to pay the amount indicated under paragraph (2) of subsection (a), and

"(2) the creditor indicates the payment of such amount is not required pending the creditor's compliance with this section.

"Nothing in this section shall be construed to prohibit any action by a creditor to collect any amount which has not been indicated by the obligor to contain a billing error.

"(d) Pursuant to regulations of the Board, a creditor operating an open end consumer credit plan may not, prior to the sending of the written explanation or clarification required under paragraph (B)(ii), restrict or close an account with respect to which the obligor has indicated pursuant to subsection (a) that he believes such account to contain a billing error solely because of the obligor's failure to pay the amount indicated to be in error. Nothing in this subsection shall be deemed to prohibit a creditor from applying against the credit limit on the obligor's account the amount indicated to be in error.

Noncompliance

"(e) Any creditor who fails to comply with the requirements of this section or section 162 forfeits any right to collect from the obligor the amount indicated by the obligor under paragraph (2) of subsection (a) of this section, and any finance charges thereon, except that the amount required to be forfeited under this subsection may not exceed $50."

15 USC 1666a.

§162. Regulation of Credit Reports

"(a) After receiving a notice from an obligor as provided in section 161(a), a creditor or his agent may not directly or indirectly threaten to report to any person adversely on the obligor's credit rating or credit standing because of the obligor's failure to pay the amount indicated by the obligor under section 161(a)(2), and such amount may not be reported as delinquent to any third party until the creditor has met the requirements of section 161 and has allowed the obligor the same number of days (not less than ten) thereafter to make payment as is provided under the credit agreement with the obligor for the payment of undisputed amounts.

88 STAT. 1514

"(b) If a creditor receives a further written notice from an obligor that an amount is still in dispute within the time allowed for payment under subsection (a) of this section, a creditor may not report to any third party that the amount of the obligor is delinquent because the obligor has failed to pay an amount which he has indicated under section 161(a)(2), unless the creditor also reports that the amount is in dispute and, at the same time, notifies the obligor of the name and address of each party to whom the creditor is reporting information concerning the delinquency.

"(c) A creditor shall report any subsequent resolution of any delinquencies reported pursuant to subsection (b) to the parties to whom such delinquencies were initially reported."

15 USC 1666b.

§163. Length of Billing Period

"(a) If an open end consumer credit plan provides a time period within which an obligor may repay any portion of the credit extended without incurring an additional finance charge, such additional finance charge may not be imposed with respect to such portion of the credit extended for the billing cycle of which such period is a part unless a statement which includes the amount upon which the finance charge for that period is based was mailed at least fourteen days prior to the date specified in the statement by which payment must be made in order to avoid imposition of that finance charge.

"(b) Subsection (a) does not apply in any case where a creditor has been prevented, delayed, or hindered in making timely mailing or delivery of such periodic statement within the time period specified in such subsection because of an act of God, war, natural disaster, strike, or other excusable or justifiable cause, as determined under regulations of the Board."

15 USC 1666c.

§164. Prompt Crediting of Payments

"Payments received from an obligor under an open end consumer credit plan by the creditor shall be posted promptly to the obligor's account as specified in regulations of the Board. Such regulations shall prevent a finance charge from being imposed on any obligor if the creditor has received the obligor's payment in readily identifiable form in the amount, manner, location, and time indicated by the creditor to avoid the imposition thereof."

15 USC 1666d.

§165. Crediting Excess Payments

"Whenever an obligor transmits funds to a creditor in excess of the total balance due on an open end consumer credit account, the creditor shall promptly (1) upon request of the obligor refund the amount of the overpayment, or (2) credit such amount to the obligor's account."

15 USC 1666e.

§166. Prompt Notification of Returns

"With respect to any sales transaction where a credit card has been used to obtain credit, where the seller is a person other than the card issuer, and where the seller accepts or allows a return of the goods or forgiveness of a debit for services which were the subject of such sale, the seller shall promptly transmit to the credit card issuer, a credit statement with respect thereto and the credit card issuer shall credit the account of the obligor for the amount of the transaction."

88 STAT. 1515
15 USC 1666f.

§167. Use of Cash Discounts

"(a) With respect to credit card which may be used for extensions of credit in sales transactions in which the seller is a person other than the card issuer, the card issuer may not, by contract or otherwise, prohibit any such seller from offering a discount to a cardholder to induce the cardholder to pay by cash, check, or similar means rather than use a credit card.

"(b) With respect to any sales transaction, any discount not in excess of 5 per centum offered by the seller for the purpose of inducing payment by cash, check, or other means not involving the use of a credit card shall not constitute a finance charge as determined under section

106, if such discount is offered to all prospective buyers and its availability is disclosed to all prospective buyers clearly and conspicuously in accordance with regulations of the Board."

15 USC 1666g.

§168. Prohibition of Tie-In Services

"Notwithstanding any agreement to the contrary, a card issuer may not require a seller, as a condition to participating in a credit card plan, to open an account with or procure any other service from the card issuer or its subsidiary or agent."

15 USC 1666h.

§169. Prohibition of Offsets

"(a) A card issuer may not take any action to offset a cardholder's indebtedness arising in connection with a consumer credit transaction under the relevant credit card plan against funds of the cardholder held on deposit with the card issuer unless—

"(1) such action was previously authorized in writing by the cardholder in accordance with a credit plan whereby the cardholder agrees periodically to pay debts incurred in his open end credit account by permitting the card issuer periodically to deduct all or a portion of such debt from the cardholder's deposit account, and

"(2) such action with respect to any outstanding disputed amount not be taken by the card issuer upon request of the cardholder.

In the case of any credit card account in existence on the effective date of this section, the previous written authorization referred to in clause (1) shall not be required until the date (after such effective date) when such account is renewed, but in no case later than one year after such effective date. Such written authorization shall be deemed to exist if the card issuer has previously notified the cardholder that the use of his credit card account will subject any funds which the card issuer holds in deposit accounts of such cardholder to offset against any amounts due and payable on his credit card account which have not been paid in accordance with the terms of the agreement between the card issuer and the cardholder.

"(b) This section does not alter or affect the right under State law of a card issuer to attach or otherwise levy upon funds of a cardholder held on deposit with the card issuer if that remedy is constitutionally available to creditors generally."

§170. Rights of Credit Card Customers

"(a) Subject to the limitation contained in subsection (b), a card issuer who has issued a credit card to a cardholder pursuant to an open end consumer credit plan shall be subject to all claims (other than tort claims) and defenses arising out of any transaction in which the credit card is used as a method of payment or extension of credit if (1) the obligor has made a good faith attempt to obtain satisfactory resolution of a disagreement or problem relative to the transaction from the person honoring the credit card; (2) the amount of the initial transaction exceeds $50; and (3) the place where the initial transaction occurred was in the same State as the mailing address previously provided by the cardholder or was within 100 miles from such address, except that the limitations set forth in clauses (2) and (3) with respect to an obligor's right to assert claims and defenses against a card issuer shall not be applicable to any transaction in which the person honoring the credit card (A) is the same person as the card issuer, (B) is controlled by the card issuer, (C) is under direct or indirect common control with the card issuer, (D) is a franchised dealer in the card issuer's products or services, or (E) has obtained the order for such transaction through a mail solicitation made by or participated in by the card issuer in which the cardholder is solicited to enter into such transaction by using the credit card issued by the card issuer.

"(b) The amount of claims or defenses asserted by the cardholder may not exceed the amount of credit outstanding with respect to such transaction at the time the cardholder first notifies the card issuer or the person honoring the credit card of such claim or defense. For the purpose of determining the amount of credit outstanding in the preceding sentence, payments and credits to the cardholder's account are deemed to have been applied, in the order indicated, to the payment of: (1) late charges in the order of their entry to the account; (2) finance charges in order of their entry to the account; and (3) debits to the account other than those set forth above, in the order in which each debit entry to the account was made."

15 USC 1666j.

§171. Relation to State Laws

"(a) This chapter does not annul, alter, or affect, or exempt any person subject to the provisions of this chapter from complying with, the laws of any State with respect to credit billing practices, except to the extent that those laws are inconsistent with any provision of this chapter, and then only to the extent of the inconsistency. The Board is authorized to determine whether such inconsistencies exist. The Board may not determine that any State law is inconsistent with any provision of this chapter if the Board determines that such law gives greater protection to the consumer.

"(b) The Board shall by regulation exempt from the requirements of this chapter any class of credit transactions within any State if it determines that under the law of that State that class of transactions is subject to requirements substantially similar to those imposed under this chapter or that such law gives greater protection to the consumer, and that there is adequate provision for enforcement."

§307. Conforming Amendments

(a) The table of chapters of the Truth in Lending Act is amended by adding immediately under item 3 the following:

"4. CREDIT BILLING ....161"

(b) Section 111(d) of such Act (15 U.S.C. 1610(d)) is amended by striking out "and 130" and inserting in lieu thereof a comma and the following: "130, and 166."

(c) Section 121(a) of such Act (15 U.S.C. 1631(a)) is amended—

(1) by striking out "and upon whom a finance charge is or may be imposed"; and

(2) by inserting "or chapter 4" immediately after "this chapter."

(d) Section 121(b) of such Act (15 U.S.C. 1631(b)) is amended by inserting "or chapter 4" immediately after "this chapter."

(e) Section 122(a) of such Act (15 U.S.C. 1632(a)) is amended by inserting "or chapter 4" immediately after "this chapter."

88 STAT. 1517

(f) Section 122(b) of such Act (15 U.S.C. 1632(b)) is amended by inserting "or chapter 4" immediately after "this chapter."

15 USC 1666 note

§308. Effective Date

This title takes effect upon the expiration of one year after the date of its enactment.

7. EXPLANATION FROM THE FEDERAL DEPOSIT INSURANCE CORPORATION ON THE FAIR CREDIT BILLING ACT

"Charge it!" Magic words—unless there's an error on your bill. If you've ever been hassled by a credit department's computer, you'll be pleased to learn about the rights you have when you think your bill is wrong.

Fair Credit Billing, an addition to the Truth in Lending Law, requires prompt correction of billing mistakes. This pamphlet tells you how to resolve a billing dispute in a way that protects your credit rating.

Billing Error

You may challenge either the purchase or the price of an item that appears on your billing statement. The law defines a billing error as any charge:

- Not made by you or by someone authorized to use your account,
- Poorly identified, for a different amount or on a different date than is shown on the statement, or
- For something you did not accept on delivery or for something not delivered according to agreement.

Billing errors also include:

- Failure to credit your account properly;
- Computational or accounting mistakes;
- Failure to mail your statement to your current address, if you notified the creditor of your address change at least 10 days before the billing period ended; and
- Questionable items for which you request explanations or information.

In Case of Error

If you think your bill is wrong, follow these steps:

1. Notify the creditor in writing within 60 days after the bill was mailed. Be sure to include:
   - Your name and account number,

- A statement that you believe the bill contains an error and an explanation of *why* you believe there is an error, and

- The suspected amount of the error.

2. While you are waiting for an answer, you do not have to pay the amount in question (the "disputed amount") or any minimum payments or finance charges that apply to it. But you *are* obligated to pay all parts of the bill that are *not* in dispute.

3. The creditor must acknowledge your letter within 30 days, unless your account is corrected. Within two billing periods—but in no case more than 90 days—either your account must be corrected or you must be told why the creditor believes the bill is correct.

4. If the creditor made a mistake, you do not pay any finance charges on the disputed amount. Your account must be corrected for either the full amount in dispute, or for a part of that amount and you must be furnished an explanation of what you still owe. You then have the time usually given on your type of account to pay any balance.

   If no error is found, the creditor must promptly send you a statement of what you owe. In this case, the creditor may include any finance charges that accumulated and any minimum payments you missed while you were questioning the bill.

5. If you are still not satisfied, you should notify the creditor within the time you have to pay your bill. However, the legal obligation of the creditor has now been fulfilled (except for the requirements that follow regarding your credit rating).

Your Credit Rating

After a creditor has received your written statement about a possible error, the creditor may not give out information to other creditors or credit bureaus or threaten to damage your credit rating. But, after the bill has been explained—and if you still disagree in writing within the time allowed for payment and do not pay—the creditor can report you as delinquent on your account and begin collection proceedings. If this is done, the creditor must also report that you challenge your bill, and you must be provided in writing the name and address of each person to whom your credit information has been given. When the matter is settled, the creditor must report the outcome to each person who received this information about you.

Until your letter is answered, the creditor also may not take any collection action on the disputed amount or restrict your account because of the dispute. A creditor can, however, apply the disputed amount against your credit limit.

Defective Merchandise or Services

The law now provides that you may withhold payment of any balance due on defective merchandise or services purchased with a credit card, provided you have made a good faith effort to return the goods or resolve the problem with the merchant from whom you made the purchase.

If the store that honored the credit card was not also the issuer of the card, two limitations apply to this right:

- The original amount of the purchase must have exceeded $50, and
- The sale must have taken place in your state or within 100 miles of your current address.

In the case of defective merchandise or services, a legal action may result to determine the validity of your claim.

Penalties and Other Provisions

The law provides that any creditor who fails to comply with these rules applying to billing errors and credit ratings automatically forfeits the amount of the item in question and any finance charges on it up to a total of $50, even if no error occurred. You as an individual may also sue for actual damages plus twice the amount of any finance charges, in any case not less than $100 or more than $1,000. Class action suits are also permitted.

The law also includes requirements for prompt reporting and crediting of payments or return of merchandise. In addition, it provides that credit card issuers may not prohibit stores which honor their cards from offering discounts to customers who pay in cash or by check.

To Find Out More

Creditors must provide you a complete statement of your Fair Credit Billing rights when you first open an account and at least twice annually (or send a shorter version with each billing). If you have any further questions about Fair Credit Billing, please contact one of the FDIC's 14 Regional Offices or the Office of Consumer Affairs and Civil Rights. These offices and other Federal agencies which enforce Fair Credit Billing for particular creditors are listed in this brochure.

8. FAIR CREDIT REPORTING ACT

Title VI

"§602. Findings and Purpose

"(a) The Congress makes the following findings:

"(1) The banking system is dependent upon fair and accurate credit reporting. Inaccurate credit reports directly impair the efficiency of the banking system, and unfair credit reporting methods undermine the public confidence which is essential to the continued functioning of the banking system.

"(2) An elaborate mechanism has been developed for investigating and evaluating the credit worthiness, credit standing, credit capacity, character, and general reputation of consumers.

"(3) Consumer reporting agencies have assumed a vital role in assembling and evaluating consumer credit and other information on consumers.

"(4) There is a need to insure that consumer reporting agencies exercise their grave responsibilities with fairness, impartiality, and a respect for the consumer's right to privacy.

"(b) It is the purpose of this title to require that consumer reporting agencies adopt reasonable procedures for meeting the needs of commerce for consumer credit, personnel, insurance, and other information in a manner which is fair and equitable to the consumer, with regard to the confidentiality, accuracy, relevancy, and proper utilization of such information in accordance with the requirements of this title.

"§603. Definitions and Rules of Construction

"(a) Definitions and rules of construction set forth in this section are applicable for the purposes of this title.

"(b) The term 'person' means any individual, partnership, corporation, trust, estate, cooperative, association, government or governmental subdivision or agency, or other entity.

"(c) The term 'consumer' means an individual.

"(d) The term 'consumer report' means any written, oral, or other communication of any information by a consumer reporting agency bearing on a consumer's credit worthiness, credit standing, credit capacity, character, general reputation, personal characteristics, or mode of living which is used or expected to be used or collected in whole or in part for the purpose of serving as a factor in establishing the consumer's eligibility for (1) credit or insurance to be used primarily for personal, family, or household purposes, or (2) employment purposes, or (3) other purposes authorized under section 604. The term does not include (A) any report containing information solely as to transactions or experiences between the consumer and the person making the report: (B) any authorization or approval of a specific extension of credit directly or indirectly by the issuer of a credit card or similar device; or (C) any report in which a person who has been requested by a third party to make a specific extension of credit directly or indirectly to a consumer conveys his decision with respect to such request, if the third party advises the consumer of the name and address of the person to whom the request was made and such person makes the disclosures to the consumer required under section 615.

"(e) The term 'investigative consumer report' means a consumer report or portion thereof in which information on a consumer's character, general reputation, personal characteristics, or mode of living is obtained through personal interviews with neighbors, friends, or associates of the consumer reported on or with others with whom he is acquainted or who may have knowledge concerning any such items of information. However, such information shall not include specific factual information on a consumer's credit record obtained directly from a creditor of the consumer or from a consumer reporting agency when such information was obtained directly from a creditor of the consumer or from the consumer.

"(f) The term 'consumer reporting agency' means any person which, **for monetary** fees, dues or on a cooperative nonprofit basis, regularly engages in whole or in part in the practice of assembling or evaluating consumer credit information or other information on consumers for the purpose of furnishing consumer reports to third parties, and which uses any means or facility of Interstate commerce for the purpose of preparing or furnishing consumer reports.

"(g) The term 'file', when used in connection with information on any consumer, means all of the information on that consumer recorded and retained by a consumer reporting agency regardless of how the information is stored.

"(h) The term 'employment purposes' when used in connection with a consumer report means a report used for the purpose of evaluating a consumer for employment, promotion, reassignment or retention as an employee.

"(i) The term 'medical information' means information or records obtained with the consent of the individual to whom it relates, from licensed physicians or medical practitioners, hospitals, clinics, or other medical or medically related facilities.

"§604. Permissible Purposes of Reports

"A consumer reporting agency may furnish a consumer report under the following circumstances and no other:

"(1) In response to the order of a court having jurisdiction to issue such an order.

"(2) In accordance with the written instructions of the consumer to whom it relates.

"(3) To a person which it has reason to believe:

"(A) intends to use the information in connection with a credit transaction involving the consumer on whom the information is to be furnished and involving the extension of credit to, or review or collection of an account of the consumer; or

"(B) intends to use the information for employment purposes; or

"(C) intends to use the information in connection with the underwriting of insurance involving the consumer; or

"(D) intends to use the information in connection with a determination of the consumer's eligibility for a license or other benefit granted by a governmental instrumentality required by law to consider an applicant's financial responsibility or status; or

"(E) otherwise has a legitimate business need for the information in connection with a business transaction involving the consumer.

"§605. Obsolete Information

"(a) Except as authorized under subsection (b), no consumer reporting agency may make any consumer report containing any of the following items of information:

"(1) Cases under title II of the United States Code or under the Bankruptcy Act that, from the date of entry of the order for relief or the date of adjudication, as the case may be, antedate the report by more than 10 years.

"(2) Suits and judgments which, from date of entry, antedate the report by more than seven years or until the governing statute of limitations has expired, whichever is the longer period.

"(3) Paid tax liens which, from date of payment, antedate the report by more than seven years.

"(4) Accounts placed for collection or charged to profit and loss which antedate the report by more than seven years.

"(5) Records of arrest, indictment, or conviction of crime which, from date of disposition, release, or parole, antedate the report by more than seven years.

(6) Any other adverse item of information which antedates the report by more than seven years.

"(b) the provisions of subsection (a) are not applicable in the case of any consumer credit report to be used in connection with—

"(1) a credit transaction involving, or which may reasonably be expected to involve, a principal amount of $50,000 or more;

"(2) the underwriting of life insurance involving, or which may reasonably be expected to involve, a face amount of $50,000 or more; or

"(3) the employment of any individual at an annual salary which equals, or which may reasonably be expected to equal $20,000, or more.

"§606. Disclosure of Investigative Consumer Reports

"(a) A person may not procure or cause to be prepared an investigative consumer report on any consumer unless—

"(1) it is clearly and accurately disclosed to the consumer that an investigative consumer report including information as to his character, general reputation, personal characteristics, and mode of living, whichever are applicable, may be made, and such disclosure (A) is made in a writing mailed, or otherwise delivered, to the consumer, not later than three days after the date on which the report was first requested, and (B) includes a statement informing the consumer of his right to request the additional disclosures provided for under subsection (b) of this section; or

"(2) the report is to be used for employment purposes for which the consumer has not specifically applied.

"(b) Any person who procures or causes to be prepared an investigative consumer report on any consumer shall, upon written request made by the consumer within a reasonable period of time after receipt by him of the disclosure required by subsection (a)(1), shall make a complete and accurate disclosure of the nature and scope of the investigation requested. This disclosure shall be made in a writing mailed, or otherwise delivered, to the consumer not later than five days after the date on which the request for such disclosure was received from the consumer or such report was first requested, whichever is the latter.

"(c) No person may be held liable for any violation of subsection (a) or (b) of this section if he shows by a preponderance of the evidence that at the time of the violation he maintained reasonable procedures to assure compliance with subsection (a) and (b).

"§607. Compliance Procedures

"(a) Every consumer reporting agency shall maintain reasonable procedures designed to avoid violations of section 605 and to limit the furnishing of consumer reports to the purposes listed under section 604. These procedures shall require that prospective users of the information identify themselves, certify the purposes for which the information is sought, and certify that the information will be used for no other purpose. Every consumer reporting agency shall make a reasonable effort to verify the identity of a new prospective user and the uses certified by such prospective user prior to furnishing such user a consumer report. No consumer reporting agency may furnish a consumer report to any person if it has reasonable grounds for believing that the consumer report will not be used for a purpose listed in section 604.

"(b) Whenever a consumer reporting agency prepares a consumer report it shall follow reasonable procedures to assure maximum possible accuracy of the information concerning the individual about whom the report relates.

"§608. Disclosures to Governmental Agencies

"Notwithstanding the provisions of section 604, a consumer reporting agency may furnish identifying information respecting any consumer, limited to his name, address, former addresses, places of employment, or former places of employment, to a governmental agency.

"§609. Disclosures to Consumers

"(a) Every consumer reporting agency shall, upon request and proper identification of any consumer, clearly and accurately disclose to the consumer:

"(1) The nature and substance of all information (except medical information) in its files on the consumer at the time of the request.

"(2) The sources of the information; except that the sources of information acquired solely for use in preparing an investigative consumer report and actually used for no other purpose need not be disclosed: *Provided,* That in the event an action is brought under this title, such sources shall be available to the plaintiff under appropriate discovery procedures in the court in which the action is brought.

"(3) The recipients of any consumer report on the consumer which it has furnished

"(A) for employment purposes within the two-year period preceding the request, and

"(B) for any other purpose within the six-month period preceding the request.

"(b) The requirements of subsection (a) respecting the disclosure of sources of information and the recipients of consumer reports do not apply to information received or consumer reports furnished prior to the effective date of this title except to the extent that the matter involved is contained in the files of the consumer reporting agency on that date.

"§610. Conditions of Disclosure to Consumers

"(a) A consumer reporting agency shall make the disclosures required under section 609 during normal business hours and on reasonable notice.

"(b) The disclosures required under section 609 shall be made to the consumer—

"(1) in person if he appears in person and furnishes proper identification; or

"(2) by telephone if he has made a written request, with proper identification, for telephone disclosure and the toll charge, if any, for the telephone call is prepaid by or charged directly to the consumer.

"(c) Any consumer reporting agency shall provide trained personnel to explain to the consumer any information furnished to him pursuant to section 609.

"(d) The consumer shall be permitted to be accompanied by one other person of his choosing, who shall furnish reasonable identification. A consumer reporting agency may require the consumer to furnish a written statement granting permission to the consumer reporting agency to discuss the consumer's file in such person's presence.

"(e) Except as provided in sections 616 and 617, no consumer may bring any action or proceeding in the nature of defamation, invasion of privacy, or negligence with respect to the reporting of information against any consumer reporting agency, any user of information, or any person who furnishes information to a consumer reporting agency, based on information disclosed pursuant to section 609, 610, or 615, except as to false information furnished with malice or willful intent to injure such consumer.

"§611. Procedure in Case of Disputed Accuracy

"(a) If the completeness or accuracy of any item of information contained in his file is disputed by a consumer, and such dispute is directly conveyed to the consumer reporting agency by the consumer, the consumer reporting agency shall within a reasonable period of time reinvestigate and record the current status of that information unless it has reasonable grounds to believe that the dispute by the consumer is frivolous or irrelevant. If after such reinvestigation such information is found to be inaccurate or can no longer be verified, the consumer reporting agency shall promptly delete such information. The presence of contradictory information in the consumer's file does not in and of itself constitute reasonable grounds for believing the dispute is frivolous or irrelevant.

"(b) If the reinvestigation does not resolve the dispute, the consumer may file a brief statement setting forth the nature of the dispute. The consumer reporting agency may limit such statements to not more than one hundred words if it provides the consumer with assistance in writing a clear summary of the dispute.

"(c) Whenever a statement of a dispute is filed, unless there is reasonable grounds to believe that it is frivolous or irrelevant, the consumer reporting agency shall, in any subsequent consumer report containing the information in question, clearly note that it is disputed by the consumer and provide either the consumer's statement or a clear and accurate codification or summary thereof.

"(d) Following any deletion of information which is found to be inaccurate or whose accuracy can no longer be verified or any notation as to disputed information, the consumer reporting agency shall, at the request of the consumer, furnish notification that the item has been deleted or the statement, codification or summary pursuant to subsection (b) or (c) to any person specifically designated by the consumer who has within two years prior thereto received a consumer report for employment purposes, or within six months prior thereto received a consumer report for any other purpose, which contained the deleted or disputed information. The consumer reporting agency shall clearly and conspicuously disclose to the consumer his rights to make such a request. Such disclosure shall be made at or prior to the time the information is deleted or the consumer's statement regarding the disputed information is received.

"§612. Charges for Certain Disclosures

"A consumer reporting agency shall make all disclosures pursuant to section 609 and furnish all consumer reports pursuant to section 611(d) without charge to the consumer if, within thirty days after receipt by such consumer of a notification pursuant to section 615 or notification from a debt collection agency affiliated with such consumer reporting agency stating that the consumer's credit rating may be or has been adversely affected, the consumer makes a request under section 609 or 611(d). Otherwise, the consumer reporting agency may impose a reasonable charge on the consumer for making disclosure to such consumer pursuant to section 609, the charge for which shall be indicated to the consumer prior to making disclosure, and for furnishing notifications, statements, summaries, or codifications to person designated by the consumer pursuant to section 611(d), the charge for which shall be indicated to the consumer prior to furnishing such information and shall not exceed the charge that the consumer reporting agency would impose on each designated recipient for a consumer report except that no charge may be made for notifying such persons of the deletion of information which is found to be inaccurate or which can no longer be verified.

"§613. Public Record Information for Employment Purposes

"A consumer reporting agency which furnishes a consumer report for employment purposes and which for that purpose compiles and reports items of information on consumers which are matters of public record and are likely to have an adverse effect upon a consumer's ability to obtain employment shall—

"(1) at the time such public record information is reported to the user of such consumer report, notify the consumer of the fact that public record information is being reported by the consumer reporting agency, together with the name and address of the person to whom such information is being reported; or

"(2) maintain strict procedures designed to insure that whenever public record information which is likely to have an adverse effect on a consumer's ability to obtain employment is reported it is complete and up to date. For purposes of this paragraph, items of public record relating to arrests, indictments, convictions, suits, tax liens, and outstanding judgments shall be considered up to date if the current public record status of the item at the time of the report is reported.

"§614. Restrictions on Investigative Consumer Reports

"Whenever a consumer reporting agency prepares an investigative consumer report, no adverse information in the consumer report (other than information which is a matter of public record) may be included in a subsequent consumer report unless such adverse information has been verified in the process of making such subsequent consumer report, or the adverse information was received within the three-month period preceding the date the subsequent report is furnished.

"§615. Requirements on Users of Consumer Reports

"(a) Whenever credit or insurance for personal, family, or household purposes, or employment involving a consumer is denied or the charge for such credit or insurance is increased either wholly or partly because of information contained in a consumer report from a consumer reporting agency, the user of the consumer report shall so advise the consumer against whom such adverse action has been taken and supply the name and address of the consumer reporting agency making the report.

"(b) Whenever credit for personal, family, or household purposes involving a consumer is denied or the charge for such credit is increased either wholly or partly because of information obtained from a person other than a consumer reporting agency bearing upon the consumer's credit worthiness, credit standing, credit capacity, character, general reputation, personal characteristics, or mode of living, the user of such information shall, within a reasonable period of time, upon the consumer's written request for the reasons for such adverse action received within sixty days after learning of such adverse action, disclose the nature of the information to the consumer. The user of such information shall clearly and accurately disclose to the consumer his right to make such written request at the time such adverse action is communicated to the consumer.

"(c) No person shall be held liable for any violation of this section if he shows by a preponderance of the evidence that at the time of the alleged violation he maintained reasonable procedures to assure compliance with the provisions of subsections (a) and (b).

"§616. Civil Liability for Willful Noncompliance

"Any consumer reporting agency or user of information which willfully fails to comply with any requirement imposed under this title with respect to any consumer is liable to that consumer in an amount equal to the sum of—

"(1) any actual damages sustained by the consumer as a result of the failure:

"(2) such amount of punitive damages as the court may allow; and

"(3) in the case of any successful action to enforce any liability under this section, the costs of the action together with reasonable attorney's fees as determined by the court.

"§617. Civil Liability for Negligent Noncompliance

"Any consumer reporting agency or user of information which is negligent in failing to comply with any requirement imposed under this title with respect to any consumer is liable to that consumer in an amount equal to the sum of—

"(1) any actual damages sustained by the consumer as a result of the failure:

"(2) in the case of any successful action to enforce any liability under this section, the costs of the action together with reasonable attorney's fees as determined by the court.

"§618. Jurisdiction of Courts: Limitation of Actions

"An action to enforce any liability created under this title may be brought in any appropriate United States district court without regard to the amount in controversy, or in any other court of competent jurisdiction, within two years from the date on which the liability arises, except that where a defendant has materially and willfully misrepresented any information required under this title to be disclosed to an individual and the information so misrepresented is material to the establishment of the defendant's liability to that individual under this title, the action may be brought at any time within two years after discovery by the individual of the misrepresentation.

"§619. Obtaining Information Under False Pretenses

"Any person who knowingly and willfully obtains information on a consumer from a consumer reporting agency under false pretenses shall be fined not more than $5,000 or imprisoned not more than one year, or both.

"§620. Unauthorized Disclosures by Officers or Employees

"Any officer or employee of a consumer reporting agency who knowingly and willfully provides information concerning an individual from the agency's files to a person not authorized to receive that information shall be fined not more than $5,000 or imprisoned not more than one year, or both.

"§621. Administrative Enforcement

"(a) Compliance with the requirements imposed under this title shall be enforced under the Federal Trade Commission Act by the Federal Trade Commission with respect to consumer reporting agencies and all other persons subject thereto, except to the extent that enforcement of the requirements imposed under this title is specifically committed to some other government agency under subsection (b) hereof. For the purpose of the exercise by the Federal Trade Commission of its functions and powers under the Federal Trade Commission Act, a violation of any requirement or prohibition imposed under this title shall constitute an unfair or deceptive act or practice in commerce in violation of section 5(a) of the Federal Trade Commission Act and shall be subject to enforcement by the Federal Trade Commission under section 5(b) thereof with respect to any consumer reporting agency or person subject to enforcement by the Federal Trade Commission pursuant to this subsection, irrespective of whether that person is engaged in commerce or meets any other jurisdictional tests in the Federal Trade Commission Act. The Federal Trade Commission shall have such procedural, investigative, and enforcement powers, including the power to issue procedural rules in enforcing compliance with the requirements imposed under this title and to require the filing of reports, the production of documents, and the appearance of witnesses as though the applicable terms and conditions of the Federal Trade Commission Act were part of this title. Any person violating any of the provisions of this title shall be subject to the penalties and entitled to the privileges and immunities provided in the Federal Trade Commission Act as though the applicable terms and provisions thereof were part of this title.

"(b) Compliance wth the requirements imposed under this title with respect to consumer reporting agencies and persons who use consumer reports from such agencies shall be enforced under—

"(1) section 8 of the Federal Deposit Insurance Act, in the case of:

"(A) national banks, by the Comptroller of the Currency;

"(B) member banks of the Federal Reserve System (other than national banks), by the Federal Reserve Board; and

"(C) banks insured by the Federal Deposit Insurance Corporation (other than members of the Federal Reserve System), by the Board of Directors of the Federal Deposit Insurance Corporation.

"(2) section 5(d) of the Home Owners Loan Act of 1933, section 407 of the National Housing Act, and sections 6(i) and 17 of the Federal Home Loan Bank Act, by the Federal Home Loan Bank Board (acting directly or through the Federal Savings and Loan Insurance Corporation), in the case of any institution subject to any of those provisions;

"(3) the Federal Credit Union Act, by the Administrator of the National Credit Union Administration with respect to any Federal credit union;

"(4) the Acts to regulate commerce, by the Interstate Commerce Commission with respect to any common carrier subject to those Acts;

"(5) the Federal Aviation Act of 1958, by the Civil Aeronautics Board with respect to any air carrier or foreign air carrier subject to that Act; and

"(6) the Packers and Stockyards Act, 1921 (except as provided in section 406 of that Act), by the Secretary of Agriculture with respect to any activities subject to that Act.

"(c) For the purpose of the exercise by any agency referred to in subsection (b) of its powers under any Act referred to in that subsection, a violation of any requirement imposed under this title shall be deemed to be a violation of a requirement imposed under that Act. In addition to its powers under any provision of law specifically referred to in subsection (b), each of the agencies referred to in that subsection may exercise, for the purpose of enforcing compliance with any requirement imposed under this title any other authority conferred on it by law.

"§622. Relations to State Laws

"This title does not annul, alter, affect, or exempt any person subject to the provisions of this title from complying with the laws of any State with respect to the collection, distribution, or use of any information on consumers, except to the extent that those laws are inconsistent with any provision of this title, and then only to the extent of the inconsistency."

EFFECTIVE DATE

SEC. 602. Section 504 of the Consumer Credit Protection Act is amended by adding at the end thereof the following new subsection:

"(d) Title VI takes effect upon the expiration of one hundred and eighty days following the date of its enactment."

Approved October 26, 1970.

9. EXPLANATION FROM THE FEDERAL DEPOSIT INSURANCE CORPORATION ON THE FAIR CREDIT REPORTING ACT

If you have a charge account, a mortgage on your home, a life insurance policy, or if you have applied for a personal loan or a job, it is almost certain that somewhere there is a "file" that shows how promptly you pay your bills, whether you have been sued or arrested, or if you have filed for bankruptcy, etc.

And such a file may include your neighbors' and friends' views of your character, general reputation, or manner of living.

The companies that gather and sell such information to creditors, insurers, employers, and other businesses are called "Consumer Reporting Agencies," and the legal term for the Report is a "Consumer Report."

If, in addition to credit information, the Report includes interviews with a third person about your character, reputation, or manner of living, it is referred to as an "Investigative Consumer Report."

THE FAIR CREDIT REPORTING ACT became law on April 25, 1971. This Act was passed by Congress to protect consumers against the circulation of inaccurate or obsolete information and to ensure that Consumer Reporting Agencies adopt fair and equitable procedures for obtaining, maintaining, and giving out information about consumers.

Under this law you can take steps to protect yourself if you have been denied credit, insurance, or employment, or if you believe you have had difficulties because of an inaccurate or an unfair Consumer Report.

You Have the Right:

1. To be told the name and address of the Consumer Reporting Agency responsible for preparing a Consumer Report that was used to deny you credit, insurance, or employment or to increase the cost of credit or insurance.

2. To be told by a Consumer Reporting Agency the nature, substance, and sources (except investigative-type sources) of the information (except medical) collected about you.

3. To take anyone of your choice with you when you visit the Consumer Reporting Agency to check on your file.

4. To obtain free of charge all information to which you are entitled if the request is made within 30 days after receipt of a notification that you have been denied credit, insurance, or employment because of information contained in a Consumer Report. Otherwise, the Consumer Reporting Agency is permitted to charge a reasonable fee for giving you the information.

5. To be told who has received a Consumer Report on you within the preceding 6 months or within the preceding 2 years if the report was furnished for employment purposes.

6. To have incomplete or incorrect information reinvestigated unless the Consumer Reporting Agency has reasonable grounds to believe that the dispute is frivolous or irrelevant. If the information is investigated and found to be inaccurate or if the information cannot be verified, you have the right to have such information removed from your file.

7. To have the Agency notify those you name (at no cost to you), who have previously received the incorrect or incomplete information, that this information has been deleted from your file.

8. When a dispute between you and the Reporting Agency about information in your file cannot be resolved, you have the right to have your version of such dispute placed in the file and included in future Consumer Reports

9. To request the Reporting Agency to send your version of the dispute to certain businesses without charge, if requested within 30 days of the adverse action.

10. To have a Consumer Report withheld from anyone who under the law does not have a legitimate business need for the information.

11. To sue a Reporting Agency for damages if the Agency willfully or negligently violates the law; and, if you are successful, to collect attorney's fees and court costs.

12. Not to have adverse information reported after 7 years. One major exception is bankruptcy, which may be reported for 14 years.

13. To be notified by a business that it is seeking information about you which would constitute an Investigative Consumer Report.

14. To request from the business that ordered an Investigative Consumer Report more information about the nature and scope of the investigation.

15. To discover the nature and substance (but not the sources) of the information that was collected for an Investigative Consumer Report.

The Fair Credit Reporting Act Does Not:

1. Give you the right to request a Report on yourself from the Consumer Reporting Agency.

2. Give you the right, when you visit the Agency, to receive a copy of your file, although some Agencies will voluntarily give you a copy.

3. Compel anyone to do business with an individual consumer.

4. Apply when you request commercial (as distinguished from consumer) credit or business insurance.

5. Authorize any Federal agency to intervene on behalf of an individual consumer.

How to Deal with Consumer Reporting Agencies

If you want to know what information a Consumer Reporting Agency has collected about you, either arrange for personal interview at the Agency's office during normal business hours or call in advance for an interview by telephone. Some Agencies will voluntarily make disclosures by mail.

The Consumer Reporting Agencies in your community can be located by consulting the *Yellow Pages* of your telephone book under such headings as "Credit" or "Credit Rating or Reporting Agencies."

If you decide to visit a Consumer Reporting Agency to check on your file, the following checklist may be of help.

For instance, in checking your credit file DID YOU:

1. Learn the nature and substance of all the information in your file?

2. Find out the name of each of the businesses (or other sources) that supplied information on you to the Reporting Agency?

3. Learn the name of everyone who received reports on you within the past six months (or the last two years if the Reports were for employment purposes)?

4. Request the Agency to reinvestigate and correct or delete information that was found to be inaccurate, incomplete, or obsolete?

5. Follow up to determine the results of the reinvestigation?

6. Ask the Agency, at no cost to you, to notify those you name who received Reports within the past six months (two years if for employment purposes) that certain information was deleted?

7. Follow up to make sure that those named by you did in fact receive notices from the Consumer Reporting Agency?

8. Demand that your version of the facts be placed in your file if the reinvestigation did not settle the dispute?

9. Request the Agency (if you are willing to pay a reasonable fee) to send your statement of the dispute to those you name who received Reports containing the disputed information within the past six months (two years if received for employment purposes)?

The FDIC has published the following pamphlets which are available upon request.

Your Insured Deposit
Equal Credit Opportunity for Women
Equal Credit Opportunity and Age
Truth in Lending
Fair Credit Billing
Consumer Information
Fair Credit Reporting Act

10. PRESERVATION OF CONSUMERS' CLAIMS AND DEFENSES

Title 18, Section 433 of the U.S. Code

"§433.1 Definitions

(a) *Person.* An individual, corporation, or any other business organization.

(b) *Consumer.* A natural person who seeks or acquires goods or services for personal, family, or household use.

(c) *Creditor.* A person who, in the ordinary course of business, lends purchase money or finances the sale of goods or services to consumers on a deferred payment basis; provided such person is not acting, for the purposes of a particular transaction, in the capacity of a credit card issuer.

(d) *Purchase money loan.* A cash advance which is received by a consumer in return for a "Finance Charge" within the meaning of the Truth in Lending Act and Regulation Z, which is applied, in whole or substantial part, to a purchase of goods or services from a seller who (1) refers consumers to the creditor or (2) is affiliated with the creditor by common control, contract, or business arrangement.

(e) *Financing a sale.* Extending credit to a consumer in connection with a "Credit Sale" within the meaning of the Truth in Lending Act and Regulation Z.

(f) *Contract.* Any oral or written agreement, formal or informal, between a creditor and a seller, which contemplates or provides for cooperative or concerted activity in connection with the sale of goods or services to consumers or the financing thereof.

(g) *Business arrangement.* Any understandinng, procedure, course of dealing, or arrangement, formal or informal, between a creditor and a seller, in connection with the sale of goods or services to consumers or the financing thereof.

(h) *Credit card issuer.* A person who extends to cardholders the right to use a credit card in connection with purchases of goods or services.

375

(i) *Consumer credit contract.* Any instrument which evidences or embodies a debt arising from a "Purchase Money Loan" transaction or a "financed sale" as defined in paragraphs (d) and (e) of this section.

(j) *Seller.* A person who, in the ordinary course of business, sells, or leases goods or services to consumers.

§433.2 Preservation of Consumers' Claims and Defenses, Unfair or Deceptive Acts or Practices.

In connection with any sale or lease of goods or services to consumers, in or affecting commerce as "commerce" is defined in the Federal Trade Commission Act, it is an unfair or deceptive act or practice within the meaning of section 5 of that Act for a seller, directly or indirectly, to:

(a) Take or receive a consumer credit contract which fails to contain the following provision in at least ten point, boldface, type:

NOTICE

ANY HOLDER OF THIS CONSUMER CREDIT CONTRACT IS SUBJECT TO ALL CLAIMS AND DEFENSES WHICH THE DEBTOR COULD ASSERT AGAINST THE SELLER OF GOODS OR SERVICES OBTAINED PURSUANT HERETO OR WITH THE PROCEEDS HEREOF. RECOVERY HEREUNDER BY THE DEBTOR SHALL NOT EXCEED AMOUNTS PAID BY THE DEBTOR HEREUNDER.

or,

(b) Accept, as full or partial payment for such sale or lease, the proceeds of any purchase money loan (as purchase money loan is defined herein), unless any consumer credit contract made in connection with such purchase money loan contains the following provision in at least ten point, boldface, type:

NOTICE

ANY HOLDER OF THIS CONSUMER CREDIT CONTRACT IS SUBJECT TO ALL CLAIMS AND DEFENSES WHICH THE DEBTOR COULD ASSERT AGAINST THE SELLER OF GOODS OR SERVICES OBTAINED WITH THE PROCEEDS HEREOF. RECOVERY HEREUNDER BY THE DEBTOR SHALL NOT EXCEED AMOUNTS PAID BY THE DEBTOR HEREUNDER.

§433.3 Exemption of Sellers Taking or Receiving Open-End Consumer Credit Contracts Before November 1, 1977 from Requirements of Section 433.2(a).

(a) Any seller who has taken or received an open-end consumer credit contract before November 1, 1977, shall be exempt from the requirements of 16 CFR Part 433 with respect to such contract provided the contract does not cut off consumers' claims and defenses.

(b) Definitions. The following definitions apply to this exemption:

(1) All pertinent definitions contained in 16 CFR 433.1.

(2) Open-end consumer credit contract; a consumer credit contract pursuant to which "open-end credit" is extended.

(3) "Open-end credit": consumer credit extended on an account pursuant to a plan under which a creditor may permit an applicant to make purchases or make loans, from time to time, directly from the creditor or indirectly by use of a credit card, check, or other device, as the plan may provide. The term does not include negotiated advances under an open-end real estate mortgage or a letter of credit.

(4) Contract which does not cut off consumers' claims and defenses: A consumer credit contract which does not constitute or contain a negotiable instrument, or contain any waiver, limitation, term, or condition which has the effect of limiting a consumer's right to assert against any holder of the contract all legally sufficient claims and defenses which the consumer could assert against the seller of goods or services purchased pursuant to the contract.

11. FEDERAL LAW: MAILING OF UNORDERED MERCHANDISE

§39 U.S.C. 3009

(a) Except for (1) free samples clearly and conspicuously marked as such, and (2) merchandise mailed by a charitable organization soliciting contributions, the mailing of unordered merchandise or of communications prohibited by subsection (c) of this section constitutes an unfair method of competition and an unfair trade practice in violation of section 45(a)(1) of title 15 (15 U.S.C.S. Section 45(a)(1)).

(b) Any merchandise mailed in violation of subsection (a) of this section, or within the exceptions contained therein, may be treated as a gift by the recipient, who shall have the right to retain, use, discard, or dispose of it in any such manner he sees fit without any obligation whatsoever to the sender. All such merchandise shall have attached to it a clear and conspicuous statement informing the recipient that he may treat the merchandise as a gift to him and has the right to retain, use, discard, or dispose of it in any manner he sees fit without any obligation whatsoever to the sender.

(c) No mailer of any merchandise mailed in violation of subsection (a) of this section, or within the exceptions contained therein, shall mail to any recipient of such merchandise a bill for such merchandise or any dunning communications.

12. COMMUNICATION ACT

§223. Whoever—

(1) in the District of Columbia or in interstate or foreign communication by means of telephone—

(A) makes any comment, request, suggestion or proposal which is obscene, lewd, lascivious, filthy, or indecent;

(B) makes a telephone call, whether or not conversation ensues, without disclosing his identity and with intent to annoy, abuse, threaten, or harass any person at the called number;

(C) makes or causes the telephone of another repeatedly or continuously to ring, with intent to harass any person at the called number; or

(D) makes repeated telephone calls, during which conversation ensues, solely to harass any person at the called number; or

(2) knowingly permits any telephone under his control to be used for any purpose prohibited by this section,

shall be fined not more than $500 or imprisoned not more than six months, or both.

Monitoring and Taping of Telephone Calls

1. FEDERAL LAWS

A. WIRE INTERCEPTION AND INTERCEPTION OF ORAL COMMUNICATIONS—TITLE 18, §2510 OF THE U.S. CODE

§2510. Definitions—18 U.S.C. United States Code (USC)

As used in this chapter:

(1) "Wire communication" means any communication made in whole or in part through the use of facilities for the transmission of communications by the aid of wire, cable, or other like connection between the point of origin and the point of reception furnished or operated by any person engaged as a common carrier in providing or operating such facilities for the transmission of interstate or foreign communications;

(2) "Oral communication" means any oral communication uttered by a person exhibiting an expectation that such communication is not subject to interception under circumstances justifying such expectation;

(3) "State" means any State of the United States, the District of Columbia, the Commonwealth of Puerto Rico, and any territory or possession of the United States;

(4) "Intercept" means the oral acquisition of the contents of any wire or oral communication through the use of any electronic, mechanical, or other device.

(5) "Electronic, mechanical, or other device" means any device or apparatus which can be used to intercept a wire or oral communication other than:

(a) any telephone or telegraph instrument, equipment, or facility, or any component thereof (i) furnished to the subscriber or user by a communications common carrier in the ordinary course of its business and being used by the subscriber or user in the ordinary course of its business; or

(ii) being used by a communication common carrier in the ordinary course of its business, or by an investigative or law enforcement officer in the ordinary course of his duties;

(b) a hearing aid or similar device being used to correct subnormal hearing to not better than normal;

(6) "Person" means any employee, or agent of the United States or any State or political subdivision thereof, and any individual, partnership, association, joint stock company, trust, or corporation;

(7) "Investigative or law enforcement officer" means any officer of the United States or of a State or political subdivision thereof, who is empowered by law to conduct investigations of or to make arrests for offenses enumerated in this chapter, and any attorney authorized by law to prosecute or participate in the prosecution of such offenses;

(8) "Content," when used with respect to any wire or oral communication, includes any information concerning the identity of the parties to such communication or the existence, substance, purport, or meaning of that communication;

(9) "Judge of competent jurisdiction" means:

    (a) a judge of a United States district court or a United States Court of Appeals; and

    (b) a judge of any court of general criminal jurisdiction of a State who is authorized by a statute of that State to enter orders authorizing interceptions of wire or oral communications;

(10) "Communication common carrier" shall have the same meaning which is given the term "common carrier" by section 153(h) of title 47 of the United States Code; and

(11) "Aggrieved person" means a person who was a party to any intercepted wire or oral communication or a person against whom the interception was directed.

B. TITLE 18, §2511 OF THE U.S. CODE

Interception and disclosure of wire or oral communications prohibited

<u>§2511</u>

(1) Except as otherwise specifically provided in this chapter any person who:

    (a) willfully intercepts, endeavors to intercept, or procures any other person to intercept or endeavor to intercept, any wire or oral communication;

    (b) willfully uses, endeavors to use, or procures any other person to use or endeavor to use any electronic, mechanical, or other device to intercept any oral communication when

        (i) such device is affixed to, or otherwise transmits a signal through, a wire, cable, or other like connection used in wire communication; or

(ii) such device transmits communications by radio, or interferes with the transmission of such communication; or

(iii) such person knows, or has reason to know, that such device or any component thereof has been through the mail or transported in interstate or foreign commerce; or

(iv) such use or endeavor to use (A) takes place on the premises of any business or other commercial establishment the operations of which affect interstate or foreign commerce; or (B) obtains or is for the purpose of obtaining information relating to the operations of any business or other commercial establishment the operations of which affect interstate or foreign commerce; or

(v) such person acts in the District of Columbia, the Commonwealth of Puerto Rico, or any territory or possession of the United States; attack or other hostile acts of a foreign power, to obtain foreign intelligence information deemed essential to the security of the United States, or to protect national security information against foreign intelligence activities. Nor shall anything contained in this chapter be deemed to limit the constitutional power of the President to take such measures as he deems necessary to protect the United States against the overthrow of the Government by force or other unlawful means, or against any other clear and present danger to the structure or existence of the Government. The contents of any wire or oral communication intercepted by authority of the President in the exercise of the foregoing powers may be received in evidence in any trial hearing, or other proceeding only where such interception was reasonable, and shall not be otherwise used or disclosed except as is necessary to implement that power.

2. STATE LAWS

CALIFORNIA PENAL CODE

§631. Wiretapping

(a) Prohibited acts; punishment; recidivists. Any person who by means of any machine, instrument, or contrivance, or in any other manner, intentionally taps, or makes any unauthorized connection, whether physically, electrically, acoustically, inductively, or otherwise, with any telegraph or telephone wire, line cable, or instrument, including the wire, line, cable, or instrument or any internal telephonic communication system, or who willfully and without the consent of all parties to the communication, or in any unauthorized manner, reads, or attempts to read or to learn the contents or meaning of any message, report, or communication while the same is in transit or passing over any such wire, line, or cable, or is being sent from, or received at any place within this state; or who uses, or attempts to use, in any manner, or for any purpose, or to communicate in any way, any information so obtained, or who aids, agrees with, employs, or conspires with any person or persons to unlawfully do, or permit, or cause to be done any of the acts or things mentioned above in this section, is punishable by a fine not exceeding two thousand five hundred dollars ($2,500), or by imprisonment in the county jail not exceeding one year, or by imprisonment in the state prison _____ , or by both such fine and imprisonment in the county jail or in the state prison. If such person has previously been convicted of a violation of this section or Section 632 or 636, he is punishable by fine not exceeding ten thousand dollars ($10,000), or by imprisonment in the county jail not exceeding one year, or by imprisonment in the state prison _____ , or by both such fine and imprisonment in the county jail or in the state prison.

(b) Exceptions. This section shall not apply (1) to any public utility engaged in the business of providing communications services and facilities, or to the officers, employees, or agents thereof, where the acts otherwise prohibited herein are for the purpose of construction, maintenance, conduct, or operation of the services and facilities of such public utility, or (2) to the use of any instrument, equipment, facility, or service furnished and used pursuant to the tariffs of such a public utility, or (3) to any telephonic communication system used for communication exclusively within a state, county, city and county, or city correction facility.

(c) Evidence. Except as proof in an action or prosecution for violation of this section, no evidence obtained in violation of this section shall be admissible in any judicial, administrative, legislative, or other proceeding.

§632. Eavesdropping On or Recording Confidential Communications

(a) Prohibited acts; punishment; recidivists. Every person who, intentionally and without the consent of all parties to a confidential communication, by means of any electronic amplifying or recording device, eavesdrops upon or records such confidential communication, whether such communication is carried on among such parties in the presence of one another or by means of a telegraph, telephone, or other device, except a radio, shall be punishable by fine not exceeding two thousand five hundred dollars ($2,500), or by imprisonment in the county jail not exceeding one year, or by imprisonment in the state prison * * *, or by both such fine and imprisonment in the county jail or in the state prison. If such person has previously been convicted of a violation of this section or Section 631 or 636, he is punishable by fine not exceeding ten thousand dollars ($10,000), or by imprisonment in the county jail not exceeding one year, or by imprisonment in the state prison * * *, or by both such fine and imprisonment in the county jail or in the state prison.

(b) Person. The term "person" includes an individual, business association, partnership, corporation, or other legal entity, and an individual acting or purporting to act for or on behalf of any government or subdivision thereof, whether federal, state, or local, but excludes an individual known by all parties to a confidential communication to be overhearing or recording such communication.

(c) Confidential communication. The term "confidential communication" includes any communication carried on in such circumstances as may reasonably indicate that any party to such communication desires it to be confined to such parties, but excludes a communication made in a public gathering or in any legislative, judicial, executive, or administrative proceeding open to the public, or in any other circumstance in which the parties to the communication may reasonably expect that the communication may be overheard or recorded.

(d) Evidence. Except as proof in an action or prosecution for violation of this section, no evidence obtained as a result of eavesdropping upon or recording a confidential communication in violation of this section shall be admissible in any judicial administrative, legislative, or other proceeding.

(e) Exceptions. This section shall not apply (1) to any public utility engaged in the business of providing communications services and facilities, or to the officers, employees or agents thereof, where the acts otherwise prohibited herein are for the purpose of construction, maintenance, conduct, or operation of the services and facilities of such public utility, or (2) to the use of any instrument, equipment, facility, or service furnished and used pursuant to the tariffs of such a public utility, or (3) to any telephonic communication system used for communication exclusively within a state, county, city and county, or city correctional facility.

(f) Hearing aids. This section does not apply to the use of hearing aids and similar devices, by persons afflicted with impaired hearing, for the purpose of overcoming the impairment to permit the hearing of sounds ordinarily audible to the human ear.

APPENDIX C

Dishonored Checks

1. DISHONORED CHECKS— DOUBLE DAMAGES

NEW YORK

CHAPTER 921

Approved Dec. 20, 1985, effective as provided in Section 2

Message of necessity, pursuant to Art. III, sec. 14, of Const.

AN ACT to amend the general obligations law, in relation to additional liability of drawer of a check

The People of the State of New York, represented in Senate and Assembly, do enact as follows:

Section 1. The general obligations law is amended by adding a new section 11–104 to read as follows:
11–104. Additional liability of drawer.

1. Notwithstanding any contrary provision of law, a drawer negotiating a check who knows or should know that payment of such check will be refused by the drawee bank either because the drawer has no account with such bank or because the drawer has insufficient funds on deposit with such bank shall be liable, except as provided in subdivision four of this section, to the payee who has presented such check for payment, not only for the face amount of the check but also for additional, liquidated damages, where the check is dishonored and the drawer fails to pay the face amount of such check within thirty days following the date of mailing by the payee of the second written demand for payment as provided in this section.

2. In the case of a drawer negotiating a check who knows or should know that payment of such check will be refused by the drawee bank because the drawer has no account with such bank, such additional liquidated damages shall be in an amount to be determined by the court in light of the circumstances, but in no event shall such amount be greater than twice the face amount of the check or seven hundred fifty dollars, whichever is less.

3. In the case of a drawer negotiating a check who knows or should know that payment of such check will be refused by the drawee bank because the drawer has insufficient funds on deposit with such bank, such additional liquidated damages shall be in an amount to be determined by the court in light of the circumstances, but in no event shall such amount be greater than twice the face amount of the check or four hundred dollars, whichever is less.

4. The drawer shall not be liable to the payee for the additional liquidated damages provided for by this section if:

(a) The drawer gave such check as payment for the rental of residential premises; or

(b) The drawer gave such check as payment for residential service supplied by a gas, electric, steam, telephone, or water corporation; or

(c) The drawer gave such check as repayment of all, or a portion of, a debt secured by collateral which the payee has repossessed.

5. Defenses which may be asserted against any person not having the rights of a holder in due course, as specified in sections 3–306 and 3–408 of the Uniform Commercial Code, shall be available to a defendant in any action or proceeding in which additional liability is claimed under this section.

6. The additional liquidated damages provided for in this section shall be available only to those persons or entities which post or otherwise give conspicuous notice to the public of the additional liquidated damages which may be imposed pursuant to this section. Such notice shall set forth the additional liquidated damages that may be imposed if a check is dishonored and the section of law authorizing imposition of such damages, and provide notice that criminal penalties also may apply.

7. The first written demand for payment on the dishonored check shall be in the form prescribed by subdivision eight of this section and shall be sent to the drawer's last known residence address or last known place of business by first class mail and by certified mail return receipt requested with delivery restricted to the drawer, on or after the date the payee received notice that such check had been dishonored. The second written demand for payment on the dishonored check shall be in the form provided in subdivision eight of this section and shall be sent to the drawer at the drawer's last known residence address or last known place of business by first class mail on or after the fifteenth day following the date of receipt of the first written demand for payment.

8. The written demands for payment required by subdivision seven of this section shall be in the following form and shall be printed in at least ten point type in both the English and Spanish languages:

DEMAND FOR PAYMENT OF DISHONORED CHECK

DATE:

TO: _____   1ST NOTICE 2ND AND FINAL
        NAME OF DRAWER   NOTICE WARNING: YOU
                                           MAY BE SUED 30 DAYS
        _____   AFTER THE DATE OF THIS
                                           NOTICE IF YOU DO NOT
        _____   MAKE PAYMENT
        LAST KNOWN RESIDENCE
        ADDRESS OR PLACE OF
        BUSINESS

YOUR CHECK IN THE AMOUNT OF $_____ DATED _____
PAYABLE TO THE ORDER OF _____ HAS BEEN DISHONORED BY
THE BANK UPON WHICH IT WAS DRAWN, BECAUSE:
    YOU HAD NO ACCOUNT WITH THAT BANK
    YOU HAD INSUFFICIENT FUNDS ON DEPOSIT WITH THAT
BANK. IF YOU DO NOT MAKE PAYMENT, YOU MAY BE SUED UNDER
SECTION 11–104 OF THE GENERAL OBLIGATIONS LAW TO RE-
COVER PAYMENT. IF A JUDGMENT IS RENDERED AGAINST YOU IN
COURT, IT MAY INCLUDE NOT ONLY THE ORIGINAL FACE
AMOUNT OF THE CHECK, BUT ALSO ADDITIONAL LIQUIDATED
DAMAGES, AS FOLLOWS:
—IF YOU HAD NO ACCOUNT WITH THE BANK UPON WHICH THE
CHECK WAS DRAWN, AN ADDITIONAL SUM WHICH MAY BE
EQUIVALENT TO TWICE THE FACE AMOUNT OF THE CHECK OR
SEVEN HUNDRED FIFTY DOLLARS, WHICHEVER IS LESS; OR
—IF YOU HAD INSUFFICIENT FUNDS ON DEPOSIT WITH THE
BANK UPON WHICH THE CHECK WAS DRAWN, AN ADDITIONAL
SUM WHICH MAY BE EQUIVALENT TO TWICE THE FACE AMOUNT
OF THE CHECK OR FOUR HUNDRED DOLLARS, WHICHEVER IS
LESS.
PLEASE MAKE PAYMENT IN THE AMOUNT OF _____ TO:

_____

NAME OF PAYEE

ADDRESS TO WHICH PAYMENT SHOULD
BE DELIVERED

IF YOU DISPUTE ANY OF THE FACTS LISTED ABOVE, CONTACT THE
PAYEE IMMEDIATELY.

9. The public service commission shall study the extent to which checks given in payment for residential service supplied by a gas, electric, steam, telephone, or water corporation are dishonored either because the drawer had no account with the bank on which the check was written or because the drawer had insufficient funds on deposit with such bank, including the extent of chronic payment with checks that are dishonored and the impact of such dishonored checks on the operating costs of these corporations and their requests for rate increases, and whether any penalty for dishonored checks, in addition to recovery of the utilities' administrative costs, is necessary. The commission shall report to the governor and the legislature no later than one year after the effective date of this section.

Section 2. This act shall take effect on the sixtieth day after it shall have become a law and shall apply to checks drawn on or after such effective date.

NORTH CAROLINA

§6-21.3 Remedies for Returned Check

(a) Notwithstanding any criminal sanctions that may apply, a person, firm, or corporation who knowingly draws, makes, utters, or issues and delivers to another any check or draft drawn on any bank or depository that refuses to honor the same because the maker or drawer does not have sufficient funds on deposit in or credit with the bank or depository with which to pay the check or draft upon presentation, and who fails to pay the same amount in cash to the payee within 30 days following written demand therefore, shall be liable to the payee for the amount owing on the check and, in addition, for damages of the lesser of five hundred dollars ($500) or three times the amount owing on the check, but in no case less than one hundred dollars ($100) in addition to the amount owing on the check. In an action under this section the court or jury may, however, waive all or part of treble damages upon a finding that the defendant's failure to satisfy the dishonored check or draft was due to economic hardship.

The written demand shall: (i) describe the check or draft and the circumstances of its dishonor, (ii) contain a demand for payment and a notice of intent to file suit for treble damages under this section if payment is not received within 30 days, and (iii) be mailed by certified mail to the defendant at his last known address.

(b) In an action under subsection (a) of this section, the presiding judge or magistrate may award the prevailing party, as part of the court costs payable, a reasonable attorney's fee to the duly licensed attorney representing the prevailing party in such suit.

(c) It shall be an affirmative defense, in addition to other defenses, to an action under this section if it is found that:

(i) full satisfaction of the amount of the check or draft was made prior to the commencement of the action, or

(ii) that the bank or depository erred in dishonoring the check or draft, or

(iii) that the acceptor of the check knew at the time of acceptance that tnere were insufficient funds on deposit in the bank or depository with which to cause the check to be honored.

(d) The remedy provided for herein shall apply only if the check was drawn, made, uttered, or issued with knowledge there were insufficient funds in the account or that no credit existed with the bank or depository with which to pay the check upon presentation.

The Act shall become effective October 1, 1985.

2. PENAL LAW PROVIDING FOR CRIMINAL PENALTIES

NEW YORK

§190.00. Issuing a Bad Check; Definitions of Terms

The following definitions are applicable to this article:

1. "Check" means any check, draft or similar sight order for the payment of money which is not postdated with respect to the time of utterance.

2. "Drawer" of a check means a person whose name appears thereon as the primary obligor, whether the actual signature be that of himself or of a person purportedly authorized to draw the check in his behalf.

3. "Representative drawer" means a person who signs a check as drawer in a representative capacity or as agent of the person whose name appears thereon as the principal drawer or obligor.

4. "Utter." A person "utters" a check when, as a drawer or representative drawer thereof, he delivers it or causes it to be delivered to a person who thereby acquires a right against the drawer with respect to such check. One who draws a check with intent that it be so delivered is deemed to have uttered it if the delivery occurs.

5. "Pass." A person "passes" a check when, being a payee, holder, or bearer of a check which previously has been or purports to have been drawn and uttered by another, he delivers it, for a purpose other than collection, to a third person who thereby acquires a right with respect thereto.

6. "Funds" means money or credit.

7. "Insufficient funds." A drawer has "insufficient funds" with a drawee to cover a check when he has no funds or account whatever, or funds in an amount less than that of the check; and a check dishonored for "no account" shall also be deemed to have been dishonored for "insufficient funds."

§190.05. Issuing a Bad Check

A person is guilty of issuing a bad check when:

1. (a) As a drawer or representative drawer, he utters a check knowing that he or his principal, as the case may be, does not then have sufficient funds with the drawee to cover it, and

   (b) he intends or believes at the time of utterance that payment will be refused by the drawee upon presentation, and

   (c) payment is refused by the drawee upon presentation; or

2. (a) He passes a check knowing that the drawer thereof does not then have sufficient funds with the drawee to cover it, and

   (b) he intends or believes at the time the check is passed that payment will be refused by the drawee upon presentation, and

   (c) payment is refused by the drawee upon presentation.

Issuing a bad check is a class B misdemeanor.

§190.10. Issuing a Bad Check; Presumptions

1. When the drawer of a check has insufficient funds with the drawee to cover it at the time of utterance, the subscribing drawer or representative drawer, as the case may be, is presumed to know of such insufficiency.

2. A subscribing drawer or representative drawer, as the case may be, of an ultimately dishonored check is presumed to have intended or believed that the check would be dishonored upon presentation when:

   (a) The drawer had no account with the drawee at the time of utterance; or

   (b) (i) The drawer had insufficient funds with the drawee at the time of utterance, and

   (ii) the check was presented to the drawee for payment not more than 30 days after the date of utterance, and

   (iii) the drawer had insufficient funds with the drawee at the time of presentation.

3. Dishonor of a check by the drawee and insufficiency of the drawer's funds at the time of presentation may properly be proved by introduction in evidence of a notice of protest of the check, or of a certificate under oath of an authorized representative of the drawee declaring the dishonor and insufficiency, and such proof shall constitute presumptive evidence of such dishonor and insufficiency.

§190.15 Issuing Bad Check; Defenses

In any prosecution for issuing a bad check, it is an affirmative defense that:

1. The defendant or a person acting in his behalf made full satisfaction of the amount of the check within ten days after dishonor by the drawee; or

2. The defendant, in acting as a representative drawer, did so as an employee who, without personal benefit, merely executed the orders of his employer or of a superior officer or employee generally authorized to direct his activities.

APPENDIX D

State Laws
Affecting
Collection
Procedures

1. MASSACHUSETTS DEBT COLLECTION PROCEDURES

940 CMR. OFFICE OF THE ATTORNEY GENERAL

940 CMR. 7.00: DEBT COLLECTION REGULATIONS

§7.01. Purpose of Regulations

The purpose of these regulations is to establish standards, by defining unfair or deceptive acts or practices, for the collection of debts from persons within the Commonwealth of Massachusetts.

§7.02. Scope

These regulations apply only to the collection of debts, as defined herein, and no conduct which is not the collection of debts or any part thereof is affected.

§7.03. Definitions

(1) "Communication" or "communicating" means conveying information directly or indirectly to any person orally through any medium excluding nonidentifying communications.

(2) "Creditor" means any person and his agents, servants, employees, or attorneys engaged in collecting a debt owed or alleged to be owed to him by a debtor provided, however, that a person shall not be deemed to be engaged in collecting a debt, for the purpose of these regulations, if his activities are solely for the purpose of repossessing any collateral or property of the creditor securing such a debt.

(3) "Debt" means money or its equivalent which is, or is alleged to be, more than 30 days past due and owing, unless a different period is agreed to by the debtor, under a single account as a result of a purchase, lease, or loan of goods, services, or real or personal property, for personal, family, or household purposes or as a result of a loan of money which is obtained for personal, family, or household purposes; provided, however, that money which is, or is alleged to be, owing as a result of a loan secured by a first mortgage on real property, or in an amount in excess of $25,000, shall not be included within this definition of "debt."

(4) "Debtor" means a natural person, or his guardian, administrator, or executor, present or residing in Massachusetts who is allegedly personally liable for a debt.

(5) "Nonidentifying communication" means any communication with any person other than the debtor in which the creditor does not convey any information except the name of the creditor and in which the creditor makes no inquiry other than to determine a convenient time and place to contact the debtor.

(6) "Person" means any natural person, corporation, trust, partnership, incorporated or unincorporated association, and any other legal entity; provided, however, that if a creditor comprises or employs more than one natural person, all such individuals shall be deemed to be one and the same "person" with respect to any debt owed or alleged to be owed to such a creditor.

§7.04. Contact with Debtors

(1) It shall constitute an unfair or deceptive act or practice for a creditor to contact a debtor in any of the following ways:

(a) Threatening to sell or assign to another the obligation of a debtor with an attending representation or implication that the result of such sale or assignment would be that a debtor would lose any defense to the claim or would be subjected to harsh, vindictive, or abusive collection attempts;

(b) Threatening that nonpayment of a debt will result in:

1. Arrest of any debtor; or

2. Garnishment of any wages of any debtor or the taking of other action requiring judicial order without informing the debtor that there must be in effect a judicial order permitting such garnishment or such other action before it can be taken;

(c) Using profane or obscene language;

(d) Communicating by telephone without disclosure of the name of the business or company of the creditor and without disclosure of the personal name of the individual making such communication provided, however, that any such individual utilizing a personal name other than his own shall use only one such personal name at all times and provided that a mechanism is established by such creditor to identify the person using such personal name;

(e) Causing expense to any debtor in the form of long distance telephone calls, or other similar charges;

(f) Engaging any debtor in communication via telephone, initiated by the creditor, in excess of two calls in each seven-day period at a debtor's residence and two calls in each 30-day period other than at a debtor's residence, for each debt, provided that for purposes of this division, a creditor may treat any billing address of the debtor as his place of residence;

(g) Placing telephone calls at times known to be times other than the normal waking hours of a debtor called, or if normal waking hours are not known, at any time other than between 8:00 A.M. and 9:00 P.M.;

(h) Placing any telephone calls to the debtor's place of employment if the debtor has made a written or oral request that such telephone calls not be made at the place of employment, provided, that any oral request shall be valid for only 10 days unless the debtor provides written confirmation postmarked or delivered within 7 days of such request. A debtor may at any time terminate such a request by written communication to the creditor;

(i) Failing to send the debtor the following notice in writing within 30 days after the first communication to a debtor at his place of employment regarding any debt, provided that a copy of the notice shall be sent every six months thereafter so long as collection activity by the creditor on the debt continues and the debtor has not made a written request as described in the previous division, but only if such first communication is made after the effective date of these regulations:

NOTICE OF IMPORTANT RIGHTS

YOU HAVE THE RIGHT TO MAKE A WRITTEN OR ORAL REQUEST THAT TELEPHONE CALLS REGARDING YOUR DEBT NOT BE MADE TO YOU AT YOUR PLACE OF

EMPLOYMENT. ANY SUCH ORAL REQUEST WILL BE VALID FOR ONLY TEN (10) DAYS UNLESS YOU PROVIDE WRITTEN CONFIRMATION OF THE REQUEST POSTMARKED OR DE-LIVERED WITHIN SEVEN (7) DAYS OF SUCH REQUEST. YOU MAY TERMINATE THIS REQUEST BY WRITING TO THE CREDITOR.

(j) Visiting the household of a debtor at times other than the normal waking hours of such debtor, or if normal waking hours are not known, at any time other than between 8:00 A.M. and 9:00 P.M., provided however that in no event shall such visits, initiated by the creditor, exceed one in any 30-day period for each debt, excluding visits where no person is contacted in the household, unless a debtor consents in writing to more frequent visits, provided, further, that at all times the creditor must remain outside the household unless expressly invited inside by such debtor; and provided further, that visits to the household of a debtor which are solely for the purpose of repossessing any collateral or property of the creditor (including but not limited to credit cards, drafts, notes or the like), are not limited under this division.

(k) Visiting the place of employment of a debtor, unless re-quested by the debtor, excluding visits which are solely for the purpose of repossessing any collateral or property of the creditor, or confrontations with a debtor regarding the collection of a debt initiated by a creditor in a public place excluding courthouses, the creditor's place of business, other places agreed to by a debtor, offices of an attorney for the creditor, or places where the conversation between the creditor and a debtor cannot be reasonably overheard by any other person not authorized by the debtor.

(1) Stating that the creditor will take any action, including legal action, which in fact is not taken or attempted on such debtor's account, unless an additional payment or a new agreement to pay has occurred within the stated time period. For purposes of this division the time period in connection with such statement shall be presumed to expire 14 days from the date the statement is made, unless otherwise indicated by the creditor;

(2) Subject to applicable law, after notification from an attorney for a debtor that all contacts relative to the particular debt in question should be addressed to the attorney, a creditor may contact the debtor only to perfect or preserve rights against the debtor or collateral securing the debt;

(3) Divisions (j) and (1) of Subsection (1) and Subsection (2) of this section shall not apply to telephone, gas and electric utility companies regulated by Massachusetts General Laws, Chapter 164 and the Depart-ment of Public Utilities.

§7.05. Contact with Persons Residing in the Household of a Debtor

(1) It shall not constitute an unfair or deceptive act or practice for a creditor to assume that all contacts directed to the debtor's household are received either by the debtor or persons residing in the household of the debtor unless the creditor knows or should know information to the contrary.

(2) It shall constitute an unfair or deceptive act or practice for a creditor to imply the fact of a debt, orally or in writing, to persons who reside in the household of a debtor other than the debtor.

(3) It shall constitute an unfair or deceptive act or practice for a creditor or debt collector to contact or threaten to contact persons who reside in the household of a debtor, other than the debtor in any of the following ways:

(a) Using profane or obscene language;

(b) Placing telephone calls, disclosing the name of the business or company of the creditor, unless the recipient expressly requests disclosure of the business or company name;

(c) Causing expense to any person in the form of long distance telephone calls, or other similar charges;

(d) Engaging any person in nonidentifying communication via telephone with such frequency as to be unreasonable or to constitute a harassment to such person under the circumstances, and engaging any person in communications via telephone, initiated by the creditor, in excess of two calls in each seven-day period at a debtor's residence and two calls in each 30-day period other than at a debtor's residence, for each debt;

(e) Placing telephone calls at times known to be times other than the normal waking hours of the person called, or if normal waking hours are not known, at any time other than between 8:00 A.M. and 9:00 P.M.;

(f) Visits to the place of employment of any person, unless requested by such person, or confrontations regarding the collection of a debt in a public place, excluding courthouses, the creditor's place of business, places agreed to by the person, offices of the person's attorney or of the attorney for the creditor or debtor, or places where the conversation between the creditor and such person cannot reasonably by overheard by anyone not authorized by such person;

(g) Using language on printed or written materials, except materials enclosed in sealed envelopes, indicating or implying that the communication relates to the collection of a debt, which in the normal course of business may be received or examined by any such person residing in the household of a debtor.

(4) Nothing in this section shall prohibit any contact required by law to be made by a creditor or attorney acting on his behalf engaged in collection activities, including notices required prior or subsequent to repossession.

§7.06. Contact with Persons Other Than Debtors or Persons Residing in the Household of a Debtor

(1) It shall constitute an unfair or deceptive act or practice for a creditor to contact or threaten to contact persons, other than the debtor and those residing in the household of the debtor, in any of the following ways:

(a) Implying the fact of the debt to any such person;

(b) Using language on envelopes indicating or implying that the contact relates to the collection of a debt;

(c) Using language on any other printed or written materials, except materials enclosed in sealed envelopes, indicating or implying that the contact relates to the collection of a debt, which in the normal course of business, may be received or examined by persons other than the debtor.

(2) The following contacts shall not be deemed unlawful:

(a) Any contact with any such persons which results solely from efforts to contact the debtor at the debtor's place of residence or at places other than a debtor's residence pursuant to Division 7.04(1)(f), provided the creditor limits the contact to disclosing only his personal name unless the recipient expressly requests the disclosure of the business or company name, provided, however, that any such individual using a personal name other than his own shall use only one such name at all times and provided that a mechanism is established by such creditor to identify the person using such personal name; and provided further, that with respect to contacts made at the debtor's place of employment, the debtor has not made a request pursuant to Division 7.04(1)(h) that such contact not be made.

(b) Any contact with any such person made for the purpose of and limited to determining the current location of the debtor, provided the creditor, after making reasonable attempts to locate the debtor, does not have correct information as to the debtor's current residence or location and provided further, that the creditor reasonably believes that the earlier response of such person, if any, is erroneous or incomplete and that such person now has correct or complete locational information, and in no event shall such contacts exceed three per person contacted in any 12-month period for each debt. The creditor in making said contacts may reveal only his personal name unless the recipient expressly requests the disclosure of the business or company name, provided, however, that any such individual using a personal name other than his own shall use only one such personal name at all times and provided that a mechanism is established by such creditor to identify the person using such personal name. Any contacts at the debtor's place of employment, made pursuant to this division, shall be lawful, notwithstanding a request made by the debtor, pursuant to Division 7.04(1)(h), that such contacts not be made.

(c) Any contact with respect to such debt to any attorney or other person employing or employed by the creditor, or to any attorney employed by the debtor; to a consumer reporting agency; or, where there are actual negotiations or arrangements for assigning or purchasing or settling of accounts, to potential assignees or purchasers or the like; or to persons who have any interest in property securing all or part of the debt; or to any *bona fide* credit counseling agency not connected to the creditor and designated in writing by the debtor;

(d) Any communication of the fact of such debt by an attorney involved in litigation in connection with such debt, or after a judgment on the debt has been entered by a court of competent jurisdiction;

(e) Any contact required by law to be made by a creditor engaged in collection activities, including notices required prior to or subsequent to repossession.

§7.07. General Deceptive Acts or Practices

It shall constitute a deceptive act or practice to engage in any of the following practices:

(1) Any false representation that the creditor has information in his possession or something of value for the debtor;

(2) Any knowingly false or misleading representation in any communication as to the character, extent or amount of the debt, or as to its status in any legal proceeding, provided, however, that an incorrect or estimated bill submitted by a gas or electric utility company regulated by Chapter 164 of the Massachusetts General Laws, and the Department of Public Utilities shall not be prohibited by this Section;

(3) Any false or misleading representation that a creditor is vouched for, bonded by, affiliated with, or is an instrumentality, agency, or official of the state, federal, or local government;

(4) Any false or misleading representation that a creditor is an attorney or any other officer of the court;

(5) The use, distribution, or sale of any written communication which simulates, or which is falsely represented to be, or which otherwise would reasonably create a false impression that it was, a document authorized, issued or approved by a court, a government official, or other governmental authority;

(6) Any representation that an existing obligation of the debtor may be increased by the addition of attorney's fees, investigation fees, service fees, or any other fees or charges, if in fact such fees or charges may not legally be added to the existing obligation;

(7) Any solicitation or obtaining of any written statement or acknowledgment in any form containing an affirmation of any obligation by a debtor who has been adjudicated bankrupt, without clearly and conspicuously disclosing the nature and consequences of such affirmation.

§7.08. Inspection

It shall constitute an unfair or deceptive act or practice for a creditor to fail to allow a debtor or an attorney for a debtor to inspect and copy the following materials regarding a debt during normal business hours of the creditor and upon notice given to such creditor not less than five business days preceding the scheduled inspection:

(1) All papers or copies of papers in the possession of the creditor which bear the signature of the debtor and which concern the debt being collected;

(2) A ledger, account card, or similar record in the possession of a creditor which reflects the date and amount of payments, credits, and charges concerning the debt.

§7.09. Postdated Checks

It shall be an unfair or deceptive act or practice for a creditor to request or demand from a debtor a postdated check, draft, order for withdrawal, or other similar instrument in payment for the debt or any portion thereof, or for a creditor to negotiate such instrument before the due date of the instrument.

§7.10. Relation to Other Laws

This chapter does not exempt any person from complying with existing laws or canons of ethics with respect to debt collection practices. To the extent that any provision of this chapter is specifically inconsistent with the Canons of Ethics and Disciplinary Rules Regulating the Practice of Law, as currently appearing in Supreme Judicial Court Rule 3:22 and then only to the extent of inconsistency, this chapter is not applicable.

§7.11. Preemption by Federal Laws

In the event any conflict exists between the provisions of these regulations and the provisions of Federal statutes or regulations relating to the collection of debts, such Federal law shall control but only to the extent that such Federal law mandates actions or procedures prohibited by these regulations

2. NEW YORK CITY CONSUMER PROTECTION REGULATIONS

DEPARTMENT OF CONSUMER AFFAIRS
CONSUMER PROTECTION LAW REGULATION 10

Promulgation of New Rules and Regulations Regarding Debt Collection

IN COMPLIANCE WITH SECTION 1105 OF THE NEW YORK CITY CHARTER and exercising the authority vested in me as Commissioner of Consumer Affairs by Section 2203(e) of said Charter and Section 2203d-3.0 of Title A of Chapter 64 of the Administrative Code of The City of New York, a regulation regarding unconscionable and deceptive trade practices in the collection of debts is hereby promulgated and shall become effective on February 27, 1979.

10.1 Definitions.

As used in this Regulation:

A. The term 'debt collector' means an individual who, as part of his or her job, regularly collects or seeks to collect a debt owed or due or alleged to be owed or due. The term does not include:

(1) any officer or employee of the United States, any State or any political subdivision of any State to the extent that collecting or attempting to collect any debt owed is in the performance of his or her official duties;

(2) any person while engaged in performing an action required by law or regulation, or required by law or regulation in order to institute or pursue a legal remedy;

(3) any individual employed by a nonprofit organization which, at the request of consumers, performs bona fide consumer credit counseling and assists consumers in the liquidation of their debts by receiving payments from such consumers and distributing such amounts to creditors; or

(4) any individual employed by a utility regulated under the provisions of the Public Service Law, to the extent that New York Public Service Law or any regulation promulgated thereunder is inconsistent with this Regulation.

Where a provision of this Regulation limits the number of times an action may be taken by the debt collector, or establishes as a prerequisite to taking an action that the debt collector has received or done something, or prohibits an action if the debt collector has knowledge of or reason to know something, the term 'debt collector' includes any debt collector employed by the same employer.

B. The term 'creditor' means any person, firm, corporation, or organization to whom a debt is owed or due or alleged to be owed or due or any assignee for value of said person, firm, corporation or organization.

C. The term 'communication' means the conveying of information regarding a debt directly or indirectly to any person through any medium.

D. The term 'consumer' means any natural person obligated or allegedly obligated to pay any debt.

E. The term 'debt' means any obligation or alleged obligation of a consumer to pay money arising out of a transaction in which the money, property, insurance, or services which are the subject of the transaction are primarily for personal, family, or household purposes, whether or not such obligation has been reduced to judgment.

F. The term 'debt collection procedures' means any attempt by a debt collector to collect a debt after:

(1) with respect to accounts for which creditors are required to send periodic statements, the creditor has ceased sending those statements, or taken or threatened to take legal action against the consumer;

(2) with respect to 30-day accounts for which periodic statements are not required, the creditor has ceased sending bills for the debt or taken or threatened to take legal action against the consumer; and

(3) with respect to all other types of credit, the creditor has accelerated the unpaid balance of the debt or demanded the full balance due.

G. The term 'location information' means a consumer's place of abode and his telephone number at such place, or his place of employment.

H. The term 'periodic statement' means the statement of account certain creditors are required by 12 CFR 226.7(b) [Regulation Z] to send at the end of each billing cycle for which there is an outstanding undisputed debit or credit balance in excess of $1 in the account or with respect to which a finance charge is imposed.

I. The term 'reasonable period of time' means in the absence of knowledge of circumstances to the contrary, ten business days.

J. The term '30-day account' means an account on which the outstanding balance at the end of a billing period is to be paid in full within a stated period of time without imposition of any finance charge.

10.2 It is an unconscionable and deceptive trade practice for a debt collector to attempt to collect a debt owed, due, or asserted to be owed or due except in accordance with the following rules:

A. *Acquisition of Location Information.*

Any debt collector communicating with any person other than the consumer for the purpose of acquiring location information about the consumer in order to collect a debt, after the institution of debt collection procedures shall:

(1) identify himself or herself, state that he or she is confirming or correcting location information about the consumer and identify his or her employer when that identification connotes debt collection only if expressly requested;

(2) not state or imply that such consumer owes any debt;

(3) not communicate more than once, unless requested to do so by such person or unless the debt collector reasonably believes that the earlier repsonse of such person is erroneous or incomplete and that such person now has correct or complete location information; for the purposes of this subsection, the debt collector need not count as a communication returned unopened mail or a message left with a party other than the person the debt collector is attempting to reach in order to acquire location information about the consumer, as long as the message is limited to a telephone number, the name of the debt collector and a request that the person sought telephone the debt collector;

(4) not use any language or symbol on any envelope or in the contents of any communication effected by the mails or telegram that indicates that the debt collector is in the debt collection business or that the communication relates to the collection of a debt; provided that a debt collector may use his or her business name or the name of a department within his or her organization as long as any name used does not connote debt collection; and

(5) if the debt collector knows the consumer is represented by an attorney with regard to the subject debt and if the debt collector has knowledge of the attorney's name and address or can readily ascertain such attorney's name and address, not communicate with any person other than that attorney for the purpose of acquiring location information about the consumer unless the attorney fails to provide the consumer's location within a reasonable period of time after a request for the consumer's location from the debt collector and;

(a) informs the debt collector that he or she is not authorized to accept process for the consumer; or

(b) fails to respond to the debt collector's inquiry about the attorney's authority to accept process within a reasonable period of time after the inquiry.

The employer of a debt collector may not be held liable in any action brought under Section 10.2A.(3) or (5) of this Regulation if the employer shows by a preponderance of the evidence that the violation was not intentional and resulted despite the maintenance or procedures reasonably adapted to avoid any such violation.

B. *Communication in Connection with Debt Collection.*

A debt collector, in connection with the collection of a debt, shall not:

(1) After institution of debt collection procedures, without the prior written consent of the consumer given directly to the debt collector after the institution of debt collection procedures, or without permission of a court of competent jurisdiction, communicate with the consumer in connection with the collection of any debt:

(a) at any unusual time or place known, or which should be known, to be inconvenient to the consumer. In the absence of knowledge of circumstances to the contrary, a debt collector shall assume that the convenient time for communicating with a consumer is after 8 o'clock antemeridian and before 9 o'clock postmeridian time at the consumer's location;

(b) if the debt collector knows the consumer is represented by an attorney with respect to such debt and if the debt collector has knowledge of the attorney's name and address or can readily ascertain such attorney's name and address, unless the attorney fails to respond within a reasonable period of time to a communication from the debt collector or unless the attorney consents to direct communication with the consumer, except any communication which is required by law or chosen from among alternatives of which one is required by law is not hereby prohibited;

(c) at the consumer's place of employment if the debt collector knows or has reason to know that the consumer's employer or supervisor prohibits the consumer from receiving such communication; or

(d) with excessive frequency. In the absence of knowledge of circumstances to the contrary, a debt collector shall assume that more than twice during a seven-calendar-day period is excessively frequent. In making its calculation, the debt collector need not include any communication between a consumer and the debt collector which is in response to an oral or written communication from the consumer, or returned unopened mail, or a message left with a party other than one who is responsible for the debt as long as the message is limited to a telephone number, the name of the debt collector and a request that one who is responsible for the debt telephone the debt collector; or any communication which is required by law or chosen from among alternatives of which one is required by law.

The employer of a debt collector may not be held liable in any action brought under Section 10.2B.(I)(b)-(d) of this Regulation if the employer shows by a preponderance of the evidence that the violation was not intentional and resulted despite maintenance of procedures reasonably adapted to avoid any such violation.

(2) In order to collect a debt, and except as provided by Section 10.2A. of this Regulation, communicate with any person other than the consumer, his or her attorney, a consumer reporting agency if otherwise permitted by law, the creditor, the attorney of the creditor, a debt collector to whom or to whose employer the debt has been assigned for collection, a creditor who assigned the debt for collection, the attorney of that debt collector, or the attorney for that debt collector's employer, without the prior written consent of the consumer given directly to the debt collector after the institution of debt collection procedures, or without the prior written consent of the consumer's attorney or without the express permission of a court of competent jurisdiction, or as reasonably necessary to effectuate a postjudgment judicial remedy.

(3) Communicate with any person other than the consumer's attorney, a consumer reporting agency if otherwise permitted by law, the creditor, the attorney of the creditor, a debt collector to whom or to whose employer the debt has been assigned for collection, a creditor who assigned the debt for collection, or the attorney of that debt collector or the attorney for that debt collector's employer in a manner which would violate any provision of this Regulation if such person were a consumer.

(4) After institution of debt collection procedures, communicate with a consumer with respect to a debt if the consumer has notified the debt collector in writing that the consumer wishes the debt collector to cease further communication with the consumer with respect to that debt, except that any communication which is required by law or chosen from among alternatives of which one is required by law is not hereby prohibited.

The debt collector shall have a reasonable period of time following receipt by the debt collector of the notification to comply with a consumer's request, except that any debt collector who knows or has reason to know of the consumer's notification and who causes further communication shall have violated this provision.

The debt collector may, however:

(a) communicate with the consumer once in writing:

(i) to advise the consumer that the debt collector's further efforts are being terminated and/or;

(ii) to notify the consumer that the debt collector or creditor may invoke specified remedies which are ordinarily invoked by such debt collector and/or;

(iii) where applicable, to notify the consumer that the debt collector or creditor intends to invoke a specific remedy if that is a remedy he is legally entitled to invoke and if he actually intends to invoke it; and

(b) respond to each subsequent oral or written communication from the consumer.

(5) For the purpose of Section 10.2B.(1)-(4) of this Regulation, the term 'consumer' includes the consumer's parent (if the consumer is a minor), guardian, executor, administrator, spouse (unless the debt collector knows or has reason to know that the consumer is legally separated from or no longer living with his or her spouse), or an individual authorized by the consumer to make purchases against the account which is the subject of the collection efforts. A request that the debt collector cease further communication, provided for under Section 10.2B.(4), if made by the consumer's spouse or an individual authorized by the consumer to make purchases against the account, only affects the debt collector's ability to communicate further with the person making the request.

C. *Harassment or Abuse.*

A debt collector, in connection with the collection of a debt, shall not engage in conduct the natural consequence of which is to harass, oppress or abuse any person in connection with a debt. Such conduct includes:

(1) the use or threat of use of violence or other criminal means to harm the physical person, reputation, or property of any person;

(2) the use of obscene or profane language or language the natural consequence of which is to abuse the hearer or reader;

(3) the advertisement for sale of any debt to coerce payment of the debt;

(4) causing a telephone to ring or engaging any person in telephone conversation repeatedly or continuously with intent to annoy, abuse, or harass any person at the called number;

(5) the publication of a list of consumers who allegedly refuse to pay debts, except to another employee of the debt collector's employer or to a consumer reporting agency or to persons meeting the requirements of 15 USC 1681a(f) or 15 USC 1681b(3); or

(6) except as provided by Section 10.2A. of this Regulation, the placement of telephone calls without meaningful disclosure of the caller's identity.

D. *False or Misleading Representations.*

A debt collector, in connection with the collection of a debt, shall not make any false, deceptive, or misleading representation. Such representations include:

(1) the false representation or implication that the debt collector is vouched for, bonded by, or affiliated with the United States or any State, including the use of any badge, uniform or facsimile thereof;

(2) the false representation or implication that any individual is an attorney or any communication is from an attorney;

(3) the representation or implication that nonpayment of any debt will result in the arrest or imprisonment of any person or the seizure, garnishment, attachment, or sale of any property or wages of any person unless such action is lawful and the debt collector or creditor intends to pursue such action;

(4) the threat to take any action that cannot legally be taken or that is not intended to be taken;

(5) the false representation or implication that a sale, referral, or other transfer of any interest in a debt shall cause the consumer to:

(a) lose any claim or defense to payment of the debt; or

(b) become subject to any practice prohibited by this Regulation;

(6) the false representation or implication made in order to disgrace the consumer that the consumer committed any crime or other conduct;

(7) the false representation or implication that accounts have been turned over to innocent purchasers for value;

(8) the false representation or implication that documents are legal process;

(9) the false representation or implication that documents are not legal process forms or do not require action by the consumer;

(10) the false representation or implication that a debt collector operates or is employed by a consumer reporting agency as defined by 15 USC 1681a(f);

(11) the use or distribution of any written communication which simulates or is falsely represented to be a document authorized, issued, or approved by any court, official, or agency of the United States or any State, or which creates a false impression as to its source, authorization, or approval;

(12) the use of any false representation or deceptive means to collect or attempt to collect any debt or to obtain information concerning a consumer;

(13) the use of any business, company, or organization name other than the true name of the debt collector's business, company, or organization, unless the general public knows the debt collector's business, company or organization by another name and to use the true name would be confusing;

(14) after institution of debt collection procedures, the false representation of the character, amount or legal status of any debt, or any services rendered or compensation which may be lawfully received by any debt collector for the collection of a debt, except that the

employer of a debt collector may not be held liable in any action brought under this provision if the employer shows by a preponderance of the evidence that the violation was not intentional and occurred despite the maintenance of procedures reasonably adapted to avoid any such violation;

(15) except as otherwise provided under Section 10.2A. of this Regulation and except for any communication which is required by law or chosen from among alternatives of which one is required by law, the failure to disclose clearly in all communications made to collect a debt or to obtain information about a consumer, that the debt collector is attempting to collect a debt and that any information obtained will be used for that purpose;

(16) the use of any name that is not the debt collector's actual name; provided that a debt collector may use a name other than his actual name if he or she uses only the name in communications with respect to a debt and if the debt collector's employer has that name on file so that the true identity of the debt collector can be ascertained; or

(17) any conduct proscribed by New York General Law Sections 601(1), (3), (5), (7), (8), or (9).

E. *Unfair Practices.*

A debt collector may not use any unfair or unconscionable means to collect or attempt to collect a debt. Such conduct includes:

(1) the collection of any amount (including any interest, fee, charge, or expense incidental to the principal obligation) unless such amount is expressly authorized by the agreement creating the debt or permitted by law;

(2) the solicitation or use by a debt collector of any postdated check or other postdated payment instrument for the purpose of threatening or instituting criminal prosecution;

(3) causing charges to be made to any person for communications by misrepresentation of the true purpose of the communication. Such charges include collect telephone calls and telegram fees;

(4) taking or threatening to take any nonjudicial action to effect dispossession or disablement of property if:

(a) there is no present right to possession of the property claimed as collateral;

(b) there is no present intention to take possession of the property; or

(c) the property is exempt by law from such dispossession or disablement;

(5) after institution of debt collection procedures, when communicating with a consumer by use of the mails or telegram, using any language or symbol other than the debt collector's address on any envelope, or using any language or symbol that indicates the debt collector is in the debt collection business or that the communication

relates to the collection of a debt on a postcard, except that a debt collector may use his or her business name or the name of a department within his or her organization as long as any name used does not connote debt collection;

(6) after institution of debt collection procedures, communicating with a consumer regarding a debt without identifying himself or herself and his or her employer or communicating in writing with a consumer regarding a debt without identifying himself or herself by name and address and in accordance with Section 10.2E.(5) of this Regulation; or

(7) after institution of debt collection procedures, if a consumer owes multiple debts of which any one or portion of one is disputed, and the consumer makes a single payment with respect to such debts:

(a) applying a payment to a disputed portion of any debt; or

(b) unless otherwise provided by law or contract, failing to apply such payments in accordance with the consumer's instructions accompanying payment. If payment is made by mail, the consumer's instructions must be written.

Any communication by a creditor made pursuant to Section 10.2E.(7)(b) of this Regulation shall not be deemed communication for the purpose of Section 10.2B.(1)(d).

The employer of a debt collector may not be held liable in any action brought under Section 10.2E.(7) if the employer shows by a preponderance of the evidence that the violation was not intentional and resulted despite maintenance of procedures reasonably adapted to avoid any such violation; or

(8) engaging in any conduct prohibited by New York General Business Law Sections 601(2) or (4).

F. *Validation of Debts.*

(1) Upon acceleration of the unpaid balance of the debt or demand for the full balance due, the following validation procedures shall be followed by debt collectors who are creditors or who are employed by creditors as deemed by 15 USC 1602(f) [Truth in Lending Act] but who are not required to comply with 15 USC 1637(a)(8) [Fair Credit Billing Act], and who do not provide consumers with an opportunity to dispute the debt which is substantially the same as that outlined in 15 USC 1637(a)(8) and regulations promulgated thereunder:

Within five days of any further attempt by the creditor itself to collect the debt, it shall send the customer a written notice containing:

(a) the amount of the debt;

(b) a statement that unless the consumer, within thirty days after receipt of the notice, disputes the validity of the debt, or any portion thereof, the debt will be assumed valid by the debt collector;

(c) a statement that, if the consumer notifies the debt collector in writing within the thirty-day period at the address designated by the debt collector in the notice, that the debt, or any portion thereof is disputed, the debt collector shall either:

(i) make appropriate corrections in the account and transmit to the consumer notification of such corrections and an explanation of any change and, if the consumer so requests, copies of documentary evidence of the consumer's indebtedness; or

(ii) send a written explanation or clarification to the consumer, after having conducted an investigation, setting forth to the extent applicable the reason why the creditor believes the account of the consumer was correctly shown in the written notice required by Section 10.2F.(1) of this Regulation and, upon the consumer's request, provide copies of documentary evidence of the consumer's indebtedness. In the case of a billing error where the consumer alleges that the creditor's billing statement reflects goods not delivered in accordance with the agreement made at the time of the transaction, a creditor may not construe such amount to be correctly shown unless it determines that such goods were actually delivered, mailed, or otherwise sent to the consumer and provides the consumer with a statement of such determination.

(d) if the debt collector is not the original creditor, a statement that, upon the consumer's written request within the thirty-day period, sent to the address designated by the debt collector in the notice, the debt collector will provide the consumer with the name and address of the original creditor:

(e) an address to which the consumer should send any writing which disputes the validity of the debt or any portion thereof or any writing requesting the name and address of the original creditor.

(2) Within five days after the initial communication with a consumer in connection with the collection of any debt, a debt collector who is not a creditor and not employed by a creditor shall, unless the following information is contained in an initial written communication, or the consumer has paid the debt, send the consumer a written notice containing:

(a) the amount of the debt;

(b) the name of the creditor to whom the debt is owed;

(c) a statement that unless the consumer, within thirty days after receipt of the notice, disputes the validity of the debt, or any portion thereof, the debt will be assumed to be valid by the debt collector;

(d) a statement that if the consumer notifies the debt collector in writing within the thirty-day period at the address designated by the debt collector in the notice that the debt, or any portion thereof, is disputed, the debt collector will obtain verification of the debt or a copy of a judgment against the consumer and a copy of such verification or judgment will be mailed to the consumer by the debt collector;

(e) a statement that, upon the consumer's written request within the thirty-day period sent to the address designated by the debt collector in the notice, the debt collector will provide the consumer with the name and address of the original creditor, if different from the current creditor; and

(f) an address to which the consumer should send any writing which disputes the validity of the debt or any portion thereof or any writing requesting the name and address of the original creditor.

(3) If, pursuant to Section 10.2F.(1) or 10.2F.(2) of this Regulation the consumer notifies the debt collector in writing within the thirty-day period that the debt, or any portion thereof, is disputed, or that the consumer requests the name and address of the original creditor, the debt collector shall not attempt to collect the amount in dispute until the debt collector obtains and mails to the consumer verification of the debt or a copy of the judgment or the name and address of the original creditor.

The debt collector shall maintain for one-year from the date the notice was mailed, records containing documentation of the date such notice was mailed, the response was received if any, and any action taken following such response.

(4) The failure of a consumer to dispute the validity of a debt under Section 10.2F. of this Regulation shall not be construed by any court as an admission of liability by the consumer.

G. *Liability.*

The employer of a debt collector is liable for the debt collector's violation of Section 10.2 of this Regulation. A debt collector who is employed by another to collect or attempt to collect debts shall not be held liable for violation of Section 10.2.

10.3 It is a deceptive and unconscionable trade practice for any person to design, compile, and furnish any form knowing that such form would be used to create the false belief in a consumer that a person other than the creditor of such consumer is participating in the collection of or in an attempt to collect a debt such consumer allegedly owes such creditor, when in fact such person is not so participating.

10.4 If any provision of this Regulation or the application of such provision to any person or circumstances shall be held unconstitutional or invalid, the constitutionality of the remainder of the Regulation and the applicability of such provision to other persons or circumstances shall not be affected thereby.

10.5 This Regulation may be cited as Consumer Protection Law Regulation 10:

EXPLANATION

New York City consumers have been subjected to abuse and harassment at the hands of creditors and other debt collectors.

The United States Congress has found that "abusive debt collection practices contribute to the number of bankruptcies, to marital instability, to the loss of jobs and to invasions of individual privacy." In enacting the Fair Debt Collection Practices Act, 15 USC 1692 *et seq.*, Congress set comprehensive and much-needed standards for collection of debts but limited the new law's application to third-party debt collectors.

In proposing this Regulation, the Commissioner finds that:

(1) third-party collectors conduct only a small percentage of the collection efforts in New York City;

(2) a considerable percentage of the unfair debt collection practices complaints received by the Department refer to actions taken by other than third-party collectors;

(3) the practices of creditors and their agents are not materially different than those of third-party collectors; and

(4) the failure to prohibit all persons from engaging in a practice found to be deceptive or unconscionable severely mitigates the effectiveness of any prohibition, and leaves consumers prey to the same practices by persons not subject to the prohibition.

This proposed Regulation prohibits creditors and those acting on their behalf from using abusive tactics in order to collect personal, family, or household debts. Examples of such debts are money owed for the purchase of a car, for medical care or on charge accounts.

Specifically, this Regulation:

- Allows a debt collector to contact persons other than a consumer-debtor or his attorney only to locate the consumer and, generally speaking, only one time. In such situations, it prevents a debt collector from revealing that the person he is looking for owes money.

- Requires the debt collector to provide the consumer notice in writing of the amount of money that is owed, to whom it is owed, and what the consumer should do if he thinks that he does not owe the money.

- Allows the consumer to inform the debt collector that it should cease its collection efforts; in that event, the creditor must institute legal action if it wishes to collect the debt.

- Prevents a debt collector from harassing or abusing consumers. For example, a debt collector may not threaten violence, use obscene or profane language, advertise a debt, or use the telephone to annoy anyone.

- Prohibits a debt collector from making any false statements when collecting a debt. For example, the debt collector cannot imply falsely that he represents any government or that he is an attorney or that a consumer committed any crime. The debt collector may not state that papers being sent are legal forms when they're not or are not legal forms when they are.

- Prohibits a debt collector from saying that any action will be taken against a consumer when that action cannot legally be taken.
- Prohibits a debt collector from being unfair in attempting to collect any debt. For example, a debt collector may not collect any amount greater than the amount of the debt, unless allowed by law, or threaten to use a postdated check to institute criminal proceedings, or make a consumer accept collect calls or pay for telegrams.

The Regulation strengthens the existing laws and regulations in the following respects: (1) it requires written notice to and written consent of the consumer where existing law would permit oral communications; (2) it prohibits treatment of the alleged debtor's spouse as the alleged debtor for purposes of communicating with the debtor if the spouse is legally separated from or not living with the alleged debtor; (3) it allows a person collecting debts to use a pseudonym only if the name is kept on file to allow identification of the collector, if necessary; and (4) it prohibits contacting an alleged debtor with excessive frequency.

In response to questions that have been raised about the scope of the Regulation, the Department makes the following observations:

(1) Creditors who meet the requirements of Section 10.2F.(1) are required to validate debts "within five days of any further attempt by the creditor itself to collect the debt" [Section 10.2F.(1)]. That language is not intended to include the act of turning an account over to another who will continue collection efforts.

(2) Our objective in adopting this Regulation is to protect New York City consumers. This objective will guide the Department's actions in enforcement of the Regulation.

The requirements of this Regulation supplement and are not inconsistent with the federal Fair Debt Collection Practices Act and New York State law.

Filed with City Clerk January 25, 1979.
Effective February 27, 1979.

BRUCE C. RATNER, Commissioner.

Reprinted from The City Record of January 29, 1979.

3. NEW YORK STATE DEBT COLLECTION PROCEDURES

§600. Definitions

As used in this article, unless the context or subject matter otherwise requires:

1. "Consumer claim" means any obligation of a natural person for the payment of money or its equivalent which is or is alleged to be in default and which arises out of a transaction wherein credit has been offered or extended to a natural person, and the money, property or service which was the subject of the transaction was primarily for personal, family, or household purposes. The term includes an obligation of a natural person who is a co-maker, endorser, guarantor or surety, as well as the natural person to whom such credit was originally extended.

2. "Debtor" means any natural person who owes or who is asserted to owe a consumer claim.

3. "Principal creditor" means any person, firm, corporation or organization to whom a consumer claim is owed, due, or asserted to be due or owed, or any assignee for value of said person, firm, corporation, or organization.

§601. Prohibited Practices

No principal creditor, as defined by this article, or his agent shall:

1. Simulate in any manner a law enforcement officer, or a representative of any governmental agency of the state of New York or any of its political subdivisions; or

2. Knowingly collect, attempt to collect, or assert a right to any collection fee, attorney's fee, court cost, or expense unless such changes are justly due and legally chargeable against the debtor; or

3. Disclose or threaten to disclose information affecting the debtor's reputation for credit worthiness with knowledge or reason to know that the information is false; or

420

4. Communicate or threaten to communicate the nature of a consumer claim to the debtor's employer prior to obtaining final judgment against the debtor. The provisions of this subdivision shall not prohibit a principal creditor from communicating with the debtor's employer to execute a wage assignment agreement if the debtor has consented to such an agreement; or

5. Disclose or threaten to disclose information concerning the existence of a debt known to be disputed by the debtor without disclosing that fact; or

6. Communicate with the debtor or any member of his family or household with such frequency or at such unusual hours or in such a manner as can reasonably be expected to abuse or harass the debtor; or

7. Threaten any action which the principal creditor in the usual course of his business does not in fact take; or

8. Claim, or attempt or threaten to enforce a right with knowledge or reason to know that the right does not exist; or

9. Use a communication which simulates in any manner legal or judicial process or which gives the appearance of being authorized, issued, or approved by a government, governmental agency, or attorney at law when it is not.

§602. Violations and Penalties

1. Except as otherwise provided by law, any person who shall violate the terms of this article shall be guilty of a misdemeanor, and each such violation shall be deemed a separate offense.

2. The attorney general or the district attorney of any county may bring an action in the name of the people of the state to restrain or prevent any violation of this article or any continuance of any such violation.

§603. Severability

If any provision of this article or the application thereof to any person or circumstances is held invalid, the invalidity thereof shall not affect other provisions or applications of this article which can be given effect without the invalid provision or application, and to this and the provisions of this article are severable.

4. COLLECTION AGENCY ACT OF ILLINOIS

CHAPTER 111—2009 PROFESSIONS AND OCCUPATIONS

An Act to register and regulate collection agencies, to provide penalties for violations, and to amend the "Criminal Code of 1961," as amended. P.A. 78–1248, approved Sept. 8, 1974, eff. Oct. 1, 1974.

2001 Short Title

1. This Act shall be known and may be cited as the Collection Agency Act.

2002. Definitions

2. Unless the context clearly requires otherwise, the following terms have the meanings ascribed to them in Sections 2.01 through 2.02.

2003. Department

2.01 "Department" means the Department of Registration and Education, and "Director" means the Director of that Department.

2004. Collection Agency or Agency

2.02 "Collection agency" or "agency" means any person, association, partnership, or corporation who, for compensation, either contingent or otherwise, or for other valuable consideration, offers services to collect an alleged debt.

2005. Application of Act

2.03 This Act does not apply to persons whose collection activities are confined to and are directly related to the operation of a business other than that of a collection agency, and specifically does not include the following:

1. Banks, including trust departments thereof, fiduciaries, and financing and lending institutions (except those who own or operate collection agencies);

2. Abstract companies doing an escrow business;

3. Real estate brokers when acting in the pursuit of their profession;

4. Public officers and judicial officers acting under order of a court;

5. Licensed attorneys at law;

6. Insurance companies;

7. Credit unions;

8. Loan and finance companies; and

9. Retail stores collecting their own accounts.

2006. Acts Constituting a Collection Agency

3. A person, association, partnership, or corporation acts as a collection agency when he or it:

(a) Engages in the business of collection for others of any account, bill, or other indebtedness;

(b) Receives, by assignment or otherwise, accounts, bills, or other indebtedness from any person owning or controlling 20% or more of the business receiving the assignment, with the purpose of collecting monies due on such account, bill, or other indebtedness;

(c) Sells or attempts to sell, or gives away or attempts to give away to any other person, other than one registered under this Act, any system of collection, letters, demand forms, or other printed matter where the name of any person, other than that of the creditor, appears in such a manner as to indicate, directly or indirectly, that a request or demand is being made by any person other than the creditor for the payment of the sum or sums due or asserted to be due;

(d) Buys accounts, bills, or other indebtedness with recourse and engages in collecting the same; or

(e) Uses a fictitious name in collecting its own accounts, bills, or debts with the intention of conveying to the debtor that a third party has been employed to make such collection.

2007. Registration

4. No collection agency shall operate in this state, directly or indirectly engage in the business of collecting, solicit claims for others, exercise the right to collect, or receive payment for another of any account, bill, or other indebtedness, without registering under this Act.

2008. Application for Registration

5. Application for registration shall be made to the Director on forms provided by the Department, shall be accompanied by the required fee, and shall state:

(1) The applicant's name and address;

(2) The names and addresses of the officers of the collection agency and, if the collection agency is a corporation, the names and addresses of all persons owning 10 percent or more of the stock of such corporation; and

(3) Such other information as the Department may deem necessary.

2009. Certificate of Registration—Applications for Renewal

6. (a) If the Director determines that the applicant meets the qualifications for registration required by this Act, he shall issue a certificate of registration forthwith. Each application for a certificate shall be acted upon within 45 days of receipt of the application by the Department. If the application is deficient in form, the Director shall reject it and notify the applicant of the nature of the deficiency. Such rejection shall be without prejudice to the filing of a new application. If the Director finds that the applicant is not qualified under this Act, he shall reject the application and give the applicant written notice of such rejection and the reasons therefore.

(b) The expiration date and renewal period for each certificate of registration issued under this Act shall be set by rule. The holder of a certificate of registration may renew such certificate during the month preceding the expiration date thereof by paying the required fee.

(c) Upon application, accompanied by the initial fee and compliance with the financial bonding requirements herein set forth, the Director shall issue an original certificate to each entity required to have a certificate if the application is received by the Department within 60 days of the effective date of this Act. Any collection agency to whom an original license is issued under this subsection (c) must meet the requirements of Section 7 of this Act to be entitled to a renewal license.

2010. Qualifications of Agency's Officers to Obtain Certificate or Renewal Certificate

7. In order to be qualified to obtain a certificate or a renewal certificate under this Act, a collection agency's officers shall:

(a) be citizens of the United States, of good moral character, and of the age of 21 years or more;

(b) have had at least one year experience working in the credit field or a related area, or be qualified for an original license under Section 6(c) of this Act;

(c) not have been convicted of a crime involving moral turpitude;

(d) have an acceptable credit rating, have no unsatisfied judgments, and never have been adjudicated a bankrupt; and not have been officers of a former registrant under this Act whose certificates were suspended or revoked without subsequent reinstatement.

2011. Bonds

8. Before issuing a certificate or renewing one, the Director shall require each collection agency to file and maintain in force a surety bond, issued by an insurance company authorized to transact fidelity and surety business in the State of Illinois. The bond shall be for the benefit of creditors who obtain a judgment from a court of competent jurisdiction based on the failure of the agency to remit money collected on account and owed to the creditor. No action on the bond shall be commenced more than one year after the termination date of the bond. The bond shall be in the form prescribed by the Director in the sum of $25,000. The bond shall be continuous in form and run concurrently with the original and each renewal license period unless terminated by the insurance company. An insurance company may terminate a bond and avoid further liability by filing a 60-day notice of termination with the Department and at the same time sending the same notice to the agency. A certificate of registration shall be cancelled on the termination date of the agency's bond unless a new bond is filed with the Department to become effective at the termination date of the prior bond. If a certificate of registration has been cancelled under this Section, the agency must file a new application and will be considered a new applicant if it obtains a new bond. Amended by P.A. 82–148, Section 1.

2011a. Fees

8a. The following fees shall be paid to the Department for the licensing and registration functions performed by the Department under this Act:

(1) The fee to be paid by an applicant for a certificate of registration as a collection agency is $50.

(2) The fee to be paid upon the renewal of a certificate of registration as a collection agency is $40.

(3) The fee to be paid for the issuance of a duplicate certificate of registration, for the issuance of a replacement certificate for a certificate which has been lost or destroyed, or for the issuance of a certificate with a change of name or address other than during the renewal period is $10.

(4) The fee to be paid for a certification of a registrant's record for any purpose is $10.

(5) The fee to be paid by a registrant for a wall certificate showing his registration shall be the actual cost of producing such certificate.

(6) The fee to be paid for a roster of persons registered as collection agencies in this State shall be the actual cost of producing such a roster.

(7) The fee to be paid to the Department for a printed copy of this Act and of the rules and regulations promulgated for the administration of this Act is $1.

2012. Unlawful Practices

9. No debt collector, while collecting or attempting to collect a debt, shall engage in any of the Acts specified in Section 9.01 through 9.21, each of which shall be an unlawful practice.

2013. Threat of Physical Violence

9.01 To use or threaten the use of force or violence to cause physical harm to a debtor, his family, or his property.

2014. Threat of Arrest or Criminal Prosecution

9.02 To threaten arrest or criminal prosecution where no basis for a criminal complaint lawfully exists.

2015. Threat of Seizure or Sale of Debtor's Property

9.03 To threaten the seizure, attachment, or sale of a debtor's property where such action can only be taken pursuant to court order without disclosing that prior court proceedings are required.

2016. Threat to Disclose False Information to Affect Credit Worthiness

9.04 To disclose or threaten to disclose information adversely affecting a debtor's reputation for credit worthiness with knowledge the information is false.

2017. Threat of Communication with Debtor's Employer

9.05 To initiate or threaten to initiate communication with a debtor's employer unless there has been a default of the payment of the obligation for at least 30 days and at least five days' prior written notice, to the last known address of the debtor, of the intention to communicate with the employer has been given to the employee and except as expressly permitted by law or court order.

2018. Harassment of Debtor or Family Members

9.06 To communicate with the debtor or any member of his family at such a time of day or night and with such frequency as may be determined by the Director to constitute harassment of the debtor or any member of his family.

2019. Profane, Obscene, or Abusive Language in Communications

9.07 To use profane, obscene or abusive language in communicating with a debtor or his family.

2020. Disclosure of Debtor's Indebtedness to Persons Without Legitimate Business Need

9.08 To disclose or threaten to disclose information relating to a debtor's indebtedness to any other person except where such other person has a legitimate business need for the information, or except where such disclosure is regulated by law.

2021. Disclosure of Existence of Disputed Debt Without Notice of Dispute

9.09 To disclose or threaten to disclose information concerning the existence of a debt which the debt collector knows to be reasonably disputed by the debtor without disclosing the fact that the debtor disputes the debt.

2022. Conduct Causing Mental or Physical Illness

9.10 To engage in any conduct which the Director finds was intended to cause and did cause mental or physical illness to the debtor or his family.

2023. Attempt or Threat to Enforce Nonexistent Right or Remedy

9.11 To attempt to or threaten to enforce a right or remedy with knowledge or reason to know that the right or remedy does not exist.

2024. Failure to Disclose Business Name

9.12 To fail to disclose to the debtor or his family the corporate, partnership, or proprietary name or other trade or business name under which the debt collector is engaging in debt collections and which he is legally authorized to use.

2025. Communication Simulating Legal Process or Governmental Appearance

9.13 To use any form of communication which simulates legal or judicial process or which gives the appearance of being authorized, issued, or approved by a governmental agency or official or by an attorney at law when it is not.

2026. Unauthorized Use of Badge, Uniform, or Other Indicia of Governmental Agency

9.14 To use any badge, uniform, or other indicia of any governmental agency or official except as authorized by law.

2027. Conducting Business As Being Bonded or Affiliated with Government or Court

9.15 To conduct business under any name or in any manner which suggests or implies that a debt collector is bonded if it is not, or is a branch of or is affiliated with any governmental agency or court if it is not.

2028. Failure to Disclose to Whom Claim Is Owed Upon Demand for Payment

9.16 To fail to disclose at the time of making any demand for payment, the name of the person to whom the claim is owed, and, at the request of the debtor, the address where payment is to be made and the address of the person to whom the claim is owed.

2029. Misrepresentation of Amount

9.17 To misrepresent the amount of the claim or debt alleged to be owed.

2030. Representation of Increase in Debt by Addition of Other Fees or Charges That Are Illegal

9.18 To represent that an existing debt may be increased by the addition of attorney's fees, investigation fees, or any other fees or charges when such fees or charges may not legally be added to the existing debt.

2031. Representation of Collector As Attorney at Law

9.19 To represent that the debt collector is an attorney at law if he is not.

2032. Collection of Unauthorized Interest or Other Charges

9.20 To collect or attempt to collect any interest or other charge or fee in excess of the actual debt or claim unless such interest or other charge or fee is expressly authorized by the agreement creating the debt or claim or unless in a commercial transaction such interest or other charge or fee is expressly authorized in a subsequent agreement or unless expressly authorized by law.

2033. Communicating with Debtor Represented by Attorney

9.21 To communicate or threaten to communicate with a debtor when the debtor is represented by an attorney concerning the claim, where the debt collector has been informed in writing by the attorney, unless authorized by the attorney.

2034. Administrative Procedure Act—Application

9.22 The Illinois Administrative Procedure Act is hereby expressly adopted and incorporated herein as if all of the provisions of such Act were included in this Act, except that the provision of paragraph (c) of Section 16 of The Illinois Administrative Procedure Act, which provides that at hearings the licensee has the right to show compliance with all lawful requirements for retention, or continuation, or renewal of the license, is specifically excluded, and for the purposes of this Act, the notice required under Section 10 of The Administrative Procedure Act is deemed sufficient when mailed to the last known address of a party.

2035. Complaint—Investigation—Hearing

10. Upon receipt of a complaint, the Director may order an investigation to determine the validity of the complaint. If the Director finds that an investigation is necessary, he shall order a hearing to be held, and give notice to the certificate holder not later than 30 days prior to the scheduled date of the hearing, together with a list of the charges.

2036. Public Hearings

11. Public hearings of violations of this Act shall be conducted by the Director or by a qualified hearing officer appointed by him. The hearing officer shall cause a record of the hearing to be preserved. The Director or hearing officer may administer oaths, may issue subpoenas, and shall issue a reasonable number of subpoenas on behalf of the registrant. The registrant has a right to be present at the hearing, to be represented by an attorney, to call witnesses, and to cross-examine witnesses for the Department, and to appeal any adverse finding under provisions of the "Administrative Review Act," as amended.

2037. Revocation or Suspension of Certificates

12. The Director may, if a registrant:
    (a) Fails to produce books and records requested by the Director or a person whom he designates;
    (b) Acts in any manner proscribed in Sections 9 and 9.01 through 9.21 of this Act, or violates any other provision of this Act or regulations promulgated hereunder;
    (c) Fails to appear at a hearing when directed by the Director or a hearing officer appointed by him; or
    (d) Is the subject of a complaint or other allegation which is proved at a hearing, revoke or suspend for a period which he shall find proper, any certificate issued under this Act.

2038. Rules and Regulations

13. The Director shall make and file in accordance with the statutes pertaining to rules and regulations of State agencies, all reasonable procedural rules and regulations as shall be necessary for the administration of this Act. The Director is authorized and empowered to make and enforce such reasonable procedural rules and regulations, directions, decisions, and findings as may be necessary for the enforcement and execution of this Act.

2039. Violations—Penalties

14. Engaging in the collection of debts without first having obtained a certificate pursuant to this Act, or carrying on such business after expiration of the certificate or after receipt of a notice of revocation or suspension of the certificate is a Class A misdemeanor. The penalties provided by this Act shall not be exclusive, but shall be in addition to all other penalties or remedies provided by law.

2040. Partial Invalidity

15. If any clause, sentence, Section, provision, or part of this Act shall be adjudged to be unconstitutional or invalid for any reason, such judgment shall not impair, affect, or invalidate the remainder of this Act, which shall be in full force and effect thereafter.

5. UNFAIR, DECEPTIVE, OR UNREASONABLE COLLECTION PRACTICES ACT OF NEW HAMPSHIRE Chapter 358-C

358-C: 1. Definitions in This Chapter

I. "Consumer" means a natural person who seeks or acquires, or is offered property, services, or credit for personal, family, or household purposes.

II. "Consumer credit transaction" means a transaction between a creditor and a consumer in which real or personal property, services, money, or a form of money is acquired on credit and the consumer's obligation is payable in four or more installments or for which credit a finance charge is or may be imposed. The term includes consumer credit sales, consumer loans, consumer leases of personal property and transactions pursuant to a seller or lender credit card, but shall not include leases of real property.

III. "Consumer transaction" means a transaction between a consumer and a person who sells, leases, or provides property, services, or credit to consumers. The term shall not include leases of real property.

IV. "Creditor" means a person who in the ordinary course of business engages in consumer credit transactions with consumers.

V. "Credit" means the right granted by a person to a consumer to defer payment of a debt, to incur debt and defer its payment, or purchase property or services and defer payment therefore.

VI. "Debt" means any obligation or alleged obligation arising out of a consumer transaction.

VII. "Debtor" means a person who owes or allegedly owes an obligation arising out of a consumer transaction.

VIII. "Debt collector" means:

(a) any person who by any direct or indirect action, conduct, or practice enforces or attempts to enforce an obligation that is owed or due, or alleged to be owed or due, by a consumer as a result of a consumer credit transaction; or

(b)   any person, who, for any fee, commission, or charge other than wages or salary, engages in any direct or indirect action, conduct or practice to enforce or attempt to enforce an obligation that is owed or due, or alleged to be owed or due, by a consumer as a result of a consumer transaction; or

(c)   any person who, pursuant to an assignment, sale, or transfer of a claim against a consumer, engages in any direct or indirect action, conduct, or practice to enforce an obligation that is owed or due, or alleged to be owed or due, by a consumer as a result of a consumer transaction.

IX.   "Finance charge" means a charge such as interest, fees, service charges, discounts, and other charges associated with the extension of credit.

X.   "Person" means an individual, corporation, trust, partnership, incorporated or unincorporated association, or any other legal entity.

358-C:2. General Prohibition. No debt collector shall collect or attempt to collect a debt in an unfair, deceptive, or unreasonable manner as defined in this chapter.

358-C:3. Prohibited Acts. For the purposes of this chapter, any debt collection or attempt to collect a debt shall be deemed unfair, deceptive or unreasonable if the debt collector:

I.   Communicates or attempts to communicate with the debtor, orally or in writing:

(a)   by causing a telephone to ring or engaging any person in telephone conversation repeatedly or continuously or at unusual times or at times known to be inconvenient with the intent to abuse, oppress, or harass any person at the called number; or

(b)   by use of profane, obscene, or vulgar language that is intended to abuse the hearer or reader; or

(c)   at the debtor's place of employment if said place is other than the debtor's residence, provided that:

(1)   a debt collector may send a single letter to the debtor at his place of employment if he has otherwise been unable to locate the debtor; and

(2)   a debt collector may phone the debtor at his place of employment if he is unable to contact the debtor at his residence, provided that:

A.   the debtor does not inform the debt collector that he does not wish the debt collector to communicate or attempt to communicate with him at his place of employment; and

B.   the debt collector shall not inform the employer of the nature of the call unless asked by the employer; and

C.   in no event shall the debt collector make more than one phone call per month to the debtor at his place of employment unless the debtor affirmatively indicates in writing that he desires the debt collector to call him at his place of employment. (For the purposes of this subparagraph, any language in any instrument creating the debt which purports to authorize phone calls at the debtor's place of employment shall not be considered an affirmative indication that the debtor desires the debt collector to call him at his place of employment.); or

(d) using any written communication which fails to clearly identify the name of the debt collector, the name of the person (as defined in RSA 358-C: 1,X) for whom the debt collector is attempting to collect the debt, and the debt collector's business address (the foregoing shall not require the name or address of the debt collector or the person for whom the debt collector is attempting to collect the debt to be printed on any envelope containing a communication); or

(e) by placement of phone calls without disclosure of the name of the individual making the call and the name of the person (as defined in RSA 358-C: 1,X) for whom the debt collector is attempting to collect the debt, or by using a fictitious name while engaging in the collection of debts; or

(f) by causing any expense to the debtor in the form of long distance telephone calls, telegram fees or other charges incurred by a medium of communication, by concealment of the true purpose of the communication; or

II. Uses or threatens the use of force or violence; or

III. Threatens to take any unlawful action or action which the debt collector in the regular course of business does not take: or

IV. Communicates or threatens to communicate, except by proper judicial process, the fact of such debt to a person other than the person who might reasonably be expected to be liable therefor; provided that the provisions of this paragraph shall not prohibit a debt collector from:

(a) communicating information relating to a debt to a person residing with the debtor and reasonably believed to be a relative or family member over the age of 18, or to an attorney, financial counseling organization or other person who has notified the debt collector that he is representing the debtor; or

(b) from leaving a message at the residence of the debtor containing no information other than a request that the debtor contact the debt collector about the debt; or

(c) communicating information relating to the debtor's spouse or , if the debtor is a minor, to the parents or guardians of the debtor where the purpose of that communication is solely to locate the debtor; provided that:

(1) the debt collector has been unable to locate the debtor by other means for a period of 30 days; and

(2) the debt collector, having once communicated with any of said persons, shall not again attempt to locate the debtor by communicating with said person; or

(d) reporting, or notifying a debtor that the debt collector may report a debt to:

(1) a consumer reporting agency defined in RSA 359-B: 3, VI, or any lending institution, provided that if the debt collector knows the debt to

be disputed he shall notify the consumer reporting agency or lending institution that the debt is disputed; or

(2)   to an agent or attorney engaged for the purpose of collecting the debt (For the purposes of RSA 358-C: 3, IV, the use of language on envelopes other than the debt collector's name, address, or telephone number, indicating that the communication relates to the collection of a debt shall be deemed a communication of the debt.); or

V.   Communicates directly with the debtor, except through proper legal action, after notification from an attorney, financial counseling organization or other person representing the debtor that all further communication relative to the debt should be addressed to the attorney, organization or other person unless the attorney, organization or other person fails to answer correspondence, return phone calls or discuss the debt within 10 days or prior approval is obtained from the attorney, organization or other person or the communication is a response in the ordinary course of business to the debtor's inquiry; or

VI.   Communicates with the debtor through the use of forms or instruments which simulate the form and appearance of judicial process or which give the appearance of being authorized, issued or approved by a government, governmental agency or attorney-at-law when they are not; or

VII.   Makes any material false representation or implication of the character, extent or amount of the debt, or of its status in any legal proceeding; or

VIII.   Makes any representation that an existing obligation may be increased by the addition of attorney's fees, investigation fees, service fees, or any other fees or charges when in fact such fees or charges may not be legally added to the existing obligation; or

IX.   Makes any representation that an existing obligation will definitely be increased by the addition of attorney's fees, investigation fees, service fees, or any other fees or charges when the award of such fee or charge is discretionary by a court of law; or

X.   Collects or attempts to collect any interest or other charge, fee or expense incidental to the principal obligation unless such interest or incidental fee, charge or expense is expressly authorized by the agreement creating the obligation and legally chargeable to the debtor; provided that the foregoing shall not prohibit a debt collector from attempting to collect court costs in a judicial proceeding; or

XI.   Threatens that nonpayment of a debt will result in the arrest of any person or the seizure, garnishment, attachment or sale of any property or wages without indicating, when a court order is a legal prerequisite to any such action; that

(a)   there must be a court order in effect permitting such action; and, where applicable,

(b)   that the debtor will have an opportunity to appear in court to contest such action prior to any such court order being effective; or

XII.   Threatens to assign or sell to another the account of or claim against the debtor with an attending representation or implication that the result of any such sale or assignment would be that the debtor would lose any defense to the debt or would be subjected to harsh, vindictive, or abusive collection attempts.

358-C: 4 Remedies

I.   Any debt collector who violates the provisions of this chapter shall be liable in any court of competent jurisdiction to the debtor for one of the following, whichever is greater:

(a)   in an action brought by and on behalf of an individual debtor only, the sum of $200 plus costs and reasonable attorney's fees for each violation, or

(b)   for all damages proximately caused by the violation.

II.   Notwithstanding the foregoing, a debt collector shall not be held liable in any action brought under this chapter for a violation if the debt collector shows by a preponderance of the evidence that:

(a)   the violation was a result of a computation error in billing and within 15 days of notification or discovery of said error, the debt collector notified the debtor of such error and corrected such error; or

(b)   the violation was not intentional and resulted from a bona fide error or mistake notwithstanding the maintenance of procedures reasonably adapted to avoid any such error or mistake

III.   In any suit to collect a debt, the debtor may raise, by way of counterclaim, setoff or recoupment, a violation of this chapter, and upon proof of a violation by a preponderance of the evidence, the court shall award damages to the defendant pursuant to this section and shall set such damages off against any recovery by the plaintiff.

IV.   Any debtor aggrieved by a debt collector's practices in violation of this chapter may bring an action individually and/or on behalf of others similarly situated in the superior court of the county in which he resides to restrain such practices by temporary or permanent injunction. If the debtor prevails in an action authorized by this paragraph, he shall be entitled to his costs and reasonable attorney's fees.

V.   If the court finds that an action initiated under this chapter was frivolous and brought to harass the debt collector, the debtor shall pay to the debt collector the costs of said action plus reasonable attorney fees.

VI.   Any violation of the provisions of this chapter shall also constitute an unfair and deceptive act or practice within the meaning of RSA 358-A: 2 and may be enforced by the attorney general pursuant to RSA 358-A.

APPENDIX E

General Information

1. WORDS TO CLARIFY LETTERS OF THE ALPHABET

The following list is a combination of words used by the United States Army and the New York Telephone Company to clarify the letter you are using:

A — ABLE	N — NANCY
B — BAKER	O — OSCAR
C — CHARLIE	P — PETER
D — DOG	Q — QUEEN
E — EDWARD	R — ROBERT
F — FOX	S — SAM
G — GEORGE	T — THOMAS
H — HARRY	U — UNIFORM
I — IDA	V — VICTOR
J — JOHN	W — WALTER
K — KATE	X — X-RAY
L — LARRY	Y — YELLOW
M — MARY	Z — ZEBRA

2. ABBREVIATIONS FOR USE IN RECORDING COLLECTION ACTIVITY

We are listing the abbreviations our telephone workers use on their reports. Variations are suggested as a function of the particular industry. We believe these are simple to use since they are in most instances abbreviations of the words themselves.

ASST	assistant
ATT	attention
ATTY	attorney
BAL	balance
BC	bad check
BEG	beginning
BIZ	business
BKPR	bookkeeper
BR	bankrupt
BRO	brother
BS	busy
CA	Canadian client
Can't Complete	can't complete as dialed
CB	call back
CC	copy of check, money order or letter
CDP	claims direct payment to client
CHGD	changed
CK	check as in "will check"
CIR	circuits as in "circuits" busy
CNOM	claims never ordered merchandise
COMPT	comptroller
CP	claims payment
CUST	customer
CR	credit card account
CRM	claims returned merchandise
CNRM	claims never received merchandise
DCB	don't call back

DECD	Deceased
DEF	defective
DIFF	different
DIS	disconnected
DTR	daughter
DXXX	debtor requests no more calls
EMPL	employee
ES	evidence of shipment, shipping receipt, UPS receipt, post office receipt
EVE	evening debtor's time
FT	family trouble
HT	health trouble
HU	hung up
HUSB	husband
INFO	information
INT	interest
KM	moved
KU	unknown
LANG	language problem
LM	left message
LMAS	left message answering service
LMTR	left message tape recorder
MA	mother
MGR	manager
MESS	message
MO	money order or month (1Y)
MT	money trouble
NA	no answer
NG	no good
NIS	not in service
NL	no listing
NLE	no longer employed
NLG	no legal, no threat left
N/S	new set of letters
#	number
OFS	office
OOB	out of business
OOO	out of order
OPER	operator
ORIG	original
PA	father
PAY(S)	payment(s)
PC	private corporation

PD	paid
PDP	promises direct payment to client
PIF	paid in full
PL	personal letter
PM	afternoon debtor's time
POB	place of business/employment
PO	purchase order
POD	proof of delivery
PP	promises payment
PREV	previous
RECP	receptionist
REF	refused
REFD	referred
RP	refused payment
RES	residence
RESP	responsible
SAT	Saturday
SECY	secretary
SIS	sister
START	starting
SWITCHBD	switchboard
TEMP	temporary
THXXX	third party requests no more calls
TR	tape recorder
TRBL	trouble
UNP	unpublished
UPS	United Parcel Service
W/	with
WI	wants invoice
WKG	working
W/O	without
WP	wrong person
WRG	wrong
WRM	will return merchandise
WTRM	wants to return merchandise
X	times, as in two times—2X

3. CANADIAN NATIONAL AND PROVINCIAL HOLIDAYS

January 1st	New Year's Day
	Good Friday
	Easter Monday (stores may be open day after Easter)
Monday preceding May 25th	Victoria Day
July 1st	Canada Day
1st Monday in August	Civic Holiday in Ontario
Labor Day	same as United States
2nd Monday in October	Thanksgiving Day
November 11	Remembrance Day
December 25th	Christmas
December 26th	Boxing Day

APPENDIX F

The Telephone Call— How Many to Make and When

GETTING THE MOST EFFICIENT COLLECTION FOR THE LEAST COST

The telephone call is the most effective and efficient tool available in the collection of a delinquent debt. However, using the telephone call alone and without letters reduces the efficiency of the telephone call approximately 50 percent. Therefore, whenever the amount will support a telephone call, it is absolutely necessary that a telephone call be used in conjunction with properly drafted collection letters. This appendix section deals with the creditor who is handling a large volume of consumer debtors where the indebtedness on each account is below $500. Department stores, direct mail and marketing companies, companies that promote products over TV in newspapers and magazines, plus other types of business fall in this category.

One client decided to do away with letters entirely and confine his collection effort to telephone calls. The calls were made during the 45-day period after shipment. The results were phenomenal, or so the collection manager believed. The statistics disclosed receipts of about $400 collected for each hour spent on the telephone. At last, the perfect collection device. One month of telephone calling produces $75,000.

The bubble burst with just one simple question: "Compared to what?" If no collection effort of any nature was in place and the customers were left to their own devices, perhaps $25,000 would have been received, since a certain number of customers would have paid without any prodding. If letters during the 45-day period would have produced $50,000, then only $25,000 could be allocated to the telephone effort. Using three letters instead of two letters during the 45-day period might have produced $60,000 at a fraction of the cost. Two letters and one telephone call might have yielded $80,000, and, even with this combination, the cost is substantially less than two or three telephone calls.

An analysis of the last paragraph should suggest a very basic tenet of all collection procedures—one that is often overlooked by the most sophisticated collection manager, i.e., the most efficient collection for the least cost. If the amount collected during the first 45 days without letters is substantially the same as with letters, then do not use letters. For example, consider a test of 100 accounts with two dunning letters (Set A) and 100 accounts with no letters (Set B).

The graph might appear as shown in Figures F.1 and F.2.

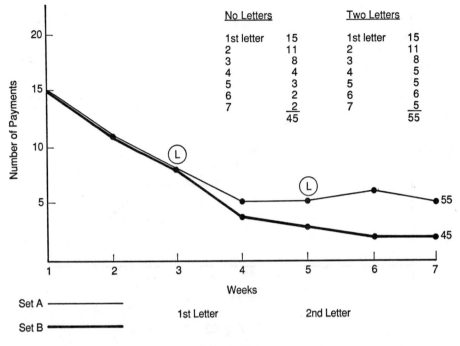

Figure F.1

The obvious conclusion is that the first letter helped very little, since the graph leveled quickly. The second letter seemed to improve payments. In addition, there is only a slight difference in results during the first three and one-half weeks despite the first letter. This may establish that no letter is warranted until after four weeks. The leveling signal toward the end of the cycle is the key to the evaluation and reading of the graph. This signal should trigger a new collection device. A typical test of 100 accounts with six letters, spaced one month apart, appears as shown in Figure F.2.

The telephone calls should commence between the third and fourth letter and a second call between the fifth and sixth letter. A letter is always mailed after a telephone call. When the debtor receives the letter, the debtor remembers the telephone call, and the net effect is two telephone calls for the price of one. This is far more efficient than telephone calls after the last letter. The graph might look like Figure F.3.

The telephone calls improved collections. The fourth letter sustained the trend after the first call, and the second call increased payments through the sixth letter. The first call also contributed to the excellent production of the second telephone call. Whether a third telephone call and another letter are warranted can only be answered by continual testing and plotting. It is usually found that the third telephone call is not generally cost effective. If a

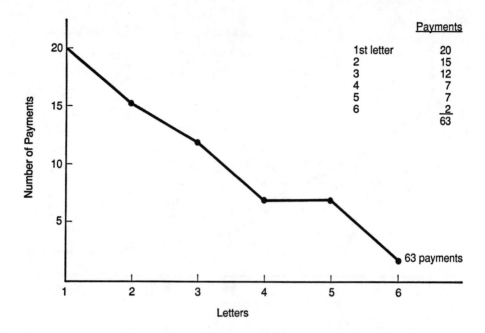

Figure F.2

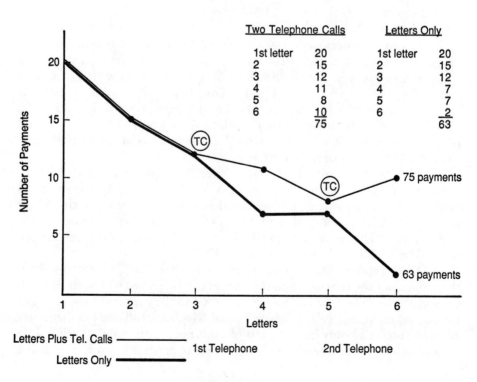

Figure F.3

debtor does not pay after two telephone calls, it is highly unlikely that the third telephone call will make a significant difference in his intentions. Nevertheless, this determination should be made by you, and not by what your competitors do. Even a second call may not be warranted. Again, the graph must be plotted. Using the same letters as in the last graph, but only one telephone call after the fourth letter, the graph might appear as shown in Figure F.4.

The net return may be almost the same, for the last two letters could very well sustain the one telephone call. Each firm is different, each product is different, each set of letters is different. Therefore, what applies to one firm does not apply to another firm. Testing and careful evaluation are the only answer.

A thorough appraisal of the results of the graphing will indicate whether a group of second calls should be implemented. This is not to be confused with circumstances that suggest that a second call would be useless, such as when the debtor refuses payment or hangs up the telephone, when the business is in bankruptcy or out of business, etc. In these individual circumstances, no second call should be made regardless of what the graph reflects.

Another point to remember is that each letter and each telephone call standing alone is economically profitable. The cost of sending letters to 100

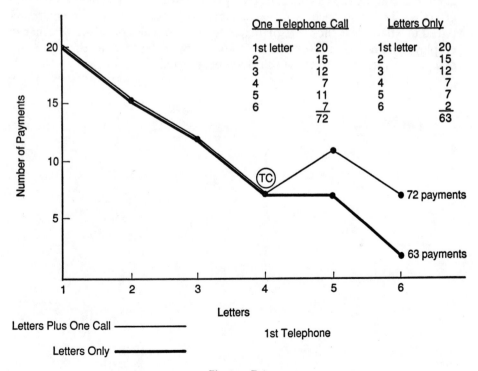

Figure F.4

accounts always will cover the payments received, whether one letter or eight letters are mailed. The argument offered by those who send eight letters is that even the last letter produces payments in excess of the cost of sending the letter. While this statement is fundamentally true, it is not necessarily justification for mailing the eighth letter. The magic formula is not to make each letter cost effective. The key is to collect the most net dollars for the least cost. Thus, if a third telephone call produces $1,000, it would far exceed the cost of about $200 to make the telephone calls (telephone charges, wages, preparation of work, etc.). But is this the most economic and efficient procedure? In the following example, if the same accounts were referred to an outside collection agency or attorney, the outside agent may collect $2,000 over the same period. The fee charged by the outside agent could be 40 percent. The amount paid to the client would be 60 percent, i.e., $1,200. The expenses to refer the accounts might be $50, so the client would net $1,150.

In-house collection	$ 1,000.00	Outside agent	$2,000.00
Cost	200.00	Fee	800.00
			$1,200.00
		Cost	50.00
	$ 800.00		$1,150.00

Thus, the firm nets $350 more referring the accounts to an outside agent. Of course, the calculations may prove that in-house collection is more effective. This approach is in accordance with our prior statement "compared to what?" It is the same principle to be used when deciding whether to employ telephone calls or letters. The only difference is that you are comparing internal efforts with different internal efforts.

Index